The Camera Lies

The Camera Lies

Acting for Hitchcock

DAN CALLAHAN

OXFORD
UNIVERSITY PRESS

Oxford University Press is a department of the University of Oxford. It furthers the University's objective of excellence in research, scholarship, and education by publishing worldwide. Oxford is a registered trade mark of Oxford University Press in the UK and certain other countries.

Published in the United States of America by Oxford University Press
198 Madison Avenue, New York, NY 10016, United States of America.

Library of Congress Cataloging-in-Publication Data
Names: Callahan, Dan, 1977– author.
Title: The camera lies : acting for Hitchcock / by Dan Callahan.
Description: New York, NY : Oxford University Press, [2020] |
Includes bibliographical references and index.
Identifiers: LCCN 2019048685 (print) | LCCN 2019048686 (ebook) |
ISBN 9780197515327 (hardback) | ISBN 9780197515341 (epub) | ISBN 9780197515358
Subjects: LCSH: Hitchcock, Alfred, 1899–1980—Criticism and interpretation. |
Motion pictures—Production and direction—Great Britain—History—20th century. |
Motion pictures—Production and direction—United States—History—20th century. |
Motion picture acting—History—20th century. | Motion picture actors and actresses—Great Britain—Biography. | Motion picture actors and actresses—United States—Biography.
Classification: LCC PN1998.3.H58 C34 2020 (print) | LCC PN1998.3.H58 (ebook) |
DDC 791.4302/33092—dc23
LC record available at https://lccn.loc.gov/2019048685
LC ebook record available at https://lccn.loc.gov/2019048686

1 3 5 7 9 8 6 4 2

Printed by Sheridan Books, Inc., United States of America

For Aleena Khan and Aiden Khan

For every answer, I like to bring up a question. Maybe I'm related to Alfred Hitchcock or maybe I got to know him too well, but I think life should be that way. I don't think you want to give all the answers, but I think every answer you do give should bring up another question, and not all questions should be answered.

Kim Novak, 1996, *The Washington Post*

Contents

Introduction ix

1. Naughty Boys and *The Pleasure Garden* 1
2. *The Mountain Eagle* and *The Lodger* 12
3. Six More in Silence: *The Ring, Downhill, The Farmer's Wife, Easy Virtue, Champagne, The Manxman* 19
4. *Blackmail* 27
5. *Juno and the Paycock, Murder!, Mary, Elstree Calling, The Skin Game* 35
6. *Rich and Strange, Number 17, Waltzes from Vienna* 44
7. *The Man Who Knew Too Much, The 39 Steps, Secret Agent, Sabotage* 55
8. *Young and Innocent, The Lady Vanishes, Jamaica Inn* 82
9. *Rebecca, Foreign Correspondent, Mr. and Mrs. Smith, Suspicion* 96
10. *Saboteur, Shadow of a Doubt, Lifeboat, Spellbound* 120
11. *Notorious, The Paradine Case, Rope, Under Capricorn, Stage Fright* 136
12. *Strangers on a Train, I Confess* 161
13. *Dial M for Murder, Rear Window, To Catch a Thief, The Trouble with Harry, The Man Who Knew Too Much* 172
14. *The Wrong Man, Vertigo, North by Northwest, Psycho, The Birds, Marnie* 190
15. *Torn Curtain, Topaz, Frenzy, Family Plot*, AFI Award 230

Notes 237
Hitchcock Bibliography 241
Index 243

Introduction

"Walt Disney had the right idea," a beaming Alfred Hitchcock told Dick Cavett on TV in 1972. "If he didn't like the actors, he tore them up!" On that same Cavett program, Hitchcock also went into his well-practiced, lugubrious elaboration on a famous remark he had supposedly made in the late 1920s and again in the mid-1930s.

"I think at the time I was accused of calling actors cattle," Hitchcock told Cavett. "I would never say such an unfeeling, rude thing about actors at all . . . what I probably said was that all actors should be *treated* like cattle." This set-up and punch line got its expected laugh from the studio audience. Hitchcock once told director Peter Bogdanovich, "Actors are like children. They have to be coddled, and sometimes spanked."

On the set of Hitchcock's romantic comedy *Mr. and Mrs. Smith* (1941), his friend Carole Lombard rented some cattle and had her name and the names of her costars, Robert Montgomery and Gene Raymond, tied on name tags around their necks. Hitchcock very much enjoyed this gag, just as he enjoyed Lombard's sense of fun and her very profane language, the free use of which was not usual for women in that period.

Lombard is an ideal Hitchcock blonde to tickle his personal fancy, or a blonde Hitchcock ideal, someone who didn't need to be menaced out of lady-like reserve. The exuberant Lombard was a liberated American woman, peppy and inventive enough to make a joke without wondering if it might backfire, and Hitchcock allows her to rule his frames just as he allowed the similarly free-spirited Tallulah Bankhead to rule *Lifeboat* (1944).

Bankhead too was an American, a Southern belle so liberated that her basso-voiced kicking over the traces became a camp joke. She had made exciting appearances on the London stage all through the 1920s, when Hitchcock was serving his apprenticeship in the British film industry, and he always saw her as an example of what a woman could be. Bankhead was a mile-a-minute talker, and an exhibitionist who liked to take all her clothes off as often as possible. To Hitchcock she was great fun, just as Lombard was, because she was so different from most of the women he had grown up with in his native England. She is mentioned by name, lovingly, as just "Tallulah" in Hitchcock's *Murder!* (1930), which is set in the theater world.

The patrician Grace Kelly, an American yet nearly British in her Philadelphia finishing school way, has come to be seen as the ultimate Hitchcock blonde on screen and in life, the one that got away, the ideal of ideals, the lady with a dirty mind of her own. It was no mistake that she really won Hitchcock's heart when she responded with pleasure to his habitual dirty talk. "I said I heard worse things when I was in convent school, and he loved that," Kelly said. Imagine Hitchcock's own pleasure when Kelly came out with that line in such a special and lightly blasphemous way. Could Kelly have sensed that it was exactly what Hitchcock wanted to hear, in exactly that way?

Lutheran-raised Tippi Hedren, who starred in *The Birds* (1963) and *Marnie* (1964) for Hitchcock, did not respond to his hushed ribaldry, his dirty mind, or his schoolboy jokes. Hitchcock had put Hedren under personal contract, and he became obsessed by her. Famed for his self-possession and his orderliness on sets and in his life, Hitchcock was in his early sixties when he was making *Marnie*. And he had reached a breaking point.

Hitchcock told many people that he had only experienced sexual intercourse once in his life, with his wife, Alma, when they wanted a child in 1927. "I did it with a fountain pen," Hitchcock quipped to Donald Spoto and several others. He had been raised in the most repressive possible Edwardian atmosphere and had been taught by Jesuit priests. He had always used food as reassurance, and his weight both protected him and closed him off.

Hitchcock vacillated between feeling superior to others when it came to sex and longing for it himself, and on his sets he constantly told naughty stories that had the ring of the schoolyard about them. They were the heavy-handed, inexact stories and jokes of an inexperienced boy who became an old man without ever having had the kind of sexual play and knowledge that many boys have enjoyed before the age of twenty. And so in his early sixties, this lifelong pressure finally became too much for Hitchcock to handle, and he behaved very badly.

Hitchcock pitted Hedren and Diane Baker against each other on the *Marnie* set at least partly because they were enemies in the movie and because Baker's character is a romantic rival of Hedren's character. Elia Kazan was noted and even celebrated for this kind of psychological manipulation on his sets, but of course there is a gender bias at work here, or a bias of desire. When Hitchcock is faced with wooden playing by John Gavin, his second male lead in *Psycho* (1960), he simply abandons both actor and character, but not before making his contempt for both of them clear. Gavin is a performer who is roughly the male equivalent of Hedren and Baker in fine looks but iffy talent, and Hitchcock has no time for him.

But Hitchcock often identified with both his male and female characters, and this is part of what makes him such a major artist and still worth writing more about. "When I shoot a terrifying scene of *Psycho* or *The Birds*, I don't go home to have nightmares all night long," Hitchcock told François Truffaut. "It's simply another day's work; I've done my best and that's all there is to it. In fact, although I'm very serious during the shooting, I might even feel like laughing about those things afterward. And that's something that bothers me because, at the same time, I can't help imagining how it would feel to be in the victim's place."

Hitchcock seeks to emotionally involve his audience and make them identify with all sorts of people, and he wants the audience to emote, not the actors. This is why if you are really involved in watching a Hitchcock film, you can accept anything that happens in them. It is only when you are detached that they might seem far-fetched or implausible. Hitchcock can put you in the place of a serenely dedicated Nazi, but he also makes you see how identity is so unstable and people are so suggestible that they can go against their own best instincts and principles, or be contaminated by contact with evil in others. He seems to believe, finally, in a sort of spiritual possession, and in people as vessels with empty spaces that can be filled by anything, by grace on one end or by evil on the other. And who are we as humans to be able to tell the difference?

Yet of course we try to tell that difference and to judge people in a movie, or people in front of a camera. The standard line is that you can hide nothing from the camera. John Barrymore once said, "If you stay in front of the movie camera long enough, it will show you not only what you had for breakfast but who your ancestors were." But this Barrymore idea of what the camera can see is maybe a bit old-fashioned. The French actress Isabelle Huppert has said that acting to her is wanting to be looked at without being seen.

There is a vast distance between someone like Barrymore, a matinee idol on stage and a famously romantic player of Hamlet, and Huppert, who unselfconsciously offers herself up to the camera but remains nearly wholly enigmatic. Most of Huppert's notable characters have no moral or ethical boundaries, and the evil that may lurk in a Huppert character cannot be anticipated. Surely Hitchcock would have relished her perverse, ground zero work in something like, say, *The Piano Teacher* (2001), for he was an acting postmodernist in this respect before his time.

George Cukor might love and caress and bring out someone like Barrymore in *A Bill of Divorcement* (1932) and *Dinner at Eight* (1933), and Barrymore's florid work still has its romantic charge in pictures like that. But Hitchcock distrusts open displays of emotion. He liked what he called "negative acting," as in a moment where a smile falls away from a face, which is most touchingly done by Sylvia Sidney in the movie house sequence in *Sabotage* (1936) where she watches a Disney cartoon.

The camera lies, Hitchcock would say to his actors. Not always, but sometimes. And he knew when he needed the camera to tell as much of the truth as possible. When Hitchcock was tasked in early 1945 with editing together footage of the liberated Nazi concentration camps for a documentary, he instructed the cameramen to film as much as possible with "long tracking shots, which cannot be tampered with," according to his editor Peter Tanner.

The camera could show the passage of time or human thought, and it could make a person look like something they weren't or like they were thinking or feeling something they weren't depending on how different shots were juxtaposed. What Hitchcock really liked were faces in some kind of transition. He liked that split-second gulf between one emotion and another, and what it might reveal to his camera.

Ingrid Bergman was maybe the ultimate female Hitchcock actor because she could dwell in that "in-between" state longer than anybody else, and her face was always alive with exciting contrasts and counterpoints of emotion. What Hitchcock could do with his camera in his montage sequences Bergman could do with her face. When she is not smiling, Bergman's face lives in dreamy uncertainty, and that's what hope can be, and carefully hidden and protected hope is what Hitchcock is all about.

He often spoke about being afraid as a boy and he made that part of his image. Hitchcock's creativity is based on fear and wanting us to be afraid with him, and fear contains an element of hope. Fear has within it the desire for the worst, which could possibly lead to change for the best, and Hitchcock wanted to live in that possibility. What is the dizziness of vertigo, after all, but the desire to fall? You can fall in love, or you can fall to your death.

"I've always wanted to be someone else," Hitchcock says in the introduction to an episode of his TV show called "None Are So Blind," and he sounds like he means it. That's what acting can be and that's what hope can be. Cary Grant was probably the ultimate male Hitchcock actor because he was edgy and never complacent and he behaved like a moving target, and so Grant was an unsettled dream come true, and a dream coming true is what Hitchcock wanted to allow room for.

Hitchcock sometimes acted scenes out for his actors, and he wanted a certain tempo in the delivery of lines, down to the second. He was often so sure of when he wanted to cut while an actor talked that he knew which syllable of a word he would be cutting on. Walter Slezak was very impressed when Hitchcock gave the stymied Mary Anderson some purely technical direction during a difficult scene in *Lifeboat*, telling her to lower her voice and let her breath give out before a certain line. "Hitch knows more about the mechanics and the physical technique of acting than any man I know," Slezak said.

Hitchcock developed his own moviemaking technique, but he remained open to chance and dreams in his writing sessions as he worked on his scripts with his wife, Alma, and whatever writer was then at hand. He liked to stealthily talk and gossip with his writers until a solution to a script problem would somehow naturally arise, for he knew that if you press hard for anything, it isn't likely to come, or if it does come it won't be very good.

It is very easy to get details wrong when writing about Hitchcock films because they move like magic acts, and they always have an element of sleight of hand. Hitchcock was generally unconcerned with plausibility, or what he called "the plausibles" out in the audience, the people who would nitpick and say later that something in the narrative "didn't ring true." He called this sort of childlike questioning "moronic logic." But he was also nervous about lack of plausibility sometimes, and this was an area where he expected and needed Alma to sometimes pull him back at the scenario stage and get his feet on the ground.

Hitchcock was basically unmoved by truth or facts, finding them too often dull and not particularly believable in the supercharged, often surreal, dreamlike sense he favored as his truth. In one of the most acute sections of his long interview with François Truffaut, Hitchcock states that if an artist actually observes or experiences something unusual or seemingly implausible in their own life that they should not put it in their film or play or novel and then cry, "But it actually happened to me!" or "It actually happened to someone I know," for that is never a good enough creative reason. Hitchcock deals in dreams, fears, and archetypes, but the richness of his work lies in his ability to also charge these non-realistic elements with realistic detail.

The Hitchcock actors had to stay within the frames and compositions he had in mind, but within these frames they were often free to do as they liked, as long as he felt that they were well cast and serious about their work. He made his "actors are cattle" statement because the English actors he was working with in the 1930s, like John Gielgud, who starred in *Secret Agent* (1936), and Michael Redgrave, who was the lead in *The Lady Vanishes* (1938), treated movie work too lightly. "I do not know whether his famous 'Actors are cattle' remark was coined for my benefit, but I well remember his saying it in my presence," Redgrave said.

Gielgud was starring on stage in *Romeo and Juliet* with Peggy Ashcroft at night while he made *Secret Agent*, and so his mind was mainly on that. Hitchcock had given Ashcroft a memorable role as the sweet and abused crofter's wife in *The 39 Steps* (1935), but Gielgud didn't take Hitchcock's movie thrillers as seriously as he did his Shakespeare, and this hurt and annoyed Hitchcock. "They're not very bright, some of them," Hitchcock said of actors.

Yet many actors gave their finest performances in Hitchcock pictures, and he sometimes guided them with his "inattention" to make them anxious (he was noted for turning his back on players doing a scene or feigning boredom or even falling asleep, or pretending to). But he also gave actors focused and detailed guidance when that was needed. By the time of *Psycho* (1960), Hitchcock was quietly touched by how seriously Anthony Perkins took the role of Norman Bates, so much so that he allowed Perkins to reword some dialogue and make some other suggestions to deepen his characterization.

Hitchcock was not a director who managed or harangued his actors as, say, Otto Preminger did. "I have a phrase for that," Hitchcock said in 1966. "I call that, 'All the drama on the set and none on the screen.'" He guided by the tone of his voice, and by indirection. And he wanted his actors to be like that, too. Indirect. Subtle. Crafty. Holding something back. Not hamming it up, which Hitchcock said was an actor "exploding all his gunpowder."

He favored major stars for his chase films because they were more likely to make the audience worry about the characters, because a star, Hitchcock said, is like one of the family. He wanted his audience to act and supply emotion to the large heads of the stars on the large screen, and so he didn't want the actors to do too much emoting. Hitchcock wanted the face of the actor to be ambiguous enough sometimes so that the audience could read thoughts or emotions into the face. Hitchcock is always asking us to wonder what might be real emotion on a face and what has to be supplied by the person watching that face.

Hitchcock would often labor to help actors in a technical sense. He said that an actor could register an emotion better if they were already in one emotion, or in the midst of some action, and then caught up quickly in another emotion. "It is more true to life and it is more believable," Hitchcock said in the 1930s. What he did not want was demonstrative acting. He would stop actors and say, "Too much, too much," if he needed to.

"Because the image is too big," Hitchcock said in the 1960s. "It's enormous on the screen there. And don't forget that you've got to keep it down so you can get a range. It's like the timbre of the voice. If the voice is too high, when you want it to go high, there is nowhere to go. And it's just the same way to keep the expression to a minimum."

Some critics felt in the early 1960s that Tippi Hedren was too deadpan and lacking in facial mobility, that she didn't act enough, but her work now looks subtle, natural, and very touchingly expressive when it needs to be. And only when it needs to be. To his credit, Hitchcock often defended Hedren's performances in his movies. They were the final refinement of what he looked for and wanted from people on screen.

Hitchcock continually said in interviews that his ideal actor was someone who could do nothing well, and this is not either simple or easy. What Hitchcock wanted was an actor who had presence but who didn't necessarily *do* anything specific as an actor has to do on stage, and so of course this made someone like John Gielgud uncomfortable. What Hitchcock lusted for is what Louise Brooks does in *Pandora's Box* (1929) and *Diary of a Lost Girl* (1929), where she dances through the films unselfconsciously and transmits emotions that are always in flux in a kind of "intense isolation," as Brooks herself put it.

Hitchcock admired the stage actor Gerald du Maurier and said that du Maurier could "do nothing" on stage for five minutes and rivet the attention of the audience. Du Maurier made one of his rare film appearances in *Lord Camber's Ladies* (1932), which Hitchcock produced but did not direct. Unprepossessing looking, du Maurier has an incisive voice and a peremptory sort of authority, and he does indeed "do nothing" while his fellow performers Nigel Bruce and Gertrude Lawrence overplay their roles. And the eye always goes to him. He is a still center that commands attention. (His writer daughter Daphne provided the basis for three Hitchcock films.)

The sense of versatility in a stage actor, of convincingly being or portraying something you are not, was anathema to Hitchcock, and to many of the best film directors from Jean Renoir to Howard Hawks. Which is why actor-auteurs like Bette Davis and Meryl Streep, who are always *doing* something and making something happen on screen, generally avoid director-auteurs who might want their presence rather than their make-believe. Streep's attempt to be a Hitchcock blonde in *Still of the Night* (1982) was particularly unhappy because she always looks like she wants to be *doing* something more.

Davis appeared on Hitchcock's TV show in 1959 as a vain, well-to-do woman who ruins the life of a young man, and her characterization is too ostentatious and self-sufficient for this context. Fear is not her thing, and she isn't neurotic in the right way; her sensibility is so strong that it becomes a Bette Davis movie rather than a Hitchcock show, even if she gets strangled in the end. This episode was directed by Paul Henreid, her costar in *Now, Voyager* (1942), and it was shot by her favored cinematographer Ernest Haller, so Davis had her own allies here.

The stage-trained Sylvia Sidney was very upset with Hitchcock's direction of her in *Sabotage* because she felt that she was being used as a puppet, especially in the scene where her Mrs. Verloc is impelled to stab her husband (Oskar Homolka) at the dinner table. Hitchcock complained to François Truffaut that it was difficult to get any "shading" into Sidney's face because it had a "mask-like" quality. But he allowed that she had "nice understatement" in the role.

What Hitchcock wanted from his actors is finally not too far from what Robert Bresson wanted from his own mainly nonprofessional actor-models: the mysterious and engaging workings of what can only be called soul. And Hitchcock wanted that from professional players, and he preferred to work with actors he liked several times if possible, whereas Bresson famously only wanted to use his models once.

Hitchcock's films are filled to bursting with memorable performances, great performances, even, understated and otherwise, and not just from leading players, and he did control and mold these performances, sometimes in a roundabout or unorthodox way. Hitchcock knew what he wanted from actors and he nearly always got it.

My hope for this book is that it will shed some light on the role of the actor in all of Hitchcock's movies, what they contribute and what Hitchcock wants and needs from them. He didn't want palpable, didactic playing in his movies, which is why he was so exasperated by Charles Laughton in the two films they made together. What he wanted, and often what he got, was sheer being, alive and flamelike, so that seemingly limited players like Joan Barry and Janet Leigh and Tippi Hedren can often be just as moving and dynamic (and often far more so) as noted stage stars like John Gielgud, Peggy Ashcroft, Michael Redgrave, Laurence Olivier, and later Method wunderkinds like Montgomery Clift.

Conversely, a Hitchcock movie can utterly fall apart if cast with weak or second-rate actors. For *Saboteur* (1942), Hitchcock wanted Gary Cooper and Barbara Stanwyck for the leads but was given Robert Cummings and Priscilla Lane instead, and they seem to be not so much second choice as third or even fourth choice. The result was one of the weakest pictures of his first American period. More often, though, Hitchcock was very lucky in his casting, particularly when it came to his villains.

The finest or at least most vivid performance in all of Hitchcock's work seems to me to be Robert Walker's Bruno Antony in *Strangers on a Train* (1951), a man bristling with sheer malicious, flipped-on presence. Walker had been an "aw shucks" male ingénue in the 1940s, and so Bruno was a casting against type and also a revelation for him and for the audience, and the perilous excitement of this performance comes because you can feel Walker go for broke at being let off his leash, even though he is supposedly working for the most restrictive of film directors.

There have been many Hitchcock books, and there will be many more because he left behind such a rich, shifting body of work that will always be open to new interpretations. This book is an investigation of the human figure in Hitchcock films, with some supplementary information and analysis of those human figures in the films they made before and after their time with the Master. It is an attempt to prove that Hitchcock was a theorist of acting as much as of filmmaking, with very insightful ideas about what a human face could or could not convey, the way it could be made to lie or the way it could be misinterpreted.

That misinterpretation of the surface seems to be at the heart of Hitchcock himself as artist and man, both as his cross to bear and his increasingly shadowed hope. The French actress Brigitte Auber, who appeared in *To Catch a Thief* (1955), was pursued by Hitchcock in the mid-1950s but had to decline his advances, though she said, "The poor cabbage had a wonderful soul, I know." Rita Riggs, who did the costumes for *Psycho*, told the author Stephen Rebello, "I always thought of him as the prince locked in the frog" and she spoke of his "frustration with his exterior."

The exterior, the surface, is all we have to go on in life, and Hitchcock wanted us to see how mistaken we could be in our judgments of that exterior. The camera lies and the surface is also often a lie. Hitchcock taught us to distrust what we see, to question it, to break it down. That was the prerogative and the necessity of a prince locked in a frog.

1

Naughty Boys and *The Pleasure Garden*

Hitchcock was born Alfred Joseph Hitchcock in Leytonstone, which was part of Essex at that time, a county northeast of London, on August 13, 1899, coming in right before the new century turned. He chose two stories to represent his infancy and childhood. In the first story, which he told Dick Cavett and many other interviewers, Hitchcock related how his mother said, "Boo!" to him in his cradle, and so this supposedly put a scare into him for life. Hitchcock's mother was the daughter of a policeman.

In the second story, which he told far more often, a very young Hitchcock was sent to a police station by his father with a note telling the police to lock him up in a cell for five minutes with the admonishment, "This is what we do to naughty boys." It was a tale that Hitchcock stuck to all his life, and when he was asked what he would like printed on his tombstone, he replied, "This is what we do to naughty boys." He hated feeling confined, and as an adult he loved to travel.

His father, William, and mother, Emma, were both half-English and half-Irish. William was a greengrocer, and Emma had borne two other children, William, who was born in 1890, and Ellen Kathleen, born in 1892, before she had her third and last child Alfred. He was close to his mother, but his weight isolated him from other children. Perhaps, though, he partly welcomed this isolation, at least as a defense mechanism. He loved to study train timetables and to figure out just when certain trains were departing and arriving.

According to biographer Patrick McGilligan, the Hitchcock family was a lively and friendly one, and full of fun and jokes. Donald Spoto paints a grimmer picture in his notorious biography *The Dark Side of Genius*, but Spoto always suspiciously twists things for a negative slant in that book, and some of his negative stories have been challenged and even proven false by McGilligan.

Hitchcock was brought up in the Roman Catholic faith and sent to be educated by the Jesuits at St. Ignatius College in Stamford Hill, London. He stayed off to the side, mainly, watching others and observing, feeling superior when he could and lonely when he had to be. Hitchcock disliked and feared the authority of the Jesuits just as he disliked and feared policemen or any authority figure. He didn't like being afraid of such figures, but he did like reading Edgar Allan Poe and getting all wrought up with fear and reassuring himself that he was actually safe in the comfort of home. What Hitchcock abhorred most was complacency. He wanted to be jolted and to jolt others out of that truly dangerous state.

Already Hitchcock loved food best of all, as a comfort. He remembered once waking up in the night as a boy of five or six and realizing his parents had gone out for a walk in Hyde Park, leaving him alone. Afraid and insecure, "nothing but night all around me," the young Hitchcock went and found himself a piece of cold meat to eat, and as he ate the piece of meat he dried his tears. He had a lifelong aversion to eggs, and as a boy at St. Ignatius, he once threw some eggs at the priests' windows, a supercharged image or incident that might have thrilled his most avid supporter, François Truffaut.

When he was fifteen, Hitchcock's father died, and so Hitchcock drew closer to his mother. He was already reading cinema trade papers from America and from Britain at this age and was studying engineering when he was excused from any active military service in World War I. In 1919, Hitchcock had a story called "Gas" published for the in-house magazine of a company called Henley's, where he worked for several years as a draftsman and was popular with the other workers, often making them laugh. This story "Gas" told of a woman who describes an assault that turns out, in a twist ending, to be a hallucination brought on by the ether she has been given in a dentist's chair.

By 1920, Hitchcock had entered the British film industry, working his way up from the bottom and doing everything he possibly could, starting first with designing elaborate title cards. He worked as an art director, a screenwriter, and an assistant to the director Graham Cutts on several films, some of which were made in Germany. Hitchcock was most influenced in this time by two films: Fritz Lang's *Destiny* (1921), in which the character of Death gives a woman three chances to save her lover, and F.W. Murnau's *The Last Laugh* (1924), a tale of humiliation done almost entirely without intertitles.

In 1922, Hitchcock had been given his first chance to direct a picture called *Number 13*, which was financed by its star Clare Greet but never finished because they ran out of money. (Hitchcock's uncle John had also provided some money for the film.) Hitchcock used Greet in small roles in six of his later pictures, the last of which was *Jamaica Inn* (1939), a movie released the year she died. Only Leo G. Carroll later matched this number of films for Hitchcock.

The footage shot for *Number 13* has never been found. The plot concerned Greet and her husband, played by the exuberantly gay character actor Ernest Thesiger, and their life together in a low-income housing building. Though the experience of shooting and then abandoning this picture was embarrassing to Hitchcock, he stayed loyal to Greet, a large character actress with a broad, beaten-down, suffering sort of face.

For some time, Hitchcock had had his eye on a young editor named Alma Reville. Born just a day after Hitchcock on August 14, 1899, Reville was already cutting movies at the age of sixteen. When Hitchcock first met Reville, she was far above him in the hierarchy at the studio, and so he waited until he had risen in the ranks before he began courting her. The story he told was that he proposed to her while they were on board a ship. Reville was badly seasick, and so, according to the family story, she merely turned her head and burped in response. Hitchcock also said in later years that Reville had asked him to marry her, which somehow sounds more likely. Reville was an active person who knew what she wanted, and she seems to have had a sense that Hitchcock was going to be an important director even from the beginning.

Reville was a major part of Hitchcock's life from this time forward as sister, mother, assistant, writer, sounding board, cutter, and companion. Her opinion meant everything to Hitchcock. She looked after him and kept him from being lonely. They did not have a conventional bond or a conventional marriage, but it lasted over fifty years and there never seems to have been any point for either of them where they seriously considered leaving each other.

"To tell the truth, she bossed him," said their friend Elsie Randolph, who emphasized that theirs was not a "grand passion." But, of course, grand passions seldom last for over fifty years. There would be many grand passions for Hitchcock, which he mainly had to keep to himself, and they usually lasted a few years and a few films or TV episodes.

Alma was there through it all, tough, managing, protective, and confrontational when she needed to be. Her status slipped somewhat as time went on, at least in comparison to her all-important role during his British period, but Hitchcock still bowed to her as a final authority on his work.

In some early photos from the 1910s that were published in Patricia Hitchcock's 2003 tribute book about her mother, Reville is dressed charmingly in Mary Pickford curls and pinafore, but she soon started dressing in a more streamlined and masculine fashion. In the 1930s, Alma often wore smart trousers and suits, which were carefully selected by her husband, who preferred simplicity in dress for himself.

"I could have been a poof if it were not for Alma," Hitchcock told the gay playwright and screenwriter Rodney Ackland, who then reported this to Hitchcock biographer John Russell Taylor, but it sounds like an idle remark made to put Ackland at ease. The subject of Hitchcock and homosexuality is a large one (whole books have been devoted to it), yet there are no stories of him expressing any desire for men. His own desire was always for a certain type of reserved and mysterious woman, and his wife Alma was decidedly not this type of woman. Alma was not, say, the character of Madeleine as played by Kim Novak in *Vertigo* (1958), but she was very close to the character of Midge (Barbara Bel Geddes), the sensible, motherly sort.

Hitchcock was fascinated by any type of sexual aberration or abnormality, which is what homosexuality was considered in his day. When he was still engaged to Alma, Hitchcock watched two lesbians make love in a brothel in Berlin, and this colored the relationship between the two lead female characters in his first film, *The Pleasure Garden* (1925).

There is an outright gay male character in *The Pleasure Garden*, a dress designer who works for the gold-digging Jill (Carmelita Geraghty). We first see this fashion-struck, angular young man fussing with a scanty stage costume he has designed for Jill, pulling at it and getting all excited by it, and smoothing his hair with his ever-active hands. He openly flirts with her impresario boss, extending a limp but dynamically tense hand toward him as they sit on a couch (see fig. 1.1). This is a man with clear sexual urges for other men, and he expresses them without hiding or shame.

Later in *The Pleasure Garden*, we see this gay dress designer holding one of Jill's frocks against his own body, and then he is sitting in a chair with his legs crossed and his dramatically limp hand holding up his chin as he stares boldly at Jill and her maids. His eyes open very wide when he gets his moment with Jill, and when she goes to her desk, the dress designer makes tense, claw-like formations with his hands as he speaks and practically climbs up the desk, his left leg crossed up over his right. The effect of all this is queerly sexy and also just plain queer.

Hitchcock allows this gay dress designer character his moment to dominate the scene and the space. He is a lovely freak, this boy, twisting himself into shapes that finally feel neither male nor female but wholly singular and artificial and expressive of a person dissatisfied with the usual, with the conventional. When he is somewhat still, we can see that this young boy has a rather beautiful face, with piercing eyes and handsome brows, and an elegant long nose.

Figure 1.1: A gay dress designer flirts with a theater mogul in Hitchcock's first film *The Pleasure Garden*.

This queer designer has nothing to do with the increasingly convoluted plot of *The Pleasure Garden*, but he has not been noted much in all of the commentary on Hitchcock, and he deserves to be. For a few moments, this young twisty boy is the star of this movie, and it's tantalizing to wonder just who he was and what his life was like, and what became of him after appearing in *The Pleasure Garden*, and also what Hitchcock thought of him while providing this little showcase. This boy dominates a scene in Hitchcock's debut film, and so that is a bit of immortality for him and also for a certain kind of 1925-style gayness.

There used to be two extant versions of *The Pleasure Garden*, a print from the German National Film Archives with German intertitles, which is a good quality copy of this movie, and the Raymond Rohauer version, which is still of good quality or more likely to be accessible, but these have been overtaken by a 2012 BFI restoration that used several different prints to add another twenty minutes to the running time.

The Pleasure Garden begins in a very prescient and Hitchcockian way with a group of chorus girls running down a spiral staircase. This is the ideal inaugural image for his career: blondes and false blondes racing down a vortex or down a drain or vertigo-spiral so that they can get out on stage of the Pleasure Garden Theatre to show their bodies to the men looking at them and appraising them out in the audience.

The unhappy-looking, unsmiling chorus girls wear white tops and tight black shorts, and we see them enter the stage and throw their arms around in an overhead shot. Hitchcock's camera moves to the right, across the faces of the men in the audience, all of them older and unattractive in different ways, from rich and puffed-up to professorial to doofish and drained of masculinity, and nearly all of them wear glasses or some aid to sight like a monocle.

The camera comes to a halt on the face of a woman who has fallen asleep before very quickly cutting away from her. Why is this sleeping woman there? Did she accompany her husband? Is she a lesbian who was on her feet all day? (She is small and young and has short dark hair like Hitchcock's wife, Alma.) Or is she actually meant to be a symbol of a female disinterested in sex, or at least in sexual display? Recall the moment in *Psycho* when Hitchcock's daughter Pat says that her mother gave her tranquilizers to take on her wedding night.

Mr. Hamilton (German actor Georg H. Schnell, who had played in Murnau's *Nosferatu* {1922}) is the top-hatted stager of the theater's revues, and he is seen smoking a cigar next to a sign that reads, "Smoking Prohibited," so that we know who has the power to set the rules and break them. In Hitchcock's movies, a character will often be both a person and a symbol of something more general he is trying to express.

We see an out-of-focus shot of the chorus girls on stage from the point of view of an older male audience member who is losing his eyesight, so that the blurred image only comes back into focus when the man lifts up his binoculars to get a closer view of the shapely legs on the girls, and this expresses the impotence and voyeuristic necessity that runs through Hitchcock's work and gets an apotheosis with James Stewart in his wheelchair in *Rear Window* (1954).

The camera settles on Patsy, played by the star of the film, Virginia Valli, a name actress of her time who had been imported from Hollywood. Her high salary, which Hitchcock very much resented, took up much of the film's budget. Valli has a harsh, blunt, nearly masculine presence, and as she kicks her legs on stage, we see that her blonde hair is actually a wig. Hitchcock himself later said that he was afraid of Valli and insecure about offering her direction until he had asked Alma about how he should approach her.

When Patsy sees the man with binoculars staring straight at her, she gives him a very unsettling, wide-eyed look that seems to say, "Well? And what do you want, huh?" This is a moment of aggression, a tough woman turning the tables on the man looking her over with the intent to make him feel guilty or scared. This look that Valli gives the man in the audience, and the camera itself, is so loaded with disdain and so close to something mentally unstable and on the edge of craziness that it stops the film dead in its tracks before she narrows her eyes again and retreats into a haughty "Why, I never" face. It's enough to make you wonder what a Hitchcock film about a fed-up chorus girl *female* murderer would be like.

There is a sense, somehow, that *The Pleasure Garden* can go no further after we see Valli's mocking, jolting face, as if it were a "Halt where you are!" warning shot in the war between men with power and women with looks, and yet this "go no further" expression in close-up is just the beginning of a major theme and dynamic for Hitchcock, and it suggests a road not taken, too. This is a face that would scare off many other male directors, but of course Hitchcock likes to be scared and he likes to scare us. By comparison, Valli's performance in King Vidor's *Wild Oranges* (1924) is ineffective because she isn't remotely believable as a waifish, sheltered girl who cannot take care of herself.

The older man who had been ogling Patsy goes backstage to see her. "I had to meet you because I was charmed by that lovely curl of hair," he tells her, whereupon she pulls the curl out from the wig she is wearing. "Then I give it to you and hope you have a nice time," Patsy tells him, handing him the curl. So here we have a woman throwing the artifice of her own "attractiveness" in the face of a man who seems a mild sort of fetishist, and this has a very satisfyingly vengeful feminist charge to it. Her admirer gives the curl back to her, bashfully, and she smiles meanly and puts it back onto the wig, leaving him looking vaguely disgruntled.

Outside of the Pleasure Garden, we see the brunette Jill (Carmelita Geraghty) at the stage door looking dewy and spacey in close-up. Her purse is coveted by two lecherous-looking crooks, one of whom is wearing a hat far too big for his head. We see a close shot of Jill's purse from the big-hatted lecher's point of view, which Hitchcock frames with an iris shot to call our full attention to it, and then we go back to a shot of these two men, both of whom are smoking cigarettes. Jill passes in front of them, and the big-hatted crook lifts some money from her bag, which is small and beaded.

The staging, acting, and shooting of this scene has an unmistakably sexual connotation that runs all the way forward to the first shot of *Marnie*, where we see Hedren's thief walking forward in a deserted train station while holding a very vaginal-looking yellow purse under her arm. The naïve Jill gets money taken from her in *The Pleasure Garden*. Marnie takes money from men in power, and in this first scene, Marnie's hair is dyed black.

Patsy comes out of her dressing room wearing a handsome suit with a tie, and she boldly rescues Jill from the wolfish attentions of two stage door johnnies, actually pushing them away physically and seeming to say, "Clear off!" She takes the younger and inexperienced Jill under her wing, so to speak, but not before Jill stops at the door and gives the men a very false-looking smile, as if this is expected of her. It's a creepy moment, and it establishes that both Patsy and Jill are united in their adversarial relationship to men. This also establishes that Jill's "dumb and helpless" vibe is actually a false front that she uses to maneuver through the world.

Jill had wanted to audition for Mr. Hamilton, but she will have to wait for that until the following day, and so Patsy takes Jill back to her flat to stay the night. Hitchcock cuts between the two girls as they undress and look at each other from opposite sides of the room, and Hitchcock also sometimes cuts to the middle of the room so that we can see them throw their clothes and scanties on the floor, all of which is very sexy. "Luckily you have me to take care of you," Patsy tells Jill, displaying some gallant female solidarity and maybe something a little randy, too.

There is only one bed in the room, which they will share for the night. Jill gets down on her knees to say her prayers, and the camera cuts to Patsy looking surprised at this and then smiling at Jill with light condescension. Patsy's dog Cuddles comes up and starts to lick Jill's feet as she prays, and Jill kicks the dog away! (Hitchcock loved animals, and so we can see just what he thinks of Jill at this moment.) This whole sequence in Patsy's room has a delightful sort of perversity, of things not being what they seem, of jokes and free-floating horniness and barely restrained lesbian attraction to Jill on the part of Patsy, and this is dependent on Valli's roguishness and Geraghty's dippy sex appeal.

Jill auditions to get into the chorus with a Charleston routine ("Take a chance, Mr. Hamilton, and I'll show you some real hot steps!," she tells the director). Mr. Hamilton is viewed from a distance, and the smoke from his cigar keeps spewing out all over the space around him, like the smoke from the train that brings Uncle Charlie (Joseph Cotten) into town in *Shadow of a Doubt* (1943).

Hitchcock shows us a girl in glasses in the audience blowing her nose as she looks at Jill's routine, the first of his glasses girls. Hitchcock had a thing for girls in glasses. What he seems to have liked, in his films and even in his professional life with his various secretaries and assistants, was for a woman to wear glasses so that she could then take them off. Hitchcock liked the contrast of that, the old "Why Miss Murgatroyd, you're beautiful without your glasses!" routine, the duckling who might be a swan, which was the female equivalent of the frog who might turn into a prince. (Later on in Hollywood, Hitchcock insisted that his secretary and business manager Carol Stevens wear glasses, which he often ordered her to take off. "He had a fetish about glasses," Stevens said.) The glasses girl applauds Jill when she finishes her dance.

Up to and including Jill's audition scene, *The Pleasure Garden* is very exciting and fraught with possibility, but Hitchcock is unable to sustain what has been set up in this opening fifteen minutes due to the weakness of the script by Eliot Stannard, which degenerates as Patsy and Jill go their separate ways with different men. Jill shows her true mettle when she deliberately burns Prince Ivan (Karl Falkenberg) with her cigarette after he makes advances to her, satisfyingly taking the phallic power that Mr. Hamilton wielded over his chorus girls into her own hands.

It is made clear that the hard-driving and managing Patsy is the good-hearted heroine here, whereas the conventionally "helpless" and yielding-looking Jill is without scruple or loyalty in her ambition for wealth and security. Jill isn't the brightest girl, maybe, but she is filled with animal-like cunning. The actor who plays Jill's fiancée Hugh, John Stuart, is conventionally good-looking and appealing in his faith in her, whereas the men who keep Jill or attempt to, like Mr. Hamilton and Prince Ivan, are seedy types she needs to manipulate for profit.

Then again, if the wages of sin include the young gay dress designer with those expressive hands, a pretty pansy boy who seems to live to design Jill outfits and hear her confidences, these men who keep her don't look all that bad purely as a price to be paid. "That girl knows exactly what she's doing, Patsy—and she likes it," emphasizes Levet (Miles Mander), a man who works with Hugh.

Though Patsy has feelings for Hugh, she is loyal to her friend Jill and falls in with the shady Levet instead. We learn that Mr. Hamilton is keeping Jill, and when we see him kiss her, very heatedly, there is a good strong sexual connection between them that seems to thrive off Jill's innate yet also sometimes feigned "out of it" quality. When we last see Jill, she is set to marry Prince Ivan, who will no doubt want her to put out cigarettes on him, at least metaphorically, for the rest of their married life.

Patsy becomes involved with Levet and marries him, and she tells him she is praying to God that they will be happy, which makes him yawn. Patsy plays with a baby that is being held in the arms of a real Italian Mama kind of older woman, and Hitchcock's camera greedily takes this woman in (one of the bonuses of going on location to Italy to shoot *The Pleasure Garden* was finding striking non-actors like this Italian lady). The bourgeois couple who run the house where Patsy lives have a sideboard with hanging teacups exactly like the one in the farmer's house in *The Birds*, but it is allowed to remain intact here.

Hitchcock stages his first murder when Patsy calls Levet a "filthy animal" for having an affair with a native girl, who is played by the German actress Elizabeth Pappritz. (This part has often been mis-credited as being played by Hollywood star Nita Naldi, who would act in Hitchcock's second film.) And so Levet drowns the poor girl in the ocean, half-heartedly pushing her head below water in a sequence that is awkwardly staged and shot. Pappritz couldn't do this scene herself because she was having her period, and a local waitress was called to stand in for her. Hitchcock later said that he hadn't known anything about female menstruation until this moment.

The ghost of the murdered girl haunts Levet, and he threatens Patsy with a sword before he gets himself shot by a male doctor character. In a hasty conclusion, Hugh declares his love for Patsy and they go home to her dog Cuddles, who is happy to see both of them. Hitchcock gives Cuddles the last shot.

The first dog who played Cuddles, the lustful pup who had licked Jill's feet in the earlier lesbian-tinged sequence, had wandered away from the set, unfortunately, and so a second dog appears thirty minutes into the film. He doesn't look much like his predecessor, and he was always licking off his own make-up. (Put in *Vertigo* terms, the second Cuddles is a kind of blunt Judy Barton canine after the more esoterically exciting Madeleine dog of the first half hour.) The last part of *The Pleasure Garden* had been shot under trying conditions in Italy, whereas the first and more persuasive part of the picture had been done at a studio in the heat of a summer in Munich.

Press reports suggest that Geraghty was cast as Jill because she had traveled to Europe with Valli. Both of them were somewhat like the characters they played in *The Pleasure Garden*, good-looking girls who retired early from their profession once the bloom of youth was gone.

Valli's last film was the independent talking picture *Night Life in Reno* (1931), which also featured Geraghty in a small role. That same year Valli married the tall and beautiful Charles Farrell, who had become a star in romantic and very sexy silent films directed by Frank Borzage like *Street Angel* (1928) and *The River* (1929). Loyal in life to his wife as he was to Janet Gaynor on screen, Farrell stayed married to Valli until her death in 1968.

Geraghty enlivened scenes as Mary Pickford's vulgar sister in the comedy *My Best Girl* (1927), but her roles got smaller until she retired in 1936. She married the writer-producer Carey Wilson in 1934 and went on to have a career as a painter until her death in 1966. Neither Valli nor Geraghty had children.

2

The Mountain Eagle and *The Lodger*

Hitchcock's second film, *The Mountain Eagle* (1926), was also filmed in Germany but set in Kentucky, and it is the only one of his features that is lost. (There used to be only six surviving stills from it, but twenty-four stills from this picture were discovered in 2012.) Hitchcock had a miserable time shooting it, and he was unhappy with the scenario he had been given and with the film itself.

Hitchcock said that he had to spend a lot of time getting his star Nita Naldi to remove her excessive make-up and false fingernails so that she would be convincing as a rural schoolteacher, and in the remaining stills Naldi is indeed de-glammed and de-vamped and outfitted in baggy dresses. Hitchcock particularly insisted on Naldi taking the curls out of her black hair and wearing it pulled back and up in a way that looks somewhat like the hairstyles of Kim Novak's Madeleine and Tippi Hedren's Melanie Daniels. A woman's hair would always be of the utmost importance to Hitchcock.

Naldi had been born Mary Dooley in New York City to an Irish family, and she had followed in the vamp footsteps of Theda Bara in her movie work, notably as a foil to John Barrymore in *Dr. Jekyll and Mr. Hyde* (1920) and to Rudolph Valentino in *Blood and Sand* (1922). Naldi arrived on the set of *The Mountain Eagle* with an older sugar daddy, likely the millionaire J. Searle Barclay, and though Hitchcock was irritated about having to urge her to look her schoolteacher part, he seems to have been fairly amused by her personally, even allowing her to take him to a brothel with Alma in tow, from which the Hitchcocks swiftly departed.

There is a famous still of Hitchcock pointing and directing on the set of *The Mountain Eagle* while Alma sits behind him and looks very concentrated and severe with script in hand. It is one of the few photos of them at work together, and even though it is staged, it expresses how he got to have the fun while she was often caught up in the details of filmmaking.

Reviews of *The Mountain Eagle* complained that it was unconvincing and far-fetched, but it is still among the most-wanted lost silent films, and surely it would be good to see for ourselves how Hitchcock handled the story and what touches he brought to it. In one still, Naldi is seated next to a man who has his hands kinkily handcuffed above his head, but the most notable still, which has been around for years, is of an old man getting strangled, his glasses falling down his nose and his mouth open and twisted in a grotesque fashion that shows most of his teeth.

In a scene where Naldi's character had to tell off the townspeople, Hitchcock egged her on and cried, "Give them all you've got!," and he was impressed with her wildness. "She gave it to them in English, Italian, American, Bowery, Park Avenue and maybe double Dutch," he said in 1937. "She called them anything and everything she could lay her tongue to. She told them where they got off, where they came from, where they were going. She used words we had never heard before. When I called 'Cut!' she was shuddering and shaking with emotion, and the whole studio—none of whom had understood a word she said—burst into spontaneous applause." When an actor was really involved with a scene in a silent film, Hitchcock knew that the exact words they said didn't matter.

Both *The Pleasure Garden* and *The Mountain Eagle* had been shown to exhibitors but had been momentarily shelved, and they only got a release after Hitchcock's third picture, *The Lodger* (1926), became a success. This was the first "real" Hitchcock picture, with most of his later themes in place, but the producers were not happy with it when the finished movie was screened for them. Hitchcock's former boss Graham Cutts had been jealously speaking out against *The Lodger* to anyone who would listen, and this definitely had a negative effect. The film was saved by Ivor Montagu, who did some cutting of unnecessary titles and some rearranging, for which he was credited with editing and titling.

The Lodger is subtitled "A Story of the London Fog," and it starred the matinee idol Ivor Novello as a man who may or may not be a killer who is strangling young blonde girls. After the stylish credits, which lean heavily on a vaginal "v" shape that keeps sexily closing and opening, we see the head of an ash-blonde girl screaming in close-up, her face irradiated by the light Hitchcock placed behind her, and the effect is deliberately artificial and abstract.

We see a sign reading, "To-Night Golden Curls" and then the girl's dead body in a sad heap at the foot of the frame, the lights of the city above her. She is the seventh victim of a killer on the loose in London who calls himself The Avenger and holds a cape in front of his face, and we see an older woman imitating the way he hides himself. The Avenger leaves a calling card next to his victims with his name and a vaginal triangle, and this detail is greedily taken up by the press. ("Murder—Wet from the Press" reads a headline.)

Hitchcock toys with the idea of making the rear of a truck carrying newspapers resemble a human face, so that the backs of male heads are made to look like eyes moving back and forth behind circular windows, and there are even piquant little "eyebrow" lines above these windows. Can we really judge the "face" of the back of this truck any more clearly than the face of Novello's mysterious lodger? Appearance is all in Hitchcock's world, and it is always slippery and deceptive, unstable.

Chorus girls in blonde wigs talk nervously about the killer, and a blonde fashion model pins a dark curl under her hat in order to repel The Avenger, who only strangles blondes. There is a shot from Novello's point of view as a shadow in a broad-brimmed hat approaches a house, and this is unsettling because we can't be sure whose point of view this is and can only assume it is the POV of the killer.

The landlady Mrs. Bunting (the fragile-looking Marie Ault) flinches when she sees Novello's lodger, who is never named, because his mouth is covered by a scarf, and he looks like the newspaper description of the killer. He seems inward, preoccupied, as if he were in a trance, like Conrad Veidt's somnambulist in *The Cabinet of Dr. Caligari* (1919). And then his eyes widen a little, which suggests mental instability.

There is a shot of his graceful hand, and when we can see more of his face it becomes clear that he is beautiful in a nearly feminine way, and weirdly abstracted. He briefly poses like a madman in the foyer, eyes staring upward, not in the way Hitchcock characters do when they are addressing God but like someone who is lost in some mentally abnormal delusion, like Mrs. Danvers in *Rebecca* (1940).

Novello was a major star, and so the producers let it be known that he could not be revealed as the killer, yet the entirety of the film is built so that we will suspect him, and this does not change over repeated viewings of *The Lodger*, which in its restored ninety-minute version moves at a slow pace. Hitchcock said in 1966 that Novello's character in *The Lodger* could be taken as just nervous or maybe a schizophrenic. "But these are rather clumsy excuses," he admitted. "Strictly speaking, you shouldn't have a matinee idol in a role of that kind."

Hitchcock finds all kinds of ways to film Novello, helping him along sometimes with a play of lights from outside passing cars in the lodger's room, and giving him a close-up where the shadow of a cross from the window is

Figure 2.1: Ivor Novello is marked by fate in *The Lodger*.

projected onto his face. This signals that he is somehow being persecuted, or is a marked man, either the wrong man or the wronged man (see fig. 2.1).

But the way he closes the window to shut out the sound of a newsboy selling papers can only be described as drama queen posturing, and some of Novello's feline hesitations look pretty silly now. He is at his best in *The Lodger* when he silently broods and trusts to presence and at his worst when most active, when he is "doing" something or trying to convey unrest or worst, and this confirms Hitchcock's liking for actors who "did nothing" well.

There are other reasons for Novello to keep still, and they have to do with seeming gay to the camera. "Anyway, I'm glad he's not keen on the girls," says Daisy's dopey policeman suitor Joe (Malcolm Keen), while Mrs. Bunting says, "Even if he is a bit queer, he's a gentleman." Novello's cringing and shuddering in *The Lodger* call to mind the English queen phrase, "My dear, I simply shuddered."

But as long as he "does nothing" in close-up and keeps his face opaque, Novello is a pleasingly ambiguous figure who invites curiosity and attention. Hitchcock, who was aware that Novello was gay, later told Rodney Ackland that he couldn't resist framing his star's head against a flower pot, but no such shot exists in the film as it stands, and so perhaps this was one of the shots that Ivor Montagu cut. "Hitch often told actors—for what mix of reasons I won't guess—that they really had to be part masculine and part feminine in order to get inside a character," said Hitchcock's friend Elsie Randolph. "He was always at ease with homosexual and bisexual people."

The daughter of Mrs. Bunting is a blonde girl named Daisy, who is played by an actress known simply as June, and at Hitchcock's request she wore a blonde wig over her own dark hair. She was another fragile beauty who married soon after her stint with Hitchcock and retired early after lending her face and figure, and her fear, to his first major picture. Hitchcock made this inexperienced actress repeat certain scenes as often as twenty times to get the reaction he wanted from her.

June later said that Hitchcock in this young period spoke in a mix of Cockney and North Country accents and that he was still struggling to emphasize dropped "h's," which is difficult to imagine given his later TV image as the proper English gentleman, or gentleman's gentleman. Acting something or someone else in England for social purposes always had a class basis, and to rise in station Hitchcock himself had to act, to create a persona, and so he understood the nature of this kind of acting, the way it can start out as artificial and become natural.

June makes little impression in *The Lodger*, except when Joe "playfully" puts his handcuffs on her and she screams, and also in an extended bathtub scene where she strips to her slip and then sits in the tub as steam rises and her feet paddle in the water and we wait for Joe or someone else to take advantage of the situation. Daisy, clever girl, has locked the bathroom door, which Novello's lodger tries to open.

And this brings up a key Hitchcockian question. Could Janet Leigh's Marion Crane have locked the bathroom door when she takes a shower in *Psycho*? Norman-in-drag-as-Mrs. Bates gets into Marion's room with his key, but is there a lock on the bathroom door Marion could have secured? Imagine "Norma" Bates's frustration, standing there with a butcher knife and unable to get in! Of course, stabbing Marion to death in her robe as she enters the bedroom after her shower just wouldn't have the same zing to it for either Mrs. Bates or the audience.

June's Daisy is a well-brought-up girl, conventional, likely popular, an easy laugher with something judgmental in her laughter, and complacent. Just the sort of powder puff of a girl that Hitchcock cannot abide, not so much "doing" nothing as being nothing much. But Daisy's mother does nothing very well. In the sequence where the lodger goes out at night and Mrs.

Bunting hears him, Ault does absolutely nothing to suggest fear and apprehension. She makes her face a blank that can be read in Hitchcock's images and in the rhythm of the editing, which do all the acting for her while we fill in the emotion.

Novello's queer beauty is highlighted in numerous close-ups, particularly one toward the end of the movie where his entire face fills the frame and light is reflected in his longing eyes, his nose appearing to be all nostril like Julie Christie's, his mouth temptingly open, coming to kiss the camera, just as Grace Kelly's Lisa Fremont later does in her famous first close-up in *Rear Window*. His lodger is in one of his "trances" here with Daisy, and he seems to be about to kiss or kill all of us watching, and yet he can be an object for our desire as well, a lovely male-female face there for the taking until we see nothing but his open mouth in close-up for the camera. That's the magic, and the magical dirtiness, of motion pictures.

Hitchcock knew that when a person paid to see a movie that they were invited to project themselves up there into the dark, and his pictures are filled with moments where we might kiss the man or woman on the screen, or share a ménage a trois with them, as in the famous kissing scene between Cary Grant and Ingrid Bergman in *Notorious* (1946).

In the scenes where June is kissing Novello, she is directed to look up, as if at God or at fate, and Hitchcock ominously frames that "To-night—Golden Curls" sign behind her in the last shot, so that we wonder just what she's in for with Novello's lodger, who has survived a vengeful mob and a sexy crucifixion where he has fallen and hung himself by handcuffs on an iron fence. In this scene, there is some fraught cutting between his helpless hands wilting, his pants from behind pulling up into the crack of his ass, and Novello's helpless, pretty face swooning with fear from the front.

The real Avenger has been caught "red-handed," but we don't see him get caught or find out anything further about him. In Hitchcock's films, beauty must be made to suffer, whether it is male or female, and Novello is both the beauty in distress here and an enigmatic figure of unspecified menace or trouble. The mob beats on him with their fists and some blood slides out of Novello's mouth before he is rescued.

Confusing actor and character can sometimes be inevitable in movies where the character finally is the actor, or vice versa, but basic distinctions can and should be made. For instance, Robert Walker was heterosexual but Bruno Antony in *Strangers on a Train* is about as gay as you can be in a movie of that period. Conversely, Anthony Perkins was gay but Norman Bates in

Psycho is heterosexual, and that movie in particular stops making any kind of sense if his tortured heterosexuality isn't definitely felt by the audience in spite of certain mannerisms from Perkins and certain tropes in Norman's back story that might have been read as gay in 1960, though they are less likely to be read as such today.

Far more neatly, John Dall and Farley Granger were gay and so are the characters they play in *Rope* (1948), and so all the signifiers there fit hand in glove. There aren't any crosscurrents showing up from their life off-camera that might confuse us or pull us in different directions. Novello's sexuality is hinted at in title cards for *The Lodger*, and his camera presence throws out other signifiers to bait and confuse us.

It is explained that Novello's character is actually a man on a mission to avenge his sister's murder, which is awkwardly shown to us toward the end of the film in a flashback. It's one of those flashbacks in Hitchcock that isn't all that convincing, maybe even a flashback that lies, like the one at the start of *Stage Fright* (1950). Yet what we see happening on screen can't be a lie. It is happening right in front of us. It is happening.

Of course you could say that *nothing* we see on a movie screen is actually happening, but that's always the trouble with flashbacks in a movie, lying or not, subjective or not (many critics have felt that the flashback of the Anne Baxter character in *I Confess* {1953} is meant to show how cheaply hearts-and-flowers her sensibility is). Hitchcock is always pushing at the bonds of his medium, but the camera can only be made to lie so much.

Was the lodger in love with his sister? Only that could explain the way he seems to sensually inhale Daisy's blonde hair, as if he is remembering his feelings for his dead sibling. Then again, he is also close to his mother, who asks him on her deathbed (and what an elaborately large, carved, and ornamented ship of a deathbed it is!) to not rest until The Avenger has been brought to justice.

The actress playing his mother looks like the upper-class, genteel version of Mrs. Buntley, and so this at least links the lodger and Daisy. A boy's best friend can be his mother, though mother might force the issue. Hitchcock himself was made to be a confidant to his own mother, Emma, who often received him in bed and expected his full attention. "All stories have an end," insists a title card at the close of *The Lodger*, yet this very insistence makes us doubt it.

3

Six More in Silence

The Ring, Downhill, The Farmer's Wife, Easy Virtue, Champagne, The Manxman

Between the success of *The Lodger* and his first talking film *Blackmail* (1929), Hitchcock made six silent pictures, all of them comparatively minor, and this is at least partly the fault of the actors that were cast in them. He himself thought fairly highly of *The Ring* (1927), a boxing drama that he wrote himself; this was the only time Hitchcock received sole credit for a screenplay.

The Ring is a film where Hitchcock experiments with different ways of telling a story and showing the passage of time, and with subjective camerawork that makes you see certain things from the vantage point of one character and then another. Not many directors, unfortunately, have done much with subjective camerawork in the years since Hitchcock made so much of his career on it.

The Ring is set in a carnival atmosphere, and it opens with shots of carnival rides meant to give the customers an enjoyable dose of contained fear, just like Hitchcock's later movies. There is a very unpleasant sequence where a black man is up on a platform and white people are throwing eggs at him to make him fall and the eggs keep hitting his face. Hitchcock makes the white people laughing look grotesque in close-ups, and one of these whites, notably, is a policeman.

The outright nastiness of this scene soon gives way to a triangle plot involving two boxers played by Carl Brisson and Ian Hunter and a girl played by Lilian Hall-Davis. These three actors basically "do nothing" in *The Ring*, but they don't do nothing well, to put it in Hitchcock's preferred terms. They present their faces and bodies to the camera, but there is no spark underneath, no inner animation. About a half hour into the film, Hitchcock rather desperately films Brisson and Davis reflected in the ripples of a pond, the only time in the movie where their images here have the necessary spark of life.

Hunter went on to play second-leads in Hollywood movies of the 1930s, and he usually got the part of a guy who doesn't get the girl, so he was a placeholder figure. Brisson was Danish and often sang and danced in Copenhagen cabarets, and so he was popular in his own country in a way that was somewhat similar to Ivor Novello's popularity in Britain, but Brisson was a stolid guy, a straight arrow, without the flaunted beauty, style, and freakish movements that made Novello so distinctive and troubling in *The Lodger*. Davis, who would go on to star for Hitchcock in *The Farmer's Wife* (1928), was a beautiful brunette, but her beauty lacked edge and charm and expressiveness, and Hitchcock was unhappy with her. She died in 1933 at the age of thirty-five, a suicide.

She had been billed as "Lillian Hall-Davis" in all the other movies she made except for her two with Hitchcock, where the second "l" in her first name became "Lilian" for him. "Lilian was a good actress, willing and very efficient, but rather fragile," Hitchcock said in 1976. "She was married and had a child, but while we were filming *The Ring* and *The Farmer's Daughter*, she had an affair with Gordon Harker. He was married, too, and involved with yet another young woman. Then Lilian had a nervous breakdown, and soon her career was over." Messy personal lives could lead to such endpoints, and this confirmed Hitchcock's need, for most of his life, to keep his desires in order and sublimate them into his films.

Hitchcock worked again with Ivor Novello on *Downhill* (1927), an adaptation of a play that Novello had written with the actress Constance Collier under the very queer pseudonym David L'Estrange. Novello's upper-class Roddy Berwick is kicked out of school after a waitress falsely accuses him of impregnating her. His stuffy family doesn't believe Roddy's story, and so he goes . . . downhill. We see him waiting on tables but then the camera dollies back so that we realize that Roddy is actually playing a waiter in a musical revue, and then the film comes alive in a sequence at a dance hall that plays with Hitchcock's interest in appearance and what it can hide.

Roddy has become a dancing gigolo with an overweight female pimp. We see an older woman (Violet Farebrother) slightly desperately staring at him from her table and quietly lusting for him, and Roddy registers that she is appraising him, but there is something more to it than that. Farebrother's character is not given a name but is billed as "Poetess." A refined Miss Lonelyhearts type, she has gray hair and looks like she was probably pretty and maybe sought after when young. She smiles and sighs at Roddy wistfully, and she makes a deal for him with his pimp.

Roddy sits down at her table, and the older poet draws him out: "My poor boy, how did you come down to—this?" She listens to the story of his life with great interest, holding her chin up with a limp wrist and looking very appealing, all at once. There seems to be a bond forming between them beyond the financial, or at least Farebrother's poet would like this to be so. There is an intensity in her manner as she holds her face with her hand that suggests a nearly crazed hunger for human contact, and that hunger is definitely partly sexual in basis (see fig. 3.1). Somehow you get the sense that her poems aren't very good, for intense desperation does not often pay dividends in either art or would-be romantic-sexual situations.

But then the windows of the dance hall are opened and the morning sun comes in, and Hitchcock catches the full horror of a debauched nighttime milieu suddenly exposed by glaring sunlight, with a lot of drunken people looking their worst and clinging on to tables for support. In this new light, Roddy suddenly sees just how old Farebrother's poet is, and the camera mercilessly keeps her in a close shot so that we can see every gray hair on her head and every wrinkle on her face. The intensity of her expression of longing is undimmed but caught in the wide-eyed look of desperation that formed our first unfortunate glimpse of her.

Figure 3.1: Violet Farebrother attempts to make contact with a young gigolo in *Downhill.*

Roddy recoils from her, and she realizes what has happened, and this makes her face collapse. This is a woman who knows about disappointment. She walks away from Roddy slowly and sadly, and the effect of all this is extremely sad. Farebrother's middle-aged poet and Roddy might have made a go of it, if only for one exciting night, if her aged surface hadn't turned him off, or been revealed by the sunlight.

This sequence has such power because Hitchcock surely identifies with this hopeful woman who gets rejected because of her age just as he was rejected because of his weight, but the effect is one of pathos spiked with a touch of sarcasm, a touch of the grotesque, even a morbid dash of humor. After all, Hitchcock insisted that *Psycho*, one of the saddest of all films, was meant to be a funny, or fun, picture.

When Roddy starts hallucinating out at sea toward the end of *Downhill*, he imagines Farebrother's character laughing at him, so that she haunts him just as she haunts the film itself. Hitchcock would use this actress again as the disapproving Mrs. Whittaker in *Easy Virtue* (1928), the first really domineering mother in his work and a very different kind of character for Farebrother.

In *Easy Virtue*, Farebrother's stares are imperious and aggressively judgmental, and her tallness is emphasized amid the grand and stodgy design of this woman's home. There are enormous religious icons staring down at everyone who sits at her dining room table, which is lit as if for a séance. Farebrother was also cast as a juror in *Murder!*, but it is in the dance hall scene with Novello in *Downhill* that she stakes her claim to cinematic immortality. She was only thirty-nine years old when she played the poet in *Downhill*, but in 1927 that was or could be seen as over-the-hill for a woman on her own who doesn't dye her hair.

Women who are un-marriageable or past their prime are the main concern of Hitchcock's next picture, *The Farmer's Wife* (1928), a gentle comedy based on a stage hit. Farmer Sweetland (Jameson Thomas) is a lonely widower looking to get married again. Thomas gives a sensitive performance, staring at the empty chair of the farmer's dead wife with touchingly restrained longing, but there isn't much comedy in the basic situation here, where the farmer interviews unsuitable women while talking about them to his loyal, young, and attractive housekeeper Araminta (Lilian Hall-Davis). It's obvious from the start that Araminta would be his ideal mate, and so we just wait to see when he will figure that out.

There is a fast dolly shot to a table filled with luscious-looking pastries that are coveted by a young boy, and this is probably the most charged moment in the whole of *The Farmer's Wife*. Hitchcock tentatively treats the parade of ladies who try out to be the farmer's new wife, and they are variously plump, thin, bossy, meek, sexually frustrated, and often trying to be something they aren't. Hitchcock doesn't mock them, exactly, and he doesn't go for pathos, either. Instead, he settles on a neither-here-nor-there tone that regards them all uneasily. You can't really laugh at them, and it won't do to cry, either, so what's to be done with them? This is a question that will be taken up far more seriously and intently in several later Hitchcock films.

Easy Virtue was again based on a play, this one by Noël Coward, whose image of comic and gay sophistication is very far from Hitchcock's own manner and tone. Coward material calls for stylized, aware playing that goes against everything that interested Hitchcock when it came to acting, and so most of the acting in *Easy Virtue* is very stiff and overly presentational.

Hitchcock used a mobile camera and point-of-view shots throughout this picture, which deals with a lady named Larita (Isabel Jeans) who acquires a tarnished reputation after she gets named as a correspondent in a divorce case. Hitchcock keeps showing a piece of paper where a member of the court is writing down thoughts about the case, one of which reads, "Love is akin to pity." We finally see that the person writing these thoughts is a stout middle-aged woman who seems to be projecting her own issues onto Larita.

Larita has been an artist's model, and Jeans does a lot of artificial posing and fussing and indicating in long shots in the first half of *Easy Virtue*, giving a vivid demonstration of outmoded Delsarte stage technique acting: slowly and stiffly raising her whole arm to her forehead to show distress, etc. In certain close-ups where she is still and not "acting," Jeans has an adult kind of reflectiveness that is dignified and intriguing, but this is always spoiled once she feels she has to do things with her body and is not controlled and boxed in by Hitchcock's camera.

Jeans improves in the second half of *Easy Virtue*, activating outmoded but still tasty theatrical poses of defiance with her rigidly held cigarette. An ominous camera is visible under the opening credits of *Easy Virtue*, which is meant to signify how Larita's life is shadowed by negative publicity, and this occasions the final title card, which Hitchcock was ashamed of having written himself. Outside a courthouse for the second time, Larita tells reporters, "Shoot! There's nothing left to kill."

Jeans had been married to Claude Rains from 1913 to 1915, and it had been a stormy relationship, with three separations before their divorce after he found that she was carrying another man's child. (Rains later said that he found her acting excessively mannered.) Jeans had some scenes with Novello in *Downhill* and Hitchcock cast her in Hollywood in *Suspicion* (1941) as a friend of Cary Grant's bounder Johnnie Aysgarth. Her most notable later role was as Aunt Alicia in Vincente Minnelli's *Gigi* (1958).

Hitchcock was most interested in a scene in *Easy Virtue* where a telephone operator (Benita Hume) listens in to a young society boy proposing marriage to Larita. Hitchcock sees this girl as an audience surrogate who goes through all kinds of vicarious emotions as Larita hems and haws over the proposal. He keeps the camera on Hume as her face alternately registers ecstasy, uncertainty, and finally relief.

The problem with this scene is that Hume forces the expressions on her face in a staccato, obvious way, as if each turn in the conversation is an electric shock that jolts her. This is a silent movie, and Hume is being asked to sustain a scene by herself in which we need to follow her emotions precisely, and so she is a little nervous and overeager. Then again, her facial expressions do get the meaning of the scene very clearly across.

If another actress had done this difficult scene in a more subtle, lifelike, legato way, some of the audience might not have known quite what she was doing or been able to follow it. And so Hitchcock, who always wanted to communicate with the largest possible audience, allows the large-eyed Hume to put across her feelings to the camera in a showy, non-Hitchcock-like fashion. It could be said that the girl Hume is playing maybe isn't the brightest and that Hume is trying to get that across, but it still feels more like acting than being.

Hitchcock himself called *Champagne* (1928) his worst movie, a bauble of a screwball comedy about a madcap heiress (Betty Balfour) with very little in the way of plot or character. Balfour has a round face and round eyes that she widens in close-up so as to appear lovably ditsy, and she wears too much jewelry and self-consciously cute, vulgar dresses with little ruffles and flowers on them. "I've always understood that simplicity was the keynote of good taste," says a beau who disapproves of her fussy outfits. Sulking at this, Balfour goes back into her room and comes out in a black dress with a scarf over her head and acts like a waif to mock him, but this rather backfires because even the scarf she selects is too loudly printed. Though charming in her own way, Balfour is not a Hitchcockian type of performer.

Like Jeans's Larita Filton in *Easy Virtue*, Balfour's heiress, who is only known as "The Girl," has a maid with a distinctly lesbian look and slicked-back haircut, and it would be pleasant to imagine them both being friendly with the gay dress designer in *The Pleasure Garden*. Hitchcock loved to fill the edges of his movies with subversive people and images like this, and sometimes he even moved them center stage.

Hitchcock continues his experiments with subjective camerawork in *Champagne*, as in a shot through the bottom of a champagne glass as it is drunk down by a man on board a ship. (We see a *very* phallic-looking champagne bottle opened and then emptied right before this, which shows how often this director had sex on the brain.) Hitchcock wanted the audience to be aware that they were watching a movie, which is why he is the opposite of someone like Howard Hawks, who favored smooth and "invisible" editing and very little camera movement.

Balfour's father pretends that they have lost their money to teach her a lesson, and so she has to apply for a modeling job, which occasions the only memorable and heated bit of *Champagne*. She is standing in a theatrical booking office filled with photos of other men and women tacked to the wall. "We're only interested in legs here," the manager tells her.

The manager has a lean-faced assistant whose interest is clearly pricked by Balfour's oblivious cuteness. He is a real wolf with a narrow, nasty-ugly-sexy face, and he looks a lot like the crook who stole money from Carmelita Geraghty's Jill in the theater-world opening of *The Pleasure Garden*. Hitchcock gives this assistant a close-up as he leans crookedly against a wall with his head tilted at an angle and looks Balfour up and down. He has a high forehead and skin that is stretched over the bones of his face, almost like Boris Karloff. Hitchcock cuts to a medium shot of Balfour and this man as she stands with her back to him and he slowly raises his right foot and lifts up her skirt in back, and then he goes over to the manager and puts in a word for her, which gets her a job. This looking-without-permission scene has an extremely erotic charge, at least in Hitchcock terms.

A regular in English music halls, the impish Balfour was far more attractively showcased in Marcel L'Herbier's *Le Diable au Coeur* (1928) as a lively girl in a fishing village, but her career ebbed away after sound came in, and her last film credit was in 1945. In 1952, Balfour attempted suicide after a failed try at a comeback, but she survived and spent the next twenty years of her life in seclusion before her death in 1977.

Hitchcock's next two films would star the beautiful Czech actress Anny Ondra, born Anna Ondrakova, a girl whose face often takes on a perverted sort of gleam. Unfortunately, her two leading men in *The Manxman* (1929),

Hitchcock's last silent film, are Carl Brisson and Malcolm Keen, who had played the dunderheaded cop boyfriend in *The Lodger*.

Extravagant claims were made for *The Manxman* in Eric Rohmer and Claude Chabrol's Hitchcock book, which was published in 1957 and eagerly tried to prove that Hitchcock was a quintessentially Catholic artist. But when François Truffaut tried to get Hitchcock to say that this was a personal film for him in his own seminal 1966 book of interviews with the Master, Hitchcock brushed this movie aside indifferently.

The Manxman is a film with very few title cards where even a crucial moment when Ondra's character says she is going to have a baby is left to us to lip-read. Hitchcock wanted to tell his stories on a purely visual basis, and this was a fine idea in theory but not in practice for *The Manxman*, a somber triangle drama that founders on the lack of animation in the two male leads. Ondra is lovely to look at, but she sometimes falls into face making and "acting" here as if to make up for the flatness of her screen partners, and sometimes her sexual leering at the camera gets a little out of hand. Her coquettish expressions of sexual hunger so inflamed Hitchcock that he doesn't seem to care that she gets slightly fussy about them for the camera.

4
Blackmail

Hitchcock made *Blackmail* (1929) as a silent movie, but then it was mostly reshot as a talking picture. Anny Ondra was the star, and her thick Czech accent was a problem because the character she was playing, Alice White, is supposed to be a working-class London girl. In a sound test that Hitchcock made with Ondra, we can see the way he liked to tease his beautiful leading ladies.

"Now, Miss Ondra, you asked me to let you hear your voice on the talking pic-shaw," Hitchcock says playfully. "But Hitch, you mustn't do that," Ondra says. "Why not?," he asks. "Well, because I can speak well!" she says, and the "au" in the word "because" comes out strangely. "Do you realize the squad van will be here *any moment*?," Hitchcock emphasizes, to get her to emote. "No, really, oh my God, I'm terribly frightened," she says non-seriously, in her sing-song accent. "Why, have you been a bad woman or something?," Hitchcock asks her. Ondra says, "Well, not this bad, but, uh . . ."

He pounces: "But you've slept with *men*?" Ondra very charmingly turns away and puts her hand on her mouth and cries, "Oh no!" She turns back around, giggling and trying to control the giggles, and he says, "You have not? Come here, stand in your place, otherwise it will not come out right . . . as the girl said to the soldier." At this Ondra breaks up laughing and turns away again, and you can see that Hitchcock is pleased with her reaction. "That's enough!," he says, smiling and holding his hand up.

The young Michael Powell, who later went on to make a string of colorful films in the 1940s, was the on-set photographer on *Champagne* and helped out on the script for *Blackmail*. In his memoir *A Life in Movies*, Powell wrote of Hitchcock, "I am sure he wanted Anny as much as I did." Powell took nature shots of Ondra, and Hitchcock urged him to get Ondra and a boy together in the hay and shoot them so that "she's pressing up against him, to feel his cock against her leg."

It was decided that Ondra would mouth the dialogue for the sound version of *Blackmail* and that the English actress Joan Barry would speak it into a microphone off-camera, and of course that leads to all kinds of awkwardness, but the awkwardness has its own fascination. Here we have Ondra, a very kittenish actress with a distinctly Eastern European flavor, like an Elisabeth Bergner with sex on the brain, with a very refined-lady type stagy British voice coming out of her. So neither the look of Ondra nor the sound of Barry is suitable for Alice White, who is supposed to be working class and torn between wanting sex and adventure and repressing that instinct in herself, which gets her into a lot of trouble.

The problem with the casting here is that Ondra looks as if she would have no problem sleeping with Crewe (Cyril Ritchard), a lecherous artist, whereas judging by the sound of Barry's genteel voice, Alice would never have gone up to "see his etchings" to begin with. What was needed was an in-between sort of actress to play Alice, someone seemingly repressed/refined but with a strong sexual desire that she is trying to hold down. This is the tension that Hitchcock desired in his dream women, the mystery, the drama. Tallulah Bankhead had played in the hit stage version of *Blackmail*, but it's hard to imagine the rowdy and uninhibited Bankhead in this part.

Hitchcock often repeated a favorite fantasy to interviewers, namely that it is the seemingly well-bred cool blonde, the librarian type who wears glasses, who is most likely to aggressively open a man's pants in the back of a cab. Hitchcock said he felt sorry for Marilyn Monroe because "sex was written all over her face," thus there was no dramatic tension with her, no reveal, nothing to hold down and then unleash by surprise. It was that surprise that turned Hitchcock on creatively and personally.

The opening of *Blackmail*, which is a high-speed chase of cops catching and apprehending a criminal, is an enormous leap forward for Hitchcock on a technical level, and he experiments with unnaturally prolonging certain moments in this opener to heighten the thrills for the audience. The cops stand in a doorway for an awfully long time as the seedy-looking criminal in bed notices them in a mirror and slowly reaches for his gun before making a grab for it. This first sequence is played with only soundtrack music and no talk or ambient noise at all aside from the brief sound of a window smashing and some car honks.

It seems as if the apprehended criminal has been brought in for a line-up, but when we see a short girl going down a long row of men, it is a different man that she identifies, gently placing her hand on his chest. This opening is so unsettling because Hitchcock is setting up just how arbitrary this system is. Is this the wrong man the girl identifies, or the right one? Does it matter?

He looks far less guilty than the man caught in bed, but does that mean he is innocent?

We see the original criminal standing at a desk in front at the station, and we see his long rap sheet. He is a thief. He is fingerprinted and he is locked in a cell, and at eight minutes in, we finally hear some dialogue. In the opening credits a real ex-Scotland Yard detective, a Sergeant Bishop, is listed as the Detective Sergeant here. Hitchcock wants this milieu to be as realistic as possible but also slightly stylized, visually and aurally.

One of the cops, Frank Webber (John Longden), meets his girlfriend Alice and takes her out on the town, and we see Hitchcock himself on the subway in one of his most memorable cameos as a fastidious chubby man trying to read a book and getting bothered by a little boy.

Though the vocal rhythms here are understandably off or unnatural, Ondra flips on her perverted and slightly grotesque face and gives Hitchcock what he needs in a series of silent close-ups at a busy restaurant that establish Alice's flightiness and her need for attention. When Frank leaves her alone for a moment, she takes a note out of her purse that reads, "I'll be here on Tuesday at 6:30 . . . will you?"

Alice sees the man who wrote her this note, an artist named Crewe. Had she gone to the restaurant by herself and flirted with this artist? Had she been with Frank and Crewe had noticed her and somehow slipped her the note? Whatever the case, Alice was intrigued enough to keep the note and keep an eye out for Crewe, but she signals to him to wait, and she tries to make up with Frank, with whom she has been lightly arguing about going to the movies. Frank stubbornly and unattractively stays mad at her and storms off. In a Hitchcock movie, dating a policeman is never a good idea.

Frank goes outside and seems to think better of his decision, but then he sees Alice leave the restaurant with Crewe, and hurt feelings register on his face. Crewe lives only around the corner from the shop owned by Alice's family, and so they walk there and flirt with each other. We see the blackmailer Tracy (Donald Calthrop, who would be used again in Hitchcock's *Murder!* and *Number 17* {1932}) listening to their conversation as Crewe talks her into going upstairs with him.

Crewe asks Alice if she is frightened to go up to his room. "It would take more than a man to frighten me!," Alice says in Barry's piping, *Alice in Wonderland*-style voice. Off screen, as Alice waits near the door of the apartment house, Tracy tries to get some money from Crewe but gets turned down. "Nothing but a sponger," Crewe says of Tracy, "pestering people all up and down the street." Are Crewe and Tracy friends, or former friends? There is something criminal-seeming about Crewe, a mysteriousness, a furtiveness.

We see Alice go up, up, up the stairs to Crewe's studio, and the visual of the two of them climbing up many flights of stairs is redolent of the famous shot of Janet Gaynor and Charles Farrell going up to their *7th Heaven* (1927), an enormous hit for director Frank Borzage that Hitchcock perverts here for his own purposes.

The scene where Alice flirts with Crewe in his rooms is uncomfortably prolonged. He seems mocking with her sometimes, in a troublesome way, and in his studio there is a painting of a laughing jester that strikes a similarly sour note. Alice draws a cartoon-like head on a canvas, and then Crewe draws a sexy nude body underneath it, complete with breasts. "Oooh, you are awful," we hear Barry's prim voice say while Ondra laughs in the exact non-prim way she did in her sound test with Hitchcock, a disconnect between voice and image that finally does express, in counterpoint, the tension in Alice.

As Alice undresses so she can pose for him, Crewe sits at the piano and plays a very Noël Coward-ish song in a Noël Coward-ish fashion, which stresses Hitchcock's sense of both Coward's liberation and aberration. (The song is about a "wild and naughty child" for whom "an awful fate" is predicted.) Ritchard's most notable credit after *Blackmail* was his very camp performance as Captain Hook in Mary Martin's perennial musical productions of *Peter Pan*, and so sometimes here there is a Norman Bates-ian confusion of a gay actor with a straight role.

In the lead-up to the struggle between Alice and Crewe, it feels like she is about to be murdered. Crewe presses down her hair and pulls it and then kisses her hard in a mean sort of way, and she has to push him off. If he had kissed her more gently, might they just have slept together? Alas, this artist seems incapable of a gentle kiss. In the silent version of *Blackmail*, Ondra's Alice has far more rapport with Crewe, even giving him a little kiss before he kisses her too hard and her mood turns.

Surely the private Hitchcock wouldn't mind seeing Ondra's Alice have a bit of fun away from her stodgy cop fiancée, but *not* with Crewe, who is given an old-time melodrama mustache when a shadow from a light fixture disfigures the right side of his face (see fig. 4.1). When he hides Alice's dress from her and she is left in her underwear, it doesn't feel sexy at all but crude and aggressive on his part.

Figure 4.1: Cyril Ritchard is disfigured by evil urges in *Blackmail.*

Finally, we only see them as struggling shadows on a wall, and we hear Barry's frantic cries of "Let me go!" and "Oh!" over and over again before we see Ondra's hand from behind a curtain grab a knife on a plate next to some bread. The curtain comes to rest, and we see Crewe's stiff hand fall out of it. Alice, who is still in her slip, comes out from behind the curtain and moves slowly and jerkily, like a robot.

Hitchcock has clearly directed Ondra to make her face a blank and move like a puppet on a string, and this is the strongest part of her performance because she becomes an abstract kind of figure: stunned, depressed, but also a figure of vengeance, a girl who has nearly been raped who has protected herself. It's an open question how far the artist has been able to get with her before getting knifed to death.

There is no blood on the knife, which aids the dreamlike quality here. What has happened? Why has it happened? As in *Psycho*, a stabbing has sent the film off one track and onto another. Alice rips the painting of the laughing jester, which had earlier made her laugh but now seems to be jeering at her. She puts her dress and coat and hat back on quickly and decisively and grabs her purse, and then she inks out her name on the painting she had made with Crewe.

There is an overhead shot of the vertiginous-looking staircase as Alice creeps out of the building. So this is a murder that takes place off screen and then, as in *Psycho*, we see and feel the long aftermath of the violence. Outside, as Alice walks home, the street sounds seem to make no impression on her as she passes through a crowd under a theater sign that reads, "A New Comedy." The world laughs at our troubles.

Alice looks up at a neon cocktail shaker sign that gradually turns into a knife stabbing downward. Hitchcock cuts between her feet walking as morning dawns and a shot of Crewe's dead hand until Alice sees the hand of a bum in the same position. She stops and opens her mouth and we hear a scream, but it is the scream of the landlady finding the artist's body, which connects the two women in their horror, if nothing else.

Frank is sent to Crewe's studio to investigate and he finds Alice's glove there. When Frank turns around, Hitchcock has the camera dolly very quickly to Crewe's dead face in bed and then this dead face is cut away from abruptly, as if Frank has shot a quick glance at the corpse and then disregarded it. This dolly shot and cutaway exactly replicates what a fast look at a dead body would feel like, just like the later famous shots of Jessica Tandy's mother quickly seeing the corpse of the farmer in *The Birds*.

Alice sneaks back into her house, running up the stairs just in the nick of time as her mother (Sara Allgood) walks out of the kitchen. Alice has movie star photographs tacked on the wall of her bedroom, and a shrill bird in a cage near her bed makes threatening sounds just to bedevil her, it seems, as she takes off her stockings in close-up and puts on new stockings and a new dress. Hitchcock's camera eyes Ondra's legs here with Crewe-like lust.

The outside world in Hitchcock's movies is always set up to underline the obsessions of the characters, as if this world is out to get them, to laugh at them, to egg them on in their disturbance. And Hitchcock himself has his obsessions. A neighbor lady (Phyllis Monkman) with a lower-class accent talks about a bathtub murder that was in the papers. "After I read about it, I didn't dare have a bath for a month!," she cries. "And for weeks after that I only had a rinse down."

The knife, the weapon she took for herself, becomes Alice's obsession, which is expressed later in the famous scene where all she hears of this neighbor woman's chatter about the murder, finally, is the word "knife," over and over again. Hitchcock had already used a lot of subjective camerawork in his silent period, and right away he proves just how subjective sound can be, too. Hitchcock's people are always so stuck in themselves, so wrapped up, so trapped, and the few times they try to reach out to someone else always go very, very badly.

Alice's father asks her to cut a bit of bread, and the litany of the word "knife" finally ends when the chatter of Monkman's neighbor and Alice's anxiety come together on the phrase, "I mean in Chelsea, you mustn't use a *knife*!," and that last "knife" is screeched in alarm as the knife Alice is holding seems to fly out of her hand. "Dear, you ought to be more careful," Alice's father says. "Might have cut somebody with that." This scene has nowhere near the same impact in the silent version of *Blackmail*, where Alice drops the knife because she hears the bell of the shop ringing.

The last third of the film where Alice and her cop fiancée are blackmailed by Tracy does not have the vitality of the first hour of this picture, though of course the same has often been said of the last third of *Psycho*. This is mainly because Tracy is one of Hitchcock's least appealing villains, a slow burning, irritating little man. When Frank has turned the tables on him and asserted his power as a policeman, Tracy tries for sympathy. "I'm not bad, really," he insists. "Only things have gone wrong lately . . . and one's got to live, you know!" But Tracy does not sound too convincing here and few hearts will be melted by his little outburst. Any attempt to switch our sympathy to Tracy, which Hitchcock might have tried for in his mature period, is blocked by Calthrop's low-life, ashcan demeanor.

In the climactic chase through the British Museum, as police are pursuing Tracy because they think he killed Crewe, there's a surreal feeling to the image where the little blackmailer shimmies down a rope next to a large stone face, a large monument and a small man standing in for tiny people and whoever or whatever might be God. On top of the roof, Tracy tries to tell the cops that Alice is guilty but falls to his death through some plate glass before he can do so.

Alice wants to turn herself in, standing up like a little girl steeling herself to take a punishment, and a shadow falls on her face like the shadow that had invaded Crewe's face earlier as she looks upward at a punishing God. But Frank stops her from confessing at the station. Hitchcock had wanted to end *Blackmail* with Frank booking Alice just like the criminal had been booked in the first sequence, but this was judged too sad. And so the wrong unappealing man perishes so that the appealing Alice is left to live with her guilt and probably get stuck forever with Frank. At the finish she sees that painting of a jester laughing at her again, and this is hardly a happy or reassuring close.

In the silent version of *Blackmail*, the ribald, jovial doorman who likes to joke with Alice says that there will soon be lady detectives at the Yard, and he'll do all right at the door then, ho ho. This adds a further touch of despair for Alice, pointing up just how restricted her life is by men from all walks of life.

Ondra married the boxer Max Schmeling and lived in Germany with him until her death in 1987. She sent Christmas cards to Hitchcock and Alma saying, "Hitchy, I'm so happy here."

5

Juno and the Paycock, Murder!, Mary, Elstree Calling, The Skin Game

After the success of *Blackmail,* Hitchcock was prevailed upon to film Seán O'Casey's Irish play *Juno and the Paycock.* Following a fairly mobile opening of a political meeting led by Barry Fitzgerald that is interrupted by gunfire, Hitchcock lets a long conversation play out in a bar without a cut for nearly four minutes. The effect is that thing he later dreaded and criticized: pictures of people talking.

Inserts of close-ups are edited into the long takes Hitchcock uses here sometimes, and this feels ungainly. The long takes in *Juno and the Paycock* tend to let the actors do what they might have done on stage, without break and without the control of Hitchcock's cutting and framing. The compositions generally box people together, often in a way that seems deliberately crowded.

The camera pans up a decrepit-looking building to give a kind of entrance to the lead and star of the film, Sara Allgood's Juno, who is seen staring out of a window. Once the camera comes into her apartment, it rarely leaves that interior, and this quickly begins to feel oppressive. Allgood, who had played the small part of Alice's mother in *Blackmail,* is fine here, in her way. She had played the part of Juno on stage, and the kind of performance she gives in *Juno and the Paycock* might still play well on stage, but for the camera her acting seems too thought-out, too conscious of shaping her behavior moment by moment.

Allgood knows who Juno is and she is showing her to us, or demonstrating her. Like the other Irish actors in this picture, including her own sister Maire O'Neill, Allgood is not doing camera-friendly work, especially in her last big scene, where she cries, "What can God do against the stupidity of men?" The camera sniffs out the removal of what all the actors are doing here, and the projected grandstanding of this climax. Hitchcock draws the camera back as Allgood raises her arms and cries to God for mercy, approximating the proscenium staging of the theater, which was never his interest.

Hitchcock contributed some brief interpolated material to the musical revue *Elstree Calling* (1930), where there is a sick-joke blackout sketch: a man and a woman are kissing with the camera close enough to be in the middle of them, Hitchcockian ménage à trois style. A menacing man enters the room, also in extreme close-up, and he fires a gun at the couple. And then he says, "My God, I'm in the wrong flat!" Otherwise, *Elstree Calling* is an often-tasteless mélange of musical numbers. As a Hitchcock curio, it does very little to repay curiosity.

Murder! was Hitchcock's next and far more congenial project, a good solid melodrama with sexual undertones. Hitchcock himself adapted the Clemence Dane/Helen Simpson play *Enter Sir John* with Walter Mycroft for this picture, with Alma credited for the scenario. There is a real crackerjack Hitchcock opening sequence here that begins with a scream and then shots of birds flying and a cat running before the camera moves along the sides of houses and people opening their windows in the middle of the night. We enter the bedroom of a man and a woman, and Hitchcock enjoys looking at this couple in very intimate moments: the man taking his teeth out of a glass in close-up, the woman putting her slip on under her nightdress, first in full-length shot and then in a close-up of her feet struggling to get the nightdress on.

The dark-haired English actress Norah Baring was chosen by Hitchcock to play the lead in this picture, and she is presented as a woman of mystery, a face to ponder and project upon. Baring plays an actress named Diana Baring, and she is first discovered, speechless and unmoving, near a dead female body that turns out to be the corpse of another actress named Edna Druce.

Baring is seen sitting in profile and not talking as neighbors and police come into her room. The camera moves down to her high-heeled foot, where we can make out a run in her stocking, and then over to the murder weapon, a poker. Norah Baring is a perfect example of someone who has camera presence, and she is best in *Murder!* when she is simply staring forward and not talking. When Baring finally speaks here in a thin, high voice, a bit of her mystery evaporates, but not for long.

Hitchcock had chosen Baring after only a three-minute conversation. "I asked him later if he always picked out his stars with as little ado as he did me," Baring said in an interview for *Film Pictorial* in 1935. "Because all he seemed to do when we first met was to play silly jokes—I thought he was having a good laugh at my expense."

But then Baring remembered what Hitchcock had told her while they were shooting. "Shows you how little you know about it," he said. "You see, there you were. You had the type of face and the personality I had in mind, but you were all tied up with nerves and so tense that at first I hadn't a ghost of an idea whether you would be any use to me at all. I didn't know if you would photograph or record well enough."

"Hitchcock used to make gentle fun of me in the studio," Baring said. "But I had to do as he wanted simply because he did not allow me to get so strung-up that I could not express the emotions the part required." So this is a first example of Hitchcock getting the performance he wanted from a somewhat inexperienced or nervous actor by teasing them out of their nerves. It wouldn't work well with everyone, but it did work for Baring in *Murder!* She made only five more films after this and lived out a long retirement until her death in 1985.

The male lead in *Murder!* was the quiet and restrained Herbert Marshall, who had lost a leg during service in World War I but got around well with a wooden leg. This was only his third picture, which immediately followed his playing the lover who is shot by Jeanne Eagels in *The Letter* (1929), but he is already a real camera player, giving just what is needed and no more. Marshall is an ideal Hitchcock actor: a little phlegmatic, maybe, but able to suggest that there are fires banked down in him, and with a speaking voice redolent of the plummy but held-back or constipated tones of James Mason.

Marshall plays an actor named Sir John Menier who has been assigned to the jury in the murder case against Diana Baring. Sir John is very taken with her dark, enigmatic beauty, and he also feels guilty because she once asked to be in his company and he sent her elsewhere. The ambitious Baring hears dialogue and applause in her head as she sits and stares in her jail cell, imagining the performance that she would like to be giving at the theater. It would seem that she is less upset about the murder of Edna Druce and more upset that she doesn't get to act her part in a farce on stage that night.

Baring had been involved with Handel Fane, a female impersonator played by Esme Percy in his first film role. Born in 1887, Percy had trained with Sarah Bernhardt and had made his theatrical debut in 1904. He was a star on stage in this period, often playing in George Bernard Shaw plays, notably as Henry Higgins in *Pygmalion* opposite Mrs. Patrick Campbell. Percy had been noted for his good looks and charm, but by the 1920s he had started to appear a little peaked. He had put on weight and his nose had been broken, and he lost an eye during a "playful mishap" with a Great Dane. So *Murder!*

stars an actor with a wooden leg and another actor with a glass eye. Very suggestive Hitchcock actors.

"This is Handel Fane, 100% he-woman," says a manager as Percy's Fane comes off stage in drag. He looks dainty at first but then disconcertingly authoritative and menacing as he walks toward the camera, and it turns out that everything about Fane is disconcerting, from his odd name (it is later spelled "Handell" in Sir John's appointment book) to his uncertain place in the theatrical firmament. "I assure you, Inspector, I'm not the other woman in the case," Fane says sportingly, in a high, precise voice, before hearing his cue to go back out to act his female part.

Hitchcock sketches in all kinds of intriguing detail at the trial. Baring has a female defense attorney, and the jurors move their heads between the main players in court as if they're at a tennis match. In the jury room, Violet Farebrother plays a well-bred upper-class woman who is portrayed as a soft-hearted and somewhat soft-headed bleeding-heart liberal. She is an enthusiast for psychoanalytic theories who wants to see Baring freed at any cost.

There is a pessimistic man who condemns the prison system and who then goes into a brief antiwar rant, and there is another man who seems simple-minded. As Farebrother's juror talks of fugue states, there is a moment of class solidarity where two female working-class co-jurors exchange a brief "Get her!" look. Farebrother wonders if Baring suffers from "split personality," if she is a killer and an ordinary person in one, like Norman Bates.

A heavyset man wonders how someone who looks as sweet as Baring could "do such a thing," because she is the sort of girl he would like for a . . . well, for a daughter. "I presume, Sir, that an ugly woman would stand very little chance at your hands," says another juror dryly. Farebrother's juror is sure that Fane is "obviously in love with the prisoner." To modern eyes, Fane would be more likely to be in love with Sir John, but in 1930 that can't even be thought of as a possibility for a leading character. Hitchcock experiments here, turning the jurors into a stylized chorus of close-up heads that he rapidly cuts among as they all try to browbeat Sir John, who is not convinced of Baring's guilt. The jurors cry his name in unison, which is a very theatrical device fitted to the theater theme.

In a scene where Marshall is shaving in a mirror back at his stylish apartment, Hitchcock tries to explore aural subjectivity with a long internal monologue played on the soundtrack as Sir John thinks things through and music from Wagner's *Tristan and Isolde* plays on the radio. This monologue of Sir John's thoughts is very detailed and well written and aided by the romantic obsessive music, which was played by a full orchestra on the set, even if Marshall's look of concentration suggests he is suffering from some stomach ailment.

Acting itself is partly the subject of *Murder!*, and it is also how Sir John solves the case when he imitates a woman's voice to prove that the landlady heard Fane at the murder scene. It is finally proved that Baring is the wrong woman and that Fane is the killer, but this takes a while, and Hitchcock fills out his canvas with many oddball characters and bustling, peculiar scenes, like the one where Sir John is beset by Una O'Connor's Mrs. Grogram and her brood of bratty kids and Marshall looks at them with slightly amused tolerance, like he looks at everyone else here. Hitchcock often films his character people eccentrically, using rather surreal cutaways to faces and objects to keep us feeling off balance.

The structure of the plot of *Murder!* could definitely do with some tightening in this later section because basically we are only watching Sir John trying to solve a case, and pure mystery like this does not interest Hitchcock. The film regains its focus when Sir John visits Baring in jail, where she tells him that a week of prison has been so bad that she welcomes her death sentence.

Baring speaks of "poisonous things" that Edna Druce tried to tell her about a man she loved, something that he "daren't have known." In this scene where she has so much to say, Baring seems like a rather dim girl, not worthy of the obsession she has inspired in Sir John. As in her first scene, Norah Baring is far more striking to Hitchcock's camera with her silent, watchful presence when she sits in German Expressionist shadows and doesn't speak.

Fane is a leading character here, and so he can't be revealed as homosexual because this is an unspeakable and even unthinkable possibility for many in 1930, and so Fane's secret is that he is "a half-caste." It turns out that Fane also works as a trapeze artist and also in drag, but the secret that Baring tells Sir John doesn't come near to explaining Percy's moist, cringing, sweaty presence in the very uncomfortable, plodding sequence where he reads for a role in a play for Sir John, who is trying to trap Fane and make him break down.

Fane is finally less a character and more an agglomeration of increasingly unlikely occupations and attributes. In another long, slow-burning sequence, we see Fane fully made up in drag again, and Percy moves in a precise, self-contained way here, his eyes looking upward, his facial expression set in a very camp "grand lady" grimace. There is a sense of exposure in this, somehow, of something we should not be seeing. Even though he is a murderer, and not a particularly appealing fellow, Fane looks like he could use some protection when he comes out to do his drag trapeze act.

Female impersonation was an accepted part of British culture at this time, but both Fane and Percy still seem brave to be doing this for an audience and for the camera. Fane's performance is partly based on the trapeze act of the American Vander Clyde, who dressed in drag as an enticingly attractive female character called "Barbette" and only revealed that he was a male at the end of his act, when he did exaggeratedly male gestures. It seems unlikely that Fane would be up for doing the super-macho close of Clyde's act.

Fane raises his hands to the audience with a strangely stiff and repressed sort of flourish before slowly climbing up a ladder and finding himself caught in Hitchcock's tight, remorseless editing between the trapeze act and Sir John looking up at it. Once he takes his feather headdress and cape off, Percy's Fane just looks like a Rick Moranis-like man in a spangled outfit, his flabby face filling with unrest and clammy fear until he finally decides to hang himself (fig. 5.1).

Figure 5.1: Police close in on Esme Percy's Handel Fane in *Murder!*

And so one more half-caste female impersonator trapeze artist bites the dust and Diana gets out of jail so that she can be Sir John's leading lady on stage, a just reward after such an ordeal. But Hitchcock's sympathy in *Murder!* winds up squarely with the freakish, outcast villain, the unaccountable Fane. It is Fane we remember when the rest of the plot has faded.

Percy's real-life sexuality is unknown at this date, though there are several fetchingly girlish photos of him as a young juvenile actor that would seem to place him on the gay side of the spectrum. He went on to do small character roles in films and started wearing an eye patch, poor fellow, after his false eye popped out and rolled down the stage during a 1949 production of Christopher Fry's fancy verse drama, *The Lady's Not For Burning*.

In the German version of this picture, which was called *Mary* (1931) and directed by Hitchcock with different actors, Sir John is played by Alfred Abel, a lean Conrad Veidt type of actor, and Fane is played by Ekkehard Arendt, a tall, cheerful, blustery actor who couldn't be more different from Percy. Olga Tschechowa acted the female lead, whose name was changed to Mary in this version, and she's a more open-faced kind of woman, older seeming, and more dignified, not as withdrawn and tempting as Norah Baring.

This Russian actress, whose aunt was Chekhov's wife Olga Knipper, stayed in Nazi Germany and was a favorite of Hitler. Tschechowa became a beautiful pawn when her brother Lev Knipper tried to use her access to set up a plan to assassinate Hitler in 1940, and so this is one Hitchcock actress whose own life was sometimes a matter of cloak and dagger. It was reported after the war that she may have been a secret agent for the Russians. Having survived both Hitler and Stalin, Tschechowa died in 1980. Knowing the end was near, she requested a glass of champagne from her granddaughter and left this world with the words, "Life is beautiful!"

Mary is far shorter than *Murder!* and was done hastily, without the often-perplexing detail of the original, and Fane is not a half-caste here but merely has "something bad in his past," and this can't be gayness because Arendt is an awfully big and butch female impersonator. *Mary* is finally a perfunctory curiosity that founders most on the miscasting of Fane.

Once again, Hitchcock was tasked with filming a successful play, John Galsworthy's *The Skin Game* (1931), and this didn't interest him unduly. Hitchcock told a story about going to Galsworthy's house for dinner where he was bemused to see that the expected topics of conversation were rigorously enforced by Galsworthy himself (in some versions of this story, the dinner talk topics were actually printed on cards at the table). This anecdote is pretty much all Hitchcock got from the experience of doing *The Skin Game*.

Donald Spoto's book *Spellbound by Beauty* suggests that *The Skin Game* was the film where Hitchcock supposedly played his cruelest practical joke. He bet unit manager Dickie Beville money that he couldn't stay in the studio all night chained to the camera. Beville said he would do it, and after cuffing him to the camera, Hitchcock gave him a laxative to drink right before leaving him there for the night.

Hitchcock's humor often took a turn to the bathroom or scatological, though he himself often said that he could leave a bathroom as if he had never been in it. Beville was a kind of class clown or court jester on Hitchcock's sets, and the story about the laxative has been told in varying versions for years without there ever being any substantial proof that it actually happened.

To keep up his interest in *The Skin Game*, which really is just pictures of people talking again, Hitchcock experiments with moving the camera quickly and jerkily back and forth to take in various reactions of people in a scene, but this device is often awkward. There is a long dolly shot away from a landscape scene that turns out to be a poster, and this neatly symbolizes the way the character played by Edmund Gwenn is ruining the land.

In a lengthy auction scene here, Hitchcock uses what look like whip pans to show us what's happening from the auctioneer's point of view. From an acting perspective, *The Skin Game* shows how much the work of many British performers from this period has dated because so many of them are trying to look and sound refined and upper crust, unlike their American 1930s counterparts across the pond.

In *The Skin Game*, the young actress Jill Esmond wears a plunging evening gown that displays her admirable décolletage, and the costumer has added little jewel-like beads on her breasts that actually make them sparkle as she moves through the later scenes. Esmond was married to Laurence Olivier, who wrote in his memoirs that he had wed her only so he could finally lose his virginity, but their sexual life was swiftly curtailed.

After Olivier divorced Esmond to marry Vivien Leigh in 1940, he had to pay alimony to his first wife for the rest of his life, for Esmond never remarried and turned to women in later years. As an elderly man, Olivier was heard to cry, "She's cost me £75,000 for every fuck!" A steep price to pay for the sparkle visible in *The Skin Game*, but that was the sexual standard of exchange for some in this period.

In the film, Esmond's character hires herself out as a correspondent in divorce cases, and when this is discovered, she drowns herself. Hitchcock made sure to dunk Esmond in her sparkle-breast gown as many times as possible before he was satisfied.

6

Rich and Strange, Number 17, Waltzes from Vienna

At last, Hitchcock made a more personal movie and one far removed from the thriller genre: *Rich and Strange* (1932), a loose and seemingly more casual picture that feels like the spontaneous cinema of the French New Wave directors of the 1960s. This movie was written with Alma and was based on some experiences they had had while traveling, and as such *Rich and Strange*, which was known as *East of Shanghai* when it was released in America, is likely the best record we have of what Hitchcock's marriage to Alma was like. It is also probably his best picture before starting his new era of thrillers with *The Man Who Knew Too Much* in 1934, and in some ways it is unlike anything else he ever tried, a rare bird in the Hitchcock aviary, very charming and pretty at first but with sharp teeth.

The married couple at the center of *Rich and Strange* were played by Henry Kendall and Joan Barry, who had dubbed Anny Ondra's voice in *Blackmail*. These are obscure names now and they were rather obscure names then, but both of them are ideal for their roles, even if Hitchcock partly blamed the film's commercial failure on the lack of well-known actors in the cast.

Kendall, who was "a fairly obvious homosexual" as Hitchcock himself put it, remembered that when he did a screen test for the film that he didn't do a scene from the script for his director. "The conversation took a very Rabelaisian turn and he kept me in fits of laughter so that I could hardly do more than stand in front of the camera and shake," Kendall said. The shooting schedule of *Rich and Strange* was prolonged when Kendall fell ill for a bit, but perhaps his illness aided him emotionally for some of his nauseated and disgruntled later scenes.

Rich and Strange begins with a lengthy silent sequence showing Kendall's Fred Hill leaving his office, where the men are just cogs in the machinery putting numbers into books and seen merely as numbers themselves. Outside in a downpour, Fred's umbrella won't open and so he gets wet, and on a crowded subway we can see his distaste for his surroundings and his vague longing for a higher life in a materialistic sense.

This opening sequence lasts about four minutes, and then we finally see and hear Fred at home with his loving wife Emily (Barry). She is making a dress for herself, and she wonders whether they should listen to the wireless or go out to the pictures, but then she quickly sees that her husband is in one of his moods, and so she anxiously returns to her sewing.

Fred peevishly throws a magazine at their cat, and then he says that the "gas oven" would be their best bet. He is childish and irritable and rather hawkish in appearance, with a staring, decadent, kingly look sometimes, and it's productive to wonder just what the sharp-edged Kendall might have been like as Handel Fane in *Murder!* if Hitchcock had wanted a more dynamic and threatening performer in that part. Emily is a lovely little blonde, tiny, self-contained, meek, and forbearing.

Fred is given some money from an uncle who wants him to have some of the adventures he seeks, and so he decides to spend it all at once on a holiday with Emily. We see them looking from right to left, and the film is slightly speeded up here to replicate the hurriedness of their gawking at various sites in Paris, and then we see them looking very shocked by Folies Bergère showgirls, just as Hitchcock and Alma were on one of their own trips.

"They're not dressed!" cries Emily. "I mean. . . ." she says, trailing off and looking down at her own modest bosom. Fred has a rather complex look on his face that seems to suggest that he *should* like this sort of thing, and maybe this is more Kendall than Fred here. A bearded man pinches Emily's rear end, which mortifies her, and then they go out to a bar and drink together.

Emily is a very shy person, but the drinks melt her inhibitions a bit, so that she seems sexually ready and holds a flimsy nightgown against herself when they get back to their room. "People will think we're not married," she says tipsily, and that's exactly what Fred wants. "Don't feel a bit as if we were," he says. But instead of having sex, they both get down to *pray* at their separate beds, Fred following Emily's lead. Do they pray before lovemaking? What kind of marriage is this? Maybe Fred and Emily don't make love anymore. Hitchcock and Alma didn't.

Fred wants to stray, mainly because he feels he should, and Emily stays tied to him even during their separate flirtations with others: Fred with a shady Princess (Betty Amann) and Emily with an upright and likable British military man named Commander Gordon (Percy Marmont). Fred is sick in bed some of the time, and Hitchcock torments him with the words "gorgonzola cheese" on a menu, which come floating up to the camera. What could be worse than the thought of smelly cheese when you're sick?

Hitchcock told François Truffaut about two scenes he planned for *Rich and Strange* that never got filmed or got cut. One was a belly dance sequence in which Emily would have stared at the rotating belly of a dancer until a vertigo-like effect was achieved, and the other was a scene between Fred and the Princess where he swam between her legs and she locked his head between them to choke him underwater. Hitchcock would have had Fred say, "You almost killed me that time," and the Princess would have answered, "Wouldn't that have been a beautiful death?"

We find out why Emily can't fully accept Gordon's attentions in an extraordinarily written and played scene where Emily talks about the particulars of her love for Fred. She says she is at ease with Gordon because he is just a nice man she has met, whereas with her husband she is always frightened of saying something foolish in front of him because she thinks he's "terribly clever." Barry plays this bit of dialogue in a sharp and vivid way, as if Emily is coming out of her shell a bit.

Compared to the way people talk in *The Skin Game*, Emily's conversation with Gordon here is very naturalistic. They interrupt each other a little and he really seems to be listening to her and to want to listen to her, and Barry and Marmont don't seem like actors acting in this scene but more like real people caught in the midst of an exciting and personal conversation where we are privileged eavesdroppers. Gordon's smiling pleasure when Emily admits that she doesn't think he is clever is particularly appealing, the reaction of a certain sort of British man who has long since vanished as a type in life and on screen.

Marmont had been a matinee idol on stage and had played Joseph Conrad's Lord Jim in a 1925 silent film for Victor Fleming. He was so well liked in Hollywood that a street was named after him called Marmont Lane, where the famous hotel the Chateau Marmont would be built. He suffered a hernia after picking up the hyperactive Clara Bow in Fleming's *Mantrap* (1926) and thereafter returned to Britain, where he played in *Rich and Strange* and then two other Hitchcock pictures, *Secret Agent* (1936) and *Young and Innocent* (1937). He spent the final years of his life nearly blind at his large country estate and died in 1977.

"Love's a very difficult business, Mr. Gordon . . . you'd be surprised," Emily says. "It makes everything difficult and dangerous. You know, I don't think love makes people brave, like they say it does in books. I think it makes them *timid* . . . I think it makes them frightened when they're happy and sadder when they're sad. You see, everything's multiplied by two, sickness, death, the future. It all means so much more."

Gordon has a very serious look on his face as he listens to this speech, and it feels as if Emily has touched some deep wound in him. He tells Emily that he has never been in love, and Emily says quickly that he should try it and that he is cut out for it . . . but that he needs to get the right girl because it would be "a crime if you were wasted." Gordon rears back at that and then he suddenly asks if she is trying to pull his leg. "Pull your leg?," she asks. Clearly she has never been more sincere in her life and she is bewildered by his response.

"I don't quite know why I said that," Gordon says, but he is just trying to save face now. He was thinking that Emily was likely laughing at him after indulging in a fairly elaborate bit of flirtation, but that is not in Emily's character. Probably a few meaner women have flirted with and then laughed at Gordon, and so he can't believe Emily is as earnest and sweet as she seems, but she is. "It was a rather foolish remark, forgive me, will you?," he says. "Yes, of course," she replies, in her simple way.

This shipboard scene is very beautifully played by Barry and Marmont on a steadily rising note of self-interrogation, as if Emily is wondering if she can allow herself to open up like this and Gordon is wondering at her wondering. This scene of give and take and things lost and gained and connections made and male feelings hurt is similar finally to the supper scene between Marion and Norman in *Psycho*, another example in Hitchcock's work of a somewhat limited and complacent woman trying to communicate with a deeply damaged man. This is some of the best acting, or pure *being* and interacting, in all of Hitchcock's work.

Emily is intimidated by her husband and feels she isn't good enough for him, and yet it is Fred who is the one in this relationship who doesn't seem good enough for her. Fred is immature in just about every way possible, like a spoiled child, whereas Emily is someone who expects very little. All Emily wants to do is guard this great love she has for Fred, who seems an unworthy object of her emotion, and this is something she cannot admit to herself. It is as if the feeling she has for Fred is outside of her control. And so she fears him and loves him and waits for him.

Did Alma write the scene between Emily and Gordon? Was it a collaboration with Hitchcock? Or was it Hitchcock who identified with both Emily and Gordon and wrote this himself, with some Alma revisions? Alma had risen as high as she could go in the British film industry in the 1920s, where there were very few female directors. She hitched her star and her talent to her husband, but it is worth wondering just what kind of films Alma might have made for herself if she had been allowed to, and if she hadn't met and married Hitchcock. Imagine the films of Alfred Hitchcock directed by Alma, or imagine the films of Howard Hawks directed by his treasured wife Slim Keith. Imagine how the view of the male characters might shift, and how the female characters might deepen in other ways.

Alma's hand is there in all of Hitchcock's work, but mainly on the level of editorial guidance. She was his final authority, and he feared her and her opinion. Her job as the years went on was to keep on the lookout for continuity errors, mistakes like Janet Leigh either gulping or blinking in a frame of *Psycho* when Marion Crane is dead on the bathroom floor (the story varies). She was "Mom" to Hitchcock, as Tippi Hedren has said, and a boy's best friend is his mother. Hitchcock is as great an artist as he is because he could put himself fully and totally into a female point of view, becoming the women and identifying with them in his films far more easily, sometimes, then he could become or identify with some of the men.

Hitchcock and Alma became fast friends with Elsie Randolph, who plays one of the most disturbing characters in all Hitchcock in *Rich and Strange*, a lady in glasses on-board ship with Fred and Emily who is billed simply on IMDb as "The Old Maid" but is called Miss Imbrie by the commander. Randolph was noted for her singing and dancing on stage in musicals with Jack Buchanan, but in *Rich and Strange* she plays a character part that is written and acted and filmed with such psychological insight that it finally becomes unnerving.

Randolph's Miss Imbrie might at first seem to be akin to Violet Farebrother's poet in *Downhill* or Judith Evelyn's Miss Lonelyhearts in *Rear Window*, but she is actually a far more problematic and disturbing figure than either of these characters. She is a freak and a reject but bossy and managing, as if she were fully aware of her status and determined to rub people's nose in it and to punish them with her presence.

There is great pathos in Farebrother's poet and in Miss Lonelyhearts, whereas Randolph's Miss Imbrie in *Rich and Strange* is not particularly pathetic: she is a pest and an infernal nuisance, determined to work her way into the social life on-board ship by hook or by crook. She is not just a bore but an aggressive, gloating bore, a social pariah who plays on pity from soft-hearted people like Emily.

Strangely, Miss Imbrie is always raising her head and squinting as she moves around the ship, as if her sight is so bad that even glasses cannot correct it. Maybe this is just a childhood mannerism that she has never gotten rid of? Or maybe she was told not to wear her glasses when she was younger?

After Gordon manages to break away from her, Miss Imbrie says to herself, "What a perfect gentle knight you are, Commander," in an absent, dry, sarcastic voice. She sits frozen in her deck chair, one of the rejects of life, and what's to be done about her? Nothing. Miss Imbrie snaps out of her reverie and says, "Good evening!" to some ladies sitting at another table, but her tone of voice is so loud and false that it is easily ignored by these ladies. She takes out some cards to play solitaire, and Hitchcock finally cuts away from her. If he had held his camera on her aloneness much longer, the effect might have been intolerable (fig. 6.1).

Hitchcock shows Emily and Commander Gordon slowly walking together and keeps the camera on their feet as they stroll along over chains and ropes on the ship deck, and the effect of this is very sexy. At last they kiss, but Emily quickly breaks this off and she feels guilty about going so far. Randolph's Miss

Figure 6.1: The outcast Miss Imbrie (Elsie Randolph) is at loose ends in *Rich and Strange*.

Imbrie has sized up their situation, and when she accosts them, she is obviously relishing the fact that their flirtation can't last.

Miss Imbrie pats Gordon's jacket and treats him with contempt, saying that he will go "right into the background" when Fred is on his feet . . . right into the woodwork, where she herself is always being consigned. And then she defensively says, "I'm only joking! Just my high spirits! Just my fun!" Finally it has to be wondered just how close the practical joker Hitchcock himself was to Miss Imbrie.

Miss Imbrie is somewhat like Miss Bates in Jane Austen's *Emma*, a lady who is happy to guilt trip or use any weapon at her disposal if it means that she can more firmly lodge herself into the social lives of others, like a burr or a barnacle that clings and will not let go, a kind of social terrorist using all of her drawbacks to her advantage. This is a Hitchcock woman in glasses who always keeps her glasses on, because there would be no transformation if she took them off. Miss Imbrie was probably meant at first as "comic relief," but she is actually one of his scariest characters, and the fear she creates is based in the knowledge that both Hitchcock and Alma might have become someone like Randolph's unavoidable Miss Imbrie if they hadn't found each other.

Hitchcock uses silent film-style title cards sometimes in *Rich and Strange*. "Fred had met a Princess!" reads one of them, and then we see a shot of Emily smiling. The title card playfully tells us what Emily is thinking in words, but this thought is visible on Barry's face, too, and so this feels very much like an experimentally meta effect in a French New Wave film. Emily seems pleased at first that someone exotic and titled desires her husband.

Fred treats Emily with contempt and strolls on-board ship himself with the rather obviously sexy Princess, who puts Fred's hand on her breast to feel how he makes her heart "jump so." Fred takes a lot of trouble to remove her veil to give her a kiss, and her smile at him when he gets it off is so obviously false that Fred doesn't seem at all clever for being taken in by her. Then again, horniness has been known to impair the cleverness of men, and it should be said that Kendall is very convincing in this sequence as a man who is so in lust for a woman that he can barely stand it.

As always in Hitchcock, it is the person that is inaccessible who is the person that is most highly valued and coveted, even if (or especially if) the inaccessible coveted person is clearly a phony. The lure of an illusion trumps mother-love reality in Hitchcock only for a time in this early film. It is in his later films that illusion will triumph over reality in a definitively tragic way.

The Princess tells Fred to have his dance with "the gossip woman," which is what she calls Miss Imbrie. "Then she will not look for you," says the Princess. The mercenary Princess knows that Miss Imbrie is someone who will cause trouble for others if she can get away with it. At a costume ball back on the ship deck, Miss Imbrie rifles her hand under Fred's vest as they dance, hungrily feeling his back to let us see that she has large but thwarted sexual desires.

The beauty mark Miss Imbrie wears on one cheek is part of her usual "take it and like it" rejection of her actual position. "Don't you think my shepherdess costume makes me look young?," she asks Fred. "Yes," he says distractedly, thinking of the Princess. "*How* old?," Miss Imbrie asks. "Nineteen," he tells her, which is the Princess's cabin number.

Randolph herself was only twenty-seven here, and when properly made up for her stage and film musicals she could be attractive. In *Rich and Strange*, she convincingly plays a much older woman, and so this is a very powerful example of charged acting and casting in a Hitchcock film. He knows that if Randolph took off her glasses and put on some make-up that she would be appealing enough to partner Jack Buchanan in a musical. But Randolph's *character* in *Rich and Strange* clearly cannot do that. The glasses bring out just how long and sharp Randolph's nose is, but taking them off wouldn't do Miss Imbrie any good, partly because the personality she has developed to go with her looks is so defensively managing and defiantly flirtatious in a poisonously artificial way, and it seems as if this false personality is finally all she has become. There is nothing soft or sad or real or yearning left of her.

And so appearance can be fate for some people but not for others, and this is a particularly upsetting notion in Hitchcock's work, especially as the relatively young man he was when he made *Rich and Strange*. Randolph's Miss Imbrie is a woman who goes beyond being sad or funny; she just *is*, horribly.

The other passengers laugh at Miss Imbrie as she dances around, but it is notable that Hitchcock does not linger over or underline the nervous reaction she gets from the others and keeps his camera distant from it. This sequence ends with a shot of Miss Imbrie asleep in her deck chair with her mouth open, still waiting for Fred to bring her an ice. The last time we see Miss Imbrie, she is taking part in a "hip hip hooray!" shout among the passengers, but of course she keeps shouting, "hip hip hooray!" after they have finished. Miss Imbrie is always out of step. She is the consummate outcast.

Commander Gordon tells Emily that the Princess is just "a common adventuress." But Fred cannot see that. "She never understood me . . . I was a bit too much for her," Fred says of Emily to the Princess, with his absurd and closed-off sense of self-satisfaction. Emily and Fred have been married for eight years, one year past the famed seven-year itch, and so she is understanding. "A wife's more than half a mother," Emily tells Gordon.

We may wonder why Fred and Emily are childless; could it be that they never felt they had enough money? Fred behaves in his characteristically spoiled schoolboy way when he learns the truth about the Princess, and finally even Emily is harsh with him. She says that she missed her chance with Gordon and now she sees her husband the way Gordon and the outside world see him, as a sham and a coward.

Emily is a Hitchcock woman who had romantic illusions and they seem to have been shattered, and Barry's thin voice is perhaps not quite strong enough in this climactic scene, but this technical limitation on her part does not harm the film. Fred leaves the room after Emily tells him off, and she sits on a bed with tears that look like carefully placed glycerin, yet this artificial look of grief is somehow more touching than a real one might be with red eyes and running nose, etc.

Fred comes back in and says, "Don't you dare say I told you so." Emily immediately tries to start to build him back up again, and she is allowed to be motherly to Fred when they think their ship is sinking and they see water outside their porthole and the lights go out. "Fred, do you mind very much?," Emily finally asks him in the dark. "Not now," he answers. "I did at first. I'm . . . I'm scared, Em." And then he apologizes to her, and Hitchcock cuts to water coming under their door.

The scenes that follow their acceptance of death are very strange and unsettling. They wake up to daylight, and the ship hasn't sunk but it has been deserted, and Fred and Emily are exhilarated by their reprieve, but only up to a point. "Shouldn't we better find some clothes or something?" wonders genteel Emily as she stands in her slip. "Somebody might come!," she cries. They find some oversized men's clothes to put on, and then they encounter the body of a dead old man in pajamas before Emily asks if she might use the men's room. "Yes, no sense in being suburban," Fred tells her. Hitch pokes a little gentle fun here at their unbreakable Britishness.

There's a dreamlike quality to the images when Fred and Emily are running around the deserted ship, but this shades into a nightmare when they are picked up by a Chinese junk, especially when one of the Chinese men falls into the water as they move away from the ship and the other Chinese seamen impassively let him drown. Emily comes out with a little ineffectual shout at this, but it is no use because it feels as if the Chinese men are in touch with the ultimate meaninglessness of life or death in a way that Emily and Fred are still not ready for. Their prospective death and then their renewed life still means a great deal to them.

The now reunited couple hungrily digs in to the food they are given until they see one of the Chinese men tacking up the hide of a cat, and Hitchcock holds on a shot of their dismay at what they have been eating. Back home they immediately start bickering and seem to have learned very little from their travels. They have returned to the complacency that Hitchcock condemned all his life in his work, and they seem to be planning to have a child in this last scene, but only if Fred can get a better job.

Like many early Hitchcock actresses, Barry retired soon after making *Rich and Strange* and married well to a merchant banker. Her daughter Henrietta Tiarks was a successful model before marrying the 14th Duke of Bedford, and her grandson Andrew Russell is currently the 15th Duke of Bedford. So the sensible Emily of *Rich and Strange*, content with her small life and making her own clothes, seems to have been very different from the actress who played her and what that actress herself wanted out of life.

Rich and Strange was not a success for Hitchcock at the time. Consequently, he found himself trying to adapt a muddled stage whodunit called *Number 17*, and it seemed so hopeless that Hitchcock, Alma, and Rodney Ackland thought that the only way to do this piece as a movie was to send it up. The result was *Number 17* (1932), which lasts a little over an hour and doesn't make too much sense.

Most of *Number 17* takes place in an old dark house, and in the blurred public domain prints that circulated for years, it was difficult to make out what anyone was doing or saying. A restored copy of the film makes it easier to see the images, at least, but it still doesn't make the narrative much more intelligible. *Number 17* is best taken as a pure exercise in style, with nearly subliminal cuts to objects and faces purposely adding to the confusion of the plot.

The jokes, when you can hear them, don't make much sense, either. The lower-class Ben (Leon M. Lion) says he's never seen a pair of handcuffs before: "I was raised Baptist!," he cries. Non-sequiturs in dialogue are matched by non-sequitur imagery and wax dripping from candles and things that go bump in the night.

This is a dreamy, manipulative, weird, subjective sort of picture, and it is set mainly in one enclosed space until a last-minute chase with miniature cars and trains. To use one of Hitchcock's favorite terms, *Number 17* is nearly all MacGuffin, or the thing the spies are after that the audience doesn't care about, and it seems to revolve around some kind of necklace theft.

There is a sexy shot in *Number 17* of the leading man (John Stuart, who had played Hugh in *The Pleasure Garden*) and the leading lady (Anne Grey) with their hands tied to a banister that gets even sexier when the banister gives way and they are left hanging and swooning in space. "It's like the pictures, isn't it?," asks Grey's Nora, right before swinging out on the banister into midair. Nora keeps fainting and then waking up and then fainting again, like a parody of a heroine always in a distressful tizzy. Grey tried Hollywood but retired by the late 1930s and went back to England, where she married in 1940 and stayed married until her death in 1987.

By 1933, Hitchcock had turned to what he termed "the lowest ebb in my output," a frothy musical called *Waltzes from Vienna*, which starred the charming, rabbitty Jessie Matthews. If Hitchcock's name were not in the credits, you would not be likely to know that he had directed this little-seen picture in which Johann Strauss (Esmond Knight) writes his waltzes in the expected inane moments of movie composer "inspiration."

Hitchcock was very unhappy with the project and he took this out on Matthews. "He sent me up mercilessly," Matthews said, "and I was always anticipating some ghastly practical joke he was about to play on me. He was just an imperious young man who knew nothing about musicals. I felt unnerved when he tried to get me to adopt a mincing operetta style. He was out of his depth, and he showed that he knew it by ordering me around." She found the film itself "perfectly dreadful." Perhaps Hitchcock wanted his leading lady to parody the material, as he himself had tried to do with *Number 17*, but Matthews insisted on taking the movie seriously.

The opening of *Waltzes from Vienna* features some tepid suspense over whether a cake will make it through a street without getting squashed, and Hitchcock's camera leers at a group of beautiful girls at a window and then cuts to a shot of them from behind so that you can see the panties beneath their underthings. Matthews loses her skirt and she gets carried down a ladder in her own frilly underthings, but this emphasis on female behinds leads nowhere much except in an elaborate scene where the women clearly yield, in a very sexual way, to their male partners as they are led out onto the dance floor for a Strauss waltz.

7

The Man Who Knew Too Much, The 39 Steps, Secret Agent, Sabotage

With the aid of many writers, including the actor-playwright Emlyn Williams, Hitchcock put together the script for *The Man Who Knew Too Much* (1934), a movie that would count as his comeback. This picture was a resounding success and established a template for certain future Hitchcock movies: a spy narrative of some sort that moved over many different and colorful locations and allowed for any imaginative set piece or idea that Hitchcock wanted to try.

This first version of *The Man Who Knew Too Much*, which would later be remade by Hitchcock in 1956, runs only seventy-five minutes, and there is a sense, sometimes, that points of character or plot are being left out or skipped over so that it is a ripping yarn and cut to the bone. Leslie Banks and Edna Best play Bob and Jill Lawrence, the married couple at the center of the film, and they are asked to establish a note of marital teasing in their first scenes at a ski lodge where Best's Jill is carrying on an above-board little flirtation with Louis Bernard (Pierre Fresnay).

These first scenes are stylized and tense, with all kinds of edgy vibes in the dialogue and the manner it is spoken by Bob and Jill, who joke about their marriage and their child Betty (Nova Pilbeam). And so I must partly disagree with Robin Wood's formulation of the Lawrence marriage in the updated version of his seminal and provocative book *Hitchcock's Films,* where he compares and contrasts the two versions of *The Man Who Knew Too Much*.

Wood is certainly worth taking very seriously on this issue, particularly because he himself was an Englishman born in 1931 who could remember being a child in England in the 1930s. To Wood, Jill's teasing of her husband and child "testifies to the absolutely solid base of the Lawrences' marriage." Wood then writes that the shakier marriage between Ben McKenna (James Stewart) and Jo Conway (Doris Day) in the 1956 remake could not possibly withstand such a flirtation or such teasing. The American Jo cannot hide what she feels as the British Jill does so immaculately, and Jo protests her own unhappy marriage by punishing herself and by fighting with Ben. Wood is right when he says that Jo could never flirt with another man to punish or test her husband.

Speaking as an American of a different generation, I think Wood is underestimating the unrest that might be lying underneath Jill's manner in the 1934 version. The way that Best's Jill indulges in raillery with her husband in the 1934 version has an air of Noël Coward sophistication to it. She is brittle and stylish, and there is not a chink in her armor. There is no way that Banks's Bob could call her out on her behavior, which is what makes it, finally, so really and actually dangerous. Jill could be feeling anything underneath her dry, noncommittal poses in the first scenes at the ski lodge, where we learn that she is a crack shot with a rifle. And so it is worth thinking over the possibility that Jill is not happy with her marriage or her child underneath her mask.

We never learn what Bob does or how he met Jill or too much else about them as a couple, and so all we can go on is their behavior before the plot swiftly kicks in. The Lawrences continually joke and say what they supposedly don't mean, and perhaps that could be taken as a sign of their cozy security with each other, but it might also be "joking" that contains a kernel of truth somewhere.

It seems to me that in the initial scenes of this first *The Man Who Knew Too Much* that the bantering between Jill and her husband Bob and Louis Bernard, with Pilbeam's teenaged girl taking it all in, somehow invites or brings on what happens to them in the way that Melanie Daniels's presence somehow triggers the bird attacks in *The Birds*. This couple both simultaneously spoil and ignore their child Betty and seem to use her as a pawn in their "teasing" relationship, and Betty looks a little troubled by this sometimes. Best herself was married to *Murder!* lead Herbert Marshall, and she was putting up with Marshall's affair with Gloria Swanson in real life.

Betty says that when Louis Bernard leaves that Jill will "cry her eyes out," and Bob agrees to this in his closed-off fashion, and it's hard to know just how we should take this remark or why Betty makes it. Could Jill cry over another man? She seems incapable of that, but we cannot be too sure. It should also be noticed that a second man flirts with Jill here, a shady character named Ramon (Frank Vosper) who is up against Jill in a shooting competition, and she takes his flirtation in her usual impregnable, impassive way as Betty disparages Ramon's brilliantined hair and plentiful teeth. And so Jill has other options, it seems. "You are as comical as your charming wife!," Ramon cries when Bob makes a silly show over Jill "going off" with Louis. Somehow all this joking feels uneasy, too much.

We see Jill and Louis dancing together, and her teasing of her husband is at its most blithe and complacent here while Louis looks genuinely taken with Jill as they speak of the "coldness" of Englishmen. And then there is a gag where Bob puts a piece of Jill's knitting onto the back of Louis's coat so that he gets himself and many other dancers into a tangle.

Why Jill has brought her knitting to a dinner dance is a mystery in the film, but in an earlier version of the script for *The Man Who Knew Too Much*, the knitting had belonged to two disapproving yet titillated spinsters who have been watching the Lawrences and Louis Bernard. When these characters were cut, Hitchcock couldn't resist retaining the yarn gag because this joke with the yarn is the sort of thing that Hitchcock himself might have done as a boyish prank.

But then there is a nearly imperceptible gunshot noise on the soundtrack, like something popping, nearly silent. Louis sees some blood start to come out on his shirtfront and he takes Jill's hand and says, "I'm sorry," very touchingly. The terror of this scene, which can still be felt so many years after it was shot, comes in a murder happening when you least expect it during a very public moment, so that the joking complacency of the preceding scenes is shattered.

Reality comes crashing through the jokes, which is finally what the jokes seem to be about; you can't continually joke about things without actually wanting them to happen. Hitchcock gets his effects by the juxtaposition of moods and actions, by the playing of an old gag followed by a sudden death. We all go along thinking that we are safe, and then at the height of our complacency, some evil we can't know about comes along and pricks our balloon, and *pop!* the game is over.

Louis tells Jill a secret that will get her daughter kidnapped by Peter Lorre's gentle-mannered Abbott, the first really major Hitchcock villain. Lorre had been the child murderer in Fritz Lang's *M* (1931) and he had acted in roles in Bertolt Brecht plays on stage. He had recently fled from Germany and spoke little English, and Lorre later said that he got the part of Abbott by listening to Hitchcock's stories and laughing uproariously as if he understood them. Lorre had to learn his role in *The Man Who Knew Too Much* phonetically, and in his first scene Abbott smiles and jokes that his English is poor.

Lorre's Abbott is traveling with a severe-looking older woman (Cicely Oates) whom he calls his "nurse," and he wears a fur collar and white gloves.

He looks and seems like a dandy who is detached from life, above it all, but that detachment of his is actually the detachment of a sociopath and an anarchist who wants to cause trouble on a rather grand scale. He laughs at Bob's knitting gag, of course. And it turns out that Ramon, who had been flirting with Jill, is one of his gang.

Lorre's Abbott is planning to assassinate an ambassador during a concert at Albert Hall, and so he needs to keep Jill and Bob quiet about that. When Jill realizes that their daughter has been kidnapped, she looks up, as so many Hitchcock characters do, and he cuts to the room rushing away from her before she faints.

As the Lawrences try to find their daughter, all we really learn about them is that the décor in their home is very busy. The pattern on the fabric of a couch clashes with the pattern on a screen behind it, and there is a small "modern" abstract painting right near these loud furnishings, and this makes a telling comparison to the spare and elegant abode of Sir John in *Murder!* Then again, maybe deliberate ugliness in furnishings is part of the British hale-and-hearty coziness of the Lawrence family. The drama of the film is in seeing how far that stiff-upper-lip manner can be pushed in a time of trouble.

Hitchcock indulges here in what today would be called "smash cuts" to ratchet up the tension between scenes, like when Bob's alarmed turn when a police inspector says the word "kidnapped" is broken off fast by a shot of Betty's toy train going along the tracks in her room. There is a lengthy sequence where Bob and the amiable "Uncle" Clive (Hugh Wakefield), who seems to be a family friend rather than actual family, have to deal with a malevolent dentist who seems to have come out of an early Universal horror movie setting with harsh lighting. Poor Clive gets a tooth yanked out offscreen without warning or anesthetic.

After he has learned some information at the dentist's office from Abbott and his henchman, Bob deals with a sort of cult or sect of older females led by the hypnotic looking "nurse" who had been traveling with Abbott. A glum old lady played by Hitchcock regular Clare Greet pulls a gun on Bob and keeps him hostage, whereupon Lorre's Abbott is revealed again. Lorre is always getting colorful and unnerving entrances in this movie, never walking in or up to anything but just suddenly appearing like Judith Anderson's Mrs. Danvers in *Rebecca*.

Evil happens so suddenly in Hitchcock, with no warning or build-up. Overcome by anger at one point, Abbott pushes Bob's head, but then he takes back control of himself and smiles slightly. "Sorry," Abbott tells Bob seductively. "Please forgive me." Hitchcock himself never liked to show his emotions, which was part of his British heritage. Kim Novak said that on the set of *Vertigo* he always had a smile on his face even when he was furious about something.

Abbott is seen planning the assassination. He has his hat off now so that we can see the white skunk stripe in his hair and a scar over his right eye, which makes him look like a twice-marked man (fig. 7.1). The scary thing about Lorre's performance in this scene is that it hasn't changed from when we first met the smiling Abbott, but he smiles and jokes now about killing a child if it is necessary, and he eats his dinner with cool relish.

Abbott is displaying another form of troubling sophistication here to match Jill's in the opening scenes, an above-it-all connoisseurship. He quotes from Shakespeare when speaking of killing Bob and Betty, getting a faraway look in his eyes as he speaks of that journey "from which no traveller returns." Abbott is charismatic, sensual, tactile, and deadly, a master of the unexpected, the kind of man who when driven to resort to physical violence will apologize sheepishly afterward. After all, he seems to say, what can be

Figure 7.1: The malevolence of a dandy: Peter Lorre in *The Man Who Knew Too Much*.

done? And Banks's coolness and light touch about the fraught situation is a match for Lorre's malicious humor. "If you expect a scene from me, you're going to be disappointed!," Bob tells Abbott, refusing to play the tormented father for this obvious voyeur.

If Lorre's performance is complex, filled with secret little compartments and original detail and sinister private laughter, the performances of Best and Banks start to become flat. They do nothing, yes, but they don't do nothing well, so that Hitchcock's camera seems to get fixated by the waves of Best's marcelled hair rather than her somewhat bland facial expression in extreme close-up as she talks on the phone to the kidnappers. There is maybe a withheld nastiness in Banks's look and manner, for he had memorably played the villain in *The Most Dangerous Game* (1932) in Hollywood, but it is too withheld to make an impact. Hitchcock said that he had trouble with Pilbeam, who was a professional child actress and had her own notions about how she wanted to do things.

In the somewhat curtailed sequence where Best's Jill goes to Albert Hall, her motivations are not adequately dramatized, whereas Hitchcock gives Doris Day lavish amounts of time and space in the remake to feel her way through the conflict that her character is experiencing between saving her child and saving the life of the ambassador. The *Storm Clouds Cantata* by the Australian composer Arthur Benjamin is an inspired choice of music in both versions of this film, always liable to raise the gooseflesh with its swelling male and female answering chorus and menacing horns, the way it tightens and intensifies as it goes on until the cymbal clash that will mean death for the ambassador.

Hitchcock keeps Best in isolated close-ups in this Albert Hall sequence and shows some shots from her point of view that are blurred by tears. Best is the sort of obvious actress who can only do one emotion at a time, and she makes sure to underline them for us, but this only has the effect of making her clear and selected emotions seem smaller and vaguer; even Best's scream to save the ambassador sounds small and cut off. When Betty finally takes up her gun to save her daughter in the climax, there is an extreme close-up of Best's swooning face as she fires a decisive shot, and so Hitchcock makes us feel with his camera what it's like for her to kill someone rather than just *seeing* what it's like from the outside.

But somehow none of this is as touching or suggestive as the moment when the unflappable Abbott is suddenly very moved by the death of his older "nurse" accomplice. He embraces her tenderly after she is shot and he looks at her with love, and he is flooded by anger after this woman's death. Lorre's Abbott gradually lets this anger go and then loosens his collar before getting up to shoot at the police, an ambiguous gesture that somehow feels exactly right.

This unexpected moment of humanity for Abbott was Lorre's own idea according to his biographer Stephen Youngkin. The transfixingly intense Cicely Oates, the gaunt actress who played the fanatic character beloved by Lorre, died the same year that this movie came out. Frank Vosper, the actor who played Ramon, died under mysterious circumstances in 1937 when he fell from an ocean liner into the sea.

A great actor like Lorre can get sympathy for the devil, whereas journeyman players like Best and Banks are often just placeholders in Hitchcock. It is the people who least expect trouble in his films that get it in the neck in the worst way. Live without alertness or vigilance, he says, and you will pay a steep price.

Hitchcock then made a nearly perfect film and a perfect entertainment: *The 39 Steps* (1935), a picture about an innocent man on the run that is perfectly cast from fore to aft. It begins and ends in a music hall where the popular performer Mr. Memory (Wylie Watson) answers any question that his working-class audience puts to him, and this music hall is where Robert Donat's Richard Hannay first meets a Woman of Mystery played by the German actress Lucie Mannheim.

Mannheim was a favorite of Emil Jannings, who had wanted her cast as Lola Lola in *The Blue Angel* (1930) because she had a "juicy behind," according to Marlene Dietrich in her daughter Maria Riva's memoir. While Dietrich took that part herself and became a star, Mannheim had to settle for the immortality of starting off one of Hitchcock's best thrillers.

Mannheim's Mysterious Lady calls herself Miss Smith when she speaks to Hannay outside on the sidewalk. She says, "May I come home with you?" right away, and so it seems like just a sexual pick-up to Hannay, who brings her back to his apartment. She is wearing a fur collar and a black hat with a little veil, and there is a gaunt Dietrich look about Mannheim's face. Her slight foreign accent promises sexual delights that would not be likely from, say, Joan Barry's Emily in *Rich and Strange* or Jill in *The Man Who Knew Too Much*. "Well, it's your funeral," Hannay tells her.

Hannay is from Canada, and he is staying at a furnished flat so that he can live in the moment and can pick up at any time, a fantasy for Hitchcock and for most men. But as Donat plays him, Hannay is a gentleman who turns a sympathetic face to people and really looks at them and waits to act, and the sensitivity that Donat brings to the part makes Hannay an enormously attractive figure. Hitchcock had seen Donat on stage and had much admired his "queer combination of determination and uncertainty."

Mannheim's Woman of Mystery tells Hannay that she fired shots in the music hall to get away from two men who are trying to kill her. She is a spy and an opportunist when it comes to which country she will spy for, which is part of her enticing air of promiscuity. "You may call me Annabella," she tells Hannay. And so "Miss Smith" or Annabella tells Hannay that she is involved in keeping a secret vital to England's air defense, and that the top man in the organization trying to kill her has half of a little finger missing.

Annabella spends the night, and in the morning she staggers into Hannay's room and collapses with a knife sticking out of her back. Hannay must escape his building and give the slip to two men outside, and he is aided in this by a delightfully seedy milkman, who won't believe the far-fetched truth from Hannay but will believe a made-up story about a sexual assignation with a married woman.

Hannay's landlady opens her mouth to scream but we hear a train whistle instead, which means that Hannay is off to Scotland to find out just who killed his Mysterious Lady. On the train there is some comic relief from a girdle salesman who also sells brassieres and a clergyman who is put off by this man's talk but gives a long look at a bra before leaving.

This is the first Hitchcock thriller to sprinkle humor all over the place, which is what audiences came to expect from his pictures. *The Lodger, Blackmail,* and *Murder!* are all fairly solemn, and *The Man Who Knew Too Much* doesn't have the time for too many jokes. *The 39 Steps* is a more expansive sort of movie with time, it seems, for everything and anything, yet the proportions are exactly right, with never a pinch too much or too little of anything.

To evade detection, Hannay forces a kiss on haughty Pamela, who is played by Madeleine Carroll, a remarkably beautiful blonde who was ideally proportioned in every way herself. The actress Jane Baxter had been considered for the role of Pamela, as had Anna Lee, who went on to play in many John Ford movies. Alma was enthusiastic about Carroll, who had starred in *The First Born* (1928), a movie that Alma had cowritten. But Hitchcock was uncertain about her.

He arranged a meeting with Carroll ostensibly to discuss her wardrobe, but he really wanted to see what she was like as a person. He handed her a script to read for him. "Madeleine Carroll suddenly became another person," Hitchcock said. "She played in a kind of mesmeric trance. I asked what had become of the gay person I'd met at our first interview. She said, 'But I thought I had to act.' I told her, 'For God's sake, be yourself.' "

Carroll wears glasses in her first scene in *The 39 Steps*, but she takes them off right away and the glasses fall out of her hands in close-up, so that she is made to very quickly reveal both her lush looks and her panicked response to Hannay's kiss. Carroll's Pamela is the ultimate stuck-up blonde, no doubt very popular at school and fond of herself and not likely to confer the favor of her company on just anyone. "Someone's having a free meal in there!," says a male passerby as he sees Hannay forcing this kiss on Pamela.

Hitchcock drastically switches the tone of *The 39 Steps* when Hannay hides out in the cottage of a stern crofter or tenant farmer (John Laurie) and his much younger wife, Margaret, who is played by the great theater actress Peggy Ashcroft. This sequence with the crofter and his wife enters immediately into the area of intense psychological drama, and it is sustained by the quick empathetic connection made between Donat and Ashcroft, who could not stop giggling when they were shooting their scenes until Hitchcock calmly walked over to a lamp on the set and smashed it.

Hannay realizes almost instantly how miserable Margaret is, and he would like to do something about it. Margaret is not an obvious beauty, like Pamela. She has a dark, melancholy face with large soulful eyes, and her physical effect is almost mousey at first (she has a mole or facial bump on her forehead) until you notice her sensual mouth and her dignified, reflective emotions (fig. 7.2). Margaret is a kind of surprise beauty, someone who might easily be overlooked for the flashy Pamelas of this world, and Hitchcock juxtaposes the surface pop of Pamela's beauty being revealed when her glasses fall off and Margaret's much deeper beauty being revealed slowly during her movements and glances.

Ashcroft was twenty-eight years old in *The 39 Steps* and at the start of a remarkable theater career in England that saw her tackle most of the classic parts in Shakespeare, Chekhov, Ibsen, and Greek tragedy. She was a modern, forward-thinking woman who got her first chance playing Desdemona in *Othello* opposite Paul Robeson in 1930, and she was disgusted by the hate mail she received for appearing on stage with a black actor and also by the treatment that Robeson endured in hotels and restaurants. She had a love affair with Robeson that hastened the end of her first marriage, and she had a passionate nature.

Figure 7.2: Peggy Ashcroft's farm wife longs to escape to the city in *The 39 Steps*.

Ashcroft barely worked in films as a young woman and rarely as an older woman, though she did pick up an Oscar for Best Supporting Actress for her soulful Mrs. Moore in David Lean's *A Passage to India* (1984). Hitchcock luckily got this rare bird in front of his camera, and he is alert to her every movement and nuance. It might be said that he is more deeply stirred, finally, by Ashcroft and the *idea* of her as an actress, the way she can transform her appearance from moment to moment, than he is by Carroll's luscious but restricted and obvious beauty.

Ashcroft's Margaret is a lesson in just how tricky appearance can be to the camera. She is not on screen for very long, only around seven minutes. Pamela is the leading lady and will soon be reintroduced, but Margaret and her dramatic vignette haunts the film because of the depth that Ashcroft brings to it, and also because of Donat's own sensitive responsiveness to her.

Margaret is from Glasgow, and Ashcroft uses a pleasing light Scottish accent here. This trapped woman helps Hannay to escape, unlike Pamela, who gave him up right away. And she makes it very clear to Hannay that she longs to escape herself and to go to the city again and the cinema and taste all the urban pleasures and have all the hot lunches that she can eat.

"Is it true that all the ladies paint their toenails?," Margaret asks Hannay, who has suddenly moved behind her in the kitchen in a way that feels openly sexual, but this connection is broken off when the gloomy crofter interrupts them and speaks of the countryside, which he says God made. Ashcroft's movements are slightly stagy in that she makes her physical actions decisively, underlining them a bit rather than letting them happen naturally. It is as if she needs to hold the attention of a live audience and keep them under her control, but this is easy to overlook in the overall impression she makes.

Margaret's husband is a religious hypocrite who quickly accepts money from Hannay when he finds out Hannay is wanted for murder. The crofter is a jealous and vindictive man, someone who wants to punish others for enjoying things he himself cannot have. Margaret gives Hannay her husband's coat, and when he asks if she will get in trouble, she reassures him that the crofter will just pray at her. "What's your name?," Hannay asks her, and when she tells him it's Margaret, he gives her a light kiss and says, "I'll never forget you for this!"

In the rush to get away, Hannay has had to forget his own impulse to rescue Margaret from her situation. Hitchcock gives Ashcroft a few beats of a close-up in profile to let us see Margaret's frustration and resignation, and this is all the more powerful for not being lingered over. Hitchcock holds it for just the right amount of time to make it sting.

This close-up is the last we see of this woman, for we only hear poor Margaret, finally, when her husband asks where his coat went. When she tells him, he starts to beat her, and the agonized sound she makes in response is harrowing, and hard to forget. It is an open question if Margaret will ever manage to escape the servile, cruel life she has to endure with this hard, religious man on a farm. Ashcroft's Margaret is so deeply attractive that thoughts of rescue are inevitable, but Hitchcock has to get on with his plot, and so he leaves her to her own devices and an ultimate fate that cannot be predicted.

Hannay meets the man with part of his pinky finger missing, which is held up to the camera as a physical symbol of impotence or oddity. This man has a daughter in glasses and an unpleasant wife, and they are giving a party when Hannay drops in. 45 minutes into *The 39 Steps*, our star gets shot, which is startling, but it turns out that Hannay was saved because the crofter's coat had a hymn book in its vest pocket. This feels ironic rather than a call for reverence given the crofter's mean and ungiving character.

Hannay is forced up on a podium to give a political speech, and he improvises one with admirable adroitness, saying nothing really but getting the audience riled up with slogans and double-talk as good-girl Pamela tries to get him arrested in a way that suggests that she was probably a snitch at school. Donat is at his very best in this scene, for he always excelled at speeches and filibusters and he lightly sends up this skill here. He had just had a success in Hollywood in *The Count of Monte Cristo* (1934), but his remaining career would be limited due to a serious asthma condition, which left him gasping for breath and sometimes unable to take work.

Donat was known on screen for his lyric speaking voice and for his air of openness and vulnerability, but this was always counterbalanced by a doggedly combative quality. He was such a touching figure because he obviously had to fight against his own illness in order to work at all, and this fight comes across on screen. In *The 39 Steps*, Donat is nearly Clark Gable-like sometimes in his authority, and the mustache he wears helps this roguish quality come out in him.

Hitchcock delights in handcuffing Donat and Carroll together, for he is well aware of the sexual connotation of such restraints and their deeper relation to the chains that bind Margaret to her older husband. He handcuffed Donat and Carroll on the set and then pretended to lose the key for quite some time until they had become comfortable with being bound to each other. According to Carroll, Hitchcock also sadistically enjoyed their predicament when they had to ask to use the restroom but were both too shy to say so outright in front of everyone. But Carroll related this humorously, calling Hitchcock a "sly old devil," which suggests that she found it funny after the fact.

"I like your pluck," Hannay tells Pamela, who continually stands up to him. Carroll has a childlike sense of surprise in these scenes that is very sexy in its simplicity and credulousness. Restraint can be sexy in the moment or as part of play, but it gets to be torturous if prolonged past a certain point, and of course that interests Hitchcock, too. He is in fetishist heaven as his camera watches Carroll roll down her stockings in close-up, one hand still handcuffed to Donat so that his hand has to lightly brush her bare legs.

Some of the handcuff scenes with Carroll in *The 39 Steps* might be unpleasant if Donat hadn't already established Hannay as a good egg and sensitive to others; if a more macho actor had played this role, it might not have worked so well. When Donat has to drag Carroll along and call her "my lovely" and so forth, it is clear that he is treating this situation ironically and distantly, so that we can enjoy it as a movie fantasy.

There are sometimes notes of the future Cary Grant in Donat's vocal delivery when he is being playful with Carroll's Pamela and putting her on. At one point, Hitchcock had trouble getting a look of surprise on Carroll's face, and Carroll told her friend Googie Withers that he finally came up to her and began to unbutton his trousers, and this got the desired effect.

The 39 Steps winds up back with Mr. Memory and with Hannay in the audience shouting, "What are the 39 steps? Come on, answer up, what are the 39 steps?" The rhythm of the dialogue here is very musical as Mr. Memory hesitates and then quietly says, "The 39 steps . . . is an organization of spies . . . collecting information on behalf of the foreign office of. . . . "

Mr. Memory is shot. Some women start screaming, again very musically, and the crowd goes wild, and a theater manager says, "Get the girls on straight away!" Hannay, still handcuffed to Pamela, hears the rest of what Mr. Memory has to tell him. Watson is quietly touching as Mr. Memory finally says, "I'm glad it's off me mind, at last." The film ends with Hannay and Pamela's hands clasping with the handcuffs still dangling from his wrist.

In later interviews, Hitchcock often said that he had made mistakes with his next two films *Secret Agent* (1936) and *Sabotage* (1936) and had abused the trust of his audience, but it is the so-called mistakes in these two pictures that makes them so intriguing and troubling. *Secret Agent* was based on W. Somerset Maugham's Ashenden spy stories and starred John Gielgud, who had already made his reputation as a classical stage actor.

Gielgud had played Hamlet at the Old Vic in 1930 in a production that used the entire text of the play, and this performance was particularly praised at the time. "I have no hesitation whatsoever in saying that it is the high water-mark of English Shakespearean acting of our time," wrote the influential drama critic James Agate of Gielgud's Hamlet.

Gielgud would play Hamlet again in 1934, and to equal acclaim. Though he had made his mark already in Shakespeare, Chekhov, and Oscar Wilde on the stage, the thirty-two-year-old Gielgud had only made a few films when he headlined *Secret Agent*. It was clear to Hitchcock that Gielgud took the theater more seriously than moviemaking, but this was only part of the problem they had.

Gielgud in *Secret Agent* looks abashed and slightly worried, as if he doesn't want to be found out. He has a rather hooded face here, a touch odd looking but strangely beautiful, too. In *The 39 Steps*, Robert Donat is restrained throughout, but his face is minutely responsive to stimuli so that thoughts and feelings register on multiple levels and very smoothly. Gielgud did not have a film face at this point, and he moves cautiously, but this sometimes works out all right because he is playing a spy in *Secret Agent* who isn't sure of what he's doing.

Gielgud was gay, and on the stage he had the parts and the scope to control his physical and vocal effects. He seems scared of Hitchcock's camera in *Secret Agent*, as if it might reveal something about him. A prince or king in the theater, Gielgud could be a very awkward man in life, and he was famous for putting his foot in his mouth. In some moments in *Secret Agent*, the young Gielgud falls back on clipped, mandarin, knifelike Noël Coward mannerisms, for he had been Coward's understudy in *The Vortex* in the 1920s and seems to have been influenced by him, for modern parts, at least.

Like Peggy Ashcroft, Gielgud's looks were unprepossessing until you really took him in and listened to his poetically resonant voice, one of the greatest of all such instruments and most at home with verse. On the stage, Gielgud was sometimes said to have been all voice, or, as Kenneth Tynan wrote, he was England's greatest actor from the neck up. It was not until he was in his sixties that Gielgud really took up film acting with relish because by that point he was beyond leading man roles and could take any character part that suited his fancy. It was only in 1977, when he played the raging novelist in Alain Resnais's tricky *Providence*, that Gielgud fully relaxed and really came into his own as a movie actor.

"I only worked for him once, and I don't think he fancied me much," Gielgud wrote of Hitchcock in a letter to a friend in 1991. "I admired his films, but only for their ingenuity and expertise. He never seemed very interested, I thought, in his actors and I was rather shocked when he made jokes about Madeleine Carroll having an affair with Robert Donat in front of the whole unit! Long before we all became impervious to the modern scatological fashion of conversation." A great actor on the stage and as an older man in films, the younger Gielgud mainly tries to be anonymous in his Hitchcock movie.

Secret Agent opens with a funeral for a soldier/novelist named Brodie that is presided over by a one-armed officer, and the coffin turns out to be empty. Gielgud's Brodie has been reported dead so that he can go on a difficult spy mission under the name Ashenden, and he is aided in this mission by Peter Lorre's The General, who is also known as the "hairless Mexican" because he isn't a Mexican and he has lots of curly hair. Lorre goes so exuberantly big with this part, popping his eyes and emphasizing volatile emotional transitions, that he makes Gielgud look cowed and disdainful in response.

Ashenden is set up in a sham marriage to the beauteous Elsa, a girl who longs for thrills, played by Madeleine Carroll in her second and last film for Hitchcock. Lorre's General gets enormously annoyed that Ashenden has been given Elsa as a fake partner, and soon Ashenden and Elsa are quarreling and smacking each other. "Married life has begun," jokes Elsa afterward.

Carroll is very close to Grace Kelly's later Hitchcock performances here: pleased with herself, smooth, pampered, irresistible, most likely, but limited. This early part of *Secret Agent* is awash in uneasy sophisticated attitudes and overall bad vibes, and Gielgud and Carroll are helpless whenever Lorre is in the frame with them and shamelessly stealing every scene, and Hitchcock seems to relish their discomfort.

Lorre is wearing a mustache and a little earring in *Secret Agent*, and he is doing very flashy work and giving his all to outlandish and even cartoonish ideas, and his performance doesn't really jell the way it did with his far more withheld camera playing in *The Man Who Knew Too Much*. To use Hitchcock's acting terminology, Lorre comes on and explodes all his gunpowder all at once so that he has nowhere to go afterward, and there's nothing to discover for us in the man he is playing. Hitchcock is maybe a little uncertain about Lorre here because at one point he cuts to a close-up of Gielgud laughing at the General as a kind of goad to the audience.

Lorre was in the grip of an addiction to morphine in this period, and he would often leave the set to shoot up what he needed. "Lorre was a great scene-stealer," Gielgud said. "He had all sorts of tricks, like adding an extra line when it came to the take, or he'd move an inch and I realized I'd been upstaged by a very clever actor."

There is an iris in to the man Ashenden and the General are supposed to kill, Mr. Caypor, who is played by Percy Marmont, the gentlemanly would-be lover from *Rich and Strange*. Carroll's Elsa is supposed to keep this man's severe German wife (Florence Kahn) occupied while they do the deed, and this becomes a very unpleasant task for her. (Kahn was a retired stage actress who had never been in a film studio and had never even seen a movie, and this was her only film credit.) The General pushes Caypor off a mountain while Ashenden looks on through a telescope, impotent and unhappy and protesting it from afar, and it turns out that they have killed the wrong man. "The wrong man!" the General cries, going into fits of hysterical giggles.

Before this has been found out, Carroll has a scene where she is sitting at a table and her face is registering deep dismay and remorse over the killing. It's a curious image because it looks like Hitchcock took his hands and arranged Carroll's face into this expression that does not come naturally to her, and it's effective but just slightly too extreme, too obvious. The camera slowly dollies into this face and right before it cuts, Carroll looks gaunt and tormented, like some sharp object is chipping away at her inside. With her chin down to her chest and her eyes looking up like this, Carroll's face is also Marlene Dietrich-like here, maybe because she is so clearly carrying out directorial instructions (fig. 7.3).

Carroll had a face that the camera eats up and she had a girlish charm, but she was not a subtle actress. Asked to do something more emotionally complex for this scene after the murder, she can only allow her face to assume a mask of disgust that has been imposed on her. Hitchcock didn't much like Carroll, even if she was ideal in her way for the two pictures he made with her. During World War II she worked bravely and tirelessly for the Red Cross,

Figure 7.3: The moral disgust of Madeleine Carroll's Elsa is shown through a very static facial expression in *Secret Agent*.

and she retired from acting soon after the war. When there was a chance to meet with her in the late 1960s, Hitchcock declined.

Robert Young, who usually played the affable second lead or part of a triangle in American films, turns out to be the villain in *Secret Agent*, and this is effectively unexpected, even if there is something "off" in his character's manner and banter, especially when he asks if he can bite Carroll's Adam's apple, a very queer request. "When Robert Young came to England to work for me in *Secret Agent* he had never appeared in a film as anything more than himself," Hitchcock said. "In this picture I gave him a chance to give a genuine characterization, with the result that, in the final sequences of the picture, he developed a power and a conviction that would have done credit to Spencer Tracy." So Hitchcock was fine with men not being just themselves if they were playing a villain for him.

Secret Agent ends up with a train crash so that blood can drip down Carroll's forehead and Hitchcock can mess her up again. There is a troubling pair of close-ups between Gielgud and Young as they stare at each other amid the wreckage, and the meaning of this is ambiguous. These close-ups are a bit like the swooning close-up of Jill when she shoots Ramon in *The Man Who Knew Too Much*, an expression of moral terror or dismay.

Young's Robert shoots Lorre's General and then dies himself as Gielgud and Carroll look on, helpless as ever, voyeurs who can never seem to do the right thing. And then Gielgud looks his most uncomfortable in the would-be smiling extreme close-up he has to share with Carroll in the last unconvincing shot of the film.

Secret Agent is a bit like the sour B-side of the far more cheerful *The 39 Steps*. It is a film that gets out of hand with dark portents and stricken consciences, and it has the effect of a hangover or an illness. *Secret Agent* was decidedly *not* a good time at the picture show, not a roller-coaster ride like *The 39 Steps*. It was an experiment for Hitchcock in how far he could go with his idea that we are all the wrong men and that original sin is strong and that evil is like a disease, ready to widely spread and contaminate people.

Joseph Conrad's very grim novel *The Secret Agent* was the basis for Hitchcock's next project, which was called *Sabotage* to avoid confusion with his previous film, and the American movie star Sylvia Sidney was imported to play the lead part of Mrs. Verloc. In her American films, Sidney was always being sent to jail and otherwise persecuted so that her eyes would glow with tears on the lam or behind bars, and of course such confinement was always Hitchcock's worst personal fear.

In Hitchcock's version of Conrad's novel, which had a lot of writers credited with the script, Mrs. Verloc runs a cinema with her husband Mr. Verloc, who turns out to be a terrorist. Mr. Verloc was cast with the Austrian actor Oskar Homolka, a character player with a truculent manner and a sinister face. Robert Donat had been cast to play Ted, the cop who is after Verloc, but he had to drop out due to his asthma, and John Loder was substituted.

Surely if Donat had stayed in this part, it would have had to have been built up for him, and probably to the detriment of the film. If Donat had been the cop, he would have brought his charm and authority to *Sabotage* and given it some hope. Loder in *Sabotage* is somewhat like John Gavin in *Psycho* because his callowness as an actor makes the character he is playing seem limited and even somewhat sleazy.

As it stands at seventy-five minutes, *Sabotage* is a potent, concentrated, unhopeful, unsparing movie, one of Hitchcock's harshest and saddest of all, a tragic picture in which he leaves you with absolutely nothing by the end, and in this it is unusually loyal to Conrad's book. The musical score, mainly by Louis Levy, is very ominous, with a quiet cymbal crash as its anxious leitmotif.

Hitchcock begins his film with a definition of the word "sabotage," and then the credits misspell the names of the two lead actors as Sylvia Sydney and Oscar Homolka, though Homolka used this spelling for some later credits. It is revealed that Verloc is the saboteur-terrorist right away as he walks into close-up after a series of shots establishing that the city of London is in a blackout. We also find out fairly early that Loder's somewhat inane grocer is a policeman spying on Verloc, and this shows Hitchcock's liking for suspense rather than surprise. Hitchcock wants the audience to know right away what's going on so that they can worry and emote through the rest of the picture.

Sabotage is not a movie that allows itself to linger much over anything, and so it is established quickly that Sidney's Mrs. Verloc has made a marriage of convenience to Mr. Verloc (she calls him Carl) mainly so that her younger and beloved brother Stevie (Desmond Tester) can be looked after. Sidney was twenty-five here and Homolka was thirty-eight, but he seems far older than she is.

Verloc doesn't particularly want to kill people, but he wants money and he doesn't care how he gets it. His movie theater doesn't cover its expenses, and so Verloc is helping out some sort of anarchist group. He goes to meet his anarchist contact at an aquarium, and Hitchcock allows for some on-the-fly humor here. "After laying a million eggs the female oyster changes her sex," says a bespectacled boy walking along at the aquarium, to which his female companion replies, "Hm, I don't blame her."

Much of the delight of these Hitchcock films in Britain is their inclusion of dry, ribald London humor, working class, teasing, and rude, the sort of humor Hitchcock himself was drawn to as a boy. But then Hitchcock cuts to Verloc after he has been given further orders to plant a bomb at Piccadilly Circus. Verloc is thinking about what it would be like to see a whole city collapse, and this is expressed visually when Hitchcock makes one of the tanks with the fish seem to smear and collapse from Verloc's point of view.

Tester's Stevie is established as a lovable little scamp when he breaks a dish and then hides the broken pieces in a drawer. Stevie has an awkward quality that needs protection (this character is mentally handicapped in the Conrad novel), but when he smiles he is radiant, angelic even. Hitchcock was not too nice to Tester on the set, calling him "The Testicle," as in, "Where is The Testicle?" or "Is The Testicle ready?" But Hitchcock's camera loves Stevie, who loves food as much as Hitchcock does.

It is easy to see why Sidney's Mrs. Verloc will do anything to protect Stevie, even enduring a somewhat loveless marriage to a glowering older man. "Mr. Verloc is very kind to Stevie," Mrs. Verloc tells Loder's Ted, who has taken her out to eat to get some information. "It means everything," she says, and she further says that she thinks Verloc is quiet and "harmless" and "home-loving."

Mrs. Verloc has economic worry written all over her face, for Sidney was one of the key faces of the American 1930s Depression on screen, and so she badly misjudges her husband's character and pays a heavy price for that. Everything about Homolka seems heavy, charmless, and menacing in *Sabotage*—even his bushy eyebrows look mean. And so it seems as if Mrs. Verloc is deliberately ignoring warning signs, but it may also be that she just isn't too bright. Sidney does allow for that possibility.

In the midsection of the film before Stevie is killed, Mrs. Verloc's doubts start to show a bit on her face, but they are doubts that she cannot place, vague premonitions of disaster. She tells her husband how good he is to her and to Stevie, but her depressed-scared face says something else entirely and totally contradicts her words, an example of the kind of counterpoint that Hitchcock favored between sound and image as expressed in Sidney's very skillful acting. Sidney is as subtle and nuanced in *Sabotage* as Robert Donat is in *The 39 Steps*.

Like Hitchcock, Stevie hates poached eggs and would like to have steak three times a day, and like Hitchcock he loves movies, always going into the theater to watch what is playing. Mr. Verloc gives Stevie a can of film that contains a bomb and tells him that he needs to get it to a certain place at a certain time. The can of film reads *Bartholomew the Strangler*, which is a two-reeler that Stevie says he has seen fourteen times.

So Hitchcock sets up suspense around this very lovable child character as he walks through London with the bomb. Stevie does dawdle a little, but he also passively and unhappily submits to a bullying crowd who force him to sit and try out some toothpaste and hair oil as the clock keeps ticking. Stevie gets stuck watching a parade, but at least he gets some pleasure out of that, and then he attempts to get on a bus. Film was flammable nitrate then and so it wasn't allowed on buses, but the bus driver lets Stevie on board because he likes the title of the film, and this is a bad mistake for all involved.

Stevie sits next to an old lady who has a cute dog, and he is playing with this dog as Hitchcock keeps cutting to the minutes ticking away and getting closer and closer to the point where the bomb will go off, 1:45 p.m. And then Hitchcock does the unthinkable from an audience point of view. After making them suffer suspense over Stevie, which might be classified as sadistic in itself, Hitchcock lets the bomb go off, killing not only a child character we have come to love but a cute dog, an old lady, and lots of other people on the bus.

Many at the time were outraged at this scene. Hitchcock remembered that the film critic for the *Observer*, C. A. Lejeune, came up to him in a rage after the press showing of *Sabotage* and started to pound on his chest. Lejeune herself had a young son Stevie's age, and she couldn't believe that Hitchcock had killed Stevie off so brutally. Lejeune was at the *Observer* for years afterward, but she finally quit her job after seeing Michael Powell's *Peeping Tom* and then Hitchcock's *Psycho* in 1960, both of which so offended her that she felt it was time to throw in the towel.

The negative reaction to the bomb going off made an impression on Hitchcock, who thereafter termed the killing of Stevie in *Sabotage* a mistake. In an article printed in *Good Housekeeping* in 1949, Hitchcock even wondered if he should have kept the audience unaware of what was in the reel of film so that the bomb going off would have been a surprise. This goes against all his rules of suspense, but clearly this was a special case for him.

Sidney's Mrs. Verloc reads in the paper about what has happened, and Sidney registers this in that special way she had on screen of taking the worst news as if it has been somehow expected. After hearing the bus has blown up, Verloc is briefly triumphant when he says to Loder's Ted, "After all, I can't be at two places at the same time, can I?"

Yes, Mr. Verloc is the sort of man who can accidentally kill his wife's sweet young brother and a busload of people and smile broadly afterward if he thinks it can't be proven. He is the sort of person who can say, "But it was not my fault!" to anything. Mr. Verloc is perhaps the least sympathetic of all Hitchcock's villains. He seems semi-stupid and often motivated by a very unpleasant and heavy sort of vanity, which shows up briefly sometimes on Homolka's scowling face.

Mrs. Verloc faints on the street when she learns the bus has blown up. In a daze when she comes to, and seeing her dead brother's forlorn face everywhere in the crowd around her, she says, "I want Mr. Verloc . . . I want to see Mr. Verloc." Her face has hardened into an expression of accusation and disbelief as she listens to Verloc saying things like, "Come on, you've got to think of tomorrow." Verloc is saying this to his wife right after her young and beloved brother has been killed, which is his fault entirely, and Mrs. Verloc's face says, "This didn't happen, this can't be happening."

Verloc blames Ted for hanging around and spying on him so that he couldn't deliver the bomb himself, a truly twisted line of reasoning. Stevie's death is just a minor irritation to him. He is a man without any feeling for others at all, a man who sickeningly turns to a paternal and cozy mode with his grieving wife, condescendingly telling her to have "a good cry." Stevie is dead and it is his fault, yet he wants everything to return to normal at home right away. When he suggests replacing Stevie with "a kid of our own," this makes Mrs. Verloc jump up from her chair. And so we want him dead, as she does. This is where it becomes a true Hitchcockian sort of situation.

Mrs. Verloc staggers away from her husband and takes refuge in the cinema, where people are laughing at a cartoon, which was provided by Walt Disney, who could just tear up his actors if he didn't like them. Desperate for some relief, she sits down and looks at the cartoon and starts to try to laugh herself. Hitchcock keeps Sidney in close-up as Mrs. Verloc watches this Disney movie.

We have seen how Sidney's face can be transformed by a smile that comes over her features like a sunburst, puffing out her cheeks and nearly closing her eyes. Sidney's smile is wonderful here in the earlier scenes, and in many of her other films, because it is such a total smile, 100 percent joy, like Ingrid Bergman's smile. And as with Bergman, Sidney's smile is so heartening

Figure 7.4: Mrs. Verloc (Sylvia Sidney) tries to forget her troubles in *Sabotage*.

because it allows her to entirely do away with the worries that clearly eat away at her. She is trying for this smile here as Mrs. Verloc watches the cartoon, where a Mae West-like bird tempts a male bird pitching woo below her.

But the male bird gets shot in the cartoon and a bass voice sings out, "Who . . . killed Cock Robin? Who . . . killed Cock Robin?" The attempts at her transformative smile fall entirely away from Sidney's face. This is a classic example of Hitchcock's method and use of actors and his love for "negative acting." He has shots of Sidney trying to smile in extreme close-up alternating with shots of the cartoon that makes her smile (fig. 7.4), and then when the song reminds her of her dead brother, he cuts from the dead bird falling and falling in the cartoon to Sidney's totally still and unsmiling face (fig. 7.5). "Who, who, who, who, *who* killed Cock Robin?," asks the bass singing voice from the screen, insistently.

It only takes a moment for the smile to fall away from her face, and so Hitchcock and Sidney are showing us how instantaneously our evasive joy can be totally destroyed. Mrs. Verloc wants the joy of forgetting, the joy of

Figure 7.5: A smile falls away from Sylvia Sidney's face in *Sabotage*, a classic example of Hitchcock's preference for negative acting.

being wrapped up in a childish movie, but she never saw the truth about her husband and now she is not allowed to escape from that; even the escapist movies seem to be taunting her, laughing at her. Her own fatal character flaw is dramatized and encapsulated in this short scene, and so Hitchcock's way of looking at people deepens in *Sabotage*. And it deepens partly because he is working with an actress who can convey such extremes.

Hitchcock had problems with Sidney, who had been trained on the stage in the 1920s and liked to have the control of playing out a scene as she would have in the theater. She thought she was being reduced to a puppet in the bits of film that make up the famous sequence where Mrs. Verloc serves dinner and is impelled, somehow, to stick a knife into her husband. That murder scene is broken up into many short pieces and shots all cut together so that the effect is nearly as dizzyingly controlled as the shower murder in *Psycho*.

Sidney had a heart-shaped face that was ideal for the camera, but in her 1930s movies she had a tendency to want to work up her emotions and to do them for us, to act them and send them out to us, not in any bad or dated way but in a way that is not conducive to Hitchcock's cinema. Sidney herself was a brassy, confrontational sort of person, not at all like her suffering, passive screen persona of this time, and she felt that Hitchcock didn't allow her to be "creative."

"She could not piece together in her mind what Hitchcock was after, the meaning of separate shots and how the scene could be constructed from them," said Ivor Montagu. "She had always acted a scene right through, and she badly needed words, a single sentence or even a phrase, to start a mood off for her, as a singer needs a note to find a key."

Sidney burst into tears during the filming of the killing of Mr. Verloc and threatened to quit because she felt powerless and irrelevant, and she was only mollified when Hitchcock showed her a rough cut of the sequence. But she was very unhappy again when Hitchcock called her back for disconnected retakes where she was simply to look down at her hands.

Here was an American actress who took her craft very seriously, and so Sidney was different from nearly all of Hitchcock's British actresses, most of whom were just in movies for a brief time before marrying and retiring. Sidney's career would go on over many decades, and she made the tough transition from star and leading lady to character actress. As an older woman, she worked all the time in movies and on TV, all the way up to her death in 1999 at age eighty-eight.

Sabotage contains probably Sidney's finest screen work along with the first two movies she made with Fritz Lang, *Fury* (1936) and *You Only Live Once* (1937). She was at her best as a young woman for martinet directors like Lang and Hitchcock and Josef von Sternberg, who got a very touching performance from her in *An American Tragedy* (1931). Sidney hated Sternberg and she was ambivalent about Hitchcock, but she liked Lang when almost no one else who worked with him did.

So Mrs. Verloc is cutting a roast after that smile fell away from her face in the cinema. Mr. Verloc is acting as if nothing has happened, even complaining again about the cabbage not being green enough for him. When he says this, Sidney's face registers a severe and wide-awake look of reproach, and this look, which feels specifically and strongly and righteously feminine in nature, stops the movie cold. Mrs. Verloc is being made to realize, all at once, just who and what she is married to.

Mr. Verloc is a sociopath, and Mrs. Verloc cannot stand much more of her knowledge of that. What is even worse, he's a *dumb* sociopath and his attempts at manipulation are insultingly clumsy. She is starting to hate herself for allowing Stevie near this wretched man, and she is taking on that responsibility because Verloc himself is so incapable of it. Sidney is stuck by Hitchcock in the machinery of his framing and cutting, which builds up a rhythm between her hands holding the carving knife, which she keeps looking down at, and Verloc's face.

"In an older style of acting Sylvia would have had to show the audience what was passing in her mind by exaggerating facial expression," Hitchcock said in 1937. "But people today in real life often don't show their feelings in their faces: so the film treatment showed the audience her mind through her hand, through its unconscious grasp on the knife."

Mrs. Verloc puts down the carving knife in a panicked way, and then she picks it up again. Mr. Verloc wonders if they can send next door for some lettuce, and this makes them both look at Stevie's empty chair, for it had been Stevie's job to run errands like that. Mrs. Verloc puts down the carving knife again. The camera dollies into her face, which seems to be saying, "I can't stand another moment of this, of hating you so much. How *can* you be so hate-able?"

There is an all-pervasive disgust in Mrs. Verloc's face, too, and this is powerfully expressed by Sidney. All of the emotions she is playing in this scene are not comfortable or flattering or easy emotions. Most actors don't like to go near the self-loathing that Mrs. Verloc is feeling here because once a dangerous feeling like this starts, you might not be able to stop it. The feelings of Mrs. Verloc in this dinner scene are gnarly and barbed and unsympathetic, so that you feel almost as sorry for the actress playing her as for the character.

Somehow it is the dim Verloc himself who sees what Mrs. Verloc is trying to push away: that she wants to kill him. So on the one hand, Mrs. Verloc is feeling her full responsibility for her brother's death, and on the other hand she is typically trying to smother and evade her real emotion, which is murderous anger. But Verloc picks up on this anger of hers, which cannot be expressed, and it is like he is transfixed by it, just as she is. He stares at her, in that blunt way of his. She looks like she is suffering torments, her face riven by conflicting emotions of self-hate and the anger that she is trying so hard to press down.

Mr. Verloc rises. He is magnetized by what he sees in her, and he advances on her, menacingly, and the camera advances on Sidney from his point of view; she looks scared and pleading now. They stand at the table with the tension mounting and the camera slowly moves down as he reaches for the knife . . . but then the camera goes up again very quickly as she *very* quickly grabs the knife with a decisive sound of that grabbing on the soundtrack to amplify the quickness of her movement, and this is all done in such a tight, smooth way that it is exactly calibrated to make an audience gasp. The camerawork here is making the audience emote and making *them* play the scene.

Yet this is Sidney's scene, too, because when she somehow sticks the knife into Mr. Verloc below camera range, she lets out a little helpless cry that is her own contribution to this moment. It's an unforgettable little sound, this cry Sidney makes, birdlike and ambiguous, met by Homolka's low, shocked noise as the knife enters his body. This is like a love scene between them, as intimate as you can get between two people in a Hitchcock picture.

Mrs. Verloc looks up and around in a panic and cries, "Stevie! Stevie!" in a musically urgent way. And then Hitchcock cuts to a very low angle as Mrs. Verloc walks away from Verloc's dead body. Sidney's foot trembles slightly in one of her high heel shoes, another detail of her performance that is hard to forget, and she has to stop to steady herself for a moment before sitting down. This is as eloquent a bit of purely physical acting as has ever been done for the camera.

In a way, this murder scene in *Sabotage* has been staged like this because Sidney is the star of the film and cannot be seen as purely vengeful or murderous without incurring some kind of punishment in the end. Yet this imperative makes the murder scene enormously complex, with all kinds of transfers of emotions between Verloc and Mrs. Verloc.

After the murder scene is over, Mrs. Verloc still feels like she is seeing Stevie everywhere. This will no doubt go on for the rest of her life in one way or another, and Loder's greengrocer-cop is cold comfort. Another bomb goes off in her house right before Mrs. Verloc is about to confess her crime, and so she is saved, in a fashion. But clearly her life is over, just as it is in the tough conclusion to Conrad's novel.

Mrs. Verloc confesses that her husband is dead to a cop right as the bomb goes off and afterward the cop can't remember if she said that Verloc was dead before or after the explosion because she said this *as* the bomb went off. That false remembering on the part of the cop is a key theme in Hitchcock and part of the re-watchable fabric of his films, too, where we cannot be too sure of what we just saw or heard. And of course the cop not being able to remember is also finally a matter of convenience and of not complicating matters for himself.

Did Mrs. Verloc actually kill Mr. Verloc? She wanted to, in her heart. But Mr. Verloc is the one who forced the issue, who insisted on that feeling she was suppressing. He brings on his own death, almost walking into the knife, and not because he feels he deserves it. Instead, Mr. Verloc is like someone who has been hypnotized. So evil himself, he cannot help marching toward the evil intention he feels in his wife. This is all very heady stuff, and a real psychological intensification in Hitchcock's work.

Eric Rohmer and Claude Chabrol unaccountably dislike *Sabotage* in their 1957 Hitchcock book, seeing it as a professional operation based on a prestigious novel that was supposed to signal Hitchcock's seriousness, and with a major American star into the bargain. They felt it was a Hitchcock movie that could be praised by people who otherwise didn't like Hitchcock, and on that level what they say has some validity. But their point of view can also be explained by the fact that these French New Wave directors, like Hitchcock himself, always said that great novels like Conrad's *The Secret Agent* almost never make great films.

Rohmer and Chabrol thought that *Sabotage* was not quite a Hitchcock film because in most Hitchcock pictures, he would have given Mr. Verloc some charm and likable qualities and he would have made Stevie unappealing or annoying, but it feels like Hitchcock sees that such complications would be intolerable with this particular story.

Homolka looks cruel and his character is cruel. Tester looks sweet and his character is sweet. Sidney looks conflicted and she is conflicted. (Oblivious as his sister, Stevie even addresses this issue at one point: "If gangsters looked like gangsters, the police would soon be after them!," he says, as Mr. Verloc glowers in a gangster-like close-up.) So the people and the actors are actually what they seem to be in *Sabotage*, but the Hitchcockian drama comes from the fact that Sidney's Mrs. Verloc can't see that. This is one of his strongest arguments of all against the perils of complacency.

Sabotage is a Hitchcock variation on Conrad, and it is a great film in its own right, done in his own way but erring more on the side of dramatic convention than usual. Far from signaling a more serious bent, it actually *is* more serious, and far more frightening, than his previous films. And his using a strong literary source as a starting point only proves that there are exceptions to rules.

8

Young and Innocent, The Lady Vanishes, Jamaica Inn

The acting in *Young and Innocent* (1937) is well below par, and this is what makes it the weakest film of this resurgent period in Hitchcock's British career. No one in this picture gets near the heights reached by Peter Lorre, Robert Donat, and Sylvia Sidney, but they aren't even in the Leslie Banks or Edna Best class, either. As a villainous drummer named Guy, George Curzon forces all of his emotions, which is evident in the first scene where Guy is in the middle of a heated argument with his ex-wife Christine Clay (Pamela Carme).

Curzon and Carme go big with this fight, starting and stopping their lines and breaking them off so that they obviously sound like written dialogue. Guy says he took Christine out of the chorus line and he won't be ignored now after her Reno divorce and her stardom in movies, and she wants to be free of him once and for all, and their voices sound weirdly clotted as they snipe at each other with their clipped British accents. Christine slaps Guy several times as thunder rumbles outside, and we see that Guy has an eye twitch problem, which is not put across subtly by Curzon. Everything is being overdone here.

Christine's dead body is found on a beach in a swimsuit and white swim cap, and there is a belt nearby that was used to strangle her. Young Robert Tisdall (Derrick De Marney) had been seeing Christine, and when he finds her body he runs to get help. Two girls see the body and see Robert running away, and these girls tell the police, and they get the situation wrong and stridently insist that they are right. Robert is swiftly implicated in Christine's murder and faints under questioning by the police when he is told Christine left him money in her will.

Tisdall is the lady in distress and sex object here, and it is intimated that he was either Christine's lover or her gigolo. Christine seems to have been a woman of somewhat easy virtue, which is discussed with relish in the press, and Hitchcock himself makes one of his more extended cameos here as a press photographer outside the courthouse who keeps making irritated and disagreeable faces.

Robert is soon on the run and taken in hand by Erica, played by the actress who was the daughter in *The Man Who Knew Too Much*, Nova Pilbeam. Erica is strong and managing with Robert, as Ingrid Bergman is with Gregory Peck in *Spellbound* (1945), but this reversal of gender roles has no emotional charge. Hitchcock nodded off to sleep sometimes on the set of *Young and Innocent*, but he once told De Marney that they'd have to retake a scene because it ran for fifty seconds instead of thirty. He knew what he wanted down to the second.

The camera style in *Young and Innocent* is restless and unsure, and the young actors are not distinctive enough to carry the picture. De Marney is a little like a grown-up version of Desmond Tester's Stevie in *Sabotage* without the charm, and Pilbeam is professional and somewhat skilled but no more. Hitchcock was gentle with Pilbeam, but he complained loudly and sarcastically on the set about De Marney's mild work.

Erica is a star part, a personality part, and Pilbeam can't bring it off. She eventually married Hitchcock's assistant director Penrose Tennyson, great-grandson of the poet Alfred Tennyson, and when he was killed during World War II, she lost her taste for filming. Pilbeam retired from acting and refused most interviews, living quietly in North London until her death in 2015 at age ninety-five.

There's a long scene in *Young and Innocent* at a meal with Erica's constable father (Hitchcock regular Percy Marmont) and her many younger brothers, and the performing rhythms are off here, even though the framing and editing are knife sharp. Hitchcock is never too interested in children on screen, or maybe it's slick and professional child actors who don't do it for him, and he can hardly be blamed for that. There is a whole swarm of annoying children to deal with in a later birthday party scene at the house of Erica's aunt (Mary Clare), and the rhythms are off here as well, too fast and artificial.

Pilbeam looks genuinely upset and hysterical in the last brief scene of *The Man Who Knew Too Much* when her parents try to reassure her, and it looks like Hitchcock actually scared her to get a response from her. There is one scary moment here that is nightmarishly effective when Erica's car falls into a mine shaft and she has to be pulled out of it, a perfect short sequence in montage of a minute or so. After Erica's rescue, it is back to trying to find the killer, which leads to one of Hitchcock's most elaborate crane and moving camera shots.

Erica and an older Cockney man who is helping her out are in a large ballroom, and all they know is that they are looking for a man with an eye twitch. The camera starts in the lobby and sweeps over most of the ballroom, taking in many people at tables and on the dance floor before starting to zero in on a band in blackface, and then the camera gets closer and closer to the drummer until his face is in an extreme close-up of just his eyes, which start to twitch.

This is all impressive technically, and the shot back over the ballroom as the villain loses control of his drumming is effective on another level of social awkwardness, but these camera stunts are negated once Guy is caught and Curzon does some really poor forced laughter in response, like a cartoon villain. Cheap acting like this can really can ruin the best-laid storyboards of even Hitchcock.

But Hitchcock was about to make the masterpiece of his British period, *The Lady Vanishes* (1938), another practically perfect entertainment, ideally judged and balanced in the style of *The 39 Steps*. The script for *The Lady Vanishes*, written by Sidney Gilliat and Frank Launder, was finished and ready to go when Hitchcock came on board, which was unusual for him, since he liked to develop his own projects. He and Alma made some adjustments to tighten the opening scenes set in a hotel, and he had Gilliat add the climactic shoot-out, but the material was already strong. The script for *The Lady Vanishes* is far richer than the sketched-in scenarios of *Secret Agent* and *Young and Innocent*, and even *The 39 Steps*, and this is a Hitchcock picture where the high and expansive quality of the writing definitely enriches everything.

The first hotel scenes immediately set up an ensemble of characters. Caldicott (Naunton Wayne) and Charters (Basil Radford) are two Englishmen who only want to get home to see a cricket match, and they are devoted to each other in a childlike Laurel and Hardy manner that hints at gayness. They sleep in the same bed, and they seem uneasy when confronted by a lively chambermaid beaming with sexual health.

There's a legal bigwig named Mr. Todhunter (Cecil Parker) and his sexy mistress, who is played by the beautiful brunette Linden Travers. There's a sweet old lady named Miss Froy played by the beloved character actress Dame May Whitty, who had just made a success in Hollywood with a film of her stage hit *Night Must Fall* (1937), where she showed acute psychological insight as a tyrannical invalid. And then there's another beautiful brunette named Iris Henderson (Margaret Lockwood), who is staying with two of her friends, one of whom is the delightful Googie Withers.

"What is there left for me but . . . marriage?" Iris asks, after standing on a table in her underwear so that the camera can appreciate her loveliness. Iris has had her fun, it seems, and now she feels she should settle down with a respectable gentleman, but her inclination to give up like this is threatened immediately, in very enjoyable 1930s movie terms, when she is bothered by a man upstairs named Gilbert, a musicologist played with rare charm and wit by Michael Redgrave.

Redgrave's naughty-minded, elegant, askew style here blends the best of Cary Grant and William Powell, an actor whom Hitchcock much admired but never worked with. Redgrave was making his film debut, and he was already working in the theater and wanted more rehearsals for his scenes in *The Lady Vanishes*, but Hitchcock valued spontaneity and this worked out well for both of them. Redgrave has just the right cheeky light touch in this picture, throwing himself into the plot as Gilbert himself does.

Iris complains about the noise Gilbert is making with his recording of folk dances above her room, and right away they start flirting and sparring in the manner of screwball comedies of this period. *The Lady Vanishes* is somewhat different from Hitchcock's previous pictures because the script finds lots of room for social satire of repressed and complacent Englishmen and also for social consciousness, which is mainly represented by Miss Froy, who is a wise old woman with a surprisingly provoking edge to her manner.

Miss Froy may look and often sound like a harmless and "whimsical" nanny, but she actually turns out to be someone you can imagine being a suffragette and agitating for workers' rights. She is that rare thing in Hitchcock: a good person, and believably so. Whitty shows that if you really want to be a good person, you have to be somewhat confrontational and spiky, and that is finally what the entire film is about. Miss Froy says that both of her parents are still alive, which must mean that they are in their nineties, and this longevity, as we will see, is cause for some hope and celebration.

About twenty-five minutes into *The Lady Vanishes*, we watch a singer get strangled, and so the lighthearted tone switches smoothly into something more menacing. All of the characters enter a train shortly afterward, and *The Lady Vanishes* is clearly one of the best of all train movies, shot on a small set in enclosed spaces where Hitchcock can control every frame and every nuance.

Iris gets hit on the head by a flowerpot before entering the train, and so when Miss Froy disappears, she is told that she just imagined this old lady due to her head injury. The dreamy feeling of the early scenes shifts into a nightmare where everyone is against Iris, but her self-confidence, or her self-love even, allows her to stand by what she knows to be true. And perhaps underneath this is the feeling that someone like Miss Froy is a rarity in this world and not to be let go of so easily.

Yet comedy keeps the narrative going, too, and this mainly falls to Redgrave, who delivers several zingers with unerringly super-fast comic timing. Redgrave even briefly sends up the soulful accented style of Paul Lukas, who plays the villain here, a brain specialist who keeps telling Iris in his "benign" and paternalistic way that she has only hallucinated Miss Froy. Hitchcock had never used this much comic material for leavening before, and it works wonderfully well. *The Lady Vanishes* is like a cake with all of the best ingredients, including a few risky spices here and there, and Hitchcock has such control of his craft at this point that he feels free to mix tones in a way that would scare off just about anyone else.

When Hitchcock is at his best, it's like he knows how long shots should be held down to the second, and yet this clockwork precision is exactly what frees him to take chances. The train really seems to be moving because the set jostles regularly, and we see lights coming from the windows, and we always hear the sound of the train on the tracks. It is a perfect illusion, even with the rear projection outside those windows.

There's an existential feeling here sometimes, as when a false Miss Froy (Josephine Wilson) is brought to Iris. Wilson is a lady who looks German or Eastern European, not English, and this was a sinister and resonant exchange in 1938, even though Wilson herself was actually English, which shows once again how you cannot trust appearance and manner. The dismaying feeling in this section of the film is that a group of people can persuade or bully a single person into thinking or feeling anything, even if it goes against something that they have seen or experienced with their own eyes. "It was so real, I'm sure it happened," Iris says.

Can she be sure? Can we be sure? Was Miss Froy only a movie? We can watch Hitchcock movies over and over again all our lives and still not be quite sure about what's coming next or what just happened. His movies, and life itself, are finally a sleight of hand. Can you be *sure* of what you saw? What if, say, Madeleine Carroll suddenly entered midway into *The Lady Vanishes* with her hair dyed black instead of its usual frothy blonde meringue, and she was as sure of herself and self-loving as Lockwood's Iris, and she told Redgrave's Gilbert that *she* was Iris? Can we really be so sure she wasn't or isn't? Maybe Hitchcock could decide to rip Lockwood up like a Walt Disney drawing and insert Carroll instead. Taken to this point, we can see how casting of actors can sometimes represent an existential dilemma.

What if in the middle of *The Lady Vanishes* as Gilbert turns a corner on that train, he suddenly finds himself face to face with Vivien Leigh, who says that *she* is Iris when he asks who she is? That might be harder to shake off than Carroll with her hair dyed black. Leigh is similar in type to Margaret Lockwood, beautiful in the same way but a little wilder, with eyes that can flicker with mental instability. If Leigh is Iris, or comes out as Iris, maybe *The Lady Vanishes* ends with her being led away to an asylum, and we never find out where Miss Froy went. It could be *The Lady Vanishes* as *L'Avventura* (1960).

In the real *The Lady Vanishes*, not the false one, Lockwood's Iris finally cries, "Leave me alone, leave me alone!" in that somewhat musical way that Hitchcock's actors often go for, her high voice blending in with the sound of the train whistle. The camera catches her in a low angle as she defiantly pulls a lever to stop the train, and when she does so Iris can stand no more and falls directly into the camera, which has a curiously upsetting yet cozy effect. People are always fainting in Hitchcock movies because they've had enough. And the movie might end there, on a black screen, the way that the TV show *The Sopranos* suddenly ended.

But there's more to this picture, of course. Hitchcock works in ever more creepy details as Iris and Gilbert search the train for the real Miss Froy, as when they stumble across a cardboard ad for an Italian magician (Philip Leaver) who is traveling with them. It seems the magician's trick is to make people disappear, like God or Death, or Hitchcock himself with a cut. Hitchcock changed the Italian character in the script from a banker to a magician so he could include magician paraphernalia, like a trunk with a trap door.

Redgrave was particularly upset with the scene where Gilbert and Iris have to do physical battle with the magician because he was given no time by Hitchcock to rehearse it, but the fight comes across as very heated and believably awkward and spontaneous. Redgrave was playing in Chekhov's *Three Sisters* for John Gielgud's company at night, and he had his mind on that. Gielgud had encouraged Redgrave to take the part in this Hitchcock movie, for the money and for the experience.

Paul Lukas saw Redgrave in *Three Sisters* as they shot *The Lady Vanishes*, and he was so impressed that he approached Redgrave privately and told him to try harder in the movie, and Redgrave said he started taking the film more seriously after this talk with Lukas. Redgrave also said later in life that he could tell the section of the film when he began trying harder, but he is likely the only one who has ever detected the difference. His performance here looks seamless. The camera lies, for some people.

What's really so intoxicating about *The Lady Vanishes* is how Hitchcock allows the romance to deepen between Iris and Gilbert as they maneuver through this difficult situation. It's particularly touching, and very romantic, when Gilbert finally lets Iris know he's on her side and she doesn't have to go it alone anymore. With Gilbert as her partner now, Iris notices that a nun is wearing high heels, and this is one of Hitchcock's richest blasphemous images, like something out of a Luis Buñuel film. Later on this false nun reveals herself to be a flinty working-class English patriot willing to help our leads, and she winds up with her hands tied.

We get the real Miss Froy back, finally, and it turns out she is a spy who has learned a crucial melody that she later teaches to Gilbert in case anything happens to her. And then the film reaches its highly resonant climax as the English are made to band together against a common enemy. It takes a bit of persuading to get Caldicott and Charters on board. "I mean, after all, people don't go about tying up nuns," says Charters dryly.

The train is finally stopped by the villains, and this has a powerful contrasting visual effect because this train has been jostling with plays of light from the windows for so long. Todhunter is an appeaser, squirming away from responsibility to the last. "Pacifist, eh?" says Caldicott to Todhunter. "Won't work, old boy, early Christians tried it and got thrown to the lions." But Todhunter is sure of himself. "They can't do anything to us, we're British subjects," he says, and he tries to wave a white flag but gets himself shot. Charters attempts to "put the matter right" but he gets shot in the hand, and so a shoot-out ensues.

When Charters and Caldicott finally decide to fight here, they do it with no fuss and with iron nerves, and this is just as wonderful as when Gilbert lets Iris know he has her back. Radford has a scar on his cheek that was sustained when he fought in World War I, and so both actor and character have had experience with having to fight. The beautiful mistress of Todhunter wants to use her lover's gun to fight as well, for this has to be, finally, a team effort, men and women fighting together with England on the brink of war with Germany. Iris, too, has nerves of steel here as she diverts a gunman verbally at great personal risk to herself.

The Lady Vanishes is a Hitchcock movie that everybody loves because it is so convincing in its depiction of good fighting against evil, and because it is so romantic and sexy (Gilbert playfully whacks Iris on the behind at one point). The story feels like it could happen, and somewhat like this, and it is a call to arms and to alertness, for that is what Hitchcock movies are aiming for, however outlandish they might get in terms of plot and detail. It is clear in this picture that the so-called jolts that Hitchcock wanted to provide his audience have a moral imperative attached to them. His entire career is devoted to calling out the passivity and complacency that allows evil action to occur unchallenged and unchecked.

The melody Miss Froy has memorized is meant to seal a pact between two foreign countries, and not a moment too soon. Hitchcock's cameo comes very late here as he walks down a street and makes a strange movement with his shoulders, and then Iris and Gilbert get to kiss in a cab at the end, at last, as she hides from her lackluster fiancée. We only have to see the fiancée for a moment from a distance to know why she has to hide from him with the wondrous Gilbert, and never has a movie kiss felt more richly earned and pleasurable. Romance and solidarity is expressed in a world on the brink of war, and this is also expressed at the very end through Miss Froy's smiling, implacable, jolly face.

Hitchcock's last film in Britain before he went to America was *Jamaica Inn* (1939), a return to far more conventional melodrama of the kind he might have seen on stage as a boy, and with Charles Laughton at its center as a wicked squire. Hitchcock had agreed to do the film as a favor to Laughton before leaving for America, but when he read the script that had been prepared, he tried to get out of his contract.

Laughton had another draft of the script done by Sidney Gilliat and Hitchcock's assistant Joan Harrison, with J. B. Priestley brought in to work solely on Laughton's character. The result is a film in which Laughton's performance is catered to and indulged, and not to advantage. *The Lady Vanishes* had moved like clockwork, but *Jamaica Inn* is like a clock out of order, booming the time irregularly and sending out cuckoos for distraction.

"Method actors are like children, they're all out of the theater," Hitchcock told Pia Lindstrom in 1972. "They're a little problem with films, especially where cutting is involved . . . Charlie Laughton was a problem when I made that film *Jamaica Inn*. It took a whole morning to get one close-up."

"He was a nice man, a charming man, he really was, but oh, he suffered so much, because he felt he couldn't get it out," Hitchcock said of Laughton.

"We were a whole morning on one close-up, and he got up, and he was crying in the corner. And I went over and sort of patted him on the shoulder. He looked up at me and said, 'Aren't you and I a couple of babies?' And I wanted to use a Goldwynism and say, 'Include me out!' "

"Finally he came back and did it," Hitchcock said. "And he said, 'All right?' And I said, 'Yes, Charles, fine.' It wasn't all that different from the other close-ups. Then he took me aside and put an arm around my shoulder and said, 'You know how I got it, don't you?' And I said, 'No, Charles.' And he said, 'I thought of myself as a small boy of ten wetting my knickers.' Now really. Absolutely true. You'd be astonished . . . I used to say the hardest things to photograph are dogs, babies, motorboats, and Charlie Laughton. Motorboats because they never come back for take two."

Laughton was a great actor and he had given many major performances all through the 1930s, but he was coming to the end of his rope a bit by the time of *Jamaica Inn*, which was released the same year as his heart-rending Quasimodo in *The Hunchback of Notre Dame*. He often compared his artistic process to a pregnancy, and in *Jamaica Inn* the character of Sir Humphrey Pengallan just would not come to him. The surviving footage of Josef von Sternberg's abandoned feature *I, Claudius* (1937) shows just how painful it was for everyone on a set when Laughton felt he was blocked. "It isn't possible to direct a Charles Laughton film," Hitchcock said. "The best you can hope is to act as referee."

In a lawless corner of nineteenth-century England, a criminal gang led from afar by Laughton's Sir Humphrey is deliberately leading ships to be wrecked for profit on the rocks of the shore. Hitchcock revels in water crashing and in human brutality in the opening to this film, and in the coachman who says that "queer things go on there" at Jamaica Inn. The atmosphere created in these first scenes is certainly effectively seedy, and as the heroine Mary the young Maureen O'Hara is so lovely that it makes sense that Sir Humphrey develops an obsessive desire for her the moment he sees her as she turns to him in extreme close-up. Sir Humphrey quotes Byron's "She walks in beauty" at Mary and frankly looks her over from stem to stern.

At Jamaica Inn, the gang is indeed a queer-looking lot with their tattoos and their gloomy attitudes, but they seem like they got their costumes from a dusty old trunk backstage in a theater. Joss, the leader of the gang, is played by Leslie Banks, who is so physically and vocally transformed into a low-minded heavy in this picture that you might not even recognize him as the same actor who played the pressured father in *The Man Who Knew Too Much*.

The gay playwright Emlyn Williams turns up here wearing an earring, and his character Harry seems sexually omnivorous and up for anything. When Harry looks Mary over as well, Joss tells him, "She's not partial to your sort."

What's intriguing about *Jamaica Inn* from a Hitchcockian point of view is that Mary is very much the voyeur protagonist, her curiosity about the gang leading her into danger. Like L.B. Jefferies in *Rear Window*, Mary is always putting herself in a position to watch what's going on, almost like a filmgoer, and O'Hara is one of Hitchcock's strongest and most formidable female leads, the ultimate proud and headstrong beauty, active and daring and righteous.

The really notable thing about *Jamaica Inn*, of course, is the standoff between the sensibilities of Laughton and Hitchcock. On the surface, they would seem to have much in common. Both came from a similar working-class English and religious background, and both were overweight. Both of them sublimated their desires into their work, but in very different ways, and this difference is crucial.

Laughton was gay and married to Elsa Lanchester, and he felt very guilty about sleeping with men, and he used this guilt in his work. He was a rhetorical sort of artist, highly conscious, and proud of his lack of professional craft, whereas Hitchcock worked from his own unconscious and prided himself on his professionalism. So Laughton and Hitchcock had many things in common as people and they started from a similar point, but they have very little in common as artists.

Hitchcock does what he can with *Jamaica Inn*, especially when it comes to the use of sound. There are some good foreboding transitions from noise to relative silence, between the crashing of the sea and then Sir Humphrey's deadly quiet house. But Laughton's labored-over characterization is nearly all external, starting with his very fake-looking eyebrows and false nose. He does a lot of face pulling and face making, and he is always "acting," everything an effort, so much so that finally it's difficult to know just what he is doing or trying for. Like the work of later Method actors, Laughton's choices here might make sense to him but they can't make much sense to the camera or to the audience.

Laughton's Sir Humphrey is a sketchbook of different bold ideas, fragments of different approaches and themes and looks that never come together or coalesce into a convincing person (fig. 8.1). If you were to only see his Sir Humphrey you would never know what Laughton was capable of as an actor, the illuminating heights of his work in *The Private Life of Henry VIII* (1933), *Les Misérables* (1935), *Mutiny on the Bounty* (1935), and *Rembrandt* (1936).

Figure 8.1: Charles Laughton offers an ostentatious and disorganized star characterization for *Jamaica Inn.*

There is a scene toward the end of *Jamaica Inn* where Hitchcock does assert himself, and it is extremely unpleasant. Sir Humphrey has Mary where he wants her and he talks softly to her as he ties her hands and gags her and puts a cloak over her head so that she looks like a tied-up and gagged Virgin Mary, and there is a gratuitously nasty shot of the gag going into O'Hara's mouth in close-up.

Laughton's voice seems post-dubbed as Sir Humphrey says, "Put your hands down . . . I shall have to tie them up, too" in a grossly solicitous, gloating voice that contains a distinct hint of the voice of Bob Rusk (Barry Foster) as he talks to his victim in Hitchcock's *Frenzy* (1972). There is another gratuitous close-up of Sir Humphrey squeezing Mary's shoulder as he leads her away, and it feels as if he were squeezing another part of her anatomy. We see the gang get arrested, and Williams's pansexual Harry goads a cop into smacking him, which makes him smirk in a frankly sexual way.

Hitchcock falls back on D.W. Griffith-type cross-cutting as men ride to save Mary from Sir Humphrey, who tells her, "The age of chivalry is gone!" He holds a gun to Mary's head and says, "Please be still" in the same sadistic and sexual way he spoke to her when he was tying her up, yet the remarkably self-possessed Mary keeps telling the men not to shoot Sir Humphrey because he's mad and "can't help himself." Finally the money-obsessed Sir Humphrey jumps from the top of a ship, putting himself, Laughton, Hitchcock, and the audience out of its misery.

Hitchcock could not function with dominant stars like Laughton. When he came to Hollywood, he spoke often in interviews of wanting to work with William Powell and Claudette Colbert, both of whom were witty and basically understated actors, though Powell could play far-out, knockabout farce. Hitchcock also said he wanted to work with the blonde and exuberant Carole Lombard, who was the exact opposite of Madeleine Carroll.

Speaking of Colbert in a rather ominously titled interview from 1939 for *Film Weekly* called "What I'd Do To The Stars," Hitchcock said, "I have often visualized her in the role of a beautiful mannequin who, having risen from the gutter, has to keep up a good appearance but who is, in her soul, lazy, good-natured, irresponsible, and slightly sluttish. This part would be rather on the lines of the one played by Jean Harlow in *Dinner at Eight*, though not quite so blatantly vulgar." He also thought of casting Colbert as the "generous, promiscuous" Rosie in an adaptation of W. Somerset Maugham's novel *Cakes and Ale*. He spoke of wanting to use Myrna Loy and Gary Cooper, both of whom were noted for underplaying.

Hitchcock had observed Emil Jannings at work on the set of F. W. Murnau's *The Last Laugh* (1924) during his apprenticeship, and he knew that a dominant actor like Jannings or Laughton or Greta Garbo was not his type of player, though at this point he wondered if he might try something with Garbo. "I expect that every director would like to have her in a picture, if only for the experience," he said.

"Garbo, it is said, works by intuition," Hitchcock reflected. "I am fully prepared to believe this, for at times she is magnificent. But I have also seen her make mistakes that Lombard could never have made. Intuitive actors, like Garbo, Laughton, and Jannings, need very special treatment. They frequently have off days where nothing will go right, but when they are really on form they can achieve things that no mere technician could ever achieve."

"I would not undertake to direct Garbo to any given schedule," Hitchcock said. "I know that to try to force her into a particular mood when she didn't feel like it would be rather like trying to force a woman to fall in love with you. For Garbo I shouldn't bother to construct my usual involved plot. I should choose some very simple story about life and love and should 'direct' the picture as little as possible, using my camera merely as a vehicle for her characterization. The greater the artist, the less directorial ingenuity is necessary."

It is unlikely that Hitchcock and Garbo could or would have made such a freestyle picture together. She was coming to the end of her career when he arrived in Hollywood in 1940 and only made one more film called *Two-Faced Woman* (1941) before retiring. Hitchcock and producer David Selznick both wanted Garbo for *The Paradine Case* (1947), but she declined, and that is likely for the best. Garbo might have been a woman of mystery in a Hitchcock film, but she would not have brought out the best in him, or he in her.

Hitchcock also spoke in this article about how he might use Katharine Hepburn, but this was really just the sort of daydreaming he liked to do in sessions with his writers. The more extravagantly particular and expressive an actor, the less they were useful for Hitchcock. His films needed people in them who could look one way and turn out to be another, and so the performances in his movies are always best and most resonant when he can cast an undervalued player against type, or a theater actor who is used to turning on a dime. The biggest and most distinctive and managing stars cannot give Hitchcock what he needs. Bette Davis is unthinkable in a Hitchcock feature because she shows too much of what she is thinking and feeling all of the time, which of course is her glory as a performer. The same goes for Garbo and Hepburn.

Could Hitchcock have worked with Barbara Stanwyck? This is trickier. Imagine Stanwyck playing Alicia Huberman in *Notorious*. It's difficult to do, isn't it? There is something helpless yet guarded and just a little vague in Ingrid Bergman that makes her so right for that part. Stanwyck is private sometimes in her movies, but private in the wrong way for Hitchcock. Like Garbo, she lets an audience in on all kinds of subtle gradations of her own thoughts and feelings, and in a Hitchcock movie this would be like showing how the magic trick is done.

Could Stanwyck have given herself up to the rapturous kissing scene with Cary Grant on the terrace? Again, this is hard to imagine. Surely she could have handled Alicia's bitterness and anger, but wouldn't Stanwyck's expression of bitterness and anger have been too immense for *Notorious*, too much like fireworks going off? For Hitchcock, the actor always needs to be holding something back, or seeming to.

Hitchcock's approach is anathema to the idea of, say, a "big scene" for an actor. There is no such thing in most of his work, as there are "big scenes" for players in the movies of George Cukor or Frank Capra or King Vidor.

Hitchcock's is not a cinema that bows down to actors, *Jamaica Inn* being a rare and negative exception to that rule. But his approach brought things out of certain players that they never showed elsewhere. Hitchcock's cinema is also a cinema of the actor, but only for a certain type of actor. The great divas, female and male, who flaunt their emotions and thoughts on camera, have no place in his films.

9

Rebecca, Foreign Correspondent, Mr. and Mrs. Smith, Suspicion

Hitchcock originally came out to Hollywood to make a movie about the sinking of the Titanic for David Selznick. "Oh yes, I've had experience with icebergs," he told a reporter in 1939 when he arrived in America. "Don't forget I directed Madeleine Carroll!" Hitchcock was inching past three hundred pounds now and eating a great deal, sometimes three steaks in a sitting with three servings of ice cream, and this was played up in his publicity.

He soon switched to an adaptation of Daphne du Maurier's best-selling novel *Rebecca* (1940), the only Hitchcock film to win a Best Picture Oscar. In the credits it is called a "picturization" of du Maurier's "celebrated" novel, and this is a purple sort of subject, florid but vital, and given the full Hollywood gloss treatment on a production design level. Selznick was a fetishist about hair and props like Hitchcock but someone who was far more dedicated to original source material and "story values."

Hitchcock himself felt that *Rebecca* was not a film that was wholly his for it belonged to Selznick, too, a high-powered producer famous for meetings in the middle of the night and interminable, micromanaging memos about every aspect of production. Hitchcock kept that mild smile on his face throughout his contract years to Selznick and kept his own counsel, enjoying for the first time the budgetary resources of Hollywood and also putting up with the interference from others, which he would not fully escape until his contract with Selznick was finished in 1947.

There was an extensive search for the nameless female lead in *Rebecca*, a good part but a difficult one to cast. Vivien Leigh was given a courtesy test even though she was all wrong for the role of the meek, put-upon heroine; Margaret Sullavan, Loretta Young, Joan Fontaine, and a very young Anne Baxter were also tested.

Of these actresses, Sullavan was the most skilled and gifted, but she was too headstrong and mature in manner to be fully convincing in the role. Still, her surviving screen test, which is riveting, shows that Sullavan might have played it, for her contradictory fragile look and slightly imperious manner make her an ideal Hitchcockian actor. Sullavan was Hitchcock's own choice, but she was nixed by Selznick. "Imagine Margaret Sullavan being pushed around by Mrs. Danvers right up to the point of suicide!," Selznick said.

Fontaine was finally chosen, mainly because Selznick was fond of her and because she did have the hypersensitive, wincing quality required. But there is a difference between having the qualities to play a role and actually being able to play it. The acting choices that Fontaine makes in her screen test are half-formed and vague, with little hints of slyness that are not in character. By all accounts, Hitchcock had his work cut out for him in getting a performance from her in *Rebecca*.

Fontaine had played some leads in B-programmers at RKO Studios, and a semi-dancing lead with Fred Astaire in *A Damsel in Distress* (1937) that hadn't worked out well. George Cukor had allowed her to overdo her telephone monologue in *The Women* (1939), which showed exactly why she needed careful handling. Alma didn't like Fontaine's tests and called her "coy and simpering." But Hitchcock handled Fontaine so minutely that he helped her shade and judge her effects and contain them so that they became winsome and charming.

There are moments in *Rebecca* when Fontaine seems right on the cusp of overdoing a reaction, especially toward the end, but the camera always cuts away from her before this can happen. Selznick thought Fontaine should emote more, telling Hitchcock he wanted some of her reactions to be "Yiddish art theater rather than British repertory theater." On this acting point, as on many others, the producer and director did not see eye to eye. The score for *Rebecca* by Franz Waxman punctuates scenes in a way that can feel old-fashioned. Scores for 1940s Hollywood films can often be noisy and intrusive, underlining things that don't need to be underlined, and some of Hitchcock's films of this period suffer from that.

Laurence Olivier was cast as the male lead, Maxim de Winter, a rich man tormented by the memory of his late wife Rebecca. He had wanted his own wife Vivien Leigh to play opposite him, and he made his unhappiness with Fontaine known on the set. Olivier was often thought to be the greatest actor of the twentieth century, and this judgment was made mainly on the basis of his theatrical work in classic parts, for which he had a ravenous and conquering appetite.

Rebecca catches Olivier in the brief period when he was a romantic Hollywood leading man, and his performance in it is all technique, which the camera does catch him out in. Olivier puts together a surface for *Rebecca* and goes through the required motions, but his mind and soul are elsewhere. Luckily, though, this removed quality is effective for the part he is playing, a brooding man who is quick to lose his temper, a man who always seems to be somewhere else.

Fontaine had recently married the actor Brian Aherne, and when Olivier heard this, he told Fontaine, "Couldn't you have done better than that?" This stung her to the quick, as did her treatment by the mainly British cast, who all snubbed her. Then again, it is an open question just how much her outcast state on the *Rebecca* set was designed, maybe instinctively by everyone, to help her give a better performance as the outcast heroine. As reported in her 1978 memoir *No Bed of Roses*, Fontaine called Hitchcock a Svengali, someone who wanted her loyalty and her attention directed solely to him. He would tell her the mean things the other cast members were saying about her behind her back and then assure her that he was on her side.

"She was not a good enough actress to play in *Rebecca*—she really was not," said Selznick's executive assistant Marcella Rabwin of Fontaine. Selznick himself, who had been infatuated with Fontaine the summer before she married Aherne, also knew that Fontaine needed work and care, but he had a very different way of looking at acting and performance than Hitchcock did. "I think we've got to be careful not to lose what little variety there is in the role by underplaying her in her emotional moments," Selznick wrote of Fontaine. "We must not make it seem as though Joan is simply not capable of the big moments."

Selznick favored the "big scene" view of acting that was crucial in the work of George Cukor, who often worked for Selznick in the 1930s. And this backfired with Fontaine, who was always at her best when she could underplay. A lot of work had to be done in the cutting room on *Rebecca* to protect her "big" moments after the fact, and Fontaine was also brought in to re-dub many of her lines. This was a performance painstakingly created by others, by camera angles, and by careful direction of every facial expression and vocal inflection.

Fontaine learned her lessons well. In *This Above All* (1942), she has a patriotic speech in which she goes way over the top, but after that misstep she found her footing. Fontaine gave many subtle and touching performances in a wide range of pictures in the 1940s and 1950s, reaching her apotheosis in Max Ophuls's classic romance *Letter from an Unknown Woman* (1948), in which her sensitivity, tact, burgeoning sophistication, and irony are often awe inspiring as she moves from a shy young girl to an assured woman of the world, always keeping true to her obsession with a pianist (Louis Jourdan) who does not recognize her lifelong ardor until it is too late.

Fontaine once asked Hitchcock to slap her so that she could get into tears for an emotional scene, and he did as she asked. To get her stirred up for one close-up, Hitchcock also did a somewhat adapted version of his pants-opening routine with Madeleine Carroll by sticking the cork of a champagne bottle in his crotch, for his mind was always in the gutter as he was looking at the stars.

Florence Bates was playing the part of Mrs. Van Hopper, the wealthy matron employer to Fontaine's character in the first scenes of *Rebecca*, and Hitchcock caught her practicing her part in a mirror. "Well, Miss Bates—when did you start playing with yourself?," Hitchcock asked her over the studio loud speaker. Bates's full-steam-ahead performance as Mrs. Van Hopper lacks shading and nuance, and it is the kind of definite acting that might have been worked out in a mirror.

Bates had been a lawyer as a young woman in Texas, and this was her first major film role. Many of her lines were also re-dubbed in the editing room after filming was done, and this is surely part of the problem with her performance here, which feels too abrupt and un-lifelike. It could also be said that the writing doesn't allow her to go beyond a caricature of a demanding, childish, older woman with money. We don't hear anything about Mr. Van Hopper, but hopefully he has passed on some time before we meet her.

Mrs. Van Hopper is a wasteful woman and a nuisance, and at one point we see her putting a cigarette out into a jar of cold cream in close-up, a really disgusting detail. Flirtatious in a heavy-spirited way with Maxim, Mrs. Van Hopper narrows her eyes and is tough and calculating when she asks Fontaine's heroine, "Tell me . . . have you been doing anything you shouldn't?" Mainly Mrs. Van Hopper is mean and unpleasant and someone to be avoided, yet we spend a lot of time with her in the first scenes of *Rebecca*.

Bates's rude American Mrs. Van Hopper is a change from what Hitchcock might have done with such a character in England. If she had been a British character, surely Hitchcock would have found a way to make her a more well-rounded person, to make her pay off in some unexpected fashion, and not necessarily by making her more sympathetic. She is a flat character. She doesn't make you think or wonder about her. Mainly, you just want to be rid of her as soon as possible, which is maybe all she is in the film for, to make us feel why Fontaine's character moves toward Maxim.

Fontaine plays these first scenes as if her chronically gauche heroine really doesn't want or need to marry the rich Maxim but feels compelled to. She is the sort of girl who will knock over a flower arrangement at a restaurant and cry, "Oh, how awkward of me!" to make it even worse for herself. Fontaine finds this odd groove in the first part of *Rebecca* where her heroine is so aware of her own deficiencies that they start to seem aggressive, somehow, or flaunted, and that's the area where she really thrives as an actress, the exaggerated shyness that is actually a cover for willfulness and bitchery and perversity. This finally is what makes Fontaine such a complex screen presence and worthy of Hitchcock's full attention.

"Still waters certainly run deep," cracks Mrs. Van Hopper after being told of this young girl's engagement to Maxim. Fontaine gives plenty of hints that her character is marrying Maxim out of sexual as much as romantic hunger. Selznick himself filmed the scene of our heroine dancing with Maxim, where she seems most sexually ready, but it becomes clear as the film goes on that Maxim and Fontaine's unnamed character do not have a successful sexual life. He is too closed off to women and too preoccupied with his anger at his dead wife.

The most memorable performance in *Rebecca* is given by the stage actress Judith Anderson, who plays the menacing housekeeper Mrs. Danvers, a woman who emerges as the key character in the film. When Maxim and Fontaine's Mrs. de Winter come back home to his estate, Manderley, after their wedding, a squadron of servants is waiting for them, and these servants are headed by the unsmiling Mrs. Danvers. Unlike Mrs. Van Hopper, Mrs. Danvers invites us to ask a whole host of questions.

For starters, just who was Mr. Danvers? Most likely he was also "in service," as they said in those days. It cannot have been pleasant for either Mr. or Mrs. Danvers, this marriage, for Mrs. Danvers was obsessively in love with her dead mistress Rebecca. Mrs. Danvers is both dominant and submissive, and this makes for a marvelously tense performing contrast that both Hitchcock and Anderson take full provocative advantage of.

Anderson's first close-up is cut off exactly at the moment when we want to see more of Mrs. Danvers, and then Fontaine's close-up in response to seeing her is rather lingered over, which creates exactly the impression we need of imbalance. Mrs. Danvers looks down at the gloves in the hands of her new mistress, which makes Fontaine's heroine drop them to the floor, whereupon there is a very charged moment when both the second Mrs. de Winter and Mrs. Danvers stoop down for the gloves. This is awkward for both of them, but it is also extremely intimate, like a sexual power game begun.

In the slight dolly in to a close-up of Mrs. Danvers, Anderson's face is both hooded and frankly curious, controlled yet vulnerable. Only a truly great actress like Anderson can convey such opposing things at once. She certainly isn't "doing nothing well" here. Anderson is doing many things in this close-up but under the control of her ironclad personal technique (see fig. 9.1). This technique of hers functions as her Hitchcockian "understatement" so that underneath it she can whip up as many different emotions as she likes.

As in *The Lady Vanishes*, an absent person once again dominates the film, but Rebecca is someone we never see or hear. She is never shown in flashback but only referred to and discussed and remembered, again and again. She was a great beauty and inclined to be promiscuous, and she would tell all about her conquests to her loyal servant Mrs. Danvers, or "Danny" as Mrs. Danvers is called by Rebecca's cousin Jack Favell. This scapegrace Favell is played by George Sanders, who makes a very winning entrance here by tripping over a windowsill. Favell seems to have been, ahem, rather close to his cousin.

Figure 9.1: Judith Anderson's Mrs. Danvers eyes her new mistress in *Rebecca*.

One day when Maxim is away, Mrs. Danvers catches Fontaine's squirming and emotionally vulnerable second wife in Rebecca's part of the house, which has been preserved exactly as she left it. Mrs. Danvers goes into a trance-like state here, and she suddenly becomes very familiar and casual with her new mistress. This is the scene in *Rebecca* that is a real Hitchcock scene. In Mrs. Danvers, he is dealing with a lesbian character, and he makes this as outright as it can possibly be in 1940.

"You've always wanted to see this room, haven't you, Madam?," Mrs. Danvers asks insinuatingly. "Why did you never ask me to show it to you? I was ready to show it to you . . . every day!" Anderson gives a hopeful and slightly crazy upward inflection to that "every day" that tips off Mrs. Danvers's intentions. She has been planning this scene ever since the new Mrs. de Winter came to the house. This is the scene Mrs. Danvers has thought about in her room at night, and maybe all during the day as she worked and intimidated the other servants.

This new girl is not Rebecca . . . but maybe she will do in a pinch. Anderson is most intriguing in *Rebecca* when Mrs. Danvers seems genuinely perplexed by the new Mrs. de Winter's inadequacies. As a rule, Mrs. Danvers's face has an impassive look suitable to her station, but she is intimidating in her submission (she is the ultimate in topping from the bottom).

"It's the loveliest room you've ever seen," Mrs. Danvers tells her new mistress when she opens the curtains of the high windows in Rebecca's bedroom. Her voice now is the voice of a fetishist, and of course being a servant is likely to make a fetishist out of anyone. What other pleasure can be had but the lustful keeping and maintaining of material things? That is all Mrs. Danvers has or likely ever has had. Sometimes here she sounds like Gloria Swanson's Norma Desmond in *Sunset Boulevard* (1950), in love with her own past and likely casting it in a rosier glow than is warranted. In the du Maurier novel, Mrs. Danvers was Rebecca's family maid when Rebecca was a child, too, and so her obsession with Rebecca has been long lasting.

When Mrs. Danvers takes a fur coat from a closet and runs the fur over her cheek, Anderson's face takes on a startlingly girlish, yielding look much like that of her new mistress. Their identities merge here, or Mrs. Danvers wants them to. She runs the fur over the new Mrs. de Winter's face, trying to share her fetishist delight with her. Hitchcock showed Anderson exactly how he wanted her to treat the fur, and he became Mrs. Danvers for her, which must have really been something to see.

Mrs. Danvers even shows the second Mrs. de Winter the lacy underwear that Rebecca wore and the see-through lingerie. "Made specially for her by the nuns of St. Clare!," Mrs. Danvers says, in a voice that implies, "How lucky those nuns were." She says she used to wait up all night sometimes for Rebecca, who wouldn't come home on certain nights until dawn. "She knew everyone that mattered," Mrs. Danvers says of Rebecca, revealing her own snobbery. "Everyone loved her," she insists, projecting her own emotion onto the whole world.

Mrs. Danvers is loyal to the memory of Rebecca and to those cherished nights when she would comb out Rebecca's hair and hear all about her mistress's adventures with men. What we wouldn't give to actually *see* some of those scenes with Vivien Leigh as Rebecca, for isn't Leigh the actress most of us think of when Rebecca is discussed?

Mrs. Danvers touches the second Mrs. de Winter for the first time since they briefly brushed each other in that electric way on first meeting, when the gloves were dropped and they both reached to pick them up. She puts her hand on Mrs. de Winter's shoulder and sets her down where Rebecca used to sit for their hair-brushing ritual, which would last "twenty minutes at a time," a process that Rebecca called "hair drill." Mrs. Danvers's own hair is worn with a long and complicated braid that she keeps on top of her head, in the same style used by Leopoldine Konstantin's Mrs. Sebastian in *Notorious*. If anything always repays close attention in Hitchcock, it is the style of the women's hair and what it might tell us about them.

When it comes to holding up her end of this crucial scene with Mrs. Danvers, Fontaine is somewhat blocked and unable to respond in a nuanced way, often falling back on a stiff sort of pride in her eyes. But then her character is not a sophisticated person. She is just bewildered by Mrs. Danvers and Rebecca's underwear, not alarmed, and this encounter only inflames her own feeling of inadequacy. She cannot bring herself to understand exactly what Mrs. Danvers is telling her, even when Mrs. Danvers brings out a flimsy nightdress and says, "Look, you can see my hand through it!"

As the new Mrs. de Winter retreats to the door of Rebecca's room in tears, Mrs. Danvers asks, "Do you think the dead come back to watch the living?" Fontaine's Mrs. de Winter sneaks away when Mrs. Danvers starts talking about the sea, where she thinks her beloved Rebecca drowned. The image of Mrs. Danvers freeze-frames here, which catches her visually in her static and Sapphic preoccupation. Maybe Mrs. Danvers was able to bring herself to orgasm while brushing Rebecca's hair, but Rebecca probably denied

"Danny" the ultimate reward. The kind of obsession that Mrs. Danvers has with Rebecca is the kind that flourishes precisely because it was never quite or exactly consummated.

Mrs. Danvers is firmly rebuffed by her new mistress after this underwear scene, which is at least partly a seduction, an attempt to share her obsession. If the new Mrs. de Winter had been more amenable or suggestible, is it possible that *Rebecca* might become a lesbian version of *Vertigo* where Mrs. Danvers manipulates the new Mrs. de Winter into dressing and behaving just like her former mistress, maybe only while Maxim is away? The possibilities really are rich when it comes to Mrs. Danvers.

Instead Mrs. Danvers behaves like a spurned lover and goes all out in trying to destroy the new Mrs. de Winter, maliciously suggesting that she wear a gown that Rebecca wore at a ball, which sends Maxim into a rage. This makes the second Mrs. de Winter go to confront Mrs. Danvers, and we see Fontaine from behind moving away from the camera down a hall so that her picture hat falls in a slightly ghostly way to her feet, a very resonant visual detail.

Mrs. Danvers makes short work of her and she collapses on a bed. Taking advantage of this chance, Mrs. Danvers opens a window. "Why don't you go, why don't you leave Manderley?," she asks. "You've nothing to stay for. You've nothing to live for, really, have you? Look down there . . . it's easy, isn't it? Why don't you?" Mrs. Danvers asks, as the second Mrs. de Winter cries near an open window. "Why don't you?," she repeats, in a soothing, hypnotic voice, urging her new mistress to throw herself out the window. "Go on . . . don't be afraid. . . ."

In this crucial scene, a tear-stained and wrung-out Fontaine rises to meet Anderson and the exchange of emotion between the two women is rich in subtext and implication, both ominous and queerly sexual. It is a love scene, in a way. Some fireworks stop Mrs. Danvers in her tracks, and then the plot kicks in where we learn the truth, or at least more, about Rebecca. And that's where Olivier has the burden of a long speech about his dead wife that Fontaine has to listen to. He handles this speech professionally, with his hushed voice and a habitual mannerism of lightly brushing his hand over his forehead, but without inspiration.

Hitchcock breaks this very long sequence up into scenes that generally run between seventy to ninety seconds, and so the responsibility for moving the narrative forward is very much on the actors here. Both Hitchcock and Selznick didn't like the way Olivier would take long pauses and then speed up his delivery of words, for these were stagy effects meant to dominate an audience rather than the truer and simpler counterpoint effects that Hitchcock favored in his actors. Olivier was known for randomly shouting a word on stage when he wanted to arrest or surprise his audience, and he often advised younger actors to do this, and such tricks are not camera friendly.

In a phone interview with Leonard Leff in 1986, when she was asked about the lesbianism of Mrs. Danvers, Anderson offered, "I wasn't aware of it then, but I certainly am now. Of course, I knew very little about lesbianism, and still don't." A statement like this from an elderly actress of her time and place is self-protective and meant for public consumption. Anderson had spent her life in the theater among gay people, and she was known for being mistrustful and difficult. She had been married herself twice and said of these marriages, "Neither experience was a jolly holiday," which sounds like what Mrs. Danvers herself might have said about her own marriage if she were speaking to trusted people like Rebecca and Jack Favell.

Anderson made herself into a great actress on stage, particularly in her famous production of *Medea*, which she played and toured in for years after *Rebecca*. She did not allow her striking, unusual looks to limit her. Her standards were of the highest, and so was her talent. Fontaine is the lead in *Rebecca*, but Anderson's Mrs. Danvers is truly the star part, the person we long to know more about. She is one of those characters in Hitchcock who are so multidimensional that she seems to lead an autonomous life outside of the film.

Hitchcock made sure that Mrs. Danvers was rarely seen walking to or from any location. She often just somehow appears, her hands folded in front of her black dress with all the buttons. Mrs. Danvers probably does not allow herself to act on her feelings for women. She has been held down and twisted, and the result is madness and finally vengeance as she burns down Manderley, her face taking on a wonderingly childlike expression as she looks at the consuming fire.

It didn't have to be this way. Imagine Mrs. Danvers (what is her first name?) born into some money and meeting some bohemian, accepting, creative people. Maybe then a smile might have bloomed on her self-denying face. Maybe she might have been a den mother, a hostess, and she might have relaxed. But she has been placed in two intolerably repressive positions as both a servant and a gay woman, and the pressure has made her into what she is.

Look at the way that Anderson relates to George Sanders in their scenes together. In these brief moments, she lets us see the possibilities that Mrs.

Danvers, or "Danny," might have had. Maybe Rebecca and Sanders's Jack laughed at their "Danny" a little, but there might have been some affection in that. Then again, maybe they were scared of her, as some of Maxim's relations are.

Maxim's sister Beatrice (Gladys Cooper) tells Fontaine's interloper that she should not have too much to do with Mrs. Danvers if she can help it. "I should think Maxim would have told you," Beatrice says. "She simply *adored* Rebecca." Cooper gives a sophisticated tinge to this line reading, leaving Fontaine to feel uncomfortable in several different ways, including deep down the way that cannot be named or even thought: that Mrs. Danvers is a lesbian. And that she might have some small interest in seducing, or destroying, this new Mrs. de Winter. In Hitchcock, seducing and destroying often look and feel like the same thing. As François Truffaut said, Hitchcock shot a scene of love as if it were a scene of murder, and he shot a scene of murder as if it were a scene of love.

Conversely, we aren't going to spend too much time wondering about Fontaine's character and her marriage to Maxim. When the film ends, somehow it doesn't seem likely that they will stay together long. After all, she no longer has "that funny young lost look" that he so loved. Maxim hated Rebecca because she led her own life and cuckolded him and laughed about him, but the glowering, needling, demanding Maxim de Winter might make a Rebecca out of any woman, even this meek second wife. In the du Maurier novel, Maxim and his second wife stay unhappily married and drift about second-class hotels where no one might recognize them, and they barely speak to each other.

Fontaine was nominated for an Oscar for Best Actress for *Rebecca* but lost to Ginger Rogers in the working girl drama *Kitty Foyle*. Rogers also beat Bette Davis in *The Letter* and Katharine Hepburn in *The Philadelphia Story*, and if we're judging on merit and level of difficulty surely Davis should have won. But it was felt that Fontaine should have had it, and she would have to wait until the following year to get awarded for Hitchcock's *Suspicion*. Anderson was nominated for supporting actress but lost to Jane Darwell's sentimental Ma Joad in *The Grapes of Wrath* (1940).

Rebecca had not been a happy experience for Hitchcock and so he was glad to be loaned out to Walter Wanger to make *Foreign Correspondent* (1940), where he was allowed to follow his natural inclinations more. He wanted Gary Cooper for the lead part of a reporter sent to cover the war in

Europe, but instead he was given the subtle and alert Joel McCrea, a fine and undervalued actor.

There were two standout sequences in *Foreign Correspondent*. The first was the murder of the ambassador Van Meer (Albert Bassermann) in the rain, where the killer makes his escape through a sea of umbrellas. Hitchcock gets away with putting in a close-up of Bassermann's bloodied and shocked face as he is shot by the gun, and the staging is truly scary once the killer is free of the umbrellas and running along the street because Hitchcock catches the sense here of a loose cannon capable of anything with bystanders all around him—two innocent onlookers get shot just for being in the wrong place at the wrong time.

The second sequence that really caught Hitchcock's attention was the climax where an airplane carrying most of the major characters gets shot down from the sky. The cutting here between the people trying to get to the back of the plane while the front of the plane comes close to hitting the ocean is very frightening, and convincing. (Hitchcock projected his nosedive footage onto a paper transparency so that when the plane hit the sea, it would immediately break and water could rush in.) Some passengers escape the plane and some of them drown, and one hardy white-haired old lady makes it through all kinds of trouble here and survives.

The thrills and the comedy and the romance between McCrea and Laraine Day's leading lady are not smoothly integrated in *Foreign Correspondent*. Hitchcock had wanted Barbara Stanwyck for the heroine but he couldn't get her, and surely this would be a far superior picture with Stanwyck in this part. Day is a particular type of innocuous, overconfident American girl that Hitchcock had not had to deal with before, and he is stuck with her for long sections of the film. As Day's father, who turns out to be the villain, Herbert Marshall is uneasy, as if he doesn't want to be unsympathetic.

Bassermann got a supporting actor Oscar nomination for his ponderous and hammy Van Meer, which turns out to be a dual role with a false Van Meer who is shot and a real Van Meer who is kept hostage in a Dutch windmill. The always-welcome George Sanders is only along for the ride here, though he does get a curiously extended close-up as his character is made to watch the torture of Van Meer.

Comedian and Algonquin round-table wit Robert Benchley is also along for the ride as a drunk reporter, and he contributed some of his own dialogue, which is not, alas, very funny. *Foreign Correspondent* got a nomination for Best Picture the same year that *Rebecca* won, but its breakneck, topical style has not aged too well. McCrea remembered that Hitchcock sometimes drank a pint of champagne at lunch and fell asleep once during one of his scenes. "Was it any good?," Hitchcock asked him.

Mr. and Mrs. Smith (1941) is a test case for auteurism. Hitchcock had nothing to do with the script, which was written by the talented Norman Krasna. He accepted the film as a favor to Carole Lombard, who wanted him to direct her. So this was an assignment in a foreign genre: American screwball comedy of remarriage made at RKO. Can you feel Hitchcock in it? Yes and no. If you didn't see Hitchcock's name in the credits, you most likely wouldn't know he had directed it. But if you do know that he was behind it, suddenly all kinds of Hitchcock inflections become apparent.

The film begins by showing us some shots of food on trays and playing cards on the floor of an apartment. David Smith (Robert Montgomery) is playing solitaire. He looks up apprehensively. There is a dolly in to Lombard's eye peeking out under the covers in her bed, and without the sprightly musical score by Edward Ward, this shot could seem like the start of a thriller. There are dark shadows from venetian blinds in many of the compositions of *Mr. and Mrs. Smith*, which is not usual for a comedy.

Lombard's Ann Smith has made it a rule that she and her husband can never leave their bedroom during a fight without making up, and she and David have been in the bedroom for three days. Their servants, a uniformed maid and a cook, let us know that they once went eight days like this. It becomes apparent as we watch this couple that Ann makes impossible demands on David when it comes to their relationship, but it is also clear that they have a robust sexual life together. Later in the film, Ann says that David "ruined" her eighty-five-dollar dress on their first date, and the urge to have constant sex is certainly the major thing that is keeping them in that bedroom for three to eight days at a time. The Smiths have been married for three years and they live in New York, and so this is Hitchcock's first Manhattan-set picture.

Finally the Smiths make up, and Lombard and Montgomery look very childishly pure and content when they do so. These two have their own world of intimacy together, even if David chafes at this sometimes. David lets Ann shave him, which allows another somewhat ominous Hitchcockian detail as she swipes at him expertly with a straight razor. Ann unreasonably expects truth at all times, and David is not without flaws himself. He had trouble getting Ann to accept his proposal, mainly because he has a tendency to be jealous.

When Ann asks David over breakfast if he would marry her again if he had everything to do over, she definitely expects him to say yes. Instead, taking her at her word about truth, David says, "Honestly, no." Lombard's face falls, a perfect example of Hitchcock's "negative acting," and her feet, which have been up under David's pants legs, slowly lower back down. There is a seeming continuity error here that is very suggestive: David's socks change style and color after he answers Ann's question.

David tries to reassure Ann but instead comes out with, "I love you, I worship you . . . I am *used* to you." A woman doesn't like to be told by her husband that he is "used to" her, of course, and especially not Ann. Among many other things, *Mr. and Mrs. Smith* shows just how large a leap in culture and sensibility Hitchcock made when he left England. This is unthinkable as a British picture, particularly when it comes to Ann's forthright, very sexual character. What a double feature this would make with *Rich and Strange*, another film about marriage with a heroine who is far more traditional and passive than Lombard's Ann but touchingly aware of her situation.

Ann is an American girl like Lombard herself, a tomboy, probably the most popular girl in school, and used to having her way in everything. This freedom has made her, it seems, more than a little bit unreasonable and manipulative. She has a difficult mother who doesn't like David, Mrs. Krausheimer (Esther Dale, who has a late Shelley Winters manner), a huffy matron who is concerned only with how things "will look."

When it turns out that Ann and David aren't legally married due to a complex technical glitch, Ann thinks that this is the perfect way to renew both their romance and their vows. But everything goes wrong. The suit Ann got married in doesn't fit her anymore, and when they go to an old restaurant that was "their place" during their courtship, it has deteriorated badly.

The scene played at "Momma Lucy's," which is the name of this old restaurant of theirs, is decidedly and unexpectedly grim. David says it smells like a livery, and there is a pesky white cat who likes to sit on the tables. The tablecloths aren't checked anymore, but they are so dirty that they might as well be. Momma Lucy herself went back to the old country, and a grouchy older man says that *he* is Momma Lucy now. He shows them reluctantly to a table outside, asking if they want the "Forty-five or the sixty-five cent dinner."

A gang of hungry children stares at the Smiths outside at their table, but the undaunted Ann tells David to just stare right back at them: "That'll make them embarrassed!," she says. This is definitely Ann's most unlikable moment in the picture, and it shows that Lombard is not afraid of being unsympathetic. Then again, there is a certain kind of busy American obliviousness to things like hungry children that insists, "Just ignore them!" in a full-steam-ahead sort of way. And the intriguing thing about *Mr. and Mrs. Smith* is that it relates Ann's inability to care about these kids with her dream of a marriage that will be always romantic yet truthful.

It could be said that there is a positive feminist aspect to Ann's obstinate American girl character here, and it emerges when she throws David out of the house and quickly gets herself a job at a store. This active show of independence proclaims, "I don't need you, I can make my own living," but we learn that she wasn't above using her looks to get that job at the store from an older man.

It is easy to see why David was ambivalent about taking on the challenge of winning Ann back at first. She is a handful, and exhausting, but *so* sexy. And so finally David loses Ann's job for her when he confronts her at the store, and her boss tells her that they don't employ married women so as to "help with the unemployment problem." This is a reminder that in 1941, even a woman like Ann is going to come up against certain limits.

The best sequence in *Mr. and Mrs. Smith* is one that belongs solely to Montgomery, with his standby "cat with the canary" face, which Hitchcock tests and finally destroys. David is out at a nightclub where Ann and his friend Jeff (Gene Raymond) have gone on a date. His own date is the vulgar and embarrassing low-class Gertie, who is played by Betty Compson, a blonde actress who was the epitome of delicate blonde beauty in Josef von Sternberg's *The Docks of New York* (1928). Compson had drastically aged out of that category by this point. She had once been the star of two silent films that Hitchcock had assistant directed for Graham Cutts in 1923, *Woman to Woman* and *The White Shadow*.

Gertie might be a prostitute or maybe just a middle-aged gal happy to put out if she gets dinner out of it. She is on David's right and there is a comely 1940s-style goddess girl seated to his left. Ann has seen him, and so David quickly decides to start mouthing words into the ear of the beautiful girl to his left to pretend that she is his date. Hitchcock builds this sequence with Montgomery as David sneaks looks at Ann and she sneaks looks right back at him until the girl and her date notice what he is doing, which makes him stop.

Wanting to escape, David induces a nosebleed by hitting himself in the face several times, a curiously slow and unpleasant process as Montgomery plays it, but when he tries to leave, Gertie insists on playing Florence Nightingale and lays him out for the whole club to see, very embarrassingly, with a knife under his nose, and Hitchcock shows us Ann and Jeff glaring down at him almost upside down from David's point of view. At this point the nightclub scene has taken on the quality of a nightmare with Hitchcockian accents that move it rather far from the formal rules and fun of screwball comedy.

"I don't care who holds the knife to him, although I'd certainly like the chance myself," Ann says to Jeff in the back of a cab. At a carnival they go up in a once-popular parachute jump ride, and there are several shots of the vertiginous view below them as they go up and up before they get stuck in midair.

The details here are more than ominous as Lombard's high cries of delight give way to an outraged, "Why don't they do something about it!" in a panicked voice. The shots from their point of view are very frightening as we see the shaky dark ground far below them with people so small that they look like dots. Ann and Jeff get rained on, and then finally they are let down and they go back to Jeff's apartment, with its knotty pine walls. He says he designed the décor himself.

Ann dries her wet hair by the fire, and no woman has ever looked lovelier or more enticing in a Hitchcock movie than in the shot where Lombard's Ann quickly turns around to look at Jeff in her prideful way, her thin hair nearly dry, her figure superb in a dark dress that looks nearly like a slip (fig. 9.2). Ann keeps talking about David, and what follows is a very strange scene where Jeff gets drunk, and we begin to wonder just what is going on with him. Raymond had been a platinum blond sex object in his early 1930s films, but here he has dark hair and has aged into a Ralph Bellamy part.

Jeff tells Ann a sinister extended story about a confrontation he witnessed in his youth between a sneaky temperance preacher and a man who was a volunteer in the audience, and there are moments here when even Ann's blithe American confidence seems a little shaky in her responses to this story. Lombard is wonderful in this scene because she is still playing in her distinctive "racing, racing, racing" style, but she expertly puts on the brakes, here and there, as Jeff throws her a curveball or two. Her face says, "I'm listening" and sometimes, "Wait, what?"

Somehow Jeff starts to seem like a genuine weirdo here, but that possibility was always inherent in second-banana parts like his, especially as Bellamy himself played them. Jeff used to be a football star at school, and he has domineering parents. That the second banana might be a pervert or even a killer is something that Hitchcock really brings out in this scene.

Figure 9.2: Carole Lombard's All-American Ann dries her hair by the fire in *Mr. and Mrs. Smith*.

Wouldn't it truly be a shocker if Jeff stabbed or strangled Ann after the first hour of this more or less conventional screwball comedy? Hitchcock had spoken in the late 1930s of starting off a film with a Keystone Cop farce sequence where cops are getting clunked on the head for laughs, but then he would have cut to one of them getting seriously injured followed by a solemn funeral. There is no such drastic switch in *Mr. and Mrs. Smith*, but there is another strange scene where Jeff tries to talk to his parents in his office restroom and loud plumbing problems keep interrupting them.

The final third of *Mr. and Mrs. Smith* plays out at a ski lodge where David and Ann try on various role-play scenarios. Finally David cries, "There's only one way to handle you!" before putting Ann in a headlock, which is standard for screwball comedy where fighting takes the place of sex or is a prelude to it. Ann reveals her bloodlust when Jeff refuses to fight David physically for her. "What kind of a man are you?," she asks. At this point, it becomes clear that Ann is an extremely attractive if difficult woman, but if she were a man, she would be a man to avoid. When Ann says she needs to leave the room "before

I forget I'm a lady," this is meant to be a joke whereas in Britain it would have been taken at least somewhat seriously.

In the last scene, Ann is stuck or "stuck" in a pair of skis as David looks on, and Lombard brings a narrow-eyed, serious intensity to the moment when she says, "Sometime, someday when your back is turned I'll stab you!" This is an unsettling line reading because she really doesn't seem to be kidding, and the way David takes off his tie has a menacing and sexual overtone. Hitchcock had been unable to do anything with the operetta *Waltzes from Vienna*, but *Mr. and Mrs. Smith* showed that his talent could illuminate and complicate a genre that might seem foreign to him on the surface.

Mr. and Mrs. Smith has often been dismissed or overlooked, and it shouldn't be. It is filled with rich and troubling detail, and bolstered by strictly controlled, first-rate farcical performances by Lombard and Montgomery that could not be bettered. If this film had been directed by, say, William A. Seiter or Garson Kanin, then the two lead actors would have given much the same performances. But having Hitchcock there on the set, smiling or dozing or what have you, probably brought out darker details in their work that would not have been there otherwise.

Hitchcock's next film, *Suspicion* (1941), was not a happy experience for anyone involved. It had an unusually prolonged shooting schedule of six months because of various illnesses that beset both Hitchcock and star Joan Fontaine, and there was some lingering indecision about the ending. In *Before the Fact*, the novel that the film was based on, the heroine comes to realize that she has married a killer who is about to do her in, but she's so crazy about him that she allows him to poison her, thus becoming an accessory to her own murder "before the fact."

Hitchcock had thought up a nifty way to punish the male lead. The heroine Lina would be seen writing a letter explaining that she was about to be murdered, and right before she drank her poisoned milk, she was to ask her husband Johnnie to mail the letter for her. The film would have ended with Johnnie happily whistling and putting the letter in a mailbox. For a title, Hitchcock favored *Johnnie*, but the title *Suspicion* reflected the new direction the project was supposed to take. Cary Grant had been cast as Johnnie, and the producers and the studio RKO did not want their male lead to be found out as a murderer.

Grant had become a real star in 1937 with *The Awful Truth*, and he had been laying down screwball comedy groundwork in films like *Bringing Up Baby* (1938) and *Holiday* (1938). He was a movie dream man with an edge and an unplaceable accent, reading his lines with a plummy yet biting voice and a needling quality just below the surface. Grant was an ideal Hitchcock actor because he never settled on one attitude for long, and this is also what makes him such a disturbing and attractive Johnnie Aysgarth, a playboy with the emphasis on play who first spots Lina McLaidlaw (Joan Fontaine) on a train.

After the credits for *Suspicion*, there are a few moments of total darkness as we hear a train whistle and then just Johnnie's voice as he apologizes for brushing Lina's leg. This strikes just the right sexy but ominous note. Lina is wearing glasses that glint in the sunlight from the train window, and she is reading a hefty tome on child psychology, and all of this gives her a forbidding look.

Hitchcock sets up this train meeting as a series of cuts between Lina and Johnnie where Lina is looking a bit distantly off-camera but the hung-over Johnnie stares into the camera directly when he needs money for the train, so that he seems to be seducing us, too (fig. 9.3). The point of view here is very tricky, shifting seamlessly between rebellious, frisky Johnnie and

Figure 9.3: Cary Grant's bad-boy Johnnie Aysgarth stares at a stranger on a train in *Suspicion*.

buttoned-up Lina and suggesting something momentous or at least inescapable happening between them. We see on Lina's face that she thinks Johnnie is probably a lot of trouble . . . but maybe he is worth it?

Lina has been carefully brought up in such a repressive way that the excitement of the ne'er-do-well Johnnie takes hold of her on a deep level. Some time after their first meeting on the train, Johnnie sees Lina on horseback, and then we see her beautiful face behind a veil in extreme close-up: "Can't be the same girl," Johnnie says. They are drawn together, and Hitchcock toys with our expectations here by showing Lina and Johnnie struggling in long shot on a hill as if he is attacking her, but then we are brought in to a close shot so that we can see Johnnie is only trying to be playful with Lina and she has reacted badly.

Or is this what has happened? It can be difficult to judge these things. Johnnie tells her that her hair has "possibilities" and that he had been reaching for her because he had suddenly become a "passionate hairdresser." Grant gives a hilariously subversive queer charge to this line, and Fontaine is right with him as she snaps shuts her very Freudian purse in close-up and goes off in a huff, or "in a huff." Fontaine uses her weakly guarded snobby look in these first scenes to excellent effect, and Grant's exciting comic authority makes Johnnie seem irresistible, or very hard to resist.

When Lina hears her stuffy parents (Sir Cedric Hardwicke and Dame May Whitty) discussing her as an incipient spinster, she throws herself right at Johnnie and kisses him. Her father talks about Johnnie at lunch and says that he is known for being wild and for cheating at cards and that there maybe was an affair Johnnie had with a married woman that led to a divorce, but this does not deter Lina. At a ball where she dances a Strauss waltz with Johnnie, Lina wears a low-cut dress and her hair is styled in a chignon. Hitchcock himself, of course, was a passionate hairdresser with women.

Johnnie has so much charm that we do not question Lina's feelings, even though his referring to her as "monkey face" doesn't exactly have the right affectionate ring to it. Johnnie takes Lina for a drive and finally stops the car. "Have you ever been kissed in a car before?," Johnnie asks Lina, who squirms pleasurably in her seat next to him. "Would you like to be?," he asks, in that marvelously clipped, larger-than-life, stylized Cary Grant voice, a real movie voice, not like anything you would hear in life.

When they speak about loving each other, Johnnie's face becomes frighteningly opaque, hard to read, slightly panicked but with maybe something satisfied and gloating underneath, something killer. A lady killer or a killer of ladies? Lina can't see his face here, but we can. Though he makes a point of being honest with her verbally, it is clear that Johnnie is not entirely honest with her, or perhaps even with himself. The camera moves around Lina and Johnnie as they kiss later back at the ball, which emphasizes her growing fixation with him. He gives her a vulnerable little boy look before kissing her. Is it genuine, or somewhat calculated?

Suspicion is a story about a woman obsessed with a man, just as *Vertigo* would be about a man obsessed with a woman. Lina and Johnnie marry, and presumably they have stupendously great sex together, for stupendously great sex is really the only reason a woman like Lina would put up with a man like Johnnie, who right away reveals how shifty and irresponsible he is after their honeymoon. This is an area where the strict censorship of 1941 rather muffles the narrative, which would be much stronger if Hitchcock were allowed to suggest or allude to Lina's sexual hunger for her husband.

Even though this crucial aspect of the story has to be assumed rather than implied, the sexual hold Johnnie has on Lina explains the depth of her disappointment as time goes on and her husband reveals himself to be not only irresponsible but probably dangerous. It also explains why she cannot stand to sever ties with Johnnie. Her sex urge becomes a death urge, or at least it moves her in that direction. And why not, if life is as dull as she knew it at home? There is a small hint of what they have sexually when Johnnie mentions all the places they went on their honeymoon and he knowingly ends this carnal litany with Paris, as if they really had quite a time sexually in Paris.

Suspicion is very good at putting us in Lina's obsessive state of mind, so that we really feel how she cannot let go of her initial feelings for Johnnie, who is a chronic liar and gambler and even a thief. Like many women with their bad-boy lovers or husbands, Lina thinks she can reform Johnnie, but he turns out to be more than she can handle. When she finds out that he has been stealing from his employer, Lina writes a letter breaking up with him but quickly tears it up, and this is followed right away by Johnnie entering to tell her that her father has died. Psychologically she's in a bind, and she can't get out of it.

In a scene where Johnnie is angry at Lina for questioning his shady business affairs, Grant dramatically switches gears, revealing a tightly coiled rage and physical menace that is the flip side of his usual springy charm. Grant's alert, restless performing style is always motivated by a deep anger that he never fully shows to us, and he shows more of it in this scene in *Suspicion* than he ever had before on screen. His dark eyes especially can be extremely intimidating and even bullying, and Fontaine looks very small and frail next to him when he bears down on her physically.

Marrying a dream movie man like Cary Grant might turn out to be a nightmare, yet it cannot be said that his murderous anger in *Suspicion* can come as much of a surprise. Actual danger was always an element of Grant's style in comedy and drama. Never does he seem like a "nice" person or a stand-up guy. He offers access to freedom and rollicking fantasy, nightclubs, and first-date teasing. But you can't "settle down" with Grant. If you do, you're likely going to find out some unsavory things about him that had been right there all along beneath the surface.

Suspicion is a film that shifts at every viewing, even more so than other Hitchcock pictures, because the performing nuances of both Fontaine and Grant are very subtle here and also very open to different questions and interpretations as German Expressionist shadows close in on Lina in her home. Is Johnnie sleeping with their very attractive young maid Ethel (Heather Angel)? Grant's Johnnie seems awfully happy when he gives Ethel a fur piece, smiling in a way that feels purely blissful. Of course, when suspicions start, there is no end to them, and Hitchcock knew a lot about that. In fact, this is the Jamesian wellspring of his art, this ceaseless asking of more and more questions. (Johnnie is indeed sleeping with Ethel in the novel, and she even gets pregnant by him.)

Hitchcock insisted on making the mystery novelist Isobel Sedbusk (Auriol Lee) into as open a lesbian character as could be shown in 1941 along with another lady in a suit and tie named Phyllis Swinghurst (Nondas Metcalf) who is seated at Isobel's small dinner party. Censors strongly objected to Phyllis wearing male clothing and what this implied and how she calls Johnnie "my dear chap," but Hitchcock somehow got away with keeping these details. He seems to like Isobel, who thinks of her villains as her heroes, as Hitchcock himself did.

Lee had only made one other film, the Ruth Chatterton vehicle *A Royal Divorce* (1938), where she played Napoleon's mother, but she had played on stage and she had directed several John Van Druten plays before she died in an automobile accident the year that *Suspicion* was released. Metcalf was in a short film in 1941, but *Suspicion* was her only other credit. Isobel and Phyllis seem very cozy, calling each other Izzy and Phil, and they are giving the dinner party together, it seems. They are the most positive gay characters in all of Hitchcock.

Auriol Lee and Nondas Metcalf. Isobel Sedbusk and Phyllis "Phil" Swinghurst. These are magic queer names. And so once again Joan Fontaine is presented with a lesbian alternative in a Hitchcock movie, and a far more enticing and healthier one than the unequal alliance between Mrs. Danvers and the dead Rebecca. These two women are Johnnie's friends, and it is very unlikely that Lina would have met people like Isobel and Phyllis if she had stayed in her original milieu. But Isobel writes books about murders, and Johnnie seems unusually urgent when he asks her about various methods of poisoning.

"Do I look like a murderer?," Johnnie asks, a key Hitchcockian question, and the answer is both yes and no. Does Lina look like one? "She has a strange glint in her eye," says Phyllis, or Phil, to Lina, and this feels flirtatious. Isobel says Johnnie is "trying to look mysterious" with the opaque face he turns on her, but he is both trying to look mysterious with this face and he also *is* mysterious, maybe even to himself. Yes and no, mysterious and not . . . and mysterious. Round and round it goes, ending on an odd little smile on Johnnie's face.

Only Grant could have made all these questions as rich as they are here, as teasing and unsettling and ambiguous. He was nominated for an Oscar in 1941 for a drama called *Penny Serenade* in which he has a big scene where his character begs to keep his adopted child, and this was obvious enough as acting to get noticed. Grant was not nominated for any of his four Hitchcock films, yet his performances in all four of them represent a height of multicolored inventiveness and of masterly, double-edged control in screen acting.

Suspicion builds to the famous moment when Johnnie slowly walks up the staircase of their home with a glass of milk on a tray for his wife, and Hitchcock drew attention to the milk by putting a light bulb in the glass. Franz Waxman's score can be intrusive in this movie, crashing in sometimes when it is not needed, but he deserves much credit here for deciding to play the waltz that Johnnie and Lina once danced to in a mournful minor key on the soundtrack as Johnnie walks up the stairs with the milk, which has a very sad effect, as if to say, "It's come to this."

If the film had ended with Lina willingly drinking the poisoned milk, *Suspicion* might be as strong and tragic a film as *Sabotage*. But RKO was in trouble and flux, and the studio forced Hitchcock to resort to a mechanical suspense sequence where Lina thinks Johnnie is about to push her out of a car and then a wholly unbelievable scene where we learn that he hasn't been so bad after all, just desperate and suicidal, none of which sounds likely coming from Cary Grant.

Fontaine won the Oscar for Best Actress for *Suspicion*, making her the only player to ever win an Oscar for a Hitchcock movie. After this second "woman's picture" cum thriller with her, Hitchcock had taken his interest in Fontaine as far as it could go. She does look a little green around the gills sometimes in *Suspicion*, as if illness and the long schedule had tired her out. In general, Hitchcock liked more spirited women with a streak of passivity, whereas Fontaine's screen image was all about hiding her own spirit and rather jaded sophistication behind a girlish and passive-aggressive style. As Fontaine's own mother said when she saw *Rebecca*, "Joan always seems rather phony in real life, but she is very believable on the screen."

10

Saboteur, Shadow of a Doubt, Lifeboat, Spellbound

Another "wrong man on the run" movie, *Saboteur* is one of Hitchcock's weakest films on every level. RKO didn't want this project, and so it was made at Universal, and Hitchcock was stuck with Robert Cummings and Priscilla Lane when he had wanted Gary Cooper and Barbara Stanwyck or Henry Fonda and Margaret Sullavan. Hitchcock later spoke of Cummings's "comedy face," which he thought made the serious situations of the film unbelievable.

Hitchcock had Peter Viertel and Dorothy Parker helping on the screenplay of *Saboteur*, and Parker herself even made a cameo with Hitchcock, croaking out, "My, they must be terribly in love," when she sees Cummings and Lane struggling from her car. But that line had been funnier when it was delivered by the hotel proprietress in *The 39 Steps*, and this American riff on *The 39 Steps* never gets anywhere near its predecessor in terms of quality. (Hitchcock later reshot this scene with professional actors when he found his own presence in it too distracting.)

The writing here is a real problem, and Viertel and Parker share responsibility for that. The dialogue throughout has an arch quality, especially in an extended interaction that Cummings has with a Wise Old Blind Man (Vaughan Glaser) that is probably the worst single scene Hitchcock ever directed, one of those "I might be blind, but I can *really* see things" routines. Glaser is playing Lane's uncle, and his character seems to be a gay guy of the benign old queen school who is enveloped in smug self-love.

There's an attempt to make Otto Kruger's big-time villain into an amalgam of both fascist and evil capitalist, but he just comes off like a bad guy in a serial. Norman Lloyd's Fry, who sets the plot in motion with an act of sabotage, is a sleazy, narrow-eyed little worm, so that we really don't care when he is hanging by a thread from the Statue of Liberty at the end. There's a promising sequence of laughter in a movie theater juxtaposed with real gunplay, but it is poorly handled because the tone and the editing rhythms here are all over the place. Nothing seems to go right in *Saboteur*.

Judging *Foreign Correspondent* and *Saboteur* against *The 39 Steps* and *The Lady Vanishes*, it's clear why some critics and fans were afraid that Hitchcock's move to America had been a mistake. But Hitchcock's follow-up to *Saboteur* was a classic that was also made for Universal, and a personal favorite of his, *Shadow of a Doubt* (1943).

In this picture, Hitchcock returned to the sort of precision that had marked his best British work, particularly with the editing, which is razor sharp here. He also made a concerted effort to deal with foreign territory for him, the life of a small American town in California called Santa Rosa. *Shadow of a Doubt* was shot on location in Santa Rosa, an unusual move for Hitchcock, who usually preferred shooting in the studio. As detailed in Bill Krohn's book *Hitchcock at Work*, the decision to go on location was mainly made because of wartime restrictions on set building.

Hitchcock relied on the playwright Thornton Wilder, the man who wrote the classic play *Our Town*, for inspiration and background on *Shadow of a Doubt*, and he was so happy with Wilder that he gave him a special mention in the credits. The writer Sally Benson, author of *Meet Me in St. Louis*, also had a major hand in the script, as did Hume Cronyn, who appears in the picture as an actor. "The camera lies, you know," Hitchcock told Cronyn. "And when it does, you have to accommodate it."

Shadow of a Doubt begins with an image of couples in turn-of-the-century garb turning and turning like mechanical figurines to Franz Lehár's Merry Widow waltz under the credits. We see boys playing ball outside on a street and then an off-kilter camera angle of a boarding house, and then we see Joseph Cotten's Charlie, or Uncle Charlie, stretched out on a bed and preoccupied in the near dark. There is cash scattered on the table and even on the floor near him, and he speaks to his landlady in a low, rather hallucinatory voice, as if he were in a private world of his own.

Cotten's Charlie brazenly escapes the policemen who are following him and calls to let his family know he is coming to Santa Rosa, and then Hitchcock cuts to shots of the idyllic town and then to young Charlie (Teresa Wright) in the exact same preoccupied pose in which we first saw her uncle, stretched out on her bed in her modest bedroom, which links niece and uncle visually. *Shadow of a Doubt* is about the way evil, or even Evil, comes to a small town, and this is visually expressed by the billowing, insistent black smoke from the train that brings Uncle Charlie to Santa Rosa and back to the family of his sister Emma (Patricia Collinge).

Hitchcock's mother was ill in England and died during the making of *Shadow of a Doubt*, and she was also named Emma, but Hitchcock's daughter Pat insisted that Collinge's Emma was nothing like Hitchcock's own mother. Still, this character was given his mother's name, and surely his mother was on his mind, for Emma in the film is lingered over almost excessively.

Collinge was a stage actress and writer, and she was best known for having played the pitiful Aunt Birdie in the stage version of *The Little Foxes* and its 1941 screen version, which had also featured Wright in her first movie role. Collinge made some contributions to the script of *Shadow of a Doubt* when she was enlisted by Wright to rewrite and improve a scene that Charlie has with a cop (Macdonald Carey) out in the family garage, and so she has a real stake in the tone of this movie.

Collinge had a dithering style as an actress that Hitchcock really presses and puts under his microscope here, notably in a late scene where Emma has a chatty, helpless, very feminist monologue about feeling trapped as a woman and as a wife, and how these roles make you "sort of forget you're you." Emma is a multidimensional character because Hitchcock also allows her to express her anger when she bosses some journalists around in her kitchen (they are really cops after her brother). The cops are pretending to do a story on a typical American family, and Emma gets increasingly annoyed with them in a jabbing, "motherly" way that expresses her own frustration with her life.

It seems like Emma's "obliviousness" might be somewhat put on as a defense mechanism that may contain a little of the contempt for life that has consumed her brother. It is clear that Emma's husband Joseph (Henry Travers) doesn't like or approve of Uncle Charlie, but Joseph is not able to express this openly, even to himself. Being a happy American small-town family means having to be very repressed about many things, and Hitchcock often strays from plot in this movie to focus on unfolding details of character and mood.

Emma deeply loves her brother Charlie in a somewhat unhealthy or at least over-intense way, and so does her daughter Charlie in her own unhealthy and nearly incestuous fashion. And so there is a real tension set up when young Charlie finds out that her uncle is a murderer of rich women, and she has to keep this from her fragile mother. The balance and give and take between Emma and her brother Charlie is very troubling, and Uncle Charlie is more than troubling. His evil is explained here by Emma, who says that he fractured his skull when he was a child and was never the same afterward, but the crocodile look on Cotten's face annihilates such tidy explanations.

Hitchcock had pursued William Powell for Uncle Charlie and Olivia de Havilland for young Charlie, and though both of them were enthusiastic, they were tied up with other projects. Wright and Cotten were both fairly new to movies when they made *Shadow of a Doubt*, and so for audiences of the time and even now, the actors *are* their characters here without any other pressing associations from other pictures. Wright's stock-in-trade was a girlish, very strained sincerity in face and voice that could become irritating in certain parts if she pressed too hard. Her face shows everything she is thinking in a clear and even obvious way. She doesn't do nuances, or complications, and so her Charlie is Good in a somewhat sexless, old-fashioned manner.

Cotten was a friend and colleague of Orson Welles, and he was under contract to David Selznick in the 1940s and mainly used for undemanding romantic leading man parts. He sometimes, very briefly, looks like a bad little boy in *Shadow of a Doubt*, but mainly he has a neither-here-nor-there sort of waiting quality that made him an ideal Hitchcock actor. Hitchcock later gave Cotten a peculiar tour de force in "Breakdown," a 1955 episode he directed personally for his TV show *Alfred Hitchcock Presents* where Cotten was a callous financier who is paralyzed after a car accident. For most of this episode, Cotton is immobilized, his eyes open and unblinking, as his thoughts are played on the soundtrack as radio-like voice over.

Before shooting with him on *Shadow of a Doubt*, Hitchcock told Cotten, "I think our secret is to achieve an effect of contrapuntal emotion. Forget trying to intellectualize about Uncle Charlie. Just be yourself." And again, Hitchcock emphasized to his lead actor that the key to Uncle Charlie should be "emotive counterpoint."

There is nothing colorful or theatrical about Cotten's Uncle Charlie as there is about, say, Robert Walker's Bruno Antony or Anthony Perkins's Norman Bates. Cotten had thick, problem hair and a deep voice and very hooded eyes, and when he smiled the smile could seem a little nasty, as if he were privately gloating over something we weren't privy to. Those hooded eyes are staring outward into nothingness when Uncle Charlie falls into a monologue about "silly, useless women" at the dinner table. He has a false nostalgia for the past that he uses as one of his many excuses.

Like his sister, Uncle Charlie is an angry person and given to expressing that verbally, but he covers himself in a way that Emma can't. He gives this misogynist, fascist speech at the dinner table in his absent, detached, hallucinatory voice, and the camera moves closer and closer to him as he airs his noxious views on "fat, greedy women" until young Charlie speaks up off-screen for humanism: "But they're alive, they're human beings!," Wright cries in that boyishly adolescent, pushed voice of hers.

Uncle Charlie looks straight into the camera, seductively. "Are they?," he asks, in his flat, croaking, unanswerable voice. The good of young Charlie is helpless here, weak and stymied compared to the way the camera gives Uncle Charlie his authority. Hitchcock knows how strong evil is, and how it can go on destroying unchecked. Uncle Charlie has strangled three rich widows, the last of whom was a famous musical comedy star in her youth.

The music for *Shadow of a Doubt* by Dimitri Tiomkin is another of those noisy, intrusive 1940s scores that punctuates and underlines moments too much, and Hitchcock isn't too interested in Charlie's young sister Ann and brother Roger, both of whom are written as precocious and aggressive in the manner of Sally Benson's Tootie, who was played by Margaret O'Brien in the 1944 film of her *Meet Me in St. Louis*. Emma seems merely amused by her younger daughter Ann in an oddly detached way that seems to represent Hitchcock's own relationship to this little girl, but he really thrives here when he emphasizes the seamy side of Santa Rosa, the sexual underbelly.

A bespectacled girl named Catherine (Estelle Jewell) looks Uncle Charlie up and down out on the street in a frankly appraising and sexual way, and she later does the exact same thing to Carey's cop and his partner. Jewell was a local Santa Rosa resident and she never made another movie, but she makes her mark here. Jewell's Catherine is like the sexually avid flip side of another unforgettable girl we meet in *Shadow of a Doubt*, a girl named Louise Finch (Janet Shaw) who waits on table at a seedy bar that Uncle Charlie forces his niece into called Til Two.

This sad young waitress, dreary voiced and slutty seeming, used to go to school with young Charlie, but Louise probably never got good grades like Charlie did. That's why she's waitressing, and waiting, and looking over this straight-A student and her uncle with some "maybe you're not so good after all" glances. "I been in half the restaurants in town," Louise says in a husky, flat voice. Why she keeps losing her jobs is not specified, but she does give Uncle Charlie a very subtle signal of her sexual willingness that finally seems not so much subtle as exhausted. It is clear that she is one of the damned (fig. 10.1).

When Charlie gives back a ring her uncle gave her, which was a trophy from one of his killings, their waitress perks up as much as she can. "I'd just die for a ring like that," Louise says, looking it over. "Yes sir, for a ring like that I'd just about die . . . I love jewelry, *real* jewelry," she emphasizes. "Notice

Figure 10.1: Uncle Charlie (Joseph Cotten) makes eye contact with Janet Shaw's Louise Finch as his niece (Teresa Wright) looks on in *Shadow of a Doubt*.

I didn't even have to ask if it was real." She just knows these things! "Who can tell?," she asks, rhetorically, and then she says, "I can." Louise's voice here has that hallucinatory quality that Uncle Charlie's voice has when he talks about women.

Louise is a hopeless case, and it feels, somehow, that she will come to a bad end. She is just floating through life, like a character in a Zola novel, waiting to be caught by someone or something down at the bottom of the barrel. Are Louise Finch and Catherine, the girl with the glasses, friends? Maybe they have a *Twin Peaks*-like "fire walk with me" operation going for them on the wrong side of the tracks of Santa Rosa. Shaw mainly played small and uncredited roles in movies, both before *Shadow of a Doubt* and afterward, but her Louise Finch is the one character here you want to follow and know more about, and surely Hitchcock would like to know more about her, too.

Shaw was born as Ellen Stuart and came from the small town of Beatrice, Nebraska, and she went out to Hollywood with her parents as a teenager. She used the stage name Ellen Clancy for a while, but Jack Warner changed her name to Janet Shaw when she was under contract to Warners. Shaw never got other parts as good or as suggestive as Louise Finch, and she had given up on acting by 1955. She died in 2001, back in Beatrice, Nebraska. Few people would remember her name or her brief career were it not for her Louise Finch, who is like a little haunting noir drama all to herself.

Hitchcock is dramatizing a very unsettling thing in *Shadow of a Doubt*: how certain kinds of behavior can be like an infectious disease. Charlie has undirected sexual longings that she had been directing at the idea of her uncle, but he takes advantage of this in a very nasty way, forcing her to see the often sordid reality of sex and how the world is a "foul sty . . . the world's a hell, what does it matter what happens in it?" (Thornton Wilder wrote both of Uncle Charlie's key negative speeches about his views on life, the earlier one at the dinner table and this one at the bar.) Later on, Uncle Charlie makes a very obnoxious comment about religion and going to church, likening it to a performance: "Show's been running such a long time I thought maybe attendance had been falling off," he says in Cotten's most incisively mean voice.

Uncle Charlie starts trying to kill off his niece as she looks up to an inactive God for help. Pushed too far, Charlie says she will kill him herself if he doesn't leave. This scene is played in silhouette, and Wright is not particularly believable here, but maybe this is just Charlie's weakness in relation to her uncle. There is a close-up shot of Emma in the back of a car where she seems to be dimly realizing that someone is trying to kill her daughter, but this cannot break through her habitual mental fog.

Finally, Charlie kills her uncle off in an extended scene on a train that is staged and played like a rape, with shots of his hand over her mouth and her shoes in very high heels, and then her frightened face in close-up in a strange moment of static panic as she waits for him to push her and then manages to push him out of the train somehow. It's finally ironic that Emma would have been "killed" by knowing her brother was a murderer but not by his sudden death, because ignorance on certain subjects is essential to a small-town American wife and mother, and on this score the film is very acute and insightful.

The last scene of *Shadow of a Doubt* is a sort of non-ending where young Charlie speaks to Carey's cop and he talks about having to be vigilant. This little scene has the same effect that the end of *Sabotage* does, leaving us with a heroine who has been marked and ruined and left with nothing. What will happen to Charlie after this movie ends? Might she self-destructively join Louise Finch and Catherine in their midnight revels? Probably not, at least not the way Wright has played Charlie. She has a "sadder but wiser" look on her face in the last scene, but surely the infection of Uncle Charlie and his evil goes deeper than that.

Hitchcock was at his heaviest when he shot *Shadow of a Doubt*, over three hundred pounds, and he took a lot of weight off before shooting his next film *Lifeboat*, which resulted in one of his most memorable cameos. By this point, a cameo was expected of Hitchcock, but this film was set on a lifeboat in mid-ocean with just a group of survivors of a shipwreck. He toyed with the idea of floating past camera range as a corpse in the opening scene, but finally he settled on putting himself in a newspaper ad for a diet system called Reduco, with before and after shots to show his weight loss.

Hitchcock liked to have prestigious authors credited for his scripts, and he pursued Ernest Hemingway for this project but got turned down. He then signed John Steinbeck as a writer for *Lifeboat*, and Steinbeck wrote a novella from the point of view of an ordinary seaman, and then he did a draft of a script that was seriously reworked by the estimable Jo Swerling. Hitchcock was making *Lifeboat* at Twentieth Century Fox, and so the cinematography has an extra clarity that was a hallmark of the visual style at that studio.

Tallulah Bankhead was placed at the center of the film as Constance Porter, a glamorous journalist who calls everyone "darling" and "my pet." Bankhead had become a star on stage in the 1920s but a brief try at making movies in the early 1930s had led to a series of flops. George Cukor, who directed Bankhead in *Tarnished Lady* (1931), said that "her eyes were not eyes for movies. They looked somehow hooded and dead. And the face didn't move as well as the most successful faces do. Being photogenic is a question of movement, how the face moves. Her smile didn't illuminate, when she spoke her mouth didn't look graceful, and her eyes never really lighted up."

Bankhead, like many theater stars, gave most of her performances with her voice, which starts out low and then just gets lower and lower for basso effect before she bursts into her starry "ba ha ha ha" laugh. The camera doesn't really like her but Hitchcock does, and he even allows her to become a kind of earth mother by the end of *Lifeboat*, which was her only decent movie showcase. She had just turned forty when she shot this film, and so there weren't too many star parts forthcoming for her afterward (fig. 10.2).

Bankhead's Constance is first seen looking remarkably chic in the lifeboat, and looking well is clearly important to her, for she seems more than a little depressed when she discovers a run in her stocking. During the course of *Lifeboat*, the journalist Connie will be divested of all of her material

Figure 10.2: Cosmopolitan Constance Porter (Tallulah Bankhead) is divested of all her worldly possessions in *Lifeboat*.

possessions, from her fancy camera to a treasured diamond bracelet that is used as fish bait. She has come up from the south side of Chicago ("Ashland Avenue, back of the yards!") moving up to the north side Gold Coast of that city and then onward and upward from there.

At first, Connie seems to be a heartless sophisticate: "Look, that's a perfect touch!," she cries as she aims her camera at a baby bottle in the water. She has a rowdy camp style of address: "You know I'm practically im*mor*tal, really," she tells C.J. Rittenhouse (Henry Hull), a ruthless capitalist. But as she is doused with water and stripped down to her essence, Connie reveals a fineness of character, within certain bounds, of course. Bankhead's bad-girl manner and very fast, surprising comic timing is vital to *Lifeboat*, which otherwise contains no humor. In fact, this is a very grim, severe movie that asks a lot of tough questions and does not provide easy answers.

Lifeboat contains some of Hitchcock's cleverest and most disturbing manipulations of our sympathies and points of view. The Nazi character Willi played by Walter Slezak is genuinely heartless, but sneakily appealing sometimes. He yawns at the nattering of a mad woman who has lost her baby, Mrs. Higley (Heather Angel), but Hitchcock himself seems to be yawning at her theatrical anguish, too. Hitchcock seems to deliberately allow William Bendix to overdo the dopiness of his character Gus, who loses his leg, so that any expected sympathy we might feel for him gets blocked.

Connie lifts her eyes heavenward and says, "God forgive me" after feeding Gus a line of malarkey to persuade him to let his leg be amputated, and Hitchcock relishes the comic charge Bankhead gives to the sort of beseeching upward look that he usually plays for utmost seriousness. Connie kisses Gus sympathetically before his leg is cut off and then she kisses hunky socialist Kovac (John Hodiak) lustily and with some tongue when they think the boat is going to sink. And Connie playfully rubs her bare foot against Kovac's bare foot, which Hitchcock shows in a close-up that celebrates her sexual freedom. Looking up at God toward the end of the film when things have gotten really desperate, earthy Connie even invigorates a standard old religious saying: "How about giving him a hand?," she asks.

Lifeboat can be dry and didactic in its moral debates in dialogue, but the way it makes victims seem unappealing and villains seem attractive, at least at first, tricks us into siding with evil. Willi pushes Gus overboard, but not before we are subjected to lots more of Bendix's laborious performance, so that we can't be too broken up about Gus going into the drink.

When they find out what Willi has done to Gus, the other passengers quickly turn into a homicidal mob, their evil need for vengeance rushing into that empty spot in all of them, and Hitchcock deliberately has the soft-spoken nurse Alice (Mary Anderson) lead the charge to kill Willi. At one point during the shoot, Anderson had guilelessly asked Hitchcock which was her best side. "My dear, you're sitting on it," he told her.

Bankhead treated Slezak as if he were a Nazi on the set. "The poor man didn't have an easy trip," Hitchcock said. "Tallulah was so vehement against the Germans in the war that she took it out on Walter. But she wasn't serious, only semi-serious." Slezak endured her taunts stoically. "Listening to her constant talk was like a Chinese water torture," Slezak said. "She told us she'd given up drinking for the duration of the war about seventy-two times a day."

"Once Tallulah tried to play a scene her way," Slezak said, "but Hitchcock said, 'No, no,' very quietly with that wonderful dead-fish face of his, and she suddenly turned to us and said plaintively, 'He won't listen to me.' And, of course, she did it his way." Bankhead's performance is always set within the strict limits of Hitchcock's framing and control here, but he does give her a kind of tribute point-of-view shot where Kovac is looking down at her and Bankhead pokes a phallic finger through his newspaper and suddenly seems like a delightfully naughty little girl. Hitchcock breaks down the components of Bankhead's performing style just as Connie herself is broken down to her essence, and he clearly likes what he sees.

Getting into and out of the boat several times a day, Bankhead always managed to lift her skirt so high that it could be seen that she wasn't wearing panties. "She carried on that tired joke for about fifteen weeks while I was on the picture," Slezak said. "Maybe I'm a prude, but I don't like vulgar women." Fielding complaints about Bankhead's no-panties entrances and exits from the boat, the unit manager told Hitchcock and asked if he should say something. "Well, I wouldn't if I were you," Hitchcock told him. "You know she's a bit of a firebrand. Don't think she's too keen on you." He always enjoyed pitting people against each other on his sets like this.

The unit manager went to Hitchcock again, who said that it wasn't his place or department to tell Tallulah to wear underwear. "Whose department is it?," the unit manager asked. "Either hairdressing or make-up," Hitchcock replied. He found Tallulah's outrageousness "healthy" and always remained fond of her. "The whole point about Tallulah was that she had no inhibitions," Hitchcock said. "Now some people can take this, others can't."

Bankhead won the New York Film Critics award for her Connie in *Lifeboat*. "At last I had licked the screen, a screen which had six times betrayed me," she wrote in her autobiography. "Did I get an Academy Oscar? No! The people who vote in that free-for-all know on which side their crepes Suzette are buttered. I wasn't under contract to any of the major studios, hence was thought an outlaw."

Hitchcock had made *Lifeboat* so complex that some of the critics who reviewed it panned it as a pro-Nazi picture, but of course Hitchcock's lifelong project was to show how evil had its attractions. He made two short French propaganda films at this time, *Bon Voyage* and *Aventure Malgache* (both 1944), intricate stories based on role-playing with an ensemble of French actors speaking very rapidly. They are both of interest, but no individual player stands out.

"Ingrid, fake it," Hitchcock told Ingrid Bergman when she complained that she didn't feel sufficiently motivated for a scene in his next movie *Spellbound* (1945). To Hitchcock, there was no such thing as "genuine" emotion, which is why he later looked on Method acting with such disdain. All emotion is a passing show, even if you are crying or laughing alone by yourself. It can be turned on and off at will and will transition to something else, or nothing much, eventually. Anyone who has ever acted professionally or even just studied acting intensively will begin to doubt their own emotional reactions in their "real" life.

Hitchcock was back to working directly for Selznick on *Spellbound*, and so once again he had to make concessions. What mainly interested him on this picture was a dream sequence for which Salvador Dalí had been hired as a visual consultant. Dalí came up with some outré ideas, like having Bergman covered in ants, but Selznick was dismayed by some of the footage that was shot, and he cut the dream section down, even bringing in William Cameron Menzies to reshoot some of it.

Spellbound is a particularly far-fetched story idea about a psychoanalyst named Constance Petersen (Bergman) who is helping the man she loves, John Ballantyne (Gregory Peck), overcome his guilt complex. Red-headed starlet Rhonda Fleming is given the whole opening of the movie to make an impression as a man-hating young minx who brags about biting off the mustache of a man who once made the mistake of proposing to her, and the tone of the writing and playing here is too nastily absurd to be taken seriously.

Bergman wears glasses in the first scenes and is at her most starry and irresistible. When she first sees Peck, Bergman chooses to look slightly hostile as if Constance is fighting against her helpless initial rush of feeling, and then she is self-conscious and nervous with him, and this is all very effective in getting across the idea that she has fallen in love at first sight. Hitchcock aids Bergman here with carefully shadowed and molded lighting of her face as she looks at Peck, and this special "love" lighting falls away when we see Constance back in a wide shot at a dinner table.

Bergman is also aided in this scene by composer Miklos Rozsa, who provided Hitchcock with his first really major musical score. This Rozsa score has specific melodies and variations on those melodies, and it was a vast improvement over the loud, unspecific, and intrusive scores that Hitchcock had been getting. Rozsa's music for *Spellbound* alternates between a spooky crypt-like melody played on a theremin for John's mental "episodes" and a main love theme that caresses Bergman's sumptuous, pliant face and her underrated hair.

Hitchcock represents Constance's complete giving herself over to love by pushing in on an extreme close-up of Bergman's face as Constance stands outside of John's bedroom, and then another close-up shot of just her vulnerable eyes, which close on a dreamy dissolve to a series of doors opening. It might be said that Rozsa's throbbing, romantic, neurotic score gives meaning here in this scene and several others where there is little to none, for it is an unusually hard-working score in that way.

The script for *Spellbound* by Ben Hecht, with Hitchcock's help and advice, has a flip, glib, slangy tone that Hitchcock increasingly favored, with a "cute" final scene for Constance and John where they are semi-recognized again by a Grand Central station ticket taker who had seen them before. Both Hecht and Selznick were in psychoanalysis themselves, but you'd never know it from this film's superficial understanding of that process. *Spellbound* was a huge financial hit in its time, mainly due to Bergman's popularity with the public, and it was sold with the tagline, "Will he kiss me or kill me?" and an image of Bergman embracing Peck as he holds a straight razor in his hand.

There are two Hitchcockian set pieces toward the end of this picture. Constance and John go on a skiing run against back projection to jog his memory, and this is interrupted by a very disturbing flashback to Peck's character as a child accidentally killing his brother. The flashback is shot in an almost documentary way with very different non-romantic lighting, and this showed Hitchcock's liking and need for contrast.

And then there is a shot of Leo G. Carroll's murderous Dr. Murchison pointing a gun at Constance from his point of view, with his enormous hand finally turning to shoot himself and the camera, whereupon Hitchcock added a subliminal splash of red to the frames of the black and white film. Carroll worked six times for Hitchcock, and Dr. Murchison was the best of the roles he played for him. He gives a fine, subtle performance here, underplaying until the doctor casually shows his inner rottenness. Watch for the barely perceptible start Carroll gives when he realizes that Peck's John is passing himself off as the man he himself murdered, Dr. Edwardes.

Hitchcock was enraptured from the first by Bergman, as everyone else was at that time. She had just won an Oscar for Best Actress for enduring an ordeal in *Gaslight* (1944), and no one suffered quite as voluptuously and somehow healthily as she did. Bergman was such an ideal Hitchcock actress because there was an element of magic about her screen presence and also something withheld from us and maybe empty. She had a rich, musical speaking voice, the lilt of her slight Swedish accent adding force and color to her line readings, and she had a very mobile face that could seem to show everything and nothing at once.

Hitchcock fell in love with Bergman, so much so that he allowed her to boss him a bit, as Alma did, and set the tone on the movies they made together. She was a very strong, hearty yet sometimes vague person, and she was adept at teasing him, which he allowed. If Bergman wanted something explained to her, Hitchcock would do so, at length, until he had had enough and told her just to "fake it."

Bergman found the script of *Spellbound* implausible, but she was excited about the possibilities of the Dalí dream sequence, and she was charmed by Hitchcock's imagination and obvious talent. In the second part of the film, Constance doesn't seem like the best or brightest or most ethical psychoanalyst in her profession, but Hitchcock's movies are filled with examples of people doing unethical things for love.

Bergman understood Hitchcock's need for distance from people and his fears, and she had a way of smiling that could calm even his deepest anxieties. That's why he loved working with her so much, but then that's why everyone loved Bergman in 1945. It finally came down to that smile of hers, how it could be made to fall away and then how it came back into bloom. She also was someone who wanted to live in her fantasy life, her creative life, just like Hitchcock did. Selznick was sometimes bewildered by Bergman's work ethic, how she never took any days off and wanted to go from one film to another without even a day of rest in between. Her real life was her working life.

Peck was twenty-nine and just getting started when he made *Spellbound*, and he had problems with Hitchcock, who wanted exact externals. "I couldn't produce the facial expressions that Hitch wanted turned on," Peck said. "I didn't have that facility. He already had a preconception of what the expression ought to be on your face, he planned that as carefully as the camera angles. Hitchcock was an outside fellow, and I had the Stanislavski training from the Neighborhood Playhouse, which means you work from the inside."

What Hitchcock wanted was for Peck to drain his young face of all expression, and Peck found this difficult to do. He's a stolid, cautious presence in *Spellbound*, and not too believably disturbed. He has especially beautiful lips and beautiful eyebrows and doe-like eyes, but he is basically uninteresting as a screen actor here, though he certainly does kiss Bergman with passion.

Michael Chekhov, a nephew of playwright Anton Chekhov, won an Oscar nomination for Best Supporting Actor for his performance here as Constance's mentor Dr. Brulov, a wise and antisocial and fussy old man something like Albert Bassermann's Van Meer in *Foreign Correspondent*. Chekhov was a renowned acting teacher who led the Moscow Art Theatre and worked closely with Stanislavski himself in Russia, but *Spellbound* doesn't allow him much scope for characterization.

Chekhov's analyst is given a lot of screen time, but his Dr. Brulov is a flat character, a plot character, and his cozy chauvinist remarks about Constance make him finally unlikable, or untenable. Chekhov sometimes indulges in the sort of cute old man mugging that marred some of the film appearances of another famed Method teacher, Lee Strasberg. Somehow preaching the need for "truth" in acting could lead its figurehead teachers into the most old-fashioned indicating when they themselves practiced the art.

Stimulated by Bergman, Hitchcock would even act scenes out for her like Ernst Lubitsch used to do with his actors. His feeling for Bergman made him experiment, which he loved to do as a filmmaker. "He watched what you're doing, he tells you what to do, and then he rearranges what he wants for information and stress and speed," Bergman said. "Sometimes he acted something out—I have so many photographs of him doing that. He doesn't want you to imitate him; he wants to hear what the intonation is." The externals of a face interested Hitchcock, and certain line readings that could be sculpted. It was an anti-psychological approach, a purely technical approach, in its way.

Hitchcock privately began telling a story that Bergman had once refused to leave his bedroom until he made love to her, a wishful fantasy. "I never got angry when it came back to me," Bergman said of this story. "People will believe what they want to believe—Hitch, just like anyone else. I loved him, but not his way. Well, I wanted to keep his friendship, and I did." Bergman saw what Hitchcock could do for her as an actress, and so she learned to handle him, to laugh off his dirty jokes and suggestions because she knew that there was the painfully unrequited love of a schoolboy underneath.

At one point in *Spellbound*, Constance is accosted by an aggressive masher (Wallace Ford) in a hotel lobby, and she deflects him with a little light disdain at first. He keeps talking about being from Pittsburgh and he calls her "snooty," and then she says, "Yeah, I'm sure you're a great social success given half a chance," which is a hilariously bitchy Ben Hecht line that Bergman can't quite put over. This line needs to be delivered faster than she can manage. Bitchery like this does not come naturally to Bergman as it would to Bankhead or Lombard.

But Bergman is marvelous when it comes to the subtle contrasts that Hitchcock liked, like the unexpected little touches of severity showing up on her face when you don't expect it. Bergman could do one thing but suggest another very easily. She could do something with her eyes and then contradict it with her mouth, and her intensely close, studious yet very sensual relation to the English language allows her to *always* be unexpected vocally, too, with her musical, pleasingly uncommon emphases of certain words. Physically she was often stiff and tense, uncomfortable with her body, but her extravagantly expressive face told a different story, a story of healthy and bold sexuality shot through with feelings of guilt. It is no wonder that Hitchcock was so crazy about her.

The masher in the hotel lobby sits close to Constance and comes on to her in a very obnoxious way, yet she is blithely above this, just as she is when coworker Dr. Fleurot (John Emery, who had been married to Tallulah Bankhead) sexually harasses her in both a verbal and physical way in Bergman's first scene.

Constance has a justifiable contempt for most of the men she encounters. She is a sensible woman, like Alma or Barbara Bel Geddes's Midge in *Vertigo*, who is overtaken by a very insensible romantic feeling that is always close to a maternal instinct. She loves John because he is beautiful and because he needs to be taken care of, because he is a boy in distress.

11

Notorious, The Paradine Case, Rope, Under Capricorn, Stage Fright

Hitchcock capitalized on his feelings for Bergman with one of his very best films, *Notorious* (1946), which, like *Spellbound*, was written by Ben Hecht. Years before Selznick had optioned a story called *The Song of the Dragon*, which involved a Mata Hari-like actress who spied during World War I. As early as 1941, Bergman wrote Selznick a letter saying that she would be happy to do this story with Hitchcock. "My great love for Hitchcock has been expressed so often that I don't need to repeat that," she told him. By 1946, this story was finally ready to go, but Selznick was preoccupied with finishing his epic *Duel in the Sun* (1946), where his girlfriend Jennifer Jones writhed about as a sexpot, and so he sold the whole *Notorious* package to RKO.

Ted Tetzlaff was on camera and Edith Head did Bergman's beautiful clothes, and so this was to be top of the line in every way. In thrall to Bergman and her talent, Hitchcock often listened to her thoughts on facial expressions and emotional transitions and let her do things her way if he liked her ideas, which were often good. Hitchcock even let her lover Robert Capa take on-set still photographs when she asked for him.

Hitchcock instructed Hecht to model the heroine's way of talking in *Notorious* on Tallulah Bankhead, but Selznick found the dialogue Hecht wrote for her in his first draft of the script to be coarse and dated in its slang, and so it was rewritten, updated, and softened accordingly for Bergman. Hecht and Hitchcock killed off the male lead, Devlin, and then the female lead, Alicia, in various drafts of the *Notorious* script, but Selznick kept insisting that they both should live.

The movie begins with the exact day and time that it starts, 3:20 p.m., April 24, 1946, when Bergman's Alicia Huberman emerges from a Miami courthouse after her Nazi father has been sentenced to jail. Tetzlaff gives everything a very spare and queasy look in black and white, so that we are down to visual and emotional essences, and Bergman plays her self-destructive party girl character with abandon. "The important drinking hasn't started yet,"

Alicia tells the guests at her "perfectly hideous party," which is dominated visually by the dark, sleek head of a man we only see from behind. Alicia keeps coming back to him, as does the camera.

Hecht's perpetually cynical attitude works very well here in dialogue because he and Bergman know how to show the deep pain underneath Alicia's posturing. "There's nothing like a love song to give you a good laugh," Alicia says, and Bergman gives this line a drunken, still, focused intensity, as if Alicia would like to be proven wrong. Hitchcock had wanted to use Noël Coward's song "Someday I'll Find You" as a leitmotif for the romance throughout the film, but negotiations with Coward broke down and so he muted the use of music here.

The dark head from behind at the party turns out to be Cary Grant's Devlin, a man of mystery who ties a scarf around Alicia's bare midriff when they go outside, one of the most erotic moments in any Hitchcock movie, a moment that is charged with sexual anticipation but also Svengali-like control as Devlin fetishistically makes sure the scarf is pulled down just right. Alicia takes Devlin for a drunken drive and they get pulled over by a cop, and she tells Devlin that this is her second drunken driving offense. "Now I go to jail," Alicia says. "Whole family in jail, who cares?"

Bergman is really taking chances with her image in *Notorious*. She had played a "bad girl" before in *Dr. Jekyll and Mr. Hyde* (1941), where she signaled sexual willingness and grief and fear in a voluptuously uninhibited, lingering way. Her Ilsa in *Casablanca* (1942) was immaculate in her beauty, without flaw, but wallowing in despair and torn between two men. Bergman had played a nun in *The Bells of St. Mary's* (1945), one of her biggest hits, but now she was playing a woman whose unhappiness has made her into a sexually promiscuous drunk, and *Notorious* doesn't hedge its bets about Alicia. There is no "she was just pretending" gambit here, as there might be in another movie of this time.

Devlin feels the need to punch Alicia when she finds out that he's a cop, or a government agent. The character of Devlin also allows Cary Grant to take chances with his own image, and this can be very disturbing, to say the least. Devlin is a buttoned-up, deeply unhappy man, rigid and hard where Alicia is loose and soft, and it is inevitable that the two will come together. It is also inevitable that they will make each other suffer.

Alicia wakes up in the morning badly hung over with her false hair sitting next to her in bed and a fizzing glass of bromo by her side. When she sees Devlin, he marches toward the camera upside down, which mimics her point of view, and this effect is very unsettling. This mysterious man looks almost vulnerable as he stares down at Alicia but he is opaque, too, basically unreadable, for federal agents need to be that way.

Devlin has come to Alicia with a mission. As the daughter of a Nazi, she is in a good position to spy for the Allies. "Waving the flag with one hand and picking pockets with the other, that's your patriotism," Alicia says to Devlin, and there is a thrill in having Bergman say such wised-up Ben Hecht lines.

There was something wholesome about Bergman that the public responded to, but this was just a surface reaction. There were many other things going on with her, and many of them had to do with sex, and of course this gets Hitchcock's full attention. Bergman's Alicia Huberman is one of the best and most complex performances in all of Hitchcock's work, and Grant's Devlin, sadistic and pained all at once, is right with her. Bergman has the flashier part, which she plays to the hilt, but Grant is just as good in his own watchful way.

As the film goes on, Devlin is a man who increasingly cannot keep the way he feels out of his face, but he is fighting with all his strength to do so, and this particular dramatic tension really suits both Grant and Hitchcock. On the plane down to Rio, where most of the story takes place, there is a highly charged, nearly unaccountable moment when Devlin reacts with fear as Alicia moves near him in profile to look out the window. Hitchcock really makes something of this image of Grant's alarmed face reacting to Bergman's profile. Is Alicia aware of what she's doing to him? She seems a little oblivious, but this obliviousness is also one of Bergman's most ambiguous modes as a performer.

Grant looks under attack here in a way that feels personal, for his Devlin has the air sometimes almost of a confession from this most stylized of performers. It is only in keeping to the fortress of his style that Grant can reveal so much under the surface of his black, glossy hair, that cleft chin, those burning black eyes of his and his thick, needling voice, which matches so well with Bergman's own Swedish-lilting coloratura.

Alicia relishes the anticipation of something momentous with this great-looking, repressed guy, and she needles him in the way Grant so often needled other people on screen. She puts herself down in a would-be humorous way that only reveals all her pain, calling herself a little tramp from Miami. A whore for the government! Of all things.

"I've always been scared of women, but I'll get over it," Devlin jokes, very seriously. He looks angry at Alicia sometimes for making him feel so much, for hurting him now as she will surely hurt him in the future. The back projection where they sit in a café is out of focus and not scaled very well, but this doesn't matter. Only those looking at *Notorious* for the hundredth time would notice such a thing.

The intimacy between Alicia and Devlin grows, and she taunts him verbally with her unhappiness and his own. She wants a maid because she doesn't mind dusting and sweeping but she hates cooking. They go for a walk, and Alicia keeps taunting Devlin until he kisses her very passionately, which was unusual for Grant. Almost always it was women who kissed him passionately on screen while he made himself a moving target.

There is the sense here that sex will have to work through and burn off all the unhappiness in both of these people, and this nearly comes to pass in the famous love scene on the balcony of Alicia's Rio apartment. Devlin goes out on the balcony and looks at the beach and the ocean coming in and the buildings in the distance. He is a solitary figure, but then he is joined by Alicia, who takes his arm, and this is one of the most romantic shots in all of Hitchcock's work, an oasis, a dream fulfilled.

Devlin doesn't have to be alone . . . but he is taking a chance on Alicia. He puts his head next to her head, almost diffidently, or cautiously, and they kiss, Alicia putting her arms around his neck and pulling him in tightly. Bergman keeps caressing and nibbling at Grant and throwing her head back in intense ecstasy while he stays very still and accepts her passion, almost grudgingly. Down deep, Devlin is feeling everything that she is, but he is a man and he has been hurt and he cannot show his feelings. Besides, everything she says about herself is basically true. And yet. . . .

Hitchcock himself wrote Alicia's murmuring dialogue about making a chicken for them to eat as she kisses and kisses Devlin and eats him up, and these added lines bewildered Hecht, but they bring just the right would-be domestic touch. "No, I don't like to cook . . . but I have a chicken in the icebox and you're eating it," Alicia says. They will stay in, together, just them. They will not go out. "We'll eat it with our fingers!," she says, shamelessly, happily. The sexiest thing here is when Bergman caresses Grant's right ear with an index finger, a moment that is more erotic than any nude thrashing around could possibly be.

This kissing scene lasts two minutes and forty seconds without music. Alicia follows Devlin to the door, her head on his shoulder, unwilling to let him go for a moment. "This is a very strange love affair," she says. He asks her why, after finally giving her an intense little kiss, and she says, "Maybe because you don't love me." She is fishing here, but she is also reeling him in. "Actions speak louder than words," he tells her. She asks him to bring back a nice bottle of wine . . . Hitchcock himself was a wine connoisseur.

Bergman is at her very best in these scenes, carefully staying on the fence emotionally as Alicia makes fun of herself but also takes all of her interactions with Devlin seriously and hopefully underneath. Alicia is a woman of appetites, a woman of depth, and she has squandered her gifts deliberately out of self-loathing and loathing for her father. Now she wonders if she might get back to what she was and what she should have been, a nice unspoiled child whose heart, she jokes, was full of "daisies and buttercups."

Bergman and Grant told Hitchcock that they felt very awkward doing the kissing scene because Hitchcock wanted them boxed in together and unable to let go of each other. It didn't feel natural to them. But an unnatural show for a camera that usually lies visually expresses in Hitchcock the truth about people and situations. And there was an element of fantasy here, too. For as Hitchcock remarked, for the length of this love scene, we the audience are privy to the embrace between two of the most attractive people in the world, enfolded in it with them, vicariously yet also actively.

There is very little musical score in *Notorious*, which aids the stripped-down intensity of the film, the mood of which can be very uncomfortable sometimes, like a hangover that leaves you unusually sensitive and vulnerable to noises. The intimacy here between the two actors, between Bergman's heartfelt and very sensual exposure and Grant's increasingly powerless, assailed gravity is kept in hushed, rapt balance by Hitchcock. The carnality on display feels like a breakthrough, momentous. Imagine Hitchcock's buried, stricken feelings as he directed this kissing scene that goes on and on, in love with Bergman and as buttoned-up as Devlin himself. . . .

Hitchcock wanted to make *Notorious* because he was intrigued by the story of a man who has to order the woman he loves to sleep with another man because of his job. Devlin leaves the wine Alicia asked for in the office of his boss (Louis Calhern), who appears to understand the whole situation between the lovers once he has explained Alicia's mission to Devlin.

The feds have targeted Alicia because a high-ranking Nazi down in Rio named Alexander Sebastian (Claude Rains) used to have a thing for her. Sebastian is in business and he helped to build up the German war machine, which is about as serious a sin as can be imagined. Hitchcock had edited together film of the liberated concentration camps right before making *Notorious*, but the footage was so upsetting that it sat unseen for decades.

Sebastian has a Nazi doctor living, and experimenting, in his house, which is not something that should be forgotten about him.

Alicia has slept with so many men for nothing, so why not one more? But this puts Devlin in a real bind. And so he lashes out at Alicia, who is resplendent in her Edith Head white blouse and heavy full skirt with wide belt as Devlin tells her about her job in Rio before making a crack about her past. “Right below the belt every time,” she says in response, looking stricken.

When Alicia goes to pour herself another drink in her kitchen, it’s as if Hitchcock cannot stand to see her suffering and so he frames her behind a window and a sheer white drape as if to protect her. Devlin’s agony is expressed by Grant very physically here, as if he wants to jump out of his skin, and every drag off his cigarette seems to burn him. Devlin and Alicia are so unkind to each other because they have been hurt badly by others and because they feel too much in their very different ways. This is what often happens between two damaged people who try to love one another.

When Alicia goes about seducing Sebastian, Hitchcock tells us all we need to know about what is happening to Devlin with a very brief shot of him sitting alone at a café where he used to meet with Alicia. In this six-second shot, Devlin is an image of proud, stiff loneliness and freezing cold bitter unhappiness, and so we can imagine what Hitchcock himself felt as Bergman’s lover Robert Capa took the photos of her on his set. This is what being in love with an actress, or a woman whose profession it is to feign affection, can be.

Hitchcock knew that all emotion was somewhat fake or acted, but he was enough of a romantic to want to believe in love between two people and also to remorselessly interrogate that love. Watching Bergman’s emotionally layered close-ups here is like drinking the richest chocolate, but with a bitter undertaste. It might be said that Bergman has a montage style of acting in close-up, a series of brief, unsettled emotions linked together on parts of her face like a collage, and so her work in *Notorious* is an acting summit and summation of Hitchcock’s early and mid-period style.

The fade out on Devlin at the café and then the fade in to Alicia waiting for Sebastian at a restaurant visually puts her where she should be in the empty chair in that café with Devlin, and this is a heartbreaking thing. *Notorious* goes very far into the most painful kinds of emotions, and it never leavens them or lets us off the hook in any way. There is no humor here at all, no funny character parts, and no jokes that aren’t sick jokes that Alicia and Devlin make against each other or against themselves.

George Sanders was the original choice for Sebastian, and surely he would have been very good, but he was busy with other projects. Hitchcock talked Selznick out of the idea of using Clifton Webb or the stage actor Alfred Lunt, and then Rains was chosen. Rains was a small man with a whispery, very incisive voice who had trained John Gielgud, Laurence Olivier, and Charles Laughton at the Royal Academy of Dramatic Art in London, and he had been married many times. He was best known for his corrupt and maybe gay Louis in *Casablanca* and for his tactfully supporting Bette Davis in several movies.

When Sebastian speaks of his "hunger" for Alicia at dinner, even her excellent acting skills need some bolstering as she takes a long sip of her champagne. Alicia says she was a brat with Sebastian once, and she probably was, but people can be bratty when they are punishing themselves. Sebastian asks if they can order dinner now, and Alicia smiles and says, "Yes, I'm starved," but then the smile falls away from her face, and this is one of the most piercing examples of Hitchcock's liking for "negative acting." *Notorious* details so many different moods of disgust, recrimination, and self-reproach, and yet they somehow never get too out of hand to spoil the film's status as an entertainment.

Sebastian is dominated by his jealous mother, who was played by the Austrian actress Leopoldine Konstantin after Ethel Barrymore turned the role down. Konstantin had been a noted actress on stage in Germany, but when she came to America in 1938, she had to get a job in a factory because she spoke no English at that time. Hitchcock had seen Konstantin on the stage in Munich in 1926, and when he heard she was living in Hollywood, he sought her out.

Konstantin was a bit taken aback by her role. "I almost frightened myself," she told a reporter for the *New York Times* when the film was finished. "Never before have I attempted such a role. When I saw it, I thought, 'My God, I'm a female Boris Karloff!' What will my friends ever think of me?"

Billed as Madame Konstantin, this actress is not visually what you would expect, somehow, for the casting of the tyrannical mother of a Nazi. She has small, sweet, gentle eyes, but the elaborate braiding of her hair gives her away (always look to the hairdos in Hitchcock to find out what you need to know about a woman). Konstantin was only fifty-nine to Rains's fifty-six, but their closeness in age adds to the incestuous feeling between their characters. "Is it so boring to sit with me alone?," Mrs. Sebastian asks her son at the racetrack, and he replies, "Not at all, not at all" in a weary voice.

Notorious has a political background that luckily fits with the reality of the time it was made. Many high-ranking Nazis were in fact escaping to Brazil, and even the MacGuffin here, bottles of uranium kept in wine bottles in the cellar of Sebastian's home, have a clear meaning now as a harbinger of the atom bomb. Alicia goes to Sebastian's house for dinner and observes the Nazi officials behaving like stone-faced gangsters as they give the order to kill Emile Hupka (Eberhard Krumschmidt) because he freaks out over the uranium in a bottle.

In the scene at a racetrack where Alicia tells Devlin what she knows, the two of them say such cruel things to each other that it becomes almost unbearable to watch. There is the Hitchcockian acting counterpoint of them falsely smiling for show while Alicia gives Devlin serious information about the Nazis, but then she lets him know she has slept with Sebastian and Devlin puts on a vicious semi-jocular mood in response in order to mask his pain.

The camera holds both Grant and Bergman in close-ups as Devlin and Alicia savage each other, but Bergman's close-ups are slightly more extreme. She holds binoculars in front of her eyes to hide her pain, and then when she lowers them, the camera eats up her face as she says, "I hate you" in the same intense way she might have said, "I love you" to Devlin. And finally, there is a jewel-like tear on the bottom of her left eye that adds immeasurably to her beauty (fig. 11.1).

Bergman used glycerin rather than actually crying in movies like *Casablanca*, and clearly this jewel tear is glycerin rather than an actual tear; an actual tear would never have stayed as round and clingy as that glycerin tear on the bottom of her left eye. The camera lies, but the lies it tells are so much more beautiful and more expressive, finally, than the truth of real tears and mucus and so forth. Bergman's face in close-up with this glycerin tear is an emblem for acting in Hitchcock's films. It is not "real," but it has style and it is better than life, just like the writing here. "Dry your eyes, baby, it's out of character," Devlin sneers to Alicia. Ben Hecht was the ultimate writer of sneering and recriminatory dialogue, and he deserves a lot of credit for the ultimate impact of *Notorious*.

Sebastian asks Alicia to marry him, and so she comes to the office where Devlin works and asks his colleagues if she should go that far. Once again, the pain between Devlin and Alicia is excruciating, and it can only find some release at a party that Devlin goes to at the Sebastian compound after Alicia has married Sebastian. There is the Hitchcockian acting counterpoint again

Figure 11.1: A glycerin tear on the face of Alicia Huberman (Ingrid Bergman) in *Notorious.*

of them smiling in a social way as Alicia laughs and says worried things to Devlin about Sebastian and he responds, still smiling.

Down in the wine cellar as the wine upstairs is running out, Alicia is terrified and Devlin remarks, "Just pretend you're a janitor . . . janitors are never terrified." They are forced to kiss in the wine cellar, and her emotion is unfettered ("Oh Dev, Dev!," she cries in enraptured close-up), and his emotion is as vulnerable as can be imagined for him. This is a rare instance of "real" feeling within something clearly "acted" in Hitchcock.

As played by Rains, Sebastian is a neat little man, self-contained, controlled both by himself and by his mother, but his sexual passion for Alicia is intense, and it is his downfall. Though Sebastian is a Nazi, Hitchcock gives his full sympathy to him, even though certain "kindly" but smug expressions sometimes show up on Rains's face that make Sebastian difficult to like, if not to sympathize with. Rains later made several appearances on Hitchcock's television show, where he was given free rein to get strenuously upset, cry, and chew the scenery in extreme close-up, but in *Notorious* he is at his acid, held-back best.

Alicia needs to go through a trial by fire to redeem herself. Sebastian finds out that she is an American agent, and he tells his mother something is wrong. "I have *expected* it," Mrs. Sebastian says, and when Sebastian tells his mother that Alicia is a spy for the Americans, Mrs. Sebastian takes a momentous pause as she lights a cigarette in a very stiff, macho sort of way. Sebastian says he hates himself for believing in Alicia's "clinging kisses," and then his formidable mother says, "Stop wallowing in your foul memories . . . we are protected by the enormity of your stupidity . . . for a time."

Mother Sebastian lays out a plan: they will poison Alicia, but slowly, very slowly, so that no one gets suspicious. Alicia begins to drink elegant little cups of coffee laced with poison, and these coffee cups have that curious power and suggestiveness that Hitchcock often gives to material objects. When things get really bad, there are shots from Alicia's point of view of Sebastian and his mother as she realizes what is happening to her, and she finally falls to the floor of their house, which looks like a chessboard in Hitchcock's overhead shot.

Devlin finally figures out what is going on, and so he comes to rescue his shady lady in distress in a rapt scene so carefully lit that you can see the pearly pores on the elegant fingers of Bergman's graceful left hand as she caresses Grant's head. Devlin apologizes to Alicia, as well he should, because this film has been a process of Devlin recognizing male sexual hypocrisy in himself and in others. His eyes have so often looked violated, and he understands now what some women have to go through. The buck stops with him.

"I was just a fat-headed guy full of pain," Devlin says, his black hair glistening from behind as it did in his first scene, but now we can see part of his face and Grant himself is unprotected, as unprotected as he would ever be on screen. He has a simplicity and a gravity here that is very touching. "It tore me up not having you," he says, in that rough, stabbing way of his.

Hitchcock amplifies the suspense as Devlin tries to get Alicia out of the house by making the staircase they are going down seem to have far more steps than it could possibly have. Somehow Hitchcock gets sympathy for both Sebastian and his mother as they walk down those steps with Devlin and Alicia, with the Nazis downstairs and ready to act on any suspicions.

Finally they are outside and Devlin locks the door against the desperate Sebastian, who is left to his fate. What's in the future for Devlin and Alicia? Amazing sex, certainly, and food . . . that roast chicken she promised him, which might catch fire but still be tasty. Maybe a family. Maybe. Or maybe just amazing sex and great food in Spain, where he has requested a transfer.

Hitchcock's last film under his Selznick contract, *The Paradine Case* (1947), found producer and director at cross-purposes because their conceptions of the film differed. This picture cost four million dollars, including four hundred thousand dollars for a lavish reconstruction of the Old Bailey courtroom, and it was filmed chaotically, with Selznick sending new script pages to the set as they shot.

Hitchcock later told François Truffaut that he had wanted to cast Robert Newton, who had been in *Jamaica Inn*, in the role of the groom Latour. His idea was that the groom should be someone really low class and repulsive so that the high-class barrister male lead Anthony Keane (Gregory Peck) would be disgusted by the choice of sex object by his client, Mrs. Paradine (Alida Valli), the woman he has become obsessed with.

But in the finished film, Latour is a valet and he is played by the young Louis Jourdan, who is first seen only in shadow and then in faraway glimpses at the Paradine estate until later he is revealed, with a burst of music, outside of the barrister's back door, ha ha. There is the shadow of a cross over his face that looks exactly like the queer shadow cross on Ivor Novello's face in *The Lodger*, and Latour speaks in a hushed way like someone in a horror movie. Hitchcock frames Latour's head under a large and ornate glass lamp, and this is one more signifier of his outsider sexual status.

Jourdan's sharp-edged, feminine beauty here is so striking because it looks so cruel, so sadistic. He hates Mrs. Paradine and calls her "bad to the bone," and though she was mad for Latour, and understandably, he had no time for her. "He despises all women," she tells Keane. Latour was only devoted to his "master," Colonel Paradine, who has been murdered.

So our female lead in *The Paradine Case* was in love with a gay man, and this is made as clear as can be in the film. Charles Coburn's barrister calls Latour a "mother hen" with Paradine. "He's a queer one, all right," says a coachman of Latour. At one point, Latour says that he would never serve a woman because "it is not in my character," and it is said that he was jilted by a woman in his youth in Canada, which muddies the waters on him a bit. Latour eventually kills himself off camera.

The Paradine Case begins with a sequence in which Valli's Mrs. Paradine is arrested in her well-appointed home, and this was meant to be done in a long take but it was cut very awkwardly by Selznick so that Mrs. Paradine's butler seems to jump into the room with her. We first see her playing the piano as a painting of her blind and rich dead husband, Colonel Paradine, looks down on her. Her glossy black hair is up in an elaborate style, but at the jail it is taken down and she is stripped of all of her clothes and jewels and put in a cell, where the door slams shut on her resoundingly.

Valli, who was billed only as "Valli" in the credits, was an Italian actress who was brought over for this part after Greta Garbo turned it down. She had a suspicious, glowering, baleful sort of face, and in later years she would often peep out of Bernardo Bertolucci movies as an older woman with an embittered attitude.

Selznick gives Valli lots of close-ups in *The Paradine Case*, and many of them are so close that they make her self-conscious and she can't really sustain them. There is the sense here that Valli doesn't know what she should be doing under all this scrutiny, and she seems lost and disconnected. After the lavishly emotional montage close-ups of Ingrid Bergman in Hitchcock's last two films, Valli is bound to suffer by comparison.

The close-ups of Valli in *The Paradine Case* are so carefully lit that you can see the pores on her beautifully molded yet somehow twisted face, for she had eyes that often looked accusing or bewildered, and these eyes of hers both mar and complicate her beauty. Valli's voice in English has the unappealingly clotted cadences and intonations of Hedy Lamarr rather than Bergman's free verbal lovemaking with the English language. "She was too impassive and didn't know her English too well, which is a tremendous handicap," Hitchcock told Charles Higham.

The Paradine Case, like many films over which Selznick had total control, is far too close-up heavy. Hitchcock was beginning his experiments with long takes, and he shot a scene between Keane and his wife Gay (Ann Todd) that lasted around five minutes without a cut, but Selznick found this too "theatrical" and ordered it edited into a more conventional sequence of shots.

Hitchcock had trouble with Todd, who was a very repressed British ice blonde married to David Lean, and at one point Hitchcock pounced on Todd and cried, "Relax!" But of course if you yell at someone to relax, you are only going to make them more tense, and Todd in *The Paradine Case* seems like the lady in the parlor who would also be a lady in the bedroom, and so she was not a Hitchcock type. He whispered dirty things in her ear before a take, as was his wont with most of his actresses, but this just made Todd more uncomfortable in the wrong way.

The Paradine Case founders most particularly on the casting of Peck as Keane, a role for which Hitchcock had wanted either Laurence Olivier or Ronald Colman. Peck is too young and stiff and too monotonously centered to be able to carry the idea that his character is so taken with Mrs. Paradine, a situation that is very similar to the one in *Murder!* between Herbert Marshall and Norah Baring but not nearly as persuasive.

Hitchcock worked again in *The Paradine Case* with Charles Laughton, who plays the mean-minded and lecherous Judge Horfield with mean-looking bushy eyebrows, and Hitchcock got Ethel Barrymore to play the judge's long-suffering wife Lady Sophie Horfield. Barrymore received an Oscar nomination for Best Supporting Actress based on her performance in the first release version of *The Paradine Case*, but by the time the film was in general release, several of Barrymore's major scenes had been deleted when many other scenes here might have been cut or shortened, particularly the ones between Todd and Peck.

In the most crucial scene with Barrymore that was cut by Selznick, Lady Horfield meets Keane at an art gallery and tells him that her husband loves to hang women, and that he always wants to go to bed with her after he has pronounced the death sentence on a female. She pleads with him to try his best to acquit Mrs. Paradine, and Lord Horfield spirits her away, telling Keane that he's going to have to commit his wife to an asylum one day given the way she talks.

Still, even in its truncated form, the marriage between the Horfields in *The Paradine Case* is a distressing one, suggesting a nightmare version of Hitchcock and Alma or an older version of the marriage between Fred and Emily Hill in *Rich and Strange*. Lord Horfield gloatingly talks about "the impermanence of beauty" after seeing a seventy-year-old former female looker at the beach, and his wife reacts to this remark in a wide-eyed and stung way. Weirdly, Lord Horfield also remarks on the great beauty of Jourdan's Latour in his courtroom. There are all kinds of troubling sexual crosscurrents in this picture.

Lady Horfield is afraid of her "clever" husband. She looks the other way when he aggressively hits on other women, as when Lord Horfield spots Gay Keane's bare shoulder and the camera dollies into it from his point of view and he sidles up to her in a very openly sexual and nasty way and takes her hand. Lord Horfield is a great gourmet, like Hitchcock, and he finds this chilly blonde wife "appetizing." Gay rejects Lord Horfield with disdain and comes back to her husband, with whom she is deeply in love.

Midway through *The Paradine Case*, the camera cuts between Mrs. Paradine, Gay Keane, and Lady Horfield, linking them all as women in a man's world and all made to suffer in different ways because of that. Barrymore is very touching when she quietly confronts Laughton's judge at the end of the film over dinner. She thinks he should be more lenient with his punishments. "Doesn't life punish us enough?," she asks, in that rich cello voice of hers.

Barrymore is working here in a sort of high-toned and more elevated version of Patricia Collinge's style in *Shadow of a Doubt*. She has a quality that is very difficult to describe, a kind of plaintive soulfulness that speaks to great understanding and great pity. It was just something Barrymore had, this quality. She might have been thinking about what she was going to have for dinner as she acted in this scene, but it doesn't matter. Both the camera and Hitchcock respect Barrymore's gravity and her authority, which was lyrical and not of this earth.

Otherwise *The Paradine Case* is a case of miscasting in central parts, close-up overdoses, messy and repetitive story structuring, promiscuous cutting in the courtroom scenes, and gaudy set design choices, like the ornate bedroom of Mrs. Paradine where there is an oval painting of her on the headboard of her bed. Who sleeps under a painting of themselves? A narcissist, and maybe someone who is contemptuously spending money. Then again, it might have been meant just as a reference to the painting that obsesses the male lead in Otto Preminger's hit *Laura* (1944).

Hitchcock was most interested here in a difficult circular shot in which Latour is seen coming in behind Mrs. Paradine in the courtroom as she sits in her prisoner's box. Hitchcock wanted to signify that she *knew* he was behind her, that she could sense him or even smell him. It was done so that Jourdan was on film behind Valli in a rear projection, as if he were a fantasy as Latour walks into the courtroom. He's her dream man and he is just a film or on film behind her until he steps into the reality of the frame of this movie, at which point Mrs. Paradine's settled image in her box, physically trapped but emotionally stirred, is whipped right off the screen.

The movement of the camera, the animal-like shifts on Valli's face, and the sudden change from the rear projection footage of Jourdan to his actual appearance in court carries a very potent emotional charge, especially since Valli's image disappears exactly when Jourdan really steps into view. This is a complex shot that says something about sexual obsession that could not have been expressed in dialogue.

Free finally of the contract to Selznick, Hitchcock acquired Patrick Hamilton's play *Rope* and decided to film it continuously in very long takes of varying length that black out whenever the camera moves into a person's back or a dark object. There were far too many cuts in *The Paradine Case*, and now Hitchcock would see what a movie would be like without any visible cuts.

Hitchcock got Hume Cronyn to do an adaptation, but then he smartly hired Arthur Laurents, a young playwright out in Hollywood. Laurents took out a lot of the "dear boy" phrases in the English play, which he thought sounded too queer, but *Rope* was a queer project from top to bottom, so to speak. The play was based on the case of Leopold and Loeb, two young gay "thrill" killers who murdered a young boy just for the excitement of it. Hitchcock cast John Dall and Farley Granger as the two young murderers.

Both Dall and Granger were gay, and Granger was living with Laurents by the time they started shooting. "Alfred Hitchcock was fun to work for and fun to be with," wrote the entertainingly prickly Laurents in his 2000 memoir *Original Story*. "He was a tough businessman; otherwise, he lived in the land of kink. Initially, I thought he was a repressed homosexual. . . . The actual word *homosexuality* was never said aloud in conference on *Rope* or on the set, but he alluded to the subject so often—slyly and naughtily, never nastily—that he seemed fixated if not obsessed.

"Sex was always on his mind; not ordinary sex, not plain homosexuality any more than plain heterosexuality," Laurents said. "Perverse sex, kinky sex, that fascinated him. In *Rope*, not just homosexuals and not just murder but a murder committed by homosexuals for a bizarre reason." Laurents was taken into Hitchcock's family circle and observed how much Alma and Hitchcock's daughter Pat loved him and how happy they seemed together. Hitchcock also invited both Laurents and Granger one night to dine at Romanoff's, making it clear that he knew they were a couple.

Hitchcock had wanted Cary Grant to play Rupert Cadell, the teacher who had corrupted the boys with his Nietzschean superman talk, but Grant turned this role down and Montgomery Clift also turned down the role of Brandon before it went to Dall, yet surely the vulnerable Clift would have made a better Philip, the part played by Granger. James Mason might have made an ideal Rupert, but it was James Stewart who was finally selected to play this role.

Rope was the first of four pictures that Stewart would make with Hitchcock, and it's the roughest fit for this actor. Stewart is excellent in *Rope* within the scope of what he can do as a focused authority figure, but he is inherently wrong for his part, and yet it is maybe that inherent wrongness that was somehow needed for this project in 1948. After all, *Rope* is a very queer movie as it is, and if Grant or Mason had played Rupert, it would have been far more so. Having the folksy and very heterosexual Stewart play Rupert threw some people off just enough for them to ignore what this movie is really about.

Hitchcock worried that the grand English actress Constance Collier was overdoing her comic relief role as a chatty dowager who comes to the party that Brandon and Philip are throwing after the murder, where they serve a meal on a chest containing the body of David Kentley (Dick Hogan), the boy they strangled. Hitchcock was also a bit worried, according to Laurents, that Collier was coming across as a lesbian, but this added another underground queer touch to go with the others.

This was Hitchcock's first film in color, which he wanted to be as muted as possible. *Rope* was his second movie set in Manhattan after *Mr. and Mrs. Smith*, and Laurents manages to give it a real Manhattan smart set tone, a brittle cross-talk feeling that is redolent of, say, the group that later formed around the poet Frank O'Hara. Laurents knew this kind of social environment and he gets it on the screen.

The Francis Poulenc piece that Granger's Philip plays at the piano, Mouvement Perpétuel No. 1, adds just the right queer culture-vulture touch, especially since it is usually played much faster than Philip plays it. This Poulenc composition is used as the basis for the score under the opening credits, too, but the film plays without any musical score otherwise, which heightens the tension.

We are only outside the single apartment set of *Rope* during the credits, after which we see a cop leading two little boys across the street. The camera moves toward a window with the drapes drawn, and we hold on them for a moment until we hear a male cry from inside. We see curly-headed David strangled with a rope in close-up, and this is a voluptuous moment that is clearly represented as a sexual act for the killers. Brandon checks David's heart and then says, "O-o-o-pen it" to Philip in his quivery yet thrusting sort of voice. They put David's body in a chest, and we see that the killers are both well-dressed and pouty young men and they both have great hair.

"The Davids of this world merely occupy space," says Brandon, who has a stutter when he's overexcited that Dall leans on in a masturbatory way. Dall and Granger were a different generation of actor and a different breed, and they both bring a kind of jangled psychological insight to their roles that feels like a step forward for Hitchcock and his actors, or at least a step into what was to come in the 1950s and 1960s.

Dall's Brandon is a villain, and he's an attractive and very sexy villain, bold and certain yet also somehow naïve. Dall hits all of these nuances in what is a very difficult role, somehow making Brandon seem like the possessed little boy in Henry James's *The Turn of the Screw*, invaded early by evil fascist ideology yet basically innocent. Imagine the nasty things he makes the semi-unwilling Philip do in bed, all with that "innocent" look on his face. Imagine the sexual experiments. . . .

Granger was discussing the subtext of Philip's relationship to Brandon with Laurents at home because gayness had to be a secret then, almost never discussed out loud except among fellow travelers. "John didn't want to talk about it," Granger said in 1996 to *The Advocate*. "He wasn't very friendly. At least not to me." Granger's Philip is the good boy who is frightened and coerced into doing something he doesn't really want to do, and this shows in the way his mouth tightens sometimes in a prissy way.

The camera movements in *Rope* are necessarily awkward a lot of the time here, but Hitchcock was doing the best he could with the equipment then available to him, and the actors all seem extra nervous throughout because they know if they make a mistake of some kind, they will have to go back to the beginning of the long take. There were cables all over the floor and furniture to be maneuvered around, so the performers in *Rope* had to keep many other things in mind besides their performances. This gives the playing a kind of tension but it is often the wrong kind of tension, actor nerves rather than the nerves of the characters.

David's mother, we later learn, had been possessive and wouldn't let him "grow up," and she had controlled him by acquiring or feigning various illnesses. (Granger himself had rebelled against his own possessive parents to move in with Laurents.) Granger's Philip is a pianist, and Brandon has wrangled him a debut at Town Hall. After the party, Brandon is supposed to drive Philip up to the home of Brandon's mother so that he can practice for a few weeks. Presumably Brandon's mother is "possessive" as well.

David had been engaged to Janet (Joan Chandler), and David's best friend Kenneth (Douglas Dick), who looks a lot like David with his curly hair and pretty face, is dating Janet now, and even Brandon had once dated Janet. So it is made very clear in the way they all relate to Janet that she is the fag hag of this group of gay boys, holding her own by being as bitchy and cutting as they are, but with a winning touch of self-deprecation to go with it.

"You smell dreamy," Janet tells Brandon, and he says that he is wearing a scent that she got him for Christmas. Janet is a theatrical girl who calls people "ducks" and "sweetie" and "chum," and her delivery is highly conscious, for queer people or people in queer milieus are never naturalistic. Janet is helplessly conscious and she is also one of the most deeply attractive women in Hitchcock's films, a girl embedded in gay culture and speaking all the lingo in her disarming way. Chandler's career didn't work out, and she was semi-retired or just plain out of work when she died at age fifty-five in 1979, but she's excellent in *Rope*, very stylish, fresh, and just stylized enough, just like Dall is. "Freud says there's a reason for everything . . . even me," Janet jokes knowingly.

Janet also makes a crack about modern art, saying that the paintings of her three-year-old sister are "really primitive," and this reiterates the bias against abstract painting that runs through many Hitchcock movies. Brandon's apartment (does Philip live there too or just stay over?) is filled with paintings, mostly still lifes, and it features a wall that has been painted at the bottom with white columns, which feels like just the right artificial, aesthetic touch.

Brandon treats his friends and acquaintances maliciously in a way that sometimes has echoes of the stories that Donald Spoto tells about Hitchcock at his social worst in the biography *The Dark Side of Genius*. Philip even condemns Brandon's macabre "touches" at the party when they are alone, and Brandon approves of people picking words for "sound rather than meaning," which also aligns him with Hitchcock.

None of the people at the party ever let the gossipy maid Mrs. Wilson (Edith Evanson) talk too much, and Laurents observed that the actors treated Evanson more like a maid than a fellow performer on the *Rope* set. Mrs. Wilson is maternal and officious in her way and tiresome sometimes, and it feels like she intuits more about what's going on than the boys realize; she keeps calling things "peculiar." She is like a servile American version of Elsie Randolph's freakish old maid in *Rich and Strange*, happy to get her digs in when she can and control what she can manage to.

Philip starts to break down under the strain of the situation and crushes a martini glass in his hand, and his mood is not helped by the entrance of Stewart's Rupert almost a half hour into this 81-minute movie. Rupert publishes books that outline his highly questionable philosophy. ("Small print, big words, no sales," says Janet neatly.) Brandon sneers at boys who died in World War II, but we learn that Rupert got a bad leg serving during that war. Stewart himself had a distinguished war record, while Dall had stayed out of fighting in World War II by telling the army that he was gay, which feels like a Brandon move.

Stewart's Rupert is a needler and about as un-gay a screen presence as it is possible to imagine, though it is said that Brandon used to sit up at "all hours" at Rupert's feet. Stewart locates a kind of bitchery in *Rope* sometimes, but it is heterosexual male bitchery, which means it isn't bitchery at all but a kind of entitled grumpiness. When Rupert speaks of the maid and says, "I may marry her," this line has no impact at all. As written, it should be a gay man's joke. As played by Stewart, it is possible to actually imagine Rupert marrying Mrs. Wilson.

It doesn't help that Collier's Mrs. Atwater brings up James Mason in conversation and calls him "so attractively sinister" and then Janet says how much she likes Cary Grant, so that it feels like the female characters in *Rope* are tantalizing us with better casting possibilities for Rupert. "He was thrilling in that new thing with Bergman," Mrs. Atwater says of Grant, referring very accurately to Hitchcock's own *Notorious*.

When David's father, Mr. Kentley (Sir Cedric Hardwicke), firmly disapproves of Rupert's superman talk and says that it was embraced by Hitler, Brandon says that Hitler and his henchmen were not really superior, as they thought they were, but "brainless," and that he would gladly start killing the remaining Nazis off because they were really inferior. This is a pretty twisted position for 1948 or any other time.

Finally Brandon has to backhand Philip to shut him up. As Rupert starts to catch on to what has happened, Stewart's performance improves and focuses, but when Rupert has to realize that his own teachings are what influenced the boys to commit murder, there is a disconnection again between Stewart's persona and Rupert's words. Rupert is a hypocrite who is also smart enough to know the wrong he did, and that needs to come across in the way he tries to defend himself, but Stewart defends himself here in his full *Mr. Smith Goes to Washington* (1939) style as an utter innocent, sick to his stomach at *them*, these boys, not at himself.

Stewart's Rupert is a touch bullying with his expression of innocence, yes, but he seems innocent all the same. And that tamps down the meaning of the drama in *Rope*, which should be tragic. The writing does deteriorate badly by the end of the film, becoming simplistic, and so Stewart presses on the accelerator of his own talent a little too hard to put it over. He was often a bit over-emphatic on screen in an "I can't help myself!" way that always seems more than a bit worked up.

Stewart is a fine enough actor to make a personal success out of his performance in *Rope*, but a more ambiguous player with easy access to emotions of self-loathing like George Sanders or Mason or Grant would be immeasurably better. For Rupert is finally a George Sanders part that Sanders didn't get to play, unfortunately.

Rope is an exercise, and not an entirely successful one, but still fascinating for its technical feats and also for its queerness. Dall's performance sometimes creeps up to the line of being overdone, but in general he and Granger, with his weak-willed, pretty mouth, are a convincing gay couple jumping from one closet to another in 1948-era Manhattan.

Dall had made his debut as the miner educated by teacher Bette Davis in *The Corn Is Green* (1945), and he was never discreet about his homosexuality. He liked sex and had a lot of it with any available man and he didn't hide it. After *Rope*, his film career didn't exactly flourish, though he did get into another intriguing movie that used very long takes, Joseph H. Lewis's *Gun Crazy* (1949).

Dall lived with his mother and escorted her to premieres, and he didn't get much work in the 1950s or beyond except for a brief role in *Spartacus* (1960). His last credits were several appearances on the *Perry Mason* show, where the far more closeted gay actor Raymond Burr presided. Dall died in 1971 at age fifty, a disappointed performer known for drinking too much, and he had been living with the actor Clement Brace at that time.

Under Capricorn (1949), shot in England but set in Australia, turned out to be Hitchcock's parting gift to Ingrid Bergman, who was consumed thereafter by a scandal where she had a baby by Italian director Roberto Rossellini out of wedlock. This movie was made for and about Bergman, in color and again using extended takes that required a lot of rehearsal and camera maneuvering. The most impressive long take in this picture was an eight minute and forty-seven second tour de force in which Bergman's character confessed her past crimes to the foppish, smirking, and voyeuristic Charles Adare (Michael Wilding).

The extended takes in *Under Capricorn* are often remarkable, but the poky, explicit script is much less so. Most Hitchcock movies are so jam-packed with characters and details that it's hard to keep up with or even notice all of them on each new viewing. *Under Capricorn* is that rare Hitchcock picture with not enough going on. The dialogue here is the sort that tells you everything so that you don't need to wonder or question.

Under Capricorn is a vehicle for Bergman in the way that Hitchcock spoke of doing a vehicle for Garbo in the 1930s, so that in many ways Bergman's performance is the whole show and Hitchcock makes himself secondary to her. Eric Rohmer and Claude Chabrol make great claims for *Under Capricorn* in their Hitchcock book as a personal project for the director or a confession, but Hitchcock showed no enthusiasm for this film when he discussed it with François Truffaut.

After they had rehearsed the long confession speech for a whole day, Hitchcock let Bergman do it her way, but she often had to stop and start again because something would go wrong technically at five minutes in or seven minutes in or six minutes in. When it was finally over and done all the way through, Bergman asked Hitchcock how it was, but he hadn't quite been watching, it seems. "How do I know?," Hitchcock asked her. "I couldn't see you for the huge camera! I hope it was good, Ingrid—we rehearsed it!"

Frustrated by the lengthy takes, Bergman sometimes yelled at Hitchcock on the set, and once he just stole quietly away while she continued yelling, and she didn't notice his absence for quite some time. But she did finally like the long confession take. "I must say much better than being cut up and edited," Bergman wrote her friend Ruth Roberts.

Under Capricorn begins with a map of Australia under the credits accompanied by Richard Addinsell's plaintive, melancholy music, which is very Irish in feeling and one of the most beautiful and expressive Hitchcock scores. Jack Cardiff is the distinguished cameraman here, and the script borrows from many other sources, particularly for the character of the cruel housekeeper Milly (Margaret Leighton), who is a low-class and far more spitefully human version of Mrs. Danvers.

Michael Wilding's Charles Adare is a queer character in every sense, a man who seems to be exhilarated by his own shortcomings, and he is an exceedingly odd person to be used as an identification figure, which is basically what he is in *Under Capricorn*. Adare is written as a rather inane man, and Wilding gives an inane, busy-faced performance, and this points up an important distinction when it comes to acting. If you're playing an inane man, you shouldn't *act* inane so much. There needs to be a slight separation between actor and role for a character like this to operate correctly.

Bergman gets a star entrance in *Under Capricorn* as the camera fixates on her bare feet in close-up and then rises to show her full figure and her glazed, abstracted face. She is Lady Henrietta Flusky, an Irish aristocrat and an alcoholic who has married beneath her to Sam Flusky (Joseph Cotten). The Fluskys are socially shunned, and their obviously tormented relationship is shrouded in secrecy and rumor. Bergman tries to do a light Irish accent through her Swedish accent in this first scene, but she pretty much gives up on that soon after, and this is all to the good. What is not to the good are the unflattering period costumes she has to wear, which bury her in fussy bows and flowers and obscuring bonnets.

Lady Henrietta is a classic Bergman part, a woman consumed by guilt who is gradually brought back to life by Charles, who treats her far more like a gay best friend than like a prospective lover, taking pains to dress her up again as if she were a doll. The triangle between Henrietta, Charles, and Sam never feels urgent or believable, and maybe the film might be better if the far more masculine and competitive Burt Lancaster had played Sam and Kirk Douglas had played Charles. The cranky Cotten disliked the film and accidentally called it *Under Cornycrap* on the set and later *Under Crapricorn.*

Henrietta is being driven crazy by Milly, who is in love with Sam. "Mr. Adare should be a lady's maid!," says Milly at one point when she is telling Sam about how Charles has chosen Henrietta's dress for a ball. "It's funny a manly young fellow like that taking so much trouble with a woman's frills. . . ." Milly has such a free-floating aptitude for nastiness that she actually shoots herself in the foot with this remark that is meant to make Sam jealous, but she has plenty more venom where that came from. (In real life, Wilding married Leighton in 1964.)

After Sam makes a scene at the ball, Henrietta confesses all to Charles in a long take that Bergman luxuriates in. She uses her full body here: her hands, her neck, her forehead, everything she is and everything she has. Henrietta takes us point by point through her love affair with Sam, evoking sounds and sights and smells in the most specific way, going back in time and viscerally capturing what she was thinking and feeling in the past during their courtship. And then she tells about shooting her own brother in self-defense and how she let Sam take the blame for it.

There is a stirring contrast here between Bergman's assumed shy manner and her discreetly signaled sexual voluptuousness, a very Hitchcockian contrast and counterpoint. Remembering her suffering when she followed Sam to Australia, Bergman's Henrietta leans back and puts her right hand to her forehead and then makes it a fist and then glides it down to her neck, and this has the effect of a series of short shots, Bergman's "montage" way of emotional acting at its best.

This long confession scene from Bergman should be shown to acting students so they can see the best way to handle a monologue where a character talks about the past, which can be tedious and un-illuminating if the actor hasn't done enough background work to make what they speak of specific, loaded, and pointed. Bergman is so gifted and prepared that very clear and detailed images really do seem to rise up in front of her as she speaks. This is some of the best acting in Hitchcock, and yet it is acting for its own sake, a tour de force for a beloved star, and far removed from what almost always interested him in his own best work.

Hitchcock remained in England for *Stage Fright* (1950), a lightweight film that featured his daughter Pat as a theater student named Chubby Bannister. ("No comment," Pat dryly wrote about this character name in her book about her mother.) This movie begins with a curtain rising and it is supposed to be about acting and theater, but Jane Wyman is insipid as Eve Gill, the plucky acting student heroine out to prove that the man she loves, Jonathan Cooper (Richard Todd), is innocent of murder. It is clear that no amount of training at the Royal Academy of Dramatic Art is going to make Wyman's Eve into anything but an also-ran ingénue.

Look to the hairstyles as always in a Hitchcock film, and you can see what is wrong with Wyman: her cutesy June Allyson bob with fluffy bangs tells you everything you need to know about both actress and character. *Stage Fright* looks rather shabby sometimes, and Hitchcock was not happy with the technical standards of his home country after his time in Hollywood. This film as a whole operates on a lower standard than his usual in every respect.

Hitchcock got himself into trouble by beginning this movie with a false flashback, an elaborate and untrue tale told by Jonathan in which his lover Charlotte Inwood (Marlene Dietrich) comes to him with blood all down the front of her white dress. He tells Eve that Charlotte had murdered her husband, "an abominable man," as Charlotte puts it, and that he helped her dispose of the incriminating dress. But by the end of the film, we learn that Jonathan is the real killer and that he, and Hitchcock, had been leading us on.

The idea of a false flashback is a tricky one. When we see something acted out on screen, we take it on faith that it has happened as we see and hear it. Perhaps Hitchcock might have toyed with the way he filmed the lie and then shown us the truth in a different visual style, but not enough thought was put into this particular idea. Alma was very much against this false flashback, but Hitchcock insisted on trying it.

On the surface, Dietrich seems like she would be one of those bold women like Carole Lombard and Tallulah Bankhead who would have delighted Hitchcock, but he was not particularly happy with her. Dietrich insisted on a wardrobe from Christian Dior and she also insisted on her own special lighting, which she had required ever since the days of her 1930s films with her Svengali and mentor Josef von Sternberg.

Hitchcock was a possessive man, and he was not pleased with having to mimic another director's visual style for Dietrich. Her tricky instinct is for mockery, for satire, and somehow this doesn't match Hitchcock's own instincts for those things. As with Charles Laughton, this collaboration with Dietrich is a "so near and yet so far" situation when it comes to sensibility.

Dietrich is about 99 percent false as an actress, which was her enclosed thing, her glamour, her mystery. It was that 1 percent she teased us with, that hint of a warm heart somewhere, that suggestion that she might be an earth mother. Actually, though, according to the 1994 memoir written by her daughter Maria Riva, Dietrich was mainly a critical destroyer with the sharpest of adder tongues.

Hitchcock's most notable comment on Dietrich ran as follows: "Miss Dietrich is a professional. A professional actress, a professional cameraman, a professional dress designer." He had not had to cede this level of control to any performer since the debacle of Charles Laughton in *Jamaica Inn*, and this shows in the fact that Dietrich seems to have her own drag act movie going on inside of *Stage Fright* that doesn't have much to do with Eve Gill and her attempts to clear Jonathan.

Dietrich's lines here are often bitchy remarks or absurd non sequiturs, and she sometimes hits that distinctive note of absurd, queer depth with which she ends Orson Welles's *Touch of Evil* (1958), particularly in her last troubling and very arbitrary scene where Charlotte speaks about a dog who bit her. She loved this dog, but he hated her and so she had him shot . . . Hitchcock had expressly asked his writer James Bridie to give Dietrich a closing speech with "a little philosophy" in it.

There is a good example of Hitchcock's "negative acting" principle here when Charlotte is languidly singing "The Laziest Gal in Town" and suddenly spots Jonathan so that her alarmed face contrasts with her "lazy" singing voice and the lyrics of that Cole Porter song, which became a Dietrich staple in her later concert career. They repeat this effect when Charlotte sings "La Vie En Rose" at a theatrical garden party and she has to stop her song when a young boy brings up a blood-spattered doll and holds it in her view. Sometimes Dietrich's contrasts mesh with Hitchcock's needs in *Stage Fright*, but not often.

According to his assistant Peggy Robertson, Hitchcock was also not pleased when Dietrich took Michael Wilding as her lover and delayed shooting of scenes while she carried on with him in her dressing room. Wilding was again the weakest part of a Hitchcock film here, playing a detective who falls in love with Eve. His character is one of the least interesting of all the uninteresting Hitchcock policemen.

Todd remembered that Dietrich often took control over directing the other actors in *Stage Fright* because Hitchcock seemed so uninterested. In her memoir *Marlene*, Dietrich recalled that Hitchcock took her and Jane Wyman out to dinner, with steaks he had had specially flown in because there was still strict rationing of food in England. "Ladies must be well fed," he told them.

Hitchcock lets some British character people do their stuff in *Stage Fright*, and for some of us the most important player in this movie after Dietrich is toothy Joyce Grenfell, a wacky comedienne who does a whole music hall routine here. She is hawking "lovely ducks" at a shooting gallery where you shoot the ducks and get a doll. "Lovely ducks, who'd like to shoot a lovely duck?," Grenfell asks, with her rabbitty overbite. "It's for the orphans," she tells Alastair Sim, who is playing Eve's father. "You *are* sorry for the orphans, aren't you? We all are, aren't we. . . ."

Overcome at one point, Grenfell cries, "We're having *such* fun over here shooting ducks." When Sim aims to shoot, Grenfell closes her eyes and squeamishly leans away in close-up. In the brief time she is on screen, *Stage Fright* becomes a film about Joyce Grenfell and her lovely ducks, as if Hitchcock were relaxing into an Ealing comedy.

12

Strangers on a Train, I Confess

"This is my real first film," Hitchcock told the cast and crew when they started shooting *Strangers on a Train* (1951), an adaptation of a Patricia Highsmith novel, and this picture really was a new beginning, partly because Hitchcock found the cinematographer that he would be working with on all his major films to come, Robert Burks.

There is an extra sharpness to the cinematography here that is especially apparent after all the motley visual style-mixing of *Stage Fright*, even a kind of deliberate gutter press harshness to some of the images, and there are some very impressive chiaroscuro shots dominated by rich and inky blacks.

Raymond Chandler worked on the script for *Strangers on a Train* at his house in La Jolla, California, but this wound up being disastrous and finally ended with Hitchcock beating a poker-faced retreat as the drunken Chandler told him off. Czenzi Ormonde, who had worked with Ben Hecht, wound up rewriting a lot of the script with the writer Barbara Keon as they shot the film, so this was a far looser production than Hitchcock generally allowed or liked.

Robert Walker had been cast throughout the 1940s as sweet, boyish, rather brittle-seeming soldiers, as in Vincente Minnelli's *The Clock* (1945). He was best known for movies at MGM where he played a soldier named Private Hargrove, and also for some leading man parts in MGM features. Walker had been married to Jennifer Jones and had been seriously damaged emotionally when she left him for David Selznick to further her career. By the mid-1940s, Walker was an alcoholic and a wreck, and prone to breakdown. He was such a mess that Judy Garland had to put her own notorious troubles on hold to make sure Walker made it through *The Clock*, and maybe that had been a relief to her.

Tabloids were always reporting on Walker's various public scenes and traumas, especially during a six-week marriage to John Ford's daughter Barbara that was quickly annulled. Walker was institutionalized for nearly a year before getting out to make *Strangers on a Train*, and Hitchcock knew he was playing with fire by casting him as the murderous dandy Bruno Antony.

Hitchcock had followed all of Walker's publicized troubles, and he knew their source was Selznick. "Wouldn't it be interesting if something happened on our film?," Hitchcock vaguely asked Farley Granger, who had been cast as Guy Haines, the tennis star co-lead of the picture. Hitchcock had wanted William Holden to play Guy but he couldn't get Holden loaned out from Columbia. If the very heterosexual Holden had played Guy, surely *Strangers on a Train* would be very different, with Bruno pursuing an uncomfortable straight stud instead of a seemingly bi-flexible opportunist, which is how Guy comes across as Granger plays him.

Aside from the first night of the shoot when Walker broke down about Jennifer Jones again and stayed up with Granger all night talking about her, he caused no trouble during the filming. Walker was professional on this comeback picture, and he was also inspired. He knew what a great part Bruno Antony was, and he was stimulated to take it into all kinds of strange and far-flung psychic areas.

Walker died the same year that *Strangers on a Train* was released when a doctor administered a sedative that mixed with the alcohol in his blood and killed him, and he was only in his early thirties when this happened. On the brink of doom and nearly totally screwed up, Walker was a man who had seen madness and experienced it and now he had the role to share that with the camera.

The first shots of *Strangers on a Train* are the shoes of the two male leads as they walk to one of those trains that Hitchcock loved, restrained and classy shoes for Granger's Guy and loud and snappy shoes for Walker's Bruno. It feels like fate and the camera have linked them together even before they meet.

Guy's foot knocks against Bruno's on the train and after that we are off to the races with them or on the carousel, because Bruno immediately recognizes this young tennis star. Bruno's name is monogrammed on his tie. "I suppose you think it's corny but my mother gave it to me, so I have to wear it to please her," Bruno tells Guy, confiding in him immediately.

This first scene on the train plays very much like a gay pickup, especially during Granger's subtle, appreciative glances at Walker. Maybe that first night of intimacy where Walker himself poured his heart out to Granger about Jennifer Jones had stirred Granger or made him feel protective, which is exactly the unexpected feeling that needs to grow between Guy and Bruno.

Bruno is a psychotic who is capable of evil thoughts and deeds, and he is very exciting. He stirs everything up. He is not complacent. He's one of those crazy people who make things happen, and that kind of energy is always attractive. Bruno convinces Guy to lunch with him on the train, and Hitchcock frames them so that Bruno's massive shoes are in the middle of the composition and sticking up like two erections.

Since Bruno is idle and rich, he has lots of time to think up crackpot ideas and theories. He has been kicked out of three colleges for drinking and gambling, speaks fluent French, and has a wealthy father who disapproves of him. "He *hates* me," Bruno says in his breathy, boyish voice, with a hilariously weird and high-going-higher inflection. And then Walker tops this with his very queeny reading of the line, "I hate him, too," a disturbing moment where Bruno immediately assumes that Guy will hate this father of his just as much as he does. Bruno might as well append the word, "Girlfriend!" to that line as he intimately pats Guy's hand and attempts to merge into one person with him, just as Mrs. Danvers tries to do in the underwear scene with the second Mrs. de Winter in *Rebecca*.

Is Bruno gay? Hitchcock hedged his bets slightly when Peter Bogdanovich asked him this question. "I would think so," Hitchcock murmured. "It wasn't specified, but he could have been, oh yes," but Bruno's most ardent physical moment is when he kisses his mother's hand. If he has had sex, it is probably of the kinkier autoerotic variety, or maybe he sometimes feels that he is above sex, as Hitchcock himself did. Czenzi Ormonde later told Patrick McGilligan that she hadn't been aware of any homosexual subtext in the film while she wrote it, and she insisted that it wasn't there. But of course it is.

Walker is so vivid in these opening scenes that he is practically radioactive, shimmering with uncapped presence and charisma. Bruno would like to kill his father, and he knows from reading the papers that Guy would like to be rid of his trashy first wife Miriam (Laura Elliott). So why not swap murders? "Criss cross!," Bruno says, in that high, boyish, perverted voice of his. Guy just laughs this off. He doesn't take Bruno seriously. He is very complacent.

Guy is going to meet with his wife in his old hometown of Metcalf because he wants a divorce from Miriam so that he can marry Anne Morton (Ruth Roman), who is the daughter of a senator (Leo G. Carroll). Guy is a social climber, and he needs to move up and away from people like Miriam, a low-class girl who is pregnant by another man.

Miriam wears thick glasses, and she works in a record store, and in her first scene she is presented as a conniving woman, knowing and venal. She talks quietly at first, but then she cries, "No man runs out on me, Guy, not even you," denying him a divorce in a voice that suddenly sounds as tough and chesty as Ann Sheridan in one of her 1940s noirs. Guy is not going to throw her away "like an old shoe," she screeches as he leaves the store, and Guy wants Miriam dead, but he would never act on that. It is Bruno who does, like some emanation from Guy's unconscious.

We see Bruno with his equally loony mother, who is played by Marion Lorne, a ditherer of a far more comic school than was usual for Hitchcock mothers. Lorne brings just the right touch to this role, playing it in her usual broad comedy style but with a slight undercurrent of anxiety underneath. Mrs. Antony is an evasive woman, and maybe she is "crazy" like a fox, just like her son. She is giving Bruno a manicure, and he is lounging in a flashy robe that features outer space-like patterns, for Bruno says he wants to go to the moon, and other planets. He is not of this earth, but he is also an anarchist who has thought of blowing up the White House.

Bruno goes to Metcalf and follows Miriam from her home, where she lives with her mother. Miriam is going out with two boys, not just one, and Bruno tails them all to a carnival. Elliott, who was born Casey Rogers and who changed her name to Kasey Rogers later in her career, was outfitted by Hitchcock with the thickest glasses that could be found, and she couldn't see anything at all while she was wearing them, which is why Miriam's boyfriends have to lead Elliott around so carefully.

But Elliott's Miriam can see enough to notice Bruno watching her, and he intrigues her. Elliott later said that Walker himself couldn't see clearly without his own thick glasses, and so we have two actors here who are playing a long sequence dependent on looks at each other but both of them are looking into a blur. (Then again, Bruno and Miriam rarely ever get close enough to read the surface of other people.) Hitchcock wanted Elliott's eyes to look small behind her lenses, "pig-eyed," he told her.

Walker plays this sequence as if Bruno is under some kind of self-hypnosis, or moving with a sense of dreamlike inevitability, as if he is finally going to put a fantasy into reality. He establishes a pickup vibe with Miriam, as he had on the train with her husband, impressing her when he wins a kewpie doll at a strength-test game, and she sadly mistakes his murderous instinct for masculine sexual hunger when Bruno does a brief "come on" waggle of his eyebrows at her. Miriam seems like a much younger and spoiled girl here, gimme, gimme, gimme. She eats a lot of ice cream and hot dogs, and so we see that she has cheap and lusty appetites. It is likely that Miriam has been indulged by her own mother, and this is probably the only thing she has in common with Bruno.

Miriam takes Bruno's bait until they are alone together on a darkened island at the carnival. He flicks a lighter in her face, illuminating it, and she smiles at him slightly, surprised but pleased. "Is your name Miriam?" he asks. "Why yes. . . ." she says, but he cuts her off and his hands are around her neck and her glasses fall off.

Elliott said that it was very difficult to do the famous shot where Miriam's death by strangling is reflected in her glasses on the ground. Hitchcock wanted her to float down slowly, and this was hard to achieve because Elliott would anticipate hitting the concrete floor they were working on and she couldn't keep from accelerating down to it. Elliott needed to still be floaty and slow right before landing hard on the ground, and finally after several takes, she managed it.

Does Hitchcock have any sympathy for Miriam? That's tough to say. His ambivalence about her is expressed in a scene where Guy has come to the Morton house after finding out about Miriam's murder and the senator's daughter Barbara, played by Hitchcock's own daughter Pat, calls Miriam a tramp in her forthright, amusing voice. But Leo G. Carroll's senator stands up for Miriam: "She was a human being," he says.

This is an exact reversal of the positions of Uncle Charlie and young Charlie in *Shadow of a Doubt* when she says the widows he kills are human beings and he croaks out that awful, "Are they?" The meaning in that movie is clear and disturbing, evil versus good with evil in ascendance. The moral positions in this scene in *Strangers on a Train* are far more complex and ambiguous.

Pat Hitchcock is very charming in her "tell it like it is" way as Barbara in *Strangers on a Train*, and very American. If she had been brought up only in England, surely she could not have played this part in this fresh way, for she probably would have been concerned over being ladylike, which is one of many reasons that Hitchcock left his native country.

Pat has no mystery in this picture but is simply and cheerfully what she is, and her character bluntly says what she thinks. As Robin Wood writes in his Hitchcock book, "We respond strongly to Barbara's no-nonsense honesty, but we are made ashamed of that response." That's a very neat formulation of the way Hitchcock can manipulate our point of view. Evil, and evil viewpoints, can be so attractive.

What are the facts about poor Miriam? She is sexually promiscuous and not too bright, or operating on a pretty low level of consciousness. What she wants most, it seems, is some fun out of life. She likes sex and wants it with as many men as she can handle, and like her husband, Guy, she looks over her shoulder to see if there might be a better lover for her, or a better catch. She is confident in her own attractiveness but aware enough to know that someone like Guy is rejecting her to move on and up socially.

Miriam was good enough for a first girlfriend in their small town but not good enough for a rise above that. She wants the money and position that Guy's nascent career in Washington would give her, but her sensibility is so limited that she doesn't have any clear idea of what this life in Washington might be like. If Bruno hadn't killed Miriam, surely her attempts to play hostess in Washington would have proved disastrous, and surely she would have had to eventually retreat back to Metcalf with her child.

Miriam's mantrap attitude might work with boys in Metcalf, but not with men in Washington. Miriam isn't socially equipped to climb upward as Guy is. Everything about her reads "cheap." She would have made Guy unhappy and she would have made herself elaborately unhappy in the manner of Barbara Stanwyck's Stella Dallas, probably. But of course she deserved the chance to make all those mistakes she doesn't get to make.

Bruno sees himself as an artist of evil, which is why immediately after strangling Miriam, he helps an old blind man across the street. He has gotten his rocks off with the murder, so why not be nice now to this old man? Before killing Miriam, Bruno had popped a little boy's balloon when the boy accosted him with a toy gun and said, "Bang, bang!" (Hitchcock lets us see the startled look on the boy's face in a separate shot.) All of Bruno's gestures, evil or good, have style and shape. An aesthete, he is trying to give meaning to life, in his way, where there is none. And that's an artistic advance on Uncle Charlie's evil in *Shadow of a Doubt*.

Lost in Eisenhower-era conformity, Bruno is an odd man out, too clever, too gay, with too much time on his hands. "I've had a *strenuous* evening," he tells Guy after murdering Miriam, rolling his eyes heavenward in a very campy way on the word "strenuous." (Did Walker know how gay these touches of his were? It's far too late to ask him, unfortunately.) Like Uncle Charlie, Bruno's hands need work, and murder by strangulation fascinated Hitchcock because of its sexual connotation. There are many photographs of Hitchcock trying out his strangling moves, including one where the murderer uses only one hand, a sort of show-off strangling.

Granger can seem wooden in *Strangers on a Train*, and Guy has been written about very negatively by most commentators on this film, to an excessive degree, so it is worth pointing out that he has moments here of genuine good nature and charm. For instance, in the scene where he is talking to a drunken man on a train, which is necessary for the plot because it could supply Guy with an alibi for Miriam's murder, Guy is very appreciative, attentive, and sweet with this drunk, and he doesn't need to be. There is nothing he needs from this man. He might have been impatient or more clearly ignored him.

This scene with the drunk might be a case where the character of the actor comes through and shades the character he is playing. In his memoir, Arthur Laurents described Granger as easy to love because he was uncomplicated: "As striking and improbable as Farley's looks were, he seemed unaware of them; and once you knew him, what you marveled at was his sweetness." Then again, the waspish Laurents also observed, "It took me a long time to realize that where Farley was really a good actor was offscreen."

Bruno stalks Guy and starts to act like a gay lover blackmailing another guy in this period. Hitchcock finds the perfect visual image to illustrate Bruno's obsessiveness and focus when he places Bruno as the one unmoving head in the audience at one of Guy's tennis matches, a fatal attraction, not to be ignored, a pickup who won't go away.

And finally, you have to ask just where Walker *found* this man he is playing. Through observation of others during his stay at a mental institution? Or is it something spookier? It sometimes feels in *Strangers on a Train* like Bruno Antony is playing Walker rather than the other way around, and Walker is excited by this possession. It's like he starts at this crazy point of invention in the first scenes and then just goes further and further with it, happily out on a limb and then up in the air doing loop-de-loops.

"Slight improvement over Miriam," Bruno says knowingly to Guy when he sees Guy's fiancée Anne, and this is an understatement. Hitchcock didn't want Ruth Roman in the part of Anne, but he was forced to take her, and he made his displeasure with her known. It cannot be said that Roman does nothing well, for she flares her eyes and nostrils to an immoderate and aimless degree. Anne is sensitive, lush looking, and rather vague, but then all Roman is given to play here is vague suspicions about Bruno. She's a little artificial in the role, but it's hard to imagine anyone else doing anything much with it. The vacant character of Anne is a flaw in *Strangers on a Train*. We spend a lot of time with her, but she is barely characterized beyond her significance to the unfolding plot.

There is a very upsetting scene here where Bruno strangles inane society dowager Mrs. Cunningham (Norma Varden) for too long at a party after he sees Barbara in her glasses and he is reminded of Miriam. There has been a buildup of social niceties between Bruno and Mrs. Cunningham, who is the wife of a judge, and the sound of her weeping is wrenching when Bruno's hands are finally pried off of her neck, at which point Bruno faints.

When Bruno is revived in another room, there is a physical fight between Bruno and Guy, and Bruno insists, "But Guy, I like you!" Guy seems to punch the camera and then we see Bruno fall back from his point of view, and this is set up by Hitchcock so that we totally identify with both of them simultaneously, a masterful technical coup that makes us feel how linked they are, like one person beset by demons. And then Guy fixes Bruno's tie and they suddenly look like a married couple.

Hitchcock is back to his best level here when it comes to minor or bit characters who seem to have a whole inner life that we wonder about, and he builds to one of his most galvanizing climaxes on a carousel gone berserk at the carnival where Miriam was killed. As in the final struggle between Uncle Charlie and young Charlie in *Shadow of a Doubt*, the struggle between Bruno and Guy comes across like a rape, like a very perverted scene of coerced sex.

As the carousel spins further and further out of control, Bruno deliberately knocks a little boy off the carousel when the boy hits out at him. It is as if the boy knows that Bruno is the villain, and so Guy has to save this boy, and then Bruno remorselessly kicks at Guy's hands as he hangs on for his life. A montage of short close-ups of carousel horses and scared riders and high-pitched screams ends with a spectacularly convincing miniature shot of the carousel coming to a stop and flying apart.

Shortly before his death, Bruno is a virtuoso of evil to the last, still trying to pin Miriam's murder on Guy, and Walker seems to be parodying his 1940s "sincere" mode here (fig. 12.1). In the last short scene, Guy and Anne are on a train and a priest tries to talk to them, but they are done with being friendly on trains with anyone and move away from the good father.)

Hitchcock dealt with his first real Method actor when he cast the beautiful and troubled Montgomery Clift as a priest who hears the confession of a murderer named Keller (O.E. Hasse) and can't tell the police what he knows in the sober and humorless *I Confess* (1953). This project had been a long time gestating, and Hitchcock had tried to get Graham Greene to do a script for it, even though Greene had written harsh reviews of Hitchcock's films in the 1930s, but Greene turned him down. Issues with censorship forced the removal of some of the most dramatic elements in the story as conceived by Hitchcock and Alma, which included the priest being the father of an illegitimate baby.

Figure 12.1: Robert Walker's Bruno pretends one more time to be boyishly sincere in *Strangers on a Train*.

Clift spent a week at a monastery to prepare and research his role, and he took everything about it very seriously. Toward the end of the film, Hitchcock needed Clift to look up at a building, and Clift wanted to know why his character was looking up. Hitchcock simply said that he needed Clift to look up to that building for plot purposes. An actor of a different school could have come up with their own reason (to escape the suffocation of the crowd, or as a plea to God), but Clift wanted every motivation to be exhaustively explored, which is why he always seems to be chewing more than he bites off as an actor.

Clift's feeling and thinking through things in *I Confess*, which he expresses mainly with his fawn-like blue eyes, can seem excessive at times, and there are moments when it feels like his large handsome head might explode from all of his inner tension. It is finally hard to know what Father Logan is thinking and feeling because Clift is thinking and feeling so much (fig. 12.2).

All of Clift's different emotions in *I Confess* are going on at once and clashing and so some of these emotions are getting cancelled out. Compare this let-'er-rip approach to Judith Anderson's super-controlled expression of conflicting emotions in *Rebecca* for contrast. Clift can't do nothing well

Figure 12.2: Montgomery Clift's priest attempts to restrain his rage in *I Confess.*

because he is doing everything possible . . .and often very well. He was a virtuoso, and he is not a Hitchcock actor. He acts with his cheeks, his mouth, his hands, his eyebrows, his forehead. Compare Father Logan's showy agony to the agony of Cary Grant's Devlin in *Notorious*, and again the difference is clear.

Hitchcock had wanted the Swedish actress Anita Bjork to play the female lead in *I Confess*, but when she arrived in Hollywood with a lover and an illegitimate baby she was rejected by the studio heads and Anne Baxter was hastily called in to be her replacement. Hitchcock had Baxter dye her hair blonde, but this didn't help much. Along with Eleanor Parker and several of the 1940s love goddesses, Baxter came from the Breathy School of Acting, putting breath and air into nearly all her words to show that she was working hard.

Baxter had a melting kind of sincerity on screen most of the time that would have seemed artificial even if she hadn't shown a much tougher character underneath these mannerisms in her most notable credit, *All About Eve* (1950). Like Ruth Roman, Baxter felt she couldn't do anything to please Hitchcock, and she earned his unmitigated dislike when she took Alma for a trip one day that ran late, which meant that he had to eat dinner alone, something he hated to do.

I Confess was shot mainly in Quebec, and it has a forbidding look, very Germanic and shadowy, very UFA, with those rich blacks Robert Burks was so skilled at getting. Hitchcock cuts to various signs pointing here and there until we see a bludgeoned body on the floor of a room. Keller, who is a German immigrant, confesses to Father Logan that he accidentally killed a man named Villette, who had caught him stealing.

It turns out that Father Logan was being blackmailed by Villette, and so when the police start investigating, the priest gets into a good deal of trouble. Hitchcock wanted Logan to be hanged for a crime he didn't commit and then be proven innocent after his death, but the censors objected to this idea and so Logan needed to live and Keller needed to be caught.

Keller has a saintly wife named Alma (Dolly Haas) who has a very sweet, slightly worn, pretty face, and he is a strange character because he seems to exist only to gloat over the torturous situation he has set up for the suffering priest. At the end of *I Confess*, when Logan has been convicted and Alma finally accuses her husband in front of an angry mob, Keller immediately shoots this wife he claims to love so much. He seems to have no guilt, though he does ask for forgiveness from the priest before he dies.

One day on the set, Clift pondered for four hours whether or not Father Logan would walk over to Keller after Keller has been shot by police, and this kind of self-indulgent motivational fussiness irritated Hitchcock immensely. At a party where Clift was already very drunk, Hitchcock gave him a glass of brandy and dared him to drink it in one gulp. Clift did so and soon collapsed to the floor.

Most of interest in *I Confess* is a long flashback told from the point of view of Baxter's romantic character Ruth, which is done in soft focus and accompanied by schmaltzy choral music to get across her limited, maudlin sensibility. Baxter's Eve Harrington was a drama queen and liar, given to exaggeration and outright fabrication, and Baxter brings this quality to Ruth's monologue about her enduring love for Father Logan. Then again, Montgomery Clift certainly seems like someone you could spend your whole life obsessing over while he obsesses over his own emotions.

13

Dial M for Murder, Rear Window, To Catch a Thief, The Trouble with Harry, The Man Who Knew Too Much

Hitchcock advised that when the batteries need recharging that a director should just buy a successful play and film it without "opening it up," which is how plays often get ruined for film. *Dial M for Murder* (1954) was shot in 3D, and Hitchcock makes you feel you are in the rooms of the apartment where it takes place even in the flat 2D version. This picture starred a new leading lady, Grace Kelly, and she was to become perhaps his favorite blonde leading lady of all. (Ingrid Bergman was a blonde, but she wasn't really a blonde blonde like Kelly.)

Kelly was the niece of playwright George Kelly, and she was the ultimate finishing school debutante, proper and well-turned out, and so refined that she almost sounded English. She had played on early TV and had been Gary Cooper's Quaker bride in *High Noon* (1952) and the rigid wife who has an affair with Clark Gable in *Mogambo* (1953). For Hitchcock, Kelly was like a perfect doll that could be molded to his specifications. She is a very stylized actress who does line readings, and she enjoys the sound of words sometimes rather than their sense, in the manner of the British actress Joan Greenwood. Kelly is not naturalistic. She is for the movies, a fantasy.

In the opening of *Dial M for Murder*, we see Ray Milland's former tennis star Tony Wendice kissing his young wife Margot (Kelly) over the breakfast table, and she is wearing a white dress. Then Hitchcock cuts to Margot kissing her lover Mark (Robert Cummings again, alas), and she is decked out in scarlet woman red lace. The Warner color is eye searing here, glaring, and it makes its point about Margot, the lady in the parlor and the tigress in the bedroom.

But Margot is curiously passive. Even though she has strayed and seems to want out of her marriage, Margot stays dimly loyal to her husband as he puts her through the worst of ordeals, and it does get pretty bad for her because

Milland plays his role with his customary sadistic edge. Milland had won an Oscar for *The Lost Weekend* (1945), where he played an alcoholic, at least partly because it was enjoyable to see *him* suffer for a change. The expert Milland was much like Rex Harrison in look and manner, and he was just as seamlessly technical as Harrison.

There are some questions here for those people that Hitchcock called "the plausibles." Tony coerces the villainous-looking Charles Swann (Anthony Dawson) to kill Margot for her money, and Swann waits behind a curtain with a stocking to strangle her with as Tony calls her from a club. Margot gets out of bed in an ice-blue nightgown and goes to the phone, and she keeps saying, "Hello . . . hello . . ." as the music swells. No one woken up in the middle of the night by a phone call would say "Hello" as many times as Margot does (she says it seven times!), but all the "Hellos" are there to build suspense.

When Swann finally attacks Margot, their struggle is very violent, with shots of her face looking like it's going to burst from the pressure and her legs sticking out and up to knock over objects. Her hand reaches back to us, and in 3D it's as if Margot wants us to give her something to fight Swann off with. She grabs a pair of scissors on the desk and somehow manages to stab Swann in the back, though it's very difficult to see how she gets the scissors into him from the angle that she does. They both start to twitch in a kind of dance and she falls to the floor and there is a close-up of Kelly reacting facially and vocally that feels overdone. Swann falls to the floor, and we see the scissors go even deeper into his back, a very nasty touch.

Tony blames the dazed Margot for the killing of Swann and so she goes through even more of an ordeal, never sticking up for herself and fading into flat hair and a brown coat before an inspector played by John Williams wraps things up in whodunit fashion. *Dial M for Murder* would be better if Margot had a bit more spirit and character. "I could have phoned it in," Hitchcock joked to reporters about this picture.

Hitchcock was intrigued by Kelly, but he felt that she was stiff in *Dial M for Murder*, even as he was impressed with her sexual appetite off camera. She had conducted an affair with Milland on *Dial M for Murder* serious enough that it nearly broke up his marriage, and she also dallied with Anthony Dawson and even the playwright and scriptwriter, Frederick Knott, which particularly amused Hitchcock.

When he was preparing his next film, *Rear Window*, Hitchcock urged his new screenwriter John Michael Hayes to spend some time with Kelly and get to know her, and Hayes found her delightfully smart, sexy, and amusing. Hayes used what he had seen of the off-screen Kelly and what he knew of his own fashion model wife to create the character of Lisa Fremont, a pampered beauty trying her best to win the hand of James Stewart's photographer L.B. Jefferies in *Rear Window*, one of Hitchcock's masterpieces, a movie about curiosity and about asking questions empathetically.

Rear Window was based on a 1942 story by the miserably inventive Cornell Woolrich that was called *It Had to Be Murder*. The basic plot was laid out in that story, but Hayes added the characters of Lisa Fremont and of Jeff's nurse Stella, who was played by the beloved character actress Thelma Ritter.

This was Hitchcock's third film set in New York, and this one would take place on a street in Greenwich Village. The address of the apartment house across the street that Jeff looks into is 125 West 9th Street, but in real life that building is actually 125 Christopher Street, which is right by the red clock tower library on Sixth Avenue that was once used as a jailhouse. (Mae West had been taken there when she was charged with obscenity for a play called *Sex*.)

The devil is in the details, and Hitchcock had reached a point in his career where he could insist on the accuracy of certain details as he created a microcosm of humanity outside of Jeff's window. Hitchcock had traveled with four photographers to Greenwich Village to take shots that could be used to re-create this location on a soundstage at Paramount, and that studio even allowed Hitchcock to cut out the lower half of the soundstage he was using to get the perspective he needed.

The set for *Rear Window* had a drainage system and a complicated wiring mechanism that changed the light for different times of day. There were thirty-one apartments built, and twelve of them were fully furnished. This really was a world of a movie set, and it does capture the hurly-burly, nonstop way of life in Greenwich Village better than nearly any other movie.

Rear Window begins with some jazzy music courtesy of Franz Waxman as three bamboo blinds are slowly pulled up for the show across the courtyard. The camera moves around this courtyard and into Jeff's apartment, where we see that his left leg is encased in a cast and that he's a photographer and that it is over ninety degrees outside. The sound design of this movie is very layered and complex, with all kinds of noises coming from different areas. There is no score after the credits save for the music from various apartments, including the apartment of Ross Bagdasarian's melancholy songwriter.

"Men, are you over forty?," asks an announcer on the radio. "When you wake up in the morning, do you feel tired and run-down . . . do you have that listless feeling?" Stewart was in his mid-forties in *Rear Window,* and Hitchcock was in his mid-fifties and Ritter was in her early fifties. Of the main characters, only Grace Kelly was in her twenties, and that is partly what this movie is about, though *Rear Window* is unusually wide open to many different interpretations, even more so than other Hitchcock films. It's partly about being middle aged and restless and hot, and having itches that are getting difficult to scratch.

Jeff has nothing to do but look at the free show outside his window, the people he sees from afar. Hitchcock had the neighbors wear earpieces so that he could give them detailed instructions and direction, and keep control of them. There's a blonde dancer whom Jeff calls Miss Torso (Georgine Darcy), a statuesque girl who always seems to be prancing around in her pink underwear and shamelessly posing as she rehearses her dances, as if she somehow knows she is being watched.

There's a middle-aged female artist who is working on a sculpture called "Hunger," which has a hole in its stomach. There's an older couple who sleep on the fire escape in the heat and dote on their little dog. There's poor Miss Lonelyhearts, played by Judith Evelyn, a middle-aged lady still pining for a knight in shining armor. There's a newly married couple who are still in the honeymoon phase.

And then there are the unhappily married Thorwalds, who occupy a center stage position outside Jeff's window. Mrs. Anna Thorwald (Irene Winston) is an invalid, and her husband Lars (Raymond Burr) is a costume jewelry salesman. Winston was in her late thirties here, and her few other credits are mainly so small as to be uncredited. She was also a writer for television, and she died in 1964 at age forty-eight from pneumonia.

We only ever see Winston's Mrs. Thorwald from a distance, but she is the character who haunts the movie. Why is she ill? How has her husband disappointed her? How has she disappointed him? She still looks attractive in her nightgown. When Thorwald brings her a tray to eat from and kisses her lightly on the head, she contemptuously tosses a flower aside, and Thorwald stiffens and reacts badly to this gesture of hers.

Maybe Mrs. Thorwald is a force of negativity, a killer of romance. She yells at Thorwald when he takes a call from another woman, and she seems to have a very sharp tongue. But there is a sense, even from the distance we see her from, that she had other possibilities. Surely this isn't the life that she would prefer to be stuck with.

For everyone that Jeff sees outside his window is stuck in some way, or waiting to be stuck. He's been in this apartment for six weeks with his broken leg and his broken camera, with his impotence. As a photojournalist, Jeff has sometimes gotten into trouble when some of his photos resulted in unfavorable publicity. His job is to nose around, to pry, and this has its good and its bad side.

Jeff exchanges bright remarks with his insurance company nurse Stella, played by Ritter with a wisecracking 1930s manner and a conservative 1950s outlook. Hayes, who would go on to write Hitchcock's next three films after *Rear Window*, had a talent for brittle repartee that had been put to use most recently in the campy Joan Crawford vehicle *Torch Song* (1953), and his 1960s credits are mainly in a trashy/campy vein. Hitchcock favored the sort of clever dialogue that Hayes could manage easily, and Ritter gets the lion's share of it here, and she makes the most of it, all with that wised-up, unsmiling face of hers.

Ritter's vocal delivery is often much faster than what might be expected, but she came from Brooklyn and things happen faster there. Stella is blunt and wordy and very funny. She says things sometimes that make Jeff and Lisa cringe, and there are limits to her sensibility, or maybe there are just things she pretends not to understand. "If Hitchcock liked what you did, he said nothing," Ritter said. "If he didn't, he looked like he was going to throw up."

"People with sense belong wherever they're put," Stella says, a complex remark that scorns both upward and downward mobility. She is against the kind of smart-set Manhattan milieu that Hitchcock showed us in *Rope*, where people went into analysis and talked their relationships to death. Stella says that when she married her husband, Miles, that they were both "maladjusted misfits . . . we are *still* maladjusted misfits, and we have *loved* every minute of it." Stella's point of view here is Hitchcock's own. If he had gone into analysis, he might have worked through his issues and let go of some of his fears, but he would have lost some or all of his creativity.

Stella speaks mainly from instinct, and she can be evasive. She is not reflective. She is a performer, a stand-up comedian, down to earth yet bigger than life. "Lisa Fremont is the right girl for any man with half a brain who can get one eye open," Stella tells Jeff, but he doesn't want to marry yet. Stewart himself played the field all through the 1930s and 1940s and finally settled down and married his wife Gloria at age forty in 1949. And Kelly was playing the field and enjoying most of the men she was meeting, some of them married. Ritter was married to the actor Joseph Moran from 1927 until her death in 1969.

Kelly's Lisa is introduced in extreme close-up as she comes in for a slow-motion kiss, and Hitchcock films it so that it feels like Kelly is going to give all of us a kiss. It's a mirage of an image, a fantasy . . . but Stewart's photographer is not taken in by it. Lisa is wearing a $1,100 dress and talks about having cocktails with Leland and Slim Hayward and planting Jeff's name in the columns, and she even brings up a whole dinner from the stylish New York restaurant "21," which Hitchcock thought looked like a jail when he first came to America. Lisa is so irresistible on the surface that we wonder, as Jeff does, why she is trying so hard.

There is a camera movement down from Mrs. Thorwald taking pills to Miss Lonelyhearts in her apartment that links them together, and then Jeff and Lisa are witnesses to just how pathetic and isolated a life can be. Miss Lonelyhearts has set her apartment up for a romantic dinner, and this gets Jeff's attention, but fairly swiftly it becomes clear that this is just an imaginary romantic dinner. Miss Lonelyhearts lives in a fantasy world most of the time because she can't stand her real life, and when she toasts her imaginary suitor, Jeff toasts her back from his window, which is probably his most sympathetic moment in this movie (fig. 13.1).

Like Hitchcock himself, Jeff pities Miss Lonelyhearts and also identifies with her. Sometimes that empty space in us can be filled by a total identification with another person, however unlikely that identification might seem on the surface. And so *Rear Window* is actually one of Hitchcock's most hopeful films even if, on the surface, it can be pessimistic about the relationships between men and women.

Stewart at this point in his career was increasingly leaning on a crankiness of manner that could sometimes shade into outright meanness. He leans also on vocal mannerisms from his past work that had matured into querulous hemming and hawing. In an argument between Jeff and Lisa, both Stewart and Kelly are doing colorful line readings rather than actually fighting, even though they both take care to stumble over words a bit, displaying a starry kind of old-fashioned stylized "naturalism." Kelly is amusing here playing the sort of character that Vivien Leigh had made her own through most of her career: the pettish, childlike, spoiled beauty, selfish but likably spirited. Georgine Darcy, who played Miss Torso, said that Kelly wore glasses off the set and that in this mode she was quiet and unrecognizable.

Figure 13.1: L.B. Jefferies (James Stewart) makes a toast to Miss Lonelyhearts (Judith Evelyn) in *Rear Window*.

Stewart is detailed and uninhibited in his facial reactions to what he sees in the windows across the way, and he explores lots of layered emotional states. He is doing a lot most of the time, and well, though just slightly overdoing things sometimes, which was always a weakness with him. Of course, Hitchcock is also pulling the strings here. If he wanted to cut Jeff's sympathetic close-up toasting Miss Lonelyhearts to a shot of Miss Torso instead, the effect from Stewart would look entirely different.

Lisa lives up on 63rd Street, and she alludes to the fact that she might be as isolated up there, in her way, as Miss Lonelyhearts. But Lisa is social enough that she also identifies with Miss Torso, who has a lot of male guests. "I'd say she's doing a woman's hardest job . . . juggling wolves," Lisa says. Lisa is sophisticated yet somehow limited, or evasive like Stella.

While the newlyweds are having nonstop sex, Mrs. Thorwald catches her husband making a phone call and her response is laughing and derisive, enough to make a man think of killing, but Hitchcock gives Mrs. Thorwald a brief moment alone that lets us see her disappointment in life, in her husband, and in herself.

Jeff hears a short, high scream and something smashing . . . and then he falls asleep in his wheelchair and wakes to see Thorwald leaving the apartment across the way in the dead of night in the rain with a briefcase. The

Rodgers and Hart song "Lover" is playing faintly somewhere as counterpoint. Thorwald comes back and then goes out again, and the composer next door comes home drunk, furiously hitting his music and falling to the floor, which makes Jeff smile. Less like a moviegoer, Jeff is more like an early TV watcher flipping channels and getting distracted. He finally falls asleep again, and there are melancholy boat noises on the soundtrack as we see something that Jeff doesn't: that Thorwald is leaving at dawn with a woman dressed in black.

Jeff gets his massage from Stella in the morning and talks about how Miss Torso is the "eat, drink, and be merry girl," and Stella says that she'll probably wind up "fat, alcoholic, and miserable," which is part prophecy (it could happen) and part wishful thinking. She says Thorwald would be a "low type of man" to run out on his invalid wife. But would walking out on her have been lower than killing her?

Jeff keeps on observing Thorwald, who sits by himself smoking at 3 a.m. and looking worryingly down at the little dog who keeps digging at his flower garden. Where is Mrs. Thorwald? As the movie goes on and Jeff becomes more and more obsessed with his theory that Thorwald murdered his wife, Lisa is shut out totally. She sits in his chair with him and kisses him in the yielding way that Ingrid Bergman kisses Cary Grant in *Notorious*, but Jeff barely seems to notice this goddess in his arms. She finally gets annoyed at this, and when he asks her what she thinks of the Thorwald matter, Lisa says, "Something too frightful to utter."

What does this mean exactly? Censorship makes the relationship between Jeff and Lisa even more difficult to parse than it might be otherwise. Have they even slept together? They are engaged, according to Lisa. Is Lisa wondering if Jeff is gay? Or, far worse, is she wondering whether he is simply not interested in sex because he can no longer have it? He is using phallic binoculars now to spy on his neighbors, which aids our own curiosity. Stella jokes that Jeff has a "hormone deficiency," but maybe it isn't such a joke.

Jeff looks at Miss Torso and wonders just how you would go about cutting up a body . . . and Lisa gets even more alarmed at this. The newlyweds next door are already falling into bad habits, with her nagging and him staring out the window like a convict. The people Jeff sees outside his window confirm his suspicions about marriage and Lisa. But he does like Stella's breakfasts. "No wonder your husband still loves you," Jeff tells Stella, the most bluntly sexist remark in all of Hitchcock's work.

We get a closer view of poor Miss Lonelyhearts through Jeff's binoculars as she puts on her glasses to apply lipstick and takes a drink for courage before going out and trying to meet someone. (The frilly little lamps on her dressing table tell us a lot about who she is.) Judith Evelyn, who played Miss Lonelyhearts, was born in 1913 in South Dakota, and she survived a shipwreck that killed her father in 1939 and was one of only six survivors of the original eighty-five on board. Evelyn worked mainly in the theater and was best known for playing the wretched wife in *The Shrike* on stage with Jose Ferrer. She played in two rather poorly written episodes of Hitchcock's TV show in 1955 and 1957, in both of which she was odd and whiny, careworn and insinuating.

The year after *Rear Window*, Evelyn played another extravagantly pathetic character, Eloise Crandall in the Joan Crawford movie *Female on the Beach*, where she paid for love from a gigolo and met a violent end. A 2005 French novel called *Mademoiselle Coeur Solitaire* by Sébastien Ortiz told the story of *Rear Window* from Miss Lonelyhearts's point of view, but in the movie, it is all from Jeff's perspective.

"He's kinda young, isn't he?," Jeff asks as he and Lisa look at Miss Lonelyhearts and the boy she has picked up. The boy kisses her and then he tries to go further, but at forty Miss Lonelyhearts still wants romance, not sex, and she has to slap him and push him out her door. This is the only time that Jeff looks uncomfortable with his peeping.

Lisa is staying the night, and she puts on a white satin nightgown . . . but then a woman's scream is heard because someone has killed the little dog. So Hitchcock killed a child in *Sabotage* and now he kills a sweet little dog, but no one complained of this except the owner of that doted-on dog on screen. "He's dead!," cries Miss Lonelyhearts. "He's been strangled, the neck is broken!" The female half of the couple who sleeps on the fire escape harangues the whole courtyard. "Did ya kill him because he liked ya?," she cries. "Just because he liked ya?"

Hitchcock gives single close-ups here to both Miss Torso and Miss Lonelyhearts, the only ones they get in the film, as they react with sympathy to this woman's lament. This is a moment of solidarity between seemingly disparate people that is again very hopeful in attitude. The neighbors soon go back into their own separate worlds, the show over, but at least they came out to watch the show. Human curiosity. Part of the point of the film seems to be that our curiosity is too promiscuous and not focused enough, but of course life offers us so much to be curious about.

To impress Jeff, Lisa takes all kinds of risks with Stella, climbing into Thorwald's garden and then entering his apartment to see if she can find evidence of Mrs. Thorwald's murder. But Jeff and Stella see that Miss Lonelyhearts is trying to kill herself with pills, and this distracts them from noticing that Thorwald is coming back, which traps Lisa. Hitchcock frames Lisa above Miss Lonelyhearts, linking two very different women in two very different situations.

Jeff is utterly impotent as Thorwald attacks Lisa and the lights go out in Thorwald's apartment. (Hitchcock told François Truffaut that at the premiere of the film, Joseph Cotten's wife turned to her husband and said, "Do something, do something!" during this scene.) This is both a male nightmare of helplessness and also a facsimile of what Hitchcock's audiences go through as they watch one of his movies.

Lisa is rescued (luckily a police station is across the street from this particular location in Manhattan in both movie life and in real life), and then Jeff does final battle with Thorwald, who is a hulking, gray-haired man in glasses. At one point when Thorwald is on the street, a car nearly hits him, and he looks at this car with scarily personal animus. Thorwald seems to be a man who has deteriorated into a "the whole world is out to get me" viewpoint.

Burr was gay, but that's not something you would likely guess from his heavy, staring screen look and presence. Thorwald is a formidable opponent, both physically and in other ways, as he enters Jeff's apartment and Jeff keeps flashing one of his cameras in his eyes. This camera warfare cannot last, and Jeff is finally struggling outside of his own window before falling to the ground and breaking his other leg.

Hitchcock gives Ritter's Stella a very ambiguous last close-up as she seems to realize that she has been morally compromised by all this vicarious sleuthing. She's very good at evading certain uncomfortable issues, but not this one. And then the film ends on a wave of goodwill as Miss Lonelyhearts has her first date with the composer (they seem very well suited to each other) and the older couple get a new dog and the Thorwald apartment is repainted and Miss Torso's very short boyfriend returns from his military service. Only the newlyweds are unhappy and bickering. "If you'd told me you'd quit your job we wouldn't have gotten married!," cries the wife.

Lisa looks over at Jeff sleeping with two casts on his legs. She has impressed him with her reckless adventurousness, and now she has him where she wants him again as she carefully puts down her mountaineering book for a fashion magazine. Lisa has proven that she is brave in a foolhardy way, and this does at least match up with a similar quality in Jeff. Pretending to be something you're not, or not quite, isn't a recipe for a good relationship, but

Lisa is a girl who gets what she wants no matter what she has to do for it, and for some reason she wants grumpy, middle-aged Jeff.

Kelly loved working on *Rear Window*. "You know, it's almost like leaving home, leaving this stage," she said when the movie was finished. Her third and last film with Hitchcock was *To Catch a Thief* (1955), a lightweight relaxation set on the French Riviera where she played a hot ice queen in thrall to Cary Grant's former cat burglar. Kelly was at her most sumptuously beautiful and assured here, and Hayes provides some amusing movie-ish dialogue for her, including a scene where she brings a picnic lunch with chicken and asks if Grant wants a leg or a breast and he says, "*You* make the choice," in that voice so thick with amusement. (She chooses a leg/thigh for him.)

Grant had been ready to retire, but he was coaxed out of that by the opportunity to star opposite Kelly. He was fifty years old here, but the script says he's thirty-five. The leading ladies got younger while the male stars stayed the same in this period, and that could sometimes be awkward in 1950s movies. Kelly and Audrey Hepburn almost never had a costar near their own age.

To Catch a Thief begins with a middle-aged woman screaming in close-up, but there is no murder here. Only her jewels have been stolen, for someone is taking valuable jewels from those older women Uncle Charlie speaks of in *Shadow of a Doubt*. Grant's suntanned, catlike John Robie was a jewel thief, but he has distinguished himself as a fighter in the French Resistance and has put lifting ice behind him. This is a champagne version of Hitchcock's wrong-man-on-the-run chase story, which he hadn't done for quite a while.

Hayes was good for bright repartee but not so solid on story and structure, and so Hitchcock amuses himself with perverse details and local color. He glorifies Kelly in her Edith Head costumes as she gets a tan and drives too fast, and he also lets Jessie Royce Landis enjoy herself as Kelly's worldly oil-widow mother, who puts out a cigarette in a plate of eggs. Landis's Jessie Stevens worries that her daughter Francie was "finished at the finishing school," and she talks a lot about missing her earthy husband Jeremiah.

There is an ominous feeling created sometimes in *To Catch a Thief* when Hitchcock fades to black and keeps the screen black longer than you would expect before opening back up to another image, which he experimented with in several subsequent movies. The effect of this device is like closing your eyes on the beach and drifting off and then opening them fast and wondering how much time has passed. *To Catch a Thief* was filmed in VistaVision, a wider frame, though Hitchcock resisted Cinemascope and the really wide frame. He liked the squarer frame he had grown up on.

Grant's John tells Kelly's Frances that she needs "two weeks with a good man at Niagara Falls," but she is the aggressor in their relationship, and this all comes to a head in a famous love scene where she wears a formfitting white gown and comes on to him as firecrackers explode outside their room. Kelly reaches a sensual, pleased-with-herself peak here, kissing each of the fingers on Grant's hand and lowering her voice to a Joan Greenwood-like sexual purr.

Less happy is Brigitte Auber's Danielle, a French girl who turns out to be the burglar the police are after. Auber's English isn't quite fluent enough, and her *Bonjour Tristesse* look does nothing for Hitchcock on screen, though he did make a play for her off screen two years later, which was recounted in Patrick McGilligan's 2003 Hitchcock biography. He was very embarrassed when she rejected him.

To Catch a Thief ends with a joke when the plot gets wound up: John and Frances plan on marrying, and she says, "Mother will love it up here!" At this point Grant offers a comic version of that agitated look he did on the plane with Bergman in *Notorious*. Soon after making this movie, Kelly retired and married Prince Rainier of Monaco. She was not a career actress as much as a beautiful girl who felt her time on screen was limited, like the many women Hitchcock had worked with during his British period. And so Hitchcock was abandoned again by his Galatea for another man.

As she filmed her last movie *High Society* (1956), Kelly told a reporter, "When I first came to Hollywood five years ago, my makeup call was at eight in the morning. On this movie, it's been put back to seven-thirty. Every day I see Joan Crawford, who's been in makeup since five, and Loretta Young, who's been there since four in the morning. I'll be God-damned if I'm going to stay in a business where I have to get up earlier and earlier and it takes longer and longer for me to get in front of the camera."

Hitchcock was starting to do his TV show, introducing macabre episodes with his unflappable face and dry humor, and that dry humor carried over into *The Trouble with Harry* (1955), a film that took full advantage of views of Vermont trees ablaze in autumn. This is one of those Hitchcock movies that really does seem storyboarded down to the last shot, and there isn't a whole lot going on in it, finally, beyond the super-dry humor of the first scene where polite spinster Mildred Natwick sees Edmund Gwenn dragging a body behind him in the woods and says, "What seems to be the trouble, Captain?"

Shirley MacLaine made her film debut here as a young widow with a small boy, and she seems uncomfortable with all the wordy dialogue provided by John Michael Hayes. She doesn't really know what she's doing, but she pretends that she does while a miscast John Forsythe tries to play a randy Abstract Expressionist painter.

Hitchcock uses those ominous fades to black for a while again, as in *To Catch a Thief*, and this film certainly looks lovely while the characters discuss very morbid memories that are supposed to act as a contrast to the setting. What was really notable about *The Trouble with Harry* was that it marked the first of eight collaborations with the composer Bernard Herrmann, a key final ingredient needed for the masterpieces to come, all in a row. Herrmann provided a "lighthearted" score for *The Trouble with Harry*, a galumphing sort of high-spirited call-and-answer session in the spirit of Richard Strauss.

Hitchcock did a remake of *The Man Who Knew Too Much* (1956), which was shot in color mainly on location in Marrakech and London and starred James Stewart and Doris Day, who plays a former singing star named Jo Conway. The daughter in the original was changed to a son named Hank (Christopher Olsen), and the buildup to his kidnapping was padded unnecessarily. Hitchcock uses the heavy, hard fade-outs to black here for a third time in a row, and this was the last script of four done for Hitchcock by John Michael Hayes.

The interesting thing about this second version of the story is its portrait of a very unhappy marriage between Stewart's Indiana doctor Benjamin McKenna and his wife Jo. Ben has a temper, and Jo is suspicious, remote, and hostile under a hard-smiling, guarded veneer. She misses her career and takes too many pills, and she and her husband have a "monthly fight." Like Lisa Fremont, Jo has her feminine intuition and she would prefer it if her husband practiced in New York so she could go on working in the theater. And in the most upsetting scene here, Ben forces Jo to take tranquilizers before telling her that their son has been kidnapped.

This scene was not taken too seriously by critics when the film was first released. Eric Rohmer and Claude Chabrol call it a scene of "cruel humor" in their early Hitchcock book, but no one is likely to laugh at it now. With time this scene has come to look like the crudest kind of sexist oppression against a woman who isn't allowed to have her own reaction before being forced into sleep. "Forgive me," Ben says, as she slips away, but not even Stewart's most anguished manner can make this moment at all palatable for his character.

Hitchcock himself was uninterested in Jo's conflict over career and family, which was very much Hayes's contribution to the project. In an earlier draft of the script, Hayes had Jo denounce her husband very angrily after he drugs her, but Hitchcock cut much of this dialogue. He had wanted the marriage in this second *The Man Who Knew Too Much* to be humorous or satirical, and he sought to insert more humor into the film as a whole, but this did not work out here. The would-be comic device of having some of Jo's friends waiting for her in a hotel room for the second half of the film is particularly awkward.

Hitchcock is probing Day's persona in *The Man Who Knew Too Much* in a way that is not always comfortable or edifying. A band canary in the 1940s, Day was one of the most popular stars of her time, and her stock-in-trade was an aggressive kind of good cheer that seemed to hide a neurotic, resentful side. She was a great singer whose main trick was hitting a note as hard as possible, very intensely, and then drawing back from it as quickly as possible, and the effect of this was dramatic and often very sexy.

Day was upset about the poverty of the people she saw in Marrakech and the starving animals, and she was reluctant to make this movie in general because working with Hitchcock made her feel inadequate. Jo is uneasy and unhappy in her marriage, and Day felt similarly on the set. She brings a lot of bad vibes underneath her over-bright smile, and Hitchcock makes ample use of them.

"He didn't direct," Day wrote in her 1975 autobiography. "He didn't say a word. He just sat next to the camera . . . all he did was start and stop the camera." She felt Hitchcock didn't "relate" to her, and that he didn't like her. Finally, she could stand no more, and when they got back to Hollywood to shoot some of her most difficult scenes, Day demanded a meeting with Hitchcock along with her agent. She needed some reassurance and told him that she was frightened and insecure.

"Everyone's frightened," Hitchcock told her. He said that he himself was as frightened as she was. "When I walk into the dining room at Paramount I'm as insecure as everyone else," he said. "Everybody's frightened and insecure, and the ones who appear not to be are just appearing not to be. Deep down, they're as frightened as the next fellow, maybe even more so."

Hitchcock wanted Day to do her "big scene" where Stewart gives her the pills in one take, and she liked the idea of this (fig. 13.2). They walked through the moves before lunch, and then after lunch she did it all just once. "What happened to me in that scene seemed very real to me," Day said. "I actually *experienced* losing my little son to a kidnapper. I was living that ordeal." But of course the whole concept of a "big scene" goes against the way Hitchcock usually works with actors.

Figure 13.2: Jo Conway (Doris Day) explodes with emotion as she is sedated and restrained by her husband (James Stewart) in *The Man Who Knew Too Much*.

Day's outburst is so histrionic that it could have been used as a clip on the Oscars, though she was not nominated. (Hitchcock's actors rarely got Oscar nominations past the initial interest in him when he first came to Hollywood.) The tension in the acting of this scene should be that the pills are beginning to work as Jo starts to flip out, but Day turns on the full faucet of her emotion and then quickly dries it all up, taking the simple route rather than the Hitchcock counterpoint route.

Day is touching in this scene in her all-out way, but so uncontrolled emotionally that she skirts right up to the edge of being ludicrous and hamola. Day had a son named Terry, and she said later that she thought, "What if it was Terry?" to get the emotion she wanted. And so there's no distance to what she does here, which might have helped her to shape the emotion more.

It isn't enough to have a lot of emotion and pour it all over the place. Impressive as this scene is on the surface level, it doesn't have that conflict that Hitchcock liked and required from his actors. Day is far more impressive, really, in the virtuoso Albert Hall sequence that uses the same music as the original movie did but with lavishly amplified orchestration and conducting by Bernard Herrmann.

This version of *The Man Who Knew Too Much* lacks a compelling villain like the one Peter Lorre played in the original. The Draytons, an English couple, were meant to be Communists in an earlier version of the script, but they don't retain much specific character in the film. (Mrs. Drayton, played by Brenda de Banzie, turns out to be rather kindhearted.) But the extra time in the Albert Hall scene does make an impact.

Day is tormented over nine minutes of playing time as the music surges forth at Albert Hall and she has to decide what to do, moving through feelings of indecision, nausea, tears, and exhaustion. Jo is like an audience member at a Hitchcock movie emoting, and she is going on a ride that she would prefer, of course, not to be on. This is Hitchcock's "negative" acting at work again, because here we have a situation where a person has to *not* do something that they feel they should do, and so this really gives Day's perpetual anxiety something immense to chew on. Finally Jo screams in close-up, and Stewart's Ben charges into the box where the assassin lurks.

Hitchcock told Reggie Nalder, the bony and scary-looking actor playing the assassin, to look at the ambassador "lovingly . . . as if you were glancing at a beautiful woman." Nalder had been a dancer in his youth, but at a certain point his face was disfigured somehow by fire. (He had several different stories about how this happened.) He was something of a man of mystery himself, and ideal visually, at least. Nalder told Donald Spoto that Hitchcock stared right at his crotch whenever he spoke to him.

Even after four years away, Jo still has fans that throng her at a London airport, and her records still sell, but she wants another child. She thinks that two children will calm some of her discontent over giving up her career, but this will only likely delay what is coming. Surely Jo is going to have to resume her career in some way because otherwise she'll be pill popping and making her family miserable with her forced good cheer. And surely the publicity Jo will gain as the foiler of an assassination attempt and the rescuer of her son will make a Jo Conway comeback all but inevitable.

Day herself said in a 1991 documentary on her life that she never wanted to be a movie star but only wanted to marry and have children and "keep house." She saw herself as a pawn, someone who was exploited, and she went into retirement when she could manage to do so financially. Day praised Hitchcock as "even-tempered" and "organized" and called him "altogether a lovely man."

"He didn't believe in rehearsals," Stewart said of Hitchcock. "He preferred to let the actor figure things out for himself. He refers to his method as 'planned spontaneity.' Of course, this is confusing to an actor who is accustomed to a director who 'participates' in the scene. In the beginning, it certainly threw Doris for a loop. Hitchcock believes that if you sit down with an actor and analyze a scene you run the danger that the actor will act that scene with his head rather than his heart, or guts." There had been a lengthy dialogue section between Day and Stewart in the Albert Hall scene, but Hitchcock had it all cut. He knew that the images and the music would carry the emotion better than words.

On his television show *Alfred Hitchcock Presents*, which ran from 1955 to 1965, Hitchcock did amusing intros and outros to the episodes that were written by James Allardice, and his comic timing was always sharp yet excitingly spontaneous; there was a sense of play and danger about these appearances, especially when Hitchcock would "break character" a few moments before he should have, which might be covered by abrupt editing. Sometimes he would slow down words until they lost all meaning, and sometimes he speeded them up just to show off, and this displayed both his mastery of the situation and his willingness to fill any time slot indicated.

There is also a sense of power about him here, for he was the king in his own macabre domain, good-humored most of the time but with a kind of coiled malevolence at his disposal. The Hitchcock TV character is vain and sometimes "vain," an exhibitionist pretending control, and he generally speaks in an exaggeratedly lugubrious voice. (His breathing sounds labored in the early seasons.) His clothes look like they have been made to accommodate fluctuations in weight, and his nose has a drinker's red tinge to it. The TV Hitchcock is a wine connoisseur, as he was in real life, and a self-made dandy, which played very well in America but would not have worked as well in his native England. A working-class Brit naturally seems classier than any American to an American, and surely this tickled Hitchcock.

The shows themselves feature a variety of locales and classes, but many of the murder plots revolve around the difficulty or impossibility of getting a divorce in this era. It is not likely that Hitchcock would be too interested in the impersonality of 21st-century evil where men try to kill as many people as possible with a gun; his poisonings and stranglings and stabbings on his television show look almost quaint by comparison, for at least they are more personal. Hitchcock wants us to do the acting most of the time, and he wants us to be jolted by the "twist" at the end of most of the stories. The trick is getting our attention with a setup and then goading our uncertainty until we can emote for him in front of the TV set just as we did for the larger movie screen.

The TV Hitchcock is sometimes like a servant or gentleman's gentleman offering asides to the audience, and he is capable of mincing in a sendup of low-class insinuation and then wincing as a man of discrimination, and so his social signifiers cover a lot of ground. His eyes are full of feeling in some light, but this hint of vulnerability often disappears behind a mask. The biggest shocker somehow is when Hitchcock will drop his humorous pose in order to offer a seemingly sincere message, as when he speaks about wanting to "help" alcoholics in the outro to "Never Again," a first-season episode of an Adela Rogers St. Johns story with Phyllis Thaxter pulling out all the stops as an alcoholic woman consumed by jealousy.

His television series showed more clearly than his features that acting was beginning to change and call attention to itself by the mid-to-late 1950s. Jo Van Fleet dominates a first-season episode called "Shopping for Death" with an all-out crazy lady characterization that is too conscious of its own virtuosity, as if she were offering a lavishly detailed scene study class turn at the Actors Studio, all fireworks. But names from the 1930s like Mary Astor, Claire Trevor, and Ann Harding were allowed to display all their deepened skill with juicy roles on his show, even as young and obvious sexpots like Jayne Mansfield and Diana Dors started to appear on episodes in the later seasons as if to announce that the "Hitchcock blonde" was near its end as a type and a dream.

Young Method actors like John Cassavetes and Rip Torn were cast as juvenile delinquents, and Robert Altman directed some episodes. Imagine Hitchcock watching Altman movies of the 1970s like *McCabe & Mrs. Miller* (1971) or the movies that Cassavetes made with his wife Gena Rowlands like *A Woman Under the Influence* (1974), where there is so much coloring outside the lines behaviorally. Likely he would have thought them self-indulgent and impractical, and too honest for his own artful hope.

14

The Wrong Man, Vertigo, North by Northwest, Psycho, The Birds, Marnie

From 1957 to 1964, Hitchcock reached the height of his artistry with six films in a row that showed all aspects of his talent, an unprecedented scaling of cinematic peaks. He had found a new leading lady on his TV show named Vera Miles, and he put her under personal contract to him for both film and TV. Edith Head was tasked with designing a wardrobe for Miles for her private life, and Hitchcock expected Miles to live and present herself exactly as he wished at all times. Hitchcock sent her many flowers with ardent notes until she married for a second time to Gordon Scott.

Miles played a disturbed wife in an episode of *Alfred Hitchcock Presents* called "Revenge" where she tells her husband (Ralph Meeker) that she has been attacked and points out the man who did it and says, "That's him!" Meeker kills this man only to have his wife point out another man right afterward and again say, "That's him!" Miles was filmed in a sexually covetous fashion in the early part of this episode, with the camera traveling down her shapely legs.

Hitchcock said that he appreciated Miles's "understatement" as an actress, but she was overdone and screechy in John Ford's *The Searchers* (1956), and just a villainous second lead to Joan Crawford in *Autumn Leaves* (1956), and neither of these performances suggested that she was ready for more serious demands. Miles had worked all through the 1950s and had sometimes been dropped by the studios she was signed to. She had a severe, reproachful look, and she needed careful direction to give the performance she did as the tormented wife in Hitchcock's *The Wrong Man* (1957).

Hitchcock comes out as himself at the beginning of *The Wrong Man*, and he is seen from a distance and in shadow but his unmistakable voice tells his audience that this is a different sort of picture for him. It is a docudrama in black and white shot on real locations in New York and based on the true story of the arrest of Emmanuel "Manny" Balestrero, a Stork Club musician who was arrested for a robbery he didn't commit when employees of an insurance office thought he looked like the man who robbed them.

Balestrero was in his early forties when this happened to him, and the ordeal of the case broke his wife Rose, who had to be committed to an institution. A title card at the end of *The Wrong Man* says that Rose eventually recovered after two years of treatment, but she had relapses through the years, and she and Manny eventually divorced. The real Balestrero was a small man, and he had a furtive, guilty look, a bit like a criminal extra sent from central casting for a lineup. The real thief, Charles James Daniell, looked almost exactly like Balestrero. So appearances can be deceiving.

Balestrero won some money when he sued the city and the insurance company that had put him in jail, and he got some money for the screen rights to his story, but most of this money went to pay for Rose's hospitalization. On January 15, 1957, Balestrero appeared on the TV program *To Tell the Truth*, where a star panel had to guess which of the three candidates on hand was the real Balestrero, and this functioned as a grotesque show-business recapitulation of his ordeal. He wears glasses and seems shy, and he is on *To Tell the Truth* to see if he can win a little money. (He got 500 dollars divided three ways courtesy of Geritol.) In some sense, Balestrero's story is all about money and the need for it and lack of it.

Bernard Herrmann provided a main samba theme and edgy, insistent musical backing to *The Wrong Man*, and Hitchcock cast upright Henry Fonda as Balestrero. Fonda was already an institution of sorts when he made *The Wrong Man*. He had played Lincoln and Tom Joad, and he had supported Bette Davis and gotten laughs with Barbara Stanwyck in *The Lady Eve* (1941). In Fritz Lang's *You Only Live Once* (1937), which is maybe his finest performance, Fonda disclosed a vivid and clean and flame-like anger as an ex-con hounded to death by police. Perhaps Hitchcock had this film in mind as he worked with Fonda here.

Casting is so crucial to the tone of a film. If Fonda's close friend James Stewart had played Manny, *The Wrong Man* would be a very different picture. Just imagine the flares of irritation and the expressions of anger and pain that Stewart would have given the scenes where Manny is taken away from his home by police and subjected to steady questioning and stripped of his whole life and his dignity. Think of the way Stewart played the interrogation scene after Louis Bernard (Daniel Gelin) is killed in *The Man Who Knew Too Much*, and then transplant even a bit of that belligerence to *The Wrong Man*.

The movie would still be as touching and infuriating as it is, but it would be far easier to take.

Fonda has an innocent, repressed, subtle, passive quality that makes *The Wrong Man* a torturous experience to watch. He has a way of both showing and not quite showing what he is thinking and feeling on his face, and this is ideal for this man caught up in a situation he cannot control. Hitchcock wants to make us see that this kind of thing could happen to any of us, for what happens to Manny was his own greatest fear. But the Master kept things light with Fonda on the set. "He was funny all the time," Fonda said. "Hitch would come in and tell a funny story just before he'd say 'Roll 'em' into a serious scene. I loved working with Hitch."

Fate plays dirty tricks in *The Wrong Man*, and there are mistakes made in life, and doppelgangers, too. Trying to establish an alibi, Manny and Rose go to find two men that Manny was playing cards with when he was on vacation, and they discover that *both* of the men have died, and so neither of them can be used as witnesses on his behalf. Now, one of them dying might be expected, but both? It is at this point that Miles's Rose laughs and starts to crack and to feel that the world has it in for her.

What Miles does in *The Wrong Man* is very realistic and not at all flashy. When we first meet Rose, she is a discreetly sexy presence in bed, a young and pretty wife and mother who is deeply in love with her husband and worried about lack of money. As the film and the ordeal go on, Hitchcock has Miles drain her face and voice of all expression, and when Rose begins to talk in a paranoid way, there is none of the expected award-baiting darting of eyes and chewing of scenery. Miles's Rose is just speaking reasonably from her own shut-down perspective, and her eyes stare inward finally and they barely blink. Rose blames herself for the troubles they are facing. She suffers finally from clinical depression and starts to become agoraphobic. And we can't blame her, given what is happening to her.

Hitchcock is at his most pitilessly subjective here, making you feel what it is like to be Manny and Rose, especially in a strange montage effect of different brief shots as she hits him with a hairbrush. The saddest thing of all is that Rose knows that there's something wrong with her after she hits her husband, but she can't get out of the mental rut she is in. *The Wrong Man* is a Kafka-esque trip to hell, with no humor and very little hope.

For the bureaucratic police, Manny is just the most likely person to pin this crime on. Hitchcock switches, very effectively, to a high angle shot when Manny finally starts to defend himself against these police who are

Figure 14.1: Henry Fonda's Manny Balestrero is locked away in *The Wrong Man.*

persecuting him, but it is no use (fig. 14.1). And Hitchcock makes very clear that a lack of money is one of the things that really ruins Manny's chances. Those people we see at the Stork Club under the opening credits wouldn't have such a tough time with the police. They'd be less likely to go along with the tactics the police use on Manny, and surely they'd get themselves a lawyer before saying anything to them.

The women in the insurance office who falsely identify Manny are portrayed as hysterics, basically. This is never underlined, but that's the feeling that comes across, particularly in the performance of Doreen Lang as the main accuser Ann James. Manny is saddled with an incompetent lawyer, and the prosecuting lawyer is seen laughing as Manny holds his rosary in court. To this prosecutor, it's just another case and it doesn't matter. No one cares about human beings and their lives in the bureaucracies that Manny passes through.

François Truffaut criticized the moment when Manny is in jail and Hitchcock has the camera start to revolve in a circle around his head to get across Manny's state of mind, a sort of Ferris wheel shot. Truffaut felt that this was too showy and that the style should have been more strictly realistic, and he spoke here as a lively critic, not a filmmaker. Hitchcock's feelings got hurt by Truffaut's fault finding, and this is the most dramatic and upsetting part of their book together, *Hitchcock/Truffaut*.

When he hears this criticism of the subjective Ferris wheel shot in jail, Hitchcock just shuts down defensively. Truffaut tries to explain himself further and get back on track, but Hitchcock has withdrawn from the discussion. It is clear that *The Wrong Man* was important to him, an experiment in just how far he could go into real newspaper story terror without any leavening.

It is notable that Jean-Luc Godard defended this same Expressionist moment in the jail cell when he reviewed the film: "Through this camera movement, he (Hitchcock) manages to express a purely physical trait: the contraction of the eyelids as Fonda closes them, the force with which they press on the eyeballs for a fraction of a second, creating in the sensory imagination a vertiginous kaleidoscope of abstractions which only an equally extravagant camera movement could evoke successfully." Godard's defense seems slightly fanciful to me because we are made too aware of the camera movement *as* a camera movement rather than as an expression of what Manny is feeling. The hand of the director is showing here in the wrong way, which is what Truffaut objected to. But it could also be argued that the audience needs some stylistic relief at this juncture.

Manny gets a mistrial due to an unruly juror. Back at home, with Rose in her institution, his warm Italian mother tells Manny to pray. Manny looks at a holy picture of Jesus on the wall and does as his mother told him to do, and as he does this the image of his face is superimposed on a street image, and then the real thief (Richard Robbins) seems to step into Manny's face. For a few moments, the outlines of this other face are there, very disturbingly, under Manny's face until Manny's face gradually disappears.

This thief has a sharper, bonier face than Manny, and a hungry look. He is apprehended while trying to rob a store, and it is only because one of the policemen who interrogated Manny notices the resemblance between them that things start to work out. ("I got kids, I didn't hurt anybody!," the thief says in the store.) It is only chance, finally, that halts the ultimate destruction of Manny and his family. Think of how many innocent people are in jail, their lives ruined and taken away from them because of chance. And think hard about how it might be you, because it might be you next.

When Manny goes to the police station, he sees the women who falsely accused him from the insurance office. They start to walk toward the camera, and when they see Manny, they look ashamed. Lang's Ann James is seen very briefly looking helpless and like she wants to say something to Manny, but Hitchcock brutally cuts away from her and we never see these women again.

It would take a different kind of artist to show the suffering of these women after they know what they have done to Manny.

With that quick cutaway from Lang's face, Hitchcock effectively gives her the back of his hand. (Whether or not you think this is a flaw in the film will depend on where you stand on the concept of forgiveness.) Unlike the men involved in the real case, the thief and Fonda really don't look *that* much alike. "Do you realize what you've done to my wife?," Manny asks the thief, and their faces are shot close together. The tone of Fonda's high voice is hard with pain and repressed anger, and the thief looks ashamed.

In *The Wrong Man*, Manny does not express anger against the police or the law or the women in the insurance office. As a religious man, he reserves his anger only for the man who did wrong to begin with, the man who terrorized those women in the office and others as well. The thief says he has a family, but somehow this just sounds like an excuse. That face of his is hawk-like and mean, the opposite of Fonda's face, which is always striving for decency. Manny is not guilty of anything except being poor and being in the wrong place at the wrong time. It is wrong to speak of a transference of guilt in this case and this movie. Guilt never really touches Manny, who remains somehow immaculate in spite of all his trouble.

The film ends with Manny going to see Rose in her institution, and she hears what he says about the thief being caught, but it does not help her. She has been broken, and she knows the score, and this film has shown that a woman who is called mad and locked away can have a perfectly reasonable position about life.

The Wrong Man is about as uncommercial a film as can be imagined. It is a tragic vision of life without relief or hope, and it is an insight into Hitchcock himself. He did not usually drive a car because he didn't want to have to deal with police or get a ticket. In a sense, he felt that people were after him, or could be, just like Rose. This had started with his education under the Jesuits. Punishment was coming, and it didn't have to have a reason.

Does Manny's prayer help him somehow? Maybe. Hitchcock calls it "an ironic coincidence" in his interview with Truffaut that the thief is caught after Manny prays. Everything we see in *The Wrong Man* is too linked to chance to make us believe that the prayer and the exoneration have too much to do with each other.

Just how religious Hitchcock himself was is an open question. He seems to have been more rebellious against his early religious upbringing than anything else, and resentful of being saddled with it, but he could not get rid of the vestiges of Catholicism. Maybe that's why *The Wrong Man* is finally so difficult to analyze from a religious perspective. The religion is present for Manny and for Manny's mother, yet somehow it is neither here nor there. Hitchcock certainly does not scorn it. But what he is trying to say in that dissolve between Manny and the thief where their faces merge remains ambiguous.

Fonda is unerring here. He is stripped down, sober, and concentrated, with that slightly rigid dignity he always had on screen, and with his primly stern and semi-limpid face he "does nothing" splendidly. And Miles is very touching, but her performance was achieved through constant rehearsal with Hitchcock, who took an intense interest in his new leading lady that she found suffocating.

Miles did wardrobe tests for Hitchcock's next movie, *Vertigo* (1958), which he thought could make her a star, but she soon dropped out of that film due to pregnancy, and Hitchcock never forgave her for that. Miles would later appear in *Psycho*, and she returned to her role in that movie in an ill-advised sequel in 1983. She worked a lot after her stint with Hitchcock, but mainly on TV, and she retired in 1995.

Miles refused interviews after retiring, even after Tippi Hedren came forward with stories of sexual harassment and abuse and said that Miles had experienced the same sort of behavior from Hitchcock, the same attempt to possess his leading lady. We will never know. Miles worked hard, and when she was done, she was done. "I tried to please him, but I couldn't," she said of her work with Hitchcock. "I was stubborn, and he wanted someone who could be molded." In the last two episodes she did for Hitchcock's TV show, Miles often tries to look warm and sympathetic but comes across as cold and rather severe instead, and so she feels like a false start for Hitchcock. Miles attempts to lie to the camera in ways that could not finally be creatively used.

In *The Morning After* (1986), Jane Fonda plays an alcoholic washed-up actress named Alex who is involved in a murder and helped by Jeff Bridges's very tolerant Turner. "They were grooming me to be the new Vera Miles," Alex tells Turner. "The new who?," Turner asks, and Alex is furious at this. "I was supposed to replace somebody the audience didn't even know was missing!" Fonda howls in her emphatic, throaty voice, making a joke over an actress who had given such a fine performance opposite her father in *The Wrong Man*. And so Miles, unlike Ingrid Bergman or Grace Kelly, was not a Galatea for Hitchcock but one of those players who make film fans vaguely say, "She was that actress who was in. . . ." This is partly what *Vertigo* is about. But then *Vertigo* is about many things.

Vertigo has become known as Hitchcock's masterpiece. It even knocked *Citizen Kane* from the top spot in the 2012 ranking of the *Sight & Sound* poll of the best films ever made. It was not well received when it was released, and this did hurt Hitchcock's feelings. It is an abstract movie in many ways, surrealist sometimes, and very meta, too, layers within layers within layers. Vera Miles, who was to have played the lead female role, posed for the first painting of Carlotta Valdes, the dead woman who haunts *Vertigo*.

Hitchcock's feminine ideal had been embodied by many actresses now, and he always lost them to another director or another man or to retirement, and always the one he imagined was beyond reach. His feelings about this dream woman of his might best be expressed in the extremely painful Kurt Weill song "It Never Was You."

Hitchcock was made to accept Kim Novak for the lead in *Vertigo*, which didn't please him at first, but this worked out beautifully for him cinematically. Miles had given birth by the time they started shooting *Vertigo*, and so she could have gone into the movie if Hitchcock had really wanted her to, but he stuck with Novak, who had been loaned out by her studio, Columbia.

Novak was the last of the studio-manufactured stars, seemingly created and controlled by Columbia and her vulgar boss Harry Cohn. In Richard Quine's noir *Pushover* (1954), which was her first starring role, Novak seems to hold nothing back from the camera, yet she is enigmatic, too, which makes her an ideal Hitchcock player, just as Henry Fonda was. Novak is catlike and somehow off-center in *Pushover*, always looking into mirrors to check or reassure herself, and she seems cool yet worried, and the camera eats all of this up. Novak is a creature of contrasts. She looks fleshy, solid, and earthy but her manner is ethereal, spacey, anxious, absent.

When Novak was interviewed by Robert Osborne for Turner Classic Movies in 2013, she went through a roller coaster of emotion: up, down, side to side, all over the place. As an older woman, Novak admitted that she was bipolar and that she had suffered sexual abuse as a girl. Her touching anxiety in her movies, which is so deep that it takes on an existential cast, is partly about holding herself together and finding some measure of control. If being filmed made her feel spied on or exploited, Novak seems to fully realize all of the ramifications of her situation as a beautiful woman in movies, and she wants to take full responsibility for it, and this specific tension and drama in her screen persona is very unusual.

The one thing Novak can't do on screen is act tough. She was at her best, as in Otto Preminger's *The Man with the Golden Arm* (1955), when she could express sympathy for others, which feels like a relief for her. It's not too much to say that Novak is a moral presence in her pictures. That's why she has remained so suggestive as an actress, and why her name and image and influence have seemed to grow with time.

Novak did not want to wear the confining gray suit that Edith Head had designed for Vera Miles for *Vertigo*, but Hitchcock insisted on it. She would have preferred to wear white or purple and something flowing that would have let her move more easily, but her very sexy body looks all the more desirable when basically hidden. The tight gray suit *suggests* the contours of her body, and this is very erotic.

Novak liked to have things explained to her in detail, and Hitchcock didn't want to do that, and so there was trouble sometimes in their relationship on the set. But she opens herself up to Hitchcock's sensibility in *Vertigo* in a way that no other player ever did. Novak was an actress who asked a lot of questions, and this is what Hitchcock is always doing, too, but he asked his questions when he worked with his writers before shooting. When he was filming, Hitchcock created the tone and the mood with his presence, but that was usually all.

Hitchcock did tell Novak that he needed her to simplify her effects. "Let me explain to you," Hitchcock told her. "If you put in a lot of redundant expressions on your face, it's like taking a sheet of paper and scribbling all over it—full of scribble, the whole piece of paper. You want to write a sentence for somebody to read. If they can't read it—too much scribble. Much easier to read if the piece of paper is blank. That's what your face ought to be when we need the expression."

Barbara Bel Geddes was cast as Midge, the former girlfriend of James Stewart's Scottie in *Vertigo*, and Midge is an important character here, the unmysterious woman on the sidelines. An Actors Studio alumnus, Bel Geddes had played the Joan Fontaine role in a TV version of *Rebecca* in 1950, and she had been Maggie the Cat for Elia Kazan on stage in *Cat on a Hot Tin Roof*, a woman sexually rejected by her husband.

Bel Geddes was in a notable TV episode for Hitchcock of Roald Dahl's macabre story "Lamb to the Slaughter," in which she seems to be doing a Method sense memory sort of exercise when her policeman husband tells her he is leaving her. Less known but far more complex is "Sybilla," a season six episode of Hitchcock's show directed by Ida Lupino in which Bel Geddes plays a wife so perfect that she allows her own death just to keep on pleasing her difficult husband. "Sybilla" was written by Margaret Manners and Charlotte Armstrong, and its point of view acts as a pioneering and very rich female counterbalance for this program.

Hitchcock didn't want deep-dish psychological delving for *Vertigo*. "Now Barbara, don't act," he told her on the set. Instead, Hitchcock told Bel Geddes to look down, look up, look left. Simple instructions like that. His editing and framing would do the rest. And so it is made to look like Midge's specific feelings for Stewart's Scottie are often kept closely guarded because they are too painful to express openly. Her face is a fortress that does not let us in, and what it says is, "I bet all my chips on one number, and if it doesn't work out finally I have nothing."

Midge is cautious with Scottie, but she makes reckless mistakes with him, too, as when she does a joke painting of herself as Carlotta Valdes. Bel Geddes does the sort of "line reading" acting that Hitchcock often liked where she enjoys the sound of words as she says them more than the sense, and this works well because Midge is always putting on an act for Scottie and protecting herself. And she is always, always failing.

Midge is such a touching character because Hitchcock identifies with her position, too. He was someone who often blundered and failed socially like she does, and he could be as glib as Midge, and like Midge he was somehow removed from the swing of life, or at least sex, yet quietly hopeful on the sidelines for some kind of reprieve.

Hitchcock's daughter Pat, a Midge type if ever there was one, revealed many times through the years that she never really understood *Vertigo* or what her father was getting at. (Pat played Bel Geddes's roommate on an *Alfred Hitchcock Presents* episode called "The Morning of the Bride" {1959}, where their sensible styles and outlooks feel very similar.) Maybe Pat didn't like *Vertigo* because Scottie so rejects Midge. That segment of Hitchcock's audience that only wanted to be entertained have never been much for *Vertigo* either, in spite (or because) of its increasing critical reputation.

Vertigo famously begins with a close-up of an anxious female face, her cheek, her mouth, her eyes, as Bernard Herrmann's score does its Wagnerian work. Who is this woman? She looks meek and compliant, a little mousy, and scared. She is a kind of halfway point between Midge and Novak's Judy Barton, the girl who is hired by Gavin Elster (Tom Helmore) to impersonate his wife Madeleine. The visual swirls in her eye, designed by Saul Bass, have a very surreal effect.

The first sequence is a nightmare based on hanging by a thread and falling and fearing to fall as Scottie chases a man and falls off a roof and is left dangling from a gutter. A policeman tries to help him but this policeman falls himself, and so Scottie is just left hanging there facing his fear of falling. We never learn how he got down.

In the next scene, which is brightly lit, Scottie is talking with Midge, who is designing brassieres. She wears glasses, of course, but there is no sense here that she could take them off and Scottie would notice that she's beautiful. She's just nice old sensible Midge, a good sport and a sexless mother figure. That's what she has become, anyway.

When Scottie politely asks about her love life, Midge says that it is "normal," which doesn't sound too hot. Scottie is wearing a corset for now. Like L. B. Jefferies, he is recovering and out of action, the impotent male, and Stewart's performing style has become more crotchety here. He is only fifty years old, but he seems older. There is very little of the innocent boy he presented to the camera in the 1930s.

Scottie is contacted to do some detective work for Elster, a man that he once knew in college with Midge. Elster has married into the shipbuilding business through his wife Madeleine, and he finds this business dull. He is a closed-off sort of man and Helmore is a closed-off sort of actor, a man you might not notice, off in a corner, with his mustache and nice clothes and his slightly wincing sort of face.

Elster looks like a man who is disappointed and seeking to deflect any kind of attention, and so Scottie can't dismiss him as a crackpot when Elster outlines an unlikely story about his wife Madeleine being possessed by the spirit of her dead grandmother, whose name was Carlotta Valdes. Elster tells this story in a way that makes it seem like he would really prefer not to, and this is very effective. But then Scottie is a fairly credulous type of guy, or wide open for something to fill his own emptiness, which makes him dizzy. Off screen, Hitchcock asked his art director Henry Bumstead to design his own office so that it would look like Elster's office . . .

This is the only Hitchcock picture that really touches on the supernatural as a theme. Even if we have seen *Vertigo* many, many times, it is impossible to not get sucked into the vortex of Scottie's feelings for Madeleine, even when we know she is really a girl named Judy Barton who has been coached by Elster the Pygmalion. In the scenes where Scottie follows Madeleine in his car, *Vertigo* is stripped down to elements of color, movement, and looking and being looked at, and Herrmann's plaintive music with its ominous undertones.

This is a dreamy soft focus world we see, this Madeleine world, and it is about watching a film and falling in love and wanting it to be real, which is what so many of us want when we first fall in love with the movies. Even when we know everything about a movie down to its shooting schedule and budget and technical tricks, we believe at some level that the magic trick is real. And of course nothing delighted Hitchcock more than explaining his tricks with the camera, his devices to make it lie. He wanted us to know it all and then still fall for it, and fall in love. Watch his films again, fall in love again, and know that we are falling in love with a mirage, with a lie.

Carlotta Valdes was a cabaret singer who was thrown over by her rich lover, a cruel man who stole her child away from her, and she fell apart and went mad and finally killed herself. The painting of Carlotta that Madeleine stares at is taunting, weird, insidious. Carlotta somehow resembles Salvador Dalí. It is easy to imagine Dalí's mustache curling up on that provoking face of hers.

Madeleine jumps into the San Francisco Bay so that Scottie can fish her out and undress her totally back at his place, which happens off screen, of course. And so Judy is likely pretending to be unconscious and she is conscious of Scottie undressing her. Does this turn her on at all? Is Judy a bit of a pervert? Hitchcock delighted in having Novak jump into the water for him again and again.

When we hear Madeleine speak, she is like the return of Hitchcock's pseudo-British Joan Fontaine heroines of the early 1940s, and this comes as rather a surprise. Fontaine is not often written about as some kind of ultimate Hitchcock woman, and yet Madeleine and Novak exactly mimic Fontaine's breathless, precious vocal stammering, and this was carefully controlled by Hitchcock. He told Novak exactly how he wanted her to say her lines, down to the breath (or lack of it) and rhythm, and Novak was a very apt pupil.

So Hitchcock's ultimate fantasy woman *sounds* like Joan Fontaine, even if the look he preferred was blonder and bustier. He had told Edith Head to give Grace Kelly falsies for her nightgown scene in *Rear Window*, but Kelly refused to wear them, and so Head worked on the nightgown and fluffed it here and there instead. Hitchcock was pleased with the result and thought that Kelly was wearing "gay deceivers," as Tennessee Williams's Amanda Wingfield memorably calls them. But she wasn't. It was an illusion created by Head, and surely Hitchcock would have appreciated that.

There is no humor in *Vertigo*. When Midge attempts to inject some humor with her own Carlotta painting, she is definitively banished by Scottie, who couldn't be more offended by this demystifying impulse of hers. This scene was difficult to get right, and Hitchcock made Bel Geddes do it many times until he was satisfied. In fact, the Midge-Scottie scenes were all difficult to get just right for Hitchcock, and Bel Geddes struggled to hit the ideal note for him.

The fascinating thing about *Vertigo* is how hard it is to see Judy in Madeleine, though it is clearly Judy speaking through Madeleine when she talks to Scottie right before going up in the bell tower. This has all been arranged by Elster so that he can throw the real Madeleine from the top. What was the real Madeleine like? Did Elster coach Judy to look and sound like his wife, or is Judy's Madeleine also Elster's fantasy woman? Or does Elster remember Scottie well enough to know that Judy's version of Madeleine would be Scottie's fantasy woman?

Questions, questions, questions, all swirling in a vortex. The Madeleine played by Judy and Novak sometimes seems to look at Scottie without really seeing him, or seeing anything, and this can be unnerving. You can see Judy sometimes and then you can't, or you can and you can't at once, and that's the ultimate in Hitchcock acting, like the "vertigo" camera move he devised, pulling back and pressing in at the same time.

Vertigo breaks down after Madeleine's death, and there is a kind of bridge at an inquest where Scottie is treated badly by the coroner, played by Henry Jones, who had been the very nasty Leroy in *The Bad Seed* (1956). (Hitchcock loathes such officials.) Elster keeps his poker face on and lets us see what a remarkably cruel man he is. The plot of *Vertigo* is unlikely when it comes to Elster and his plan, but Hitchcock has no use here for "the plausibles" who might object to this.

Any "plausible" qualms are swept away by a nightmare sequence where Scottie sees cartoon flowers pull apart and Herrmann unnervingly puts castanets on the soundtrack and an actress playing Carlotta stands near Elster and looks at Scottie reproachfully . . . and then there is an open grave and Scottie falling, falling, falling until he wakes up in terror.

Midge tries to help, but there is no use. "Mother's here," she says to Scottie as he stares vacantly in a sanitarium like the one that Rose Balestrero was sent to. "You don't even know I'm here, do you?," Midge asks him, and kisses him. "But I'm here," she says, so quietly that it breaks your heart. Midge is last seen as a lonely figure walking away from the camera, painfully rejected and superfluous, but still there, off somewhere, waiting to pick up the pieces.

Why did Midge break off her engagement with Scottie when they were younger? The look she gives him when he mentions it offers no clues. Maybe she knew when she was young that she could never be what he wanted her to be, and maybe that stung then. But Midge is a pragmatist, and she is capable of real love. Scottie is not capable of that. In an ending Hitchcock shot but then discarded, he showed Midge listening to the radio at her apartment and ready to help Scottie. So Midge might really be waiting or she might not. By the time we get to the ending beyond an ending in this picture, it really doesn't matter one way or another.

Like Mrs. Verloc seeing her dead brother Stevie everywhere at the end of *Sabotage*, Scottie seems to see Madeleine everywhere until he actually *does* see her face, but differently made up, with different dark hair and a wool dress that highlights her figure. She is Judy Barton now, a working girl, a little brassy, and not the brightest, maybe, but a cool customer. Look at Judy's face when she opens the door to her room and sees Scottie standing there. She doesn't flinch or start at all at the sight of him, not even a little bit, as Dr. Murchison does when he sees Gregory Peck's false Dr. Edwardes in *Spellbound*. But then watch how her eyes start to look like those of a trapped animal, and how they seem used to dissimulation in order to survive. Her eyes say, "Please don't hurt me" (fig. 14.2).

Judy is from Salina, Kansas, and she works at I. Magnin department store. She has purple dresses in her wardrobe. Her way of talking is brash . . . but could Judy be exaggerating her own Judy-ness to throw Scottie off the trail? It's enough to make Pirandello dizzy. Scottie begins to direct her, just as Elster did, as Hitchcock is directing Novak, until he finally gets her where he wants her. In despair, Judy says she knows that he is only with her because she reminds him of Madeleine. "And not even that very much," she says, her self-esteem at its lowest point. But Scottie needs Judy to do Madeleine again. "It can't matter to you," he tells her heartlessly.

Judy has her hair dyed blonde again and Scottie gets a gray suit for her like Madeleine used to wear, but Judy won't put the hair up. This is her final attempt to hold on to part of herself. Scottie insists she put it up. And so she comes out of the bathroom with green light behind her as Herrmann's music swells, and Judy is Madeleine again.

Vertigo is partly a movie about acting in that Judy is able to express emotions through the role of Madeleine that she could never express as herself. Like

Figure 14.2: Judy Barton (Kim Novak) does not flinch when she sees Scottie (James Stewart) at her door in *Vertigo*.

many actors, Judy is taking on this role because the people around her don't seem to think that she herself is good enough. Novak's best work is often based around this crucial actorly lack of self-worth, which she always dramatizes so upsettingly, especially in Richard Quine's *Strangers When We Meet* (1960). Hitchcock told no dirty stories to Novak and made no plays for her. "Maybe I wasn't his type," Novak said in an interview in the mid-1990s, a remark that sums up her position in *Vertigo* as both character and actress.

When Scottie and the reborn Madeleine kiss and the camera revolves around them, they seem to go back in time visually as the background behind them changes and Herrmann's music swells and swells some more, and the effect is very much like something that F. W. Murnau used for some of his silent pictures, particularly *Sunrise* (1927), one of the most admired and influential of all movies. This was a difficult shot to get, and Stewart even slipped and fell during one take of it, which necessitated him going to the studio doctor before they finally got it right at the end of the day.

Hitchcock lets these two people have their triumph, this re-creation of a romantic world of their own, and in a way the film could end right here. But we have been shown that Judy was playing Madeleine and that she is a morally compromised person who was talked into a murder plot by Elster, who then abandoned her. Judy feels guilt about this, and nobody feels guilty quite as painfully as Novak does on screen. Why does Judy wear Carlotta's necklace, which gives her crime away to Scottie? A Freudian analyst might say it was because Judy wanted to be caught and punished for her sins.

Scottie drags Judy back up that bell tower, and there is no Herrmann music playing as he does so until he is at the top. Stewart is really tremendous in this scene, particularly when Scottie yells at Judy about keeping the necklace and then stops himself and quietly says, "You shouldn't have been that sentimental," which sounds like mainly an accusation against himself. This really is killer, this line and this line reading by Stewart.

Both Scottie and Judy are morally compromised people, and Hitchcock makes you feel very bad for both of them. For just a moment, Scottie seems to feel Judy's own pain and when he kisses her for the last time, he is kissing Judy. Stewart saw how seriously Hitchcock was taking this movie, and he burrowed deeper and deeper into himself for *Vertigo*. Novak later said that both she and Stewart would have to take a while to compose themselves and come back to reality when their scenes were over.

When they get to the top of the bell tower, Scottie has cured his fear of heights but a nun startles Judy and she falls herself from the tower, maybe because her version of Madeleine must really die the way she had been scripted to by Elster. The ultimate in Method acting. The nun crosses herself and says, "God have mercy." The helpless little gesture that Stewart makes with his hands as he looks down at Judy's body is beyond killer.

Hitchcock had revealed too much of his heart in *Vertigo*, and it was rejected, as it often had been in life. Perhaps he was even starting to lose count of how many times he had been rejected personally, sometimes without even really throwing his hat into the ring or making any sign of his feelings. Many of the American reviews of *Vertigo* were bluntly negative and dismissive. Both Hitchcock and Alma suffered serious illnesses during this most creative period of Hitchcock's career, and perhaps their brushes with mortality were part of what deepened these pictures.

Hitchcock reacted by making his most colorful man-on-the-run chase entertainment, *North by Northwest* (1959), which starred Cary Grant as Roger O. Thornhill, ad man and Manhattan bon vivant. The "O" doesn't stand for anything, just like the "O" initial of Hitchcock's former employer David O. Selznick, but it does mean that Roger gets to carry around matchbooks with the monogram ROT. This movie was made for MGM, and it marked the first and only time that Hitchcock worked there. From a culinary standpoint,

North by Northwest is the tastiest of desserts, all done with fast cutting and in cool colors: grays, creams, and blues, with some red and orange for a finish.

North by Northwest begins with Hitchcock's funniest cameo right at the end of the graphic line credits when he runs up to a Manhattan bus and misses it, which usually gets a roar of laughter when this movie is shown with an audience. Roger is lean and sophisticated in his gray suit, and like Grant himself he "thinks thin." He snaps his fingers at a bar and gets mistaken for a nonexistent secret agent named George Kaplan, at which point Roger is kidnapped and taken to the home of the villainous Phillip Vandamm (James Mason).

There are all kinds of gay or bisexual undercurrents in the scenes between Thornhill and Vandamm, and these are aided or set into motion by the presence of Vandamm's jealous "secretary" Leonard (Martin Landau), who is portrayed outright as gay and in love with his boss. Roger is forcibly intoxicated with bourbon by Vandamm's henchmen, a scene that feels very much like a rape. Both men and women in Hitchcock have to deal with helplessness in the face of physical force, but this helplessness is undercut in *North by Northwest* because Grant plays drunkenness so expertly and so comically, like Fred Astaire doing a little soft shoe.

Grant had reached the same relaxed mastery over his art as Hitchcock had by this point. Contrary, fussy, the pursued fantasy male, the edgy Grant had his own method of working for Hitchcock. "All I have to do is disregard everything he says," Grant told a reporter. "But I guess what's in his mind, and then I do just the opposite. Works every time, and I find it very pleasant." Grant always strove for the unexpected, right up to the knife edge of perversity, which is why he is one of the top Hitchcock actors. Unlike James Stewart, Grant could be difficult. He griped and complained and worried things to death, and to perfection.

Roger's mother Clara (Jessie Royce Landis) is skeptical of her son's story and skeptical of her son in general, but she likely has every right to be. Roger gets himself into further trouble at the United Nations when he is mistaken for an assassin, and so he hides out on one of those trains that Hitchcock loved so much, and there he meets the fine-boned Eve Kendall (Eva Marie Saint). An alumnus of the Actors Studio but blessedly sane and non-neurotic, Saint had won an Oscar for Best Supporting Actress as the leading lady to Marlon Brando in *On the Waterfront* (1954), and she had been a pregnant wife in the working-class drama *A Hatful of Rain* (1957).

Hitchcock sought to rescue Saint from the drab surroundings of her previous films: "No more kitchen sinks for you, Eva Marie," he told her before taking her to Bergdorf Goodman to select the wardrobe for her sexy spy character. The dialogue between Roger and Eve, courtesy of Ernest Lehman, is the ultimate in sophisticated adult flirtation, though one line had to be noticeably post-dubbed when the censors objected to Eve saying, "I never make love on an empty stomach." (This became "discuss love" instead.)

"It's going to be a long night," Eve says. "I don't particularly like the book I started . . . know what I mean?" When they repair back to Eve's cabin, Hitchcock stages another love scene where the lovers are unnaturally bound together, this time moving in a circle against a wall as Roger encircles Eve's head with his hands. The effect of this couldn't be sexier, and it's all about their hands, his taking, hers caressing. She plays with his ear with her elegant fingers just as Alicia does with Devlin in *Notorious*.

The famous scene where Roger is pursued by a crop-dusting plane in broad daylight out in a field has a quality of abstraction, and surprisingly it was shot without storyboards according to Hitchcock scholar Bill Krohn. But Hitchcock was very conscious of his image of control, and so he actually went to the trouble of making up storyboards after the fact to feed the legend that everything he shot was worked out first on paper. In reality, Hitchcock could be more improvisatory than that, and with classic results.

There is barely anywhere for Roger to hide from this plane that is chasing him, and again there is a surreal quality to the images and the rhythm of the editing, and something queerly sexy, too, as Grant runs and falls to the ground and lets his torso lift in the air in his beautifully tailored gray suit. Like so much of Hitchcock, this sequence has the quality of a dream. "The fact is I practice absurdity quite religiously!," Hitchcock told Truffaut.

When Roger finds out that Eve is the mistress of Vandamm (what he doesn't know is that she is a double agent working for the American government), Grant hits Saint with recriminations in a very tense auction scene that plays somewhat like the scene at the racetrack in *Notorious*. Vandamm suggests that Roger should attend the Actors Studio because he is overplaying his various roles, but neither Grant nor Mason is ever anywhere near overplaying, even when Grant is making funny but drunkenly accurate faces when Roger tries to drive a car while under the influence of a bottle of bourbon.

Saint has a very sober face and a serene attitude, but she very stirringly assumes Eve's sexual gleam and avidity, and she gives the film an emotional weight that works very well opposite Grant's sparkle and syncopation. Her playing of anxiety is very well acted and judged, but clearly acted, whereas Novak, who was not a trained actress, is actually anxious in *Vertigo* and somehow manages to control that anxiety and show it to us with her own far less conscious technique. Still and all, Saint is one of the coolest of Hitchcock blondes, and she does a lot to suggest carnal passion roiling away under her ladylike surface.

North by Northwest runs to 136 minutes, which is long for a Hitchcock picture, and MGM executives told Hitchcock to cut a scene between Roger and Eve where she tells him about why she took her job as a double agent and the emptiness of her life before that. Hitchcock insisted on keeping the scene because he knew that it added dimension and pathos to the character of his heroine, and he got his way. He stood up for Eve and for Saint, and the film is all the better for that.

In the movies, villains often live in places that are very up-to-the-minute architecturally, and so it goes for Vandamm, who operates out of a Frank Lloyd Wright house. Roger goes to rescue Eve and drops a matchbook with his initials on the floor of the Vandamm compound. The tension of this sequence tightens and tightens as neat Leonard puts the matchbook in an ashtray without seeing the initials and gets into a lovers' quarrel with Vandamm about Eve, even referencing his "woman's intuition." (Landau, who was pure Actors Studio, is a little too conscious in his role and might "do nothing" more.) Vandamm throws a punch at the camera and then we see Leonard fall back, which is the exact way that Hitchcock filmed the punch between Guy and Bruno in *Strangers on a Train*.

Leonard is the most unappealing and nasty of all Hitchcock's gay characters, as when he sadistically steps on Roger's hand as Roger tries to pull Eve back up onto Mount Rushmore. She dangles there in her orange dress until the police shoot and Leonard's foot falls away in close-up, and it all ends with Roger and Eve back on a train and the train going into a tunnel, a bit of sexual symbolism that Lehman said was entirely Hitchcock's idea. In the trailer for this picture, Hitchcock himself promised that his master lark *North by Northwest* would be "a vacation from all your problems, as it was for me."

Hitchcock had been all set to make a film called *No Bail for the Judge* with Laurence Harvey and John Williams, but when Audrey Hepburn read the script, she turned it down due to a scene where her character was dragged into Hyde Park and nearly raped. Hitchcock never forgave Hepburn for leaving the project, but surely it was best for everyone involved that she did.

Whole books have been written about *Psycho*, which was shot in black and white because color would have been too gory but maybe also because, like *The Wrong Man*, it takes place in a world and milieu where money is a problem for the characters. Hitchcock optioned the novel by Robert Bloch and after a first unsatisfactory script by James Cavanagh, he settled in to work with the young Joseph Stefano, who was in psychoanalysis. Stefano suggested building up the part of Mary Crane, the woman who gets murdered in the shower in the novel, and Hitchcock got excited by this idea. "We could get a star to play that part," he said.

Hitchcock showed *Vertigo* to Stefano. "Here was this incredibly beautiful movie he had made that nobody went to see or said nice things about it," Stefano said. "I told him I thought it was his best film. It brought him to near-tears." Hitchcock filmed Stefano's first draft, which both he and Alma were pleased with. Mary's name was changed to Marion.

Psycho was shot cheaply on the Universal lot, like one of Hitchcock's TV shows with his TV crew. Ever the showman, Hitchcock put out items for the press that he was looking to cast the homicidal mother of Norman Bates, the young man who runs a forsaken hotel off a main road. He cast Janet Leigh as Marion Crane after briefly considering Lana Turner and gave Leigh special billing in the credits, and he cast Anthony Perkins as Norman. (Perkins was paid forty thousand dollars to play Norman, the exact amount that Leigh's Marion Crane steals.) Hitchcock was very happy with both of these actors and worked with them unusually closely, especially Leigh.

Bernard Herrmann's all-string score saws out insistently during Saul Bass's graphic credits, and afterward the camera moves toward a hotel window in drab Phoenix, Arizona. (When he heard Herrmann's *Psycho* score, the miserly Hitchcock immediately doubled his salary, a very unusual thing for him to do.) Hitchcock wanted details of the setting to be correct and suggestive, and so he had sent a crew to take photos of all kinds of Phoenix locations so that he would get the atmosphere and décor just right, and this research really pays off here. The look of *Psycho* is very convincing: southwestern, dry, lonely, with sun glaring.

Leigh's Marion is seen on her back on a hotel room bed in her white bra, her beautiful breasts sticking straight up as her gloating lover Sam (John Gavin) gets dressed. They have just finished another lunchtime assignation, and Marion says that hotels "of this sort" aren't interested in you until your time is up. Clearly she herself is beginning to think that her own time is up.

Sam is a great-looking guy but he's something of a clod, and Hitchcock emphasized this because he was unhappy with Gavin. Frustrated with Gavin's inhibitions, Hitchcock took Leigh aside and asked her to get a rise out of him, and she tried, but this was like Marion trying to get Sam to see her and really address her. Sam is an insensitive guy and mainly interested in sex. He has an ex-wife that he pays alimony to, and so he doesn't have enough money to marry Marion, who longs for a respectable life as a wife and mother and feels like it is getting too late for that. She isn't a natural blonde, and her dark roots show rather plainly.

Marion goes back to her job at a small real estate company where she works as a secretary along with a character played by the director's daughter, Pat Hitchcock, who provides some comic relief when she says her mother gave her tranquilizers on her wedding night. Marion had talked about her dead mother with Sam, and everybody in *Psycho* seems mother dominated. The office Marion works in is not air conditioned, and it's very hot out.

A crass rich man named Cassidy comes into the office waving an envelope with forty thousand dollars in it. Cassidy is portrayed by Frank Albertson, who had played working-class guys in 1930s movies. In those early credits, Albertson had been cute and fun but troublesome, as in *Alice Adams* (1935), where he embarrasses his social-climbing sister Alice (Katharine Hepburn) and ruins a dinner she is giving when it turns out that he has been stealing from his employer.

By 1960 Albertson is unrecognizable as that earlier feckless boy in *Alice Adams*. (Even if you knew his 1930s work, you'd be hard-pressed to guess that this was Albertson as Cassidy in *Psycho*.) Albertson's voice has lowered and roughened, but the mischief is still there in his face, and Cassidy seems very pleased with himself as he zeroes in on Marion, talking about how his daughter has never had an unhappy day, and if unhappiness came he would just buy it off. He's a funny guy, in his way.

Cassidy asks Marion if she has been unhappy, and she answers, "Not inordinately." Marion is the kind of girl who can use a word like "inordinately" in conversation very naturally. How did she wind up in this office and unmarried, and having nooners with a guy like Sam? Her wide eyes look hard at Cassidy, but she also seems to be looking at nothing. It's as if she finds it difficult to make her expected faces of reaction to his jokes.

Marion's prim-looking boss looks on with distaste as Cassidy tries to impress her and pick her up. But she is very distracted, preoccupied. Would she go with Cassidy to Las Vegas and accept some money from him? No. Because she doesn't see herself as "that kind of a girl," even if she does sleep with a man she isn't married to in a hotel. Marion wants to be married. She wants that security.

The way that Leigh plays her, Marion Crane seems like she was the prom queen *and* the class valedictorian, too. She was probably someone who had all the promise in the world in high school and even ruled her high school, but then something happened and she got on a trajectory that led nowhere. We learn later that Marion's mother died unexpectedly, and so she dropped out of college to work to support her sister Lila (Vera Miles), but her sacrifice was unnecessary. Lila is a tough, hard-driving sort of person, and she went to work too and didn't need Marion's help. But Marion is someone who likes to sacrifice herself, even if the sacrifice is unneeded. This is one of her fatal flaws.

Marion has been working at her dead-end job for ten years. She is supposed to put the money from Cassidy in the bank, and this money comes from a real estate deal that sounds pretty shady the way Cassidy tells it. Marion wears a black bra as she stares at the envelope with the forty thousand dollars in it, and she starts to seem hypnotized by it. Even with its harsh and dingy look, *Psycho* still has the quality of a dream, and it operates with dream logic.

When she gets in her car with the money and a suitcase, Marion sees her employer and smiles at him, but he gives her a suspicious, disapproving look, and then Herrmann's music comes crashing in. It almost feels like this look from her employer is what *really* sets Marion on another mistaken course. If he's so suspicious, why not confirm his suspicions? Really anything would be better than going back to that office again, even being a fugitive.

Marion sleeps in her car and gets waylaid by a policeman with sunglasses that shield his eyes, and this policeman has a real sadomasochistic look, like something out of a Kenneth Anger film. He is suspicious of Marion, and he follows her. Is his interest in her sexual? What is going on behind those sunglasses, which have mirrors on the front of the lenses? Marion clumsily exchanges her car for another one and sets off again, and then she starts to hear voices in her head, and imagine various scenarios. She doesn't go mad exactly, but she does become ever-so-slightly unglued. The cutting in these scenes with Marion driving to Sam is very edgy and jumpy, just like she is.

Hitchcock himself sat off camera and read the imaginary dialogue in Marion's head to Leigh to get her facial expressions, which are very exact and suggestive, especially her little smile when she imagines Cassidy's rage when he discovers the theft, and the physical, sexual punishment he expects to inflict on her. This smile almost becomes a smirk, and certainly we might read this look on her face as one that says, "Fuck you, men," even though Marion herself would never think to put it that way. This rebellion against these older men is what's propelling her and guiding her. The most powerful feelings and instincts are often ones that cannot be verbalized.

A downpour of rain makes Marion stop at the Bates Motel, where she meets the lonely and appealing Norman. (If it hadn't rained, she wouldn't have had to stop, and so water, from the sky or from a shower head, is certainly not Marion's friend.) In the Bloch novel, Norman is pudgy, bald, and nondescript, someone you'd not notice, but Perkins's Norman is cute and charming, if excessively nervous. His Norman cannot even bring himself to say the word "bathroom."

There are bird drawings on the walls of the hotel and taxidermy birds in the parlor, and Norman himself is a bird, one of those elongated birds that stand on one rail-thin leg in the shallow water. When he picks a key for Marion (the hotel has twelve rooms and twelve vacancies), Norman's hand hovers for a moment before he picks cabin one. Cabin one is for young girls he has decided to kill. But he does hesitate. Maybe if he'd given her cabin three, she would have lived.

Norman says he can bring her some dinner, and Marion hears his mother yelling at him and repressing him. Mother Bates speaks of ugly appetites, and of Norman's lack of guts. "I wish you could apologize for other people," Norman charmingly tells Marion afterward. He says eating in his office would be too "officious," and at this moment he matches up well with the girl who uses "inordinately" in conversation. Marion and Norman are both somewhat prissy like that, but she is the alpha female in a bind whereas he is the beta male to be pitied rather than a courtly rescuer. They assume the roles that they would have had in high school with each other, alas.

If Norman weren't damaged and mad, he might have been a good match for Marion, or he might have been better than Sam, anyway. But high-quality girls like Marion are often wasted on the Sams of this world, and Hitchcock certainly understands that. There is a shot of Marion outside of the office from Norman's point of view where her physical smallness in relation to Norman is deliberately emphasized, and yet she seems to loom over him intimidatingly, and this is a very striking Hitchcockian contrast. For a brief moment, Marion is Mother for him, demanding, "Well, boy?"

In the long conversation that Marion and Norman have over sandwiches in his parlor, she listens to him attentively but often condescendingly, and a bit carelessly (that's her prom queen side). "You've never had an empty moment in your whole life, have you?," Norman asks her, with his pained smile. And she responds quietly, "Only my share." This response says a lot for her grace and for her equanimity.

They connect here, very briefly. Marion listens to Norman as closely as she possibly can for a while. But she can't know who and what she is dealing with. Few people in 1960 could have known that there were people like Norman in this world. We all know now, but surface charm can be deceptive. Norman is young and attractive, and he clearly has a sweet side.

Marion is a very bright person, brainy, even, but her comprehension of this situation only goes so far. She has been trained to face facts and to put people into categories, and so when she starts to put Norman in a category, he bristles. Marion is trying to be kind to him, but in an impersonal way. This is really admirable of her, in a sense, but all Norman can feel is the effort of it, which feels to him like falseness. It is a 1950s falseness he is reacting to, and he is being unfair to Marion just as she is only going so far with him and not far enough. But of course only a trained therapist could even begin to reach the brutalized Norman, who is so damaged that he becomes possessed by the woman who once tore him to pieces while also making him a kind of lover.

Marion really does try with Norman in this scene. Is this a mistake? She strikes a nerve when she says maybe he could get his mother "put someplace." He reacts angrily to this, and the anger feels out of proportion, unreasonable. He knows what the inside of a madhouse is like, he tells her, and Marion shuts down. She realizes instinctively now that Norman is out of the ordinary and outside her ken, but she doesn't have the social tools to deal with that. "I meant well," Marion tells Norman. But he isn't buying that, and finally he smiles at her, dismissing her. And this is very unfair of him. Thus ends one of the most tragic scenes of miscommunication in movies, very sensitively played by both Leigh and Perkins.

Norman spies on Marion through a peephole on the wall while she undresses to shower in the bathroom of cabin one. And then comes the famous murder in the shower, which took seven days to film. Leigh shows us the relief that Marion feels as she showers, and how the water cleanses her. It is a sensual experience, too, this water. Marion has decided to go back and return the money. She believes the mistake she made has ended and that she has woken up from her dream, and right at that moment the shower curtain is pulled aside and a dark face is behind the water, and Marion is being stabbed over and over again. A nude body double was used for Leigh for some shots in the shower scene, and she herself wore a moleskin covering.

Hitchcock gives Leigh's Marion a moment of life after "Mother" leaves the bathroom with her bloody knife. Her face is stunned and almost blank but not quite, and she slowly reaches out and up with her right hand. This shot of her reaching out before dying is annihilatingly sad, and it isn't too much to say that it carries a very heavy weight outside of what has happened to Marion herself.

Psycho was a huge hit and a thrill ride for its first audience, who screamed and carried on in the dark. Of course they were still screaming during this shot as Marion reaches out with her hand to us and to life and to God, and Hitchcock quickly cuts away from it to Marion's hand clutching the shower curtain in close-up before she falls. But this reaching out of Marion's hand right before she dies is the most heartbreaking physical gesture in all of Hitchcock.

Leigh needed twenty or so takes for the shot of Marion's dead face on the floor because she had a hard time not reacting to the water dripping from her face. The camera moves out and her wide-open eye is a vortex just as the blood (really chocolate sauce) going down the shower drain is a vortex. Fear of falling is part of this unexpected murder, falling into an abyss, extinction. Leigh herself said that she never took a shower again after filming *Psycho*, only baths.

Norman cleans up the murder, which Hitchcock lingers over in detail because he needs to give his audience time to recover, and Norman eats candy corn as he watches Marion's car sink into a swamp, as if he's at a movie and just watching the show. When it finally sinks, he smiles. Norman is always scariest when he smiles.

It was Perkins's idea that Norman eat candy, and Hitchcock welcomed Perkins's contributions and enthusiasm for the role, even letting him rewrite some of his lines. Hitchcock was also intrigued by the spindly, sexy, weird Perkins himself, who was gay but unhappy with that and trying to be straight by the early 1970s.

Hitchcock told Stefano in a confidential voice that Perkins was "excessively shy around women," and so he let Perkins fly to New York to start rehearsing a musical called *Greenwillow* rather than putting him in Mother drag to shoot the shower scene. Hitchcock's explanation of this to Stefano was that dealing with a naked girl would have made Perkins uncomfortable. "It just wouldn't be very nice," Hitchcock told Stefano.

Norman Bates is not gay but a frustrated heterosexual, and that's important to the plot of the film. Norman would like to sleep with Marion, not Sam or the investigator Arbogast (Martin Balsam), who becomes another victim of "Mother" and her knife, but Norman does stammer much like Brandon in *Rope*, and so this sends us mixed signals.

A stuntwoman named Margo Epper played Mother for the shower scene, and her shots had to be redone when her face was too visible behind the water. The makeup man Jack Barron blackened Epper's face to make it less visible and shadowy so that it almost looks like a shrunken head that's been buried in the earth and dug up. This is exactly what "Mother" should look like.

Hitchcock used three performers for Mother's voice. Perkins suggested recording Mother Bates's lines himself since Norman is really just imagining conversations with a dead woman, but this didn't work because Hitchcock worried that the audience might guess the killer was Perkins from the start, and then Perkins suggested his friend Paul Jasmin could record the lines for Mother.

Jasmin was a young actor who was noted for doing a sort of shrewish Marjorie Main-type female character named Eunice Ayers at parties, and so Hitchcock had Jasmin do a lot of the lines we hear from Mother when she is yelling at Norman, but he blended them a bit with the voices of two other actresses, Jeanette Nolan and Virginia Gregg. In the last scene when Norman has been caught and his mother is speaking to him only in his mind, Hitchcock used mostly Gregg's voice and no Jasmin. (The very tall, thin, blonde Gregg had made several appearances on Hitchcock's television show.)

Marion's sister Lila and Sam come on to resolve the mystery, and Hitchcock is not at all interested in either of them. "Patience doesn't run in my family, Sam," Lila says, but surely Marion had to cultivate patience in those ten years in that office. Hitchcock cut some dialogue that Stefano had written where Lila talked about Marion to Sam, for they are there only to wrap things up.

Lila enters the Bates house and sees Mother's fussily furnished Victorian room and then Norman's childlike bedroom, where there are still toys and a worn stuffed rabbit with a sad and angry expression (fig. 14.3). There is a record of Beethoven's third Eroica symphony on Norman's phonograph, which has sections that sound a lot like Herrmann's jabbing score for strings for *Psycho*, and Lila also seems to discover a pornographic book.

Lila goes downstairs to the fruit cellar ("Ya think I'm fruity, huh?," Jasmin's Mother voice had said to Norman) and sees Mrs. Bates from behind in a chair. For some reason the chair turns all the way around when she touches

Figure 14.3: The stuffed rabbit on the bed of Norman Bates (Anthony Perkins) in *Psycho*.

it (does it turn this way by supernatural force?) and we see that Mother is a skeleton. Lila screams and knocks against the bare light bulb in the fruit cellar and Miles's face registers that Mother is actually Norman in drag with a knife. "I-I-I-I-I-I am *Norma* Bates!," he cries hoarsely before Sam gets the knife away from him.

Hitchcock didn't much like the explanation scene that a psychiatrist (Simon Oakland) gives about Norman's condition, though it does allow Sam to cry, "Why was he . . . dressed like that?" in a way that shows his blunt lack of imagination once again and also his male heterosexual disgust and fear.

There is a subtle jolt of sick humor here when Oakland's explainer gets a little too caught up in how Norman was "aroused" by Marion and the look on Lila's semi-confused face says, "Umm . . . could we get back to the point?" We learn that Norman had a close and incestuous bond with his mother and that he killed her and her lover ten years ago . . . just when Marion started working in that office. And he has killed two other girls who were unlucky enough to stop at the Bates Motel and get assigned cabin one.

Perkins carries the last scene as Gregg's Mother voice talks to him on the soundtrack, and his face briefly becomes a skull before Hitchcock cuts to Marion's car being pulled out of the swamp. Audiences were not allowed in to *Psycho* after it had started, and this was a new way of doing things because customers used to come in and out of movies whenever they wanted to.

Psycho was a real coup for Hitchcock and the height of his commercial success, and his critical reputation was starting to rise after years of dismissal and skepticism. He took time and trouble with his next project, *The Birds* (1963), which required intricate special effects, and for this movie he found a new leading lady.

One day, Hitchcock spotted an attractive blonde in a TV commercial where boys whistled at her, which made her turn around and look pleased. This model was Tippi Hedren, who had grown up in poverty during the Depression and had sustained a modeling career for ten years. She was thirty by 1960 and a single mother, and her modeling days were starting to wane. Hedren was surprised and happy at first when Hitchcock signed her to a personal contract and gave her the lead role of Melanie Daniels in *The Birds*.

There is no score in *The Birds*, only unsettling electronic bird sounds supervised by Bernard Herrmann, and Hitchcock is back to using those ominous fades to black that last a few moments between certain scenes here. He handles Hedren very carefully in most of *The Birds*, playing Svengali and allowing her room to subtly play various moods.

In the credits, Hitchcock had his discovery billed as "Tippi" Hedren, wanting to set her apart and make a special star of her, and he even re-creates the commercial that had first caught his eye as Melanie walks down a San Francisco street and looks back after a little boy whistles at her. She seems pleased, just as Hedren did in the commercial, but this complacent pleasure in her own allure is swiftly followed by Melanie noticing some birds gathering overhead in a somewhat unnatural way.

So Melanie's smile transitions to a foreboding look, in the "negative acting" sense that Hitchcock always wanted. Smiles always fall away from faces in Hitchcock's movies, but he never did the opposite and had a worried person suddenly smile. That kind of "positive" acting was for those with a more positive outlook, or those like Doris Day who didn't want to face the negative.

In the early 1960s, women were wearing their hair in increasingly elaborate beehives, and so Hitchcock's Hedren pictures *The Birds* and *Marnie* get to be his ultimate female hair movies. Hedren herself called this hairstyle she wears in *The Birds* "the French roll," and what's neat about this look is that every time a bird pecks Melanie, her hairdo can fall apart in a picturesque way and then afterward she can put it right back up again.

This hair is deceptive, too, because it looks like it's a complicated creation that needs a lot of volume in back but when Hedren's Melanie has her hair down, we can see that it's fairly short; it is simply cut in such a way that it can be swept up to look voluminous. And it's maybe not going too far to say that Hedren's French roll in *The Birds* represents the pleasures of civilization in its impractical and even decadent phase and that the birds themselves are the original Mother Bates, a Mother Nature that cares not one whit for living creatures.

The daughter of a newspaper tycoon, Melanie Daniels is a playgirl and practical joker, spoiled and overconfident yet insecure and rudderless. She has a run-in with Mitch Brenner (Rod Taylor) in a bird shop in San Francisco, and she follows him to his home in Bodega Bay, where the first bird attacks her twenty-five minutes into the film.

Mitch's possessive mother Lydia (Jessica Tandy) has a hairstyle that looks a lot like Melanie's, only gray rather than blonde, and we learn that Mitch is a lawyer who is defending a man who shot his wife six times in the head for changing the TV channel. As played by Taylor, Mitch is the simplest and most macho guy in all of Hitchcock, even if the situations and the script tell us that he must have some issues. Put Anthony Perkins into the Mitch part and you have an entirely different film.

Melanie and Mitch spar with each other, and Hitchcock made certain to add a scene he wrote himself where Melanie talks about how her mother abandoned her. Hedren has narrow eyes that are somewhat hidden by overelaborate false eyelashes, but she has a very expressive voice that is unmistakable in tone, sandy and tart and brittle just like her manner. The voice and the way she tilts her head make Melanie seem neurotic yet controlled, very stylish on the surface but a mess underneath. She is a very unaware sort of person, and she sounds blithe and clueless when she brags to Mitch about her charity work. Melanie is Hitchcock's glib side, and he identifies with her because Melanie is lost, but it takes an outside catastrophe to bring that fully to the surface.

The dark-haired schoolteacher Annie Hayworth (Suzanne Pleshette) is supposedly still carrying a torch for Mitch even though she gives off strong lesbian vibes in her scenes with Melanie. There is a lot going on in the non-attack scenes in *The Birds*, a lot of subtext and hints that keep us on edge as the attack scenes themselves get increasingly violent, none more so than when Lydia discovers the aftermath of an attack on a farmer named Dan Fawcett.

The critic Dave Kehr has wondered whether Lydia was having an affair with Fawcett. (Lydia does start a bit when his name is mentioned as she speaks on the phone.) When Lydia enters Fawcett's house, she turns and sees that the teacups hanging on a sideboard are broken, a surreal image that answers an image all the way back in Hitchcock's first movie *The Pleasure Garden* where a sideboard with hanging teacups is a symbol of a happy home. Lydia takes in a disaster area when she looks into Dan's bedroom, and when she looks further inside Hitchcock has his camera zoom into three fast cuts to Dan's gouged-out eyes to represent the panicked way that Lydia would see this, one of his scariest subjective shots.

Tandy was an outstanding actress who had originated Blanche DuBois in *A Streetcar Named Desire* on stage, but she had never been given much of a chance in movies before *The Birds*. (She had offered several very sensitive performances on Hitchcock's TV show in the late 1950s.) Fine as Tandy is, Hitchcock knew that no actress could sustain a reaction to what Lydia sees in Dan's bedroom. "I never show her face," Hitchcock said. "I knew I couldn't. I knew very well I could never get an expression strong enough." And so Hitchcock cuts quickly to just Lydia's shoulder moving away from the door before he allows Tandy to do a silent scream outside the farm.

Lydia, as Tandy plays her, has an over-explicit face and she cannot hide her feelings. Like Blanche DuBois, Lydia is highly strung and she wants so much to be able to relax and to rest. She is weak and she knows it, and Tandy makes all of this quite touching as Hitchcock connects Lydia in her bedroom with Hedren's Melanie through careful and sensitive editing, cutting to Hedren's face just before Tandy finishes a line.

The writing for Lydia by screenwriter Evan Hunter is very fine, or maybe Tandy just makes it seem that way because really first-rate actors can do that. Tandy was soulful like Peggy Ashcroft was in *The 39 Steps*, and so she makes a story within the story of *The Birds* until Lydia's story is allowed to take over at the very end.

Melanie is looking for the mother who abandoned her, and in some ways, *The Birds* is a love story between Melanie and Lydia, who is a very insecure and clinging mother. The bird attacks get worse and worse, and there is a long sequence in a diner where different types of people express their points of view, including an elderly English ornithologist named Mrs. Bundy (Ethel Griffies) who will not believe that birds can attack until she sees it with her own eyes. Hitchcock only shows the back of Mrs. Bundy's anguished head after she has seen a bird attack, and he cuts away from her quickly in respect for her feelings.

The decision to have Hedren's reaction to a fire spreading on gasoline represented by three static shots of her face "arranged" into an expression of panic is a strange one, but consistent with what Hitchcock wanted from his

Galatea here: only one emotion at a time. In this picture he sought strong, definite feelings from his players, and so Hitchcock uses Doreen Lang again (she gets special "and" billing in the credits) as a hysterical mother who instinctively feels that it is Melanie's presence in Bodega Bay that has somehow caused the bird attacks. "I think you're evil, evil!" this mother cries in close-up, so that Melanie has to slap her. Lang insisted that Hedren really slap her here, which aids the intensity of the scene.

The emotional upsets and tensions in *The Birds* run very deep, yet they exist hand in glove with a kind of harsh Pop Art and nearly camp element that was a new quality in Hitchcock. This is a Hitchcock movie that does *not* seem dreamlike but situated in a hostile world made up of primary colors, mainly green and red. There is ample evidence in interviews and press releases of this time that Hitchcock wanted to compete with the popular new existential art films from Europe, which is partly why he insisted on an ending to *The Birds* where nothing is resolved. Hitchcock told Peter Bogdanovich that he meant *The Birds* as a movie about "the dangers of complacency," stating one of his major themes outright, which was not usually his dandyish, epigrammatic way in interviews.

In the last scenes in *The Birds* where the surviving characters are barricaded in the Brenner house, Hitchcock had a drummer on the set insistently drumming, drumming, drumming to drive his cast to the proper emotional level of fear. Tandy reaches a peak of hysteria when Lydia yells at Mitch that is amplified by a swift dolly shot in and then a quick cut to Lydia's equally hysterical young daughter Cathy (Veronica Cartwright) that gives this conflict a really upsetting family-quarrel feeling that dries up as quickly as it erupts.

In one of the most poetic shots in all of Hitchcock's work, he has Melanie sitting with her legs folded on a couch as we hear the birds coming and she moves helplessly back against a lamp shade as if sensing an attack by a ghost, or by an immense nothingness. (Hitchcock later said that he based this image on his own experience of what he felt like during an air raid.) Melanie goes upstairs finally to investigate the attic, and Hedren asked Hitchcock why Melanie does this. "Because I tell you to do it," he told her.

And so for a week, Hedren had live birds thrown at her until one of them went for her eye and she broke down crying and said she could do no more. (She was under a doctor's care for a week afterward.) Melanie is reduced to shocked semi-catatonia by this attack, where she is nearly cut to death in quick, slashing shots. But she survives, and she finally gets the mother she always wanted in Lydia.

Hunter finished his script for *The Birds* so that the remaining characters get away, with manly Mitch being hopeful about their chances. Hitchcock toyed with the idea of them getting to San Francisco and then seeing that the whole of the Golden Gate Bridge is covered in birds, but this was too complicated an effect to achieve, and so he settled on a state of suspension, the family driving away into an uncertain fate, for it was an apocalyptic time, the early 1960s. No one knew what might happen if atomic warfare broke out between America and Russia. That uranium in those bottles in *Notorious* was more significant than Hitchcock knew or allowed. What had interested him there was the tortured love story.

Hitchcock attempted to control Hedren off the set, having her followed and wanting to know where she was at all times. According to Hedren, when they were in the back of a car that was pulling up to some of their coworkers in a parking lot, Hitchcock attempted to embrace her and she had to push him off. This scene is bungled in the very poor 2012 TV movie *The Girl* because the car isn't pulling in to a lot and coworkers aren't looking on.

The point of Hedren's story was that Hitchcock wanted people to *think* that he was involved with her. Again according to Hedren, Alma apologized to her for what she was going through with Hitchcock. Alma had always been a mother figure and a final authority, someone Hitchcock both feared and needed, but when it came to this last obsession with an actress, Alma seems to have had her hands tied.

Hitchcock had wanted Grace Kelly to return to the screen for *Marnie* (1964), and she was interested but the people of Monaco objected, and so she had to turn him down. "After all, it was only a movie," Hitchcock wrote Kelly, but of course movies were his life. The difficult lead role in *Marnie* went to Hedren, whose relations with Hitchcock deteriorated badly during the shoot.

She had shown in *The Birds* that she was very good at evoking states of extreme emotional trauma, and this would be put to the test in *Marnie*. In the trailer for that film, Hitchcock called it "a sex mystery . . . if one used such words." Hitchcock told Hedren that he was having a recurring dream where she said, "Hitch, I love you . . . I'll always love you." Hedren replied, "But it was a dream, just a dream," and excused herself from his presence. He was in love with her, or obsessed with her, and pressure was building on him and also on Hedren.

Joseph Stefano did a first draft of a script for *Marnie*, but he didn't understand the story at all and thought that Marnie herself was unsympathetic. Evan Hunter tried to write a script next, changing a jealous male character into a female character named Lil, but he refused to write the rape scene of Marnie by the rich Mark Rutland, who has coerced her into marrying him. "I knew every woman in the audience would hate him," Hunter said.

But Hitchcock was only interested in this scene, according to Hunter, and so Jay Presson Allen was hired to do a third script. Later Allen would remark on her own "insensitivity" to the issue of the marital rape. "I did not define it as rape, and Hitch never used the word 'rape' with me," Allen said. It was just "a trying marital situation," she said. The dialogue in *Marnie* has a British feeling and syntax a lot of the time, even though Allen was born in Texas and the film is set in America.

When they cast Sean Connery as Mark, Allen thought that his star charisma might redeem Mark's behavior in the rape scene, and Hedren herself told Hitchcock that it would be difficult to reject Connery and not be attracted to him throughout the film, to which Hitchcock told her, "It's called acting, my dear." The brunette Diane Baker was cast as Lil, and she remembered very external direction from Hitchcock. There were times when he even molded her face with his hands into exactly the expression he wanted. Baker had been chewing scenery pretty hard opposite Joan Crawford in the TV film *Della* (1964) and *Strait-Jacket* (1964), but Hitchcock would require a different approach.

When Lil was supposed to react to the robbed businessman Strutt (Martin Gabel) at a party, Hitchcock told Baker that if she started the scene with a serious face and then tried to react, the effect would be grotesque. It would be much better, he said, if she started with a smile and then let the smile drain away from her face. Baker also remembered that Hitchcock told Louise Lorimer, who was playing Mrs. Strutt, to "smile like you have a mouth full of broken china." Louise Latham was cast as Marnie's mother, an important role, and Hitchcock was pleased with her even though her approach to her part was very Actors Studio in its deep-dish psychological detail.

Marnie was the last time that a Bernard Herrmann score was used for a Hitchcock film, and it is one of Herrmann's very best scores for Hitchcock: alarmed, roiling, yearning. After the credits, we see a very vaginal looking yellow bag being carried under the arm of a dark-haired woman walking slowly along a deserted railway platform. The amount of $9,967 has been taken from the squat businessman Strutt by a girl he hired called Marion Holland. In a scene in Strutt's office, his secretary and the cops stifle their laughter as he remembers Marion's physical allure in detail. His hot need for vengeance against her for stealing from him has an obvious sexual basis.

Marion is actually Hedren's Marnie, who has an orderly habit of changing her name and hair color and stealing from men like Strutt. As Marnie goes to her hotel room, Hitchcock himself comes out of one room and looks directly at the camera, as he did on his TV show. We see Marnie working the black dye out of her hair in the bathroom sink and then Herrmann's music swells as Hedren's lifts her wet blonde hair and we see her proud, emotionally cloudy face in close-up, which to Hitchcock is as sexy as Rita Hayworth flipping her hair in her introductory close-up in *Gilda* (1946). Everything in *Marnie* is fetishized, from Marnie's false Social Security cards to a key that she tosses down a grate.

Marnie only relaxes when she is riding her beloved horse Forio, which Hitchcock shows us by having Hedren pretend to ride against rear projection, and this is as obvious as the matte painting of a boat next to the Baltimore apartment of Marnie's mother Bernice. Some of Hitchcock's crew were unhappy with this painting of the boat and told him that they could make it more lifelike and more detailed and less fake looking, but Hitchcock said it was fine as it was.

Hedren's hair, which was done by Alexandre of Paris, is even more elaborate in *Marnie*, and her physical splendor contrasts with the drab furnishings in Bernice's home, especially the dirty wallpaper near the staircase. Once again, Hedren has mother issues in a Hitchcock movie, and this time she is at war with a little girl named Jessie (Kimberly Beck) who is doted on by Bernice.

Marnie feels that her mother doesn't love her because Bernice flinches when Marnie touches her and moralizes a lot. "Men and a good name don't go together," Bernice says. Marnie doesn't understand her mother's coolness toward her, and she also doesn't understand why the color red sets her off into panic attacks, which Hitchcock expresses through red flashes that fill up the whole screen. The relationship between Marnie and her mother and the little girl Jessie is very complex, and troublingly unusual. It feels like Marnie is "keeping" her mother like a man would keep a mistress, and Marnie even references this in dialogue. The whole of *Marnie* is thick with sublimated urges and feelings.

Connery's Mark is written in a partly indirect Cary Grant-like way at first, but of course Connery is a very different and more direct screen presence. Mark is pursuing Marnie, tracking her even, because her thievery turns him on, and Grant was the pursued in his movies, not the pursuer. Marnie herself seems to derive a sexual satisfaction from stealing, which to her is putting men in their place. So, like Marion Crane, her stealing has a "fuck you, men" aspect that Marnie *could* verbalize, but it would most likely be, "Men are filthy pigs," which she does actually say in a later scene.

Mark's wife died at age twenty-nine, and his interest in Marnie has its tender, paternal side. It turns out that thunderstorms scare Marnie, too, which is expressed in a rigorously composed and edited and acted sequence in Mark's office where a tree comes crashing through a window. We see Mark kiss Marnie in extreme close-up, and this is both loving on his part and unfairly taking advantage of her situation, just as the tree that comes through Mark's window is both similar to the Mother Nature attacks of *The Birds* and phallic like the men Marnie fears and hates. This is all a rich brew, and it is maybe too rich for some. That tree also destroys a vase that belonged to Mark's dead wife, which is probably one symbol too many.

Marnie steals from Mark in a suspenseful sequence where she clearly takes a smirking sexual satisfaction in the stealing, a real pleasure. She creeps out of the office as a woman cleans up, and this woman is played by the maid from *Rope*, Edith Evanson. One of Marnie's shoes falls out of her pocket and hits the floor with a thud, but the cleaning woman doesn't react because it turns out that she is hard of hearing.

Hedren plays Marnie as if she is feeling her way through rooms in a house in the dark, and she really gets across how lost in a maze this woman is. She doesn't do line readings, like many Hitchcock actors do. (Diane Baker does them here in the "words as fun sounds" way of Barbara Bel Geddes in *Vertigo.*) When she talks as Marnie, Hedren is searching for exactly the right word to express what she wants to express, and she has a trapped kind of dignity and panic that is very touching. Mark calls Marnie "a cold, practiced little Method actress of a liar," but when she lies it doesn't feel either cold or practiced. Marnie is a certain kind of Method actress of this time, though, in that she is such a mess that you wouldn't know where to begin to start cleaning her up.

Marnie becomes a proto-Rainer Werner Fassbinder sort of story in which Mark is supposedly trying to help Marnie but is actually imprisoning her, and since Marnie's trouble began with violent men, there is a nasty irony in the very male way he catches her in order, he says, to help her. He *is* trying to help her, but he is also an exploitative bastard, and at one point Mark says he has to repress the urge to "beat the hell" out of her.

In an infamous *Playboy* interview from 1965, Connery said, "I don't think there is anything particularly wrong about hitting a woman—although

I don't recommend doing it in the same way that you'd hit a man. An open-handed slap is justified—if all other alternatives fail and there has been plenty of warning. If a woman is a bitch, or hysterical, or bloody-minded continually, then I'd do it." Connery, like Rod Taylor, is a very macho guy, but with a different kind of edge, and *Marnie* would be a lot easier to take sometimes if the actor playing Mark were softer and more conflicted.

On their honeymoon cruise, Marnie desperately shrinks from Mark. She says that getting married is "degrading, animal," but he can't control himself or have any pity for her condition, which is what Hunter so objected to. Hedren cries, "No!" like an outraged little girl when Mark pulls Marnie's nightgown down, and then her face becomes frozen. Like many victims of abuse, Marnie leaves her body when Mark takes her sexually and she goes somewhere else, but the look on her face, beneath the protective ice, is very angry.

Hedren's stories in recent years describe Hitchcock descending to the level of a villain in an old stage melodrama on the set of *Marnie*, practically twirling his mustache as he demanded sexual access to her. When Hedren reacted with outrage to this demand, as Marnie does, Hitchcock supposedly became Uncle Charlie in *Shadow of a Doubt*, or a heavy in one of the old penny dreadfuls he read as a boy, reminding her that she had a child to support and parents who were getting on in years. But of course Hitchcock's movie villains had usually been very sympathetic and his heroes were often unappealing.

This sexual demand from Hitchcock, according to latter-day Hedren interviews, occurred right as they were shooting Marnie's attempted suicide scene in the pool of a large ship. The attempted suicide in the pool is the lowest point for Hedren's Marnie in the film, a cry for help. When Sean Connery's Mark asks her why she didn't just jump in the ocean, Marnie feebly says that she didn't want to "feed the damn fish."

Did Hitchcock choose to make his demand on Hedren before shooting this particular scene for a reason? Had he been planning it, or was it a spur-of-the-moment lurch in the dark aided by drink? He was drinking heavily during the day now. Both his father and his brother William had been heavy drinkers, and Hitchcock often followed suit. He was known for planning everything in detail on his films and in life, but sometimes he left things to chance. Marnie tries to kill herself, but in the ship's pool rather than the ocean, and so maybe she wanted a chance still to be saved.

In her 2016 memoir *Tippi*, Hedren says that Hitchcock grabbed her and "put his hands on me" during this encounter, which had never been a part of her story before. But then she writes, "I've never gone into detail about this and I never will." Feeding and protecting the lions at her Shambala Preserve in California was Hedren's all-consuming aim in the second half of her long life, and it was an expensive calling, and so doling out information like this about her experience with Hitchcock was a way of gaining money for her animals, which is ironic given the overall theme of *The Birds*.

Marnie only really loves her horse Forio, which she has to put down after he is injured. Connery's Mark Rutland says he trained a South American cat, a jaguarondi, and he claims he made this wild animal "trust" him, so it is not too much to say that Hedren moved on from playing Marnie to play an aspect of Mark in life. She and her husband Noel Marshall put their family and a crew in danger to film *Roar* (1981) where lions and tigers roam freely with humans. (Hitchcock once did an outro for the TV episode "Together" next to a large lion, and he does not flinch or crack his façade of control even when this lion turns and looks at him curiously.)

Hitchcock told Hedren that he would destroy the career he was trying to give her, and he did keep her under contract and idle in the mid-1960s, but of course she wouldn't have had any career to begin with without him. Based on the interviews she gave in this period, Hedren wanted to star in features after she was introduced in these two Hitchcock films, but time was of the essence for her, and any momentum she had was gone by the time she turned forty in 1970. She worked a lot after that, but rarely in anything notable. Out of her ordeal, Hedren got a name as an actress and two classic films that she could dine out on and introduce for the rest of her life, a kind of devil's bargain in the long run.

"That man was physically so unattractive," Hedren said in 2012. "I think to have a mind that thought of himself as an attractive, romantic man and then to wake up in the morning and look at that face and that body was tough." As time went on, Hedren's tales about Hitchcock got more and more uncharitable. That's what happens as decades go by and you are asked to cover the same ground over and over again. Her outrage went out in many directions, but she did sometimes stop to express some understanding. "This poor man was desperate for something he never had in his lifetime," Hedren said in 2007.

Baker was also sexually harassed by Hitchcock during the making of *Marnie*, so it seems clear that Hitchcock had reached a crisis point. He had spent decades as a reserved man who was above all that, supposedly, but now something had changed and he was acting out in desperation because time was slipping away from him. Women had tolerated and teased him and none of them had ever found him attractive, and now he must have felt that he had to take drastic action before he died without having experienced any of the romantic and sexual passion that had been sublimated into his work. The result was disastrous, mean, blundering, and sad.

Hedren called Hitchcock a "fat pig" on the set of *Marnie* in front of the cast and crew, a story that often goes missing in contemporary Hedren-Hitchcock coverage, and this was the final straw for him. "She did what no one is permitted to do," Hitchcock told biographer John Russell Taylor. "She referred to my weight."

This on-set row came after Hitchcock refused to allow Hedren to fly to New York to pick up an award because he felt it would ruin her concentration on her difficult role. Of course he often made jokey references to his own weight in his introductions to his TV show, but he had a grim measure of control over that. To have Hedren call out his weight in front of his crew must have been deeply humiliating for Hitchcock. But he had humiliated her in private, and she did not react passively to that.

Marnie got negative notices when it was first released, as did Hedren, but this film has grown in stature through the years, so much so that Robin Wood, one of the most insightful of all critics on Hitchcock, made a large claim for it on a *Marnie* DVD feature documentary. "If you don't like *Marnie*, you don't really like Hitchcock," Wood said. "I would go farther than that and say, if you don't love *Marnie*, you don't really love cinema." Wood was often extreme and doctrinaire in his various positions, but that was his sexy value. And his love for this particular Hitchcock picture points to the fact that *Marnie* is somehow the queerest of Hitchcock's films, not least when Lil looks at Mark and tells him, "I'm queer for liars."

Lil is a somewhat Midge type of girl, the sensible type that the man rejects in favor of the lady in distress. "I've always thought that a girl's best friend was her mother," Lil says, linking Marnie to Norman Bates as well as Melanie Daniels and Marion Crane. There is a meta quality to *Marnie* that is part of its queerness, as when Marnie verbally sends up the film's own psychoanalytic conventions and those of *Spellbound* in the scene where Mark plays a word association game with her, but this awareness falls away when he says, "Death" and she answers, "Me." This is an extraordinarily difficult scene because it moves from playful camp posing to genuine terror, and it is beautifully played and sustained by Hedren.

The only way that Marnie can find relief is in stealing, and the film makes you intimately understand why she needs to steal, and the compulsive pleasure she gets from it. She is on the verge of being caught and sent to jail, where she would likely go down the drain for good, and Mark stops that from happening, but he exacts a cruel price for it. It is when Marnie hesitates before reaching for money in Mark's safe that she becomes more aware of herself, and when we are aware we might start to heal, and improve.

Marnie comes to its climax back at the apartment where Marnie's mother Bernice lives in Baltimore. In a flashback, we learn that Bernice had been a prostitute servicing clients while Marnie slept outside her bedroom. A sailor john (Bruce Dern) bothered Marnie, and it seems clear now that Bernice reacts so violently because the sailor was molesting her little girl. Bernice and the sailor struggle and Marnie finally kills the sailor with a poker, and Hitchcock used a full gallon of red paint on the sailor's white shirt to get across the stain of this visually.

Bernice's leg was hurt in the fight with the sailor, and she took the blame for the killing and felt grateful that Marnie didn't seem to remember it afterward. Bernice's stiff and "decent" behavior has been dictated by this incident ever since, and the repression of it has warped her daughter. Hitchcock knew the twisted results of this kind of "decency" very well.

Finally Marnie and her mother just stare at each other, and Hitchcock staged this to resemble something he had once seen in a prizefighting ring: after many rounds, he said, the boxers just slumped down in their places and looked at each other, exhausted and unable to move. Released from one prison, Marnie is ready to go back to another. "Oh Mark . . . I don't want to go to jail," she says plaintively. "I'd rather stay with you."

So many scenes in *Marnie* might have been absurd if Hedren hadn't been so emotionally involved in them, so deep into misery and disgust, so childlike and trapped. The camera stopped lying here for Hitchcock, no matter the use of artificial and stylized backdrops. Louise Latham's tears come out of her eyes for real in the last scene in *Marnie*. They are not glycerin, as they were for Ingrid Bergman at the racetrack in *Notorious* (fig. 14.4). That lack of distance in the acting meant that Hitchcock's way of working with actors was truly finished by 1964. Art and life had collided, for the misery of Marnie is also the misery of Hedren on the set of *Marnie*, and so this is a particularly unfortunate endpoint where Hitchcock's camera is not lying, or not lying enough.

Figure 14.4: Real tears on the face of Louise Latham in *Marnie* signal that Hitchcock's way of working with actors is finished.

In 2018, an eighty-eight-year-old Hedren attended the premiere of Nico Muhly's opera of *Marnie* at the Metropolitan Opera House in Manhattan. She got a standing ovation when she was brought out on stage for the curtain call, and she was wearing a bright red dress. "I thought, I'm going to wear it," Hedren told a reporter from the *New York Times*, "and see if anybody gets it." She was long past the fear of red or fear of anything else.

15

Torn Curtain, Topaz, Frenzy, Family Plot, AFI Award

The four films that Hitchcock made after *Marnie* were not happy or fortunate in most ways. He lost his favored cinematographer Robert Burks when Burks died in a fire in 1968, and he also lost his longtime editor, George Tomasini, who died in 1964. Bernard Herrmann wrote a score in his usual heavy style for *Torn Curtain* (1966), but Hitchcock was unhappy with it and he chose a more commercial, driving sort of score by John Addison instead.

Hitchcock's long-treasured film adaptation of James M. Barrie's 1920 play *Mary Rose* was officially off limits under his new Universal contract, which deprived him of the creative freedom he had recently enjoyed. Hitchcock had loved that romantic Barrie play with its supernatural theme since he first saw it as a young man, and surely *Mary Rose* would have been preferable to any of the projects he did turn to in this period.

Torn Curtain contains a notably extended murder sequence where Hitchcock shows just how hard it is to kill a man. The male lead Michael Armstrong (Paul Newman) needs to dispatch the treacherous Gromek (Wolfgang Kieling) at a farmhouse with the help of the farmer's wife, who is played by Carolyn Conwell in her film debut. Conwell has a soulful and distressed face that looks a lot like Liv Ullmann's, and she didn't work much afterward aside from a role on the soap opera *The Young and the Restless*, but she has her immortality in this murder scene in *Torn Curtain* where her German character uses every household object she can to help Armstrong murder Gromek: a knife, a shovel, and then finally a gas oven, which they drag him to.

Newman and Julie Andrews don't have chemistry with each other or with Hitchcock in *Torn Curtain*, and this is enough to ruin the film. They were both major stars at that time, and Andrews was beloved for *Mary Poppins* (1964) and *The Sound of Music* (1965), but those were films for children, family films, and from Hitchcock's point of view, Andrews is a disastrous return to the sort of bright and ladylike British actresses he had fled in England years before. (His production assistant Peggy Robertson wrote that Hitchcock had seen Julie Christie in *Billy Liar* {1963} and was keen to use her in his film, but he was nixed by Universal.) Both Andrews and Newman look depressed and bewildered sometimes in *Torn Curtain*, and Andrews is hardly helped visually by frosted hair and a dark mustard yellow suit by Edith Head, one of the last of Hitchcock's key collaborators still working for him.

The credits to *Torn Curtain* are intriguing, with anguished, disturbing, anticipatory shots of the people in the film next to a sort of fire-breathing engine, and then we are on a freezing ship in the middle of an ice-cold sea as Newman and Andrews toss in bed together. (Alas, they are both just as icy as their surroundings.) Newman asked his director all sorts of questions about character motivation, which irritated Hitchcock, and the presence Newman brings to *Torn Curtain* is alternately closed off, over-explicit, and bad-boy sullen. Andrews is merely conscientious, like a worried mother along for the ride or a hostess at a dud of a dinner party.

There is a very expressive Edward Hopper-ish shot of the leads from a distance in a hotel room and several other compositions featuring saturated colors that show Hitchcock's visual imagination still functioning, but the last long chase sequence is a long way from the precision of *The Lady Vanishes*, and Hitchcock felt compelled to cut a scene where Armstrong meets Gromek's twin brother, which sounds fascinating.

There are a lot of good ideas in *Torn Curtain*, but they are blocked by the actors, not least the shameless ham Lila Kedrova, who is allowed to take over a long section of the film as a countess desperate to get out of Communist Berlin. Hitchcock had allowed older European character actors to linger a bit over their acting in earlier films, but he lets Kedrova go on and on here, smiling and rolling her big eyes and looking for another Oscar to go with the one she got for *Zorba the Greek* (1964).

Topaz (1969) was unhappier still. It was Hitchcock's longest film, a two-and-a-half-hour adaptation of a Leon Uris cold war espionage novel, and it was begun without a script and written by his friend Samuel Taylor as they went along. Stung by Newman and Andrews and their large salaries for *Torn Curtain*, which ran close to a million apiece for each of them, Hitchcock opted in *Topaz* for a sizable cast of nonentities, with the exception of French actors Michel Piccoli and Philippe Noiret, both of whom are uncomfortable in English.

There is one memorable shot in *Topaz*, an overhead view of Karin Dor being killed by her lover where her purple dress spreads out beneath her like a blood pool, but it is a brief bit of inspiration. The original ending of *Topaz* was a duel between two of the male characters, and audiences so disliked this ending that Hitchcock had to substitute another one that was even more awkward.

It is a shame that Hitchcock never got to work with Catherine Deneuve, who was the ultimate refinement of his cool/dirty-blonde type of woman. When Luis Buñuel visited Hollywood in 1972, Hitchcock told him how impressed he was by Buñuel's film *Tristana* (1970), especially the scenes after Deneuve's character has lost a leg. "Tristana's false leg. . . ." he kept murmuring.

Surely Hitchcock enjoyed Buñuel's *Belle de Jour* (1967) as well, and he very much admired Michelangelo Antonioni's *Blow-Up* (1966), saying afterward to screenwriter Howard Fast that Antonioni was "a hundred years ahead of me in terms of technique." In his article about filmmaking that was published in the *Encyclopedia Britannica* in 1965, Hitchcock offered, "Everything, as Ingmar Bergman has said, begins with the actor's face."

This was a period when Hitchcock and his earlier films were being much celebrated, revived, and analyzed, and so *Frenzy* (1972), a return to England, was overpraised on its release. The crude side of Hitchcock's own personality was revealed here for the first time, and the non-name British cast are often painfully off in their too-fast delivery of the jocular, rough dialogue by playwright Anthony Shaffer.

Frenzy can be seen as an elderly misstep or a revelation of things that studio-era censorship had kept under wraps in Hitchcock. It features a blunt, unlikable protagonist, Richard Blaney (Jon Finch), and an even more blunt, unlikable villain, Robert Rusk (Barry Foster), an impotent man who strangles women with his neckties.

Blaney's ex-wife Brenda (Barbara Leigh-Hunt) runs a marriage bureau, which is perhaps why she is so brutally punished in the scene where Rusk assaults and murders her. Brenda is portrayed as a curiously passive person in her relation to her husband, but when Rusk comes into her office she is coldly dismissive of his sadomasochistic sexual taste, expressing her disgust for him vehemently.

Somehow it feels like Brenda is less a person at this moment and more a symbol of the kind of repressive sexual attitudes that Hitchcock had hated since his youth, and so in killing her off in such a gross and lingering way, he is killing off what she symbolizes to him: marriage, judgmental lack of understanding about certain sexual urges, ladylike gentility, and denial. That's the charitable way to view this scene.

Rusk pulls Brenda's dress and brassiere down in front, and there is a close-up of her breast, but then she pulls the bra back up as she starts quoting a Bible verse. Hitchcock keeps Brenda and Rusk totally separate visually at this point, emphasizing her helplessness and his sweaty anger as he cries, "Lovely! Lovely!" but can't get an erection. She screams when she realizes he is the strangler, and it takes a while to kill her. Hitchcock finally shows Brenda with her tongue sticking out of her mouth, a grotesque image that might have been worse had he not been persuaded by Shaffer to drop a shot he had planned of saliva dripping from her red tongue.

Hitchcock felt that he had missed out on the sexual and romantic side of life because of the way he looked but also because of the sexually repressive time and place he had grown up in, and so in *Frenzy* he expresses his anger about that and also about the new freedom and relaxation of sexual mores. And so he made just about as unpleasant a movie as can be imagined, which even extends to the serving of unappetizing food by the gourmet wife (Vivien Merchant) of the detective (Alec McCowen) investigating the case.

Hitchcock knows that the second murder of Babs (Anna Massey) will be far worse if we just imagine it rather than see it, and so he follows Babs and Rusk to Rusk's room and then slowly takes his camera out and back onto the street so that we are as helpless as Brenda. But we do see bits of Babs's murder when Rusk remembers it, and the sight of her horrified corpse face when she is found is very hard to take, as is the expendable character played by Billie Whitelaw, who does little but yell at Blaney. At the end of this movie, Blaney discovers a slain nude girl who looks like a strangled *Playboy* model, at which point Rusk finally gets caught.

Elsie Randolph, who was the unavoidable spinster in *Rich and Strange*, turns up in *Frenzy* briefly as a hotel manager, and though she is not recognizable, she is at least a link to an earlier and gentler and far more creatively fertile time in Hitchcock's youth, where so much could be romantically imagined and not shown or fully disclosed.

Hitchcock's last film was the mild *Family Plot* (1976), which was cast with Bruce Dern, Barbara Harris, Karen Black, and William Devane, all quirky character actors. Hitchcock told Devane to think of William Powell as he played his jewel thief character in *Family Plot*, but of course Devane is far more redolent of Jack Nicholson than Powell. Al Pacino was the first choice for Dern's role, but Hitchcock didn't want to pay high star prices anymore and instead went with people he felt he could afford. Hitchcock was a very rich man by this point but still fearful about money, or wanting to keep control of it.

The actors in *Family Plot* are mannered and neurotic in a way far removed from Hitchcock's earlier work. At one point, Devane was being shot a lot from behind, and so he told Hitchcock that his mother wouldn't like going to this movie and only seeing the back of his head. "Have her destroyed," Hitchcock told him.

Harris has amusing moments in this last Hitchcock picture as a false medium. Hitchcock kissed her on the cheek when he noticed that she was nervous before a scene. "Barbara, *I'm* scared," he told her. "Now go and act. Many are called but few are frozen." Harris ends the film, and Hitchcock's career, with a wink to the camera, a "that's all folks" image that signaled that the magic show was over. To promote *Family Plot* at a press conference, Hitchcock had all the names of the invited reporters put on tombstones. He was a showman to the last.

Hitchcock and Alma were both in ill health when he was given the American Film Institute Lifetime Achievement Award in 1979, and no finessing in later editing could make the camera lie about that fact. Ingrid Bergman, ill herself with cancer but seemingly blooming with health, was the mistress of ceremonies, and she was distressed about what she saw of Hitchcock, telling François Truffaut backstage, "Why do they always organize this kind of ceremony when it's too late?"

Both Hitchcock and Alma seemed to be physically present but mainly mentally absent at the AFI ceremony, though Hitchcock did praise Bergman's "spontaneity" in a letter to Elsie Randolph afterward. At a later meeting at his home, Hitchcock tearfully told Bergman that he was going to die. "But of course you are going to die sometime, Hitch—we are all going to die," Bergman told him in her sensible, cheerful way. Bergman talked to Hitchcock about her own illness and continuing treatment and how she was thinking about leaving, too, and this made him feel somewhat peaceful, finally. Bergman had managed to quell some of his fears.

But perhaps Hitchcock found ways to enjoy his fear and waiting, as we all try to. For he needed Alma and feared her, and maybe he needed his fear. In 1959 in an article printed in *Guideposts Magazine*, Hitchcock had related the workings of his films to life itself. "Take the concept of heaven, for instance—wouldn't we tend to lose some of our interest in it if we knew exactly what it was like?," Hitchcock asked. "So when God keeps the future hidden, He is saying that things would be very dull without suspense."

Stony-faced and barely aware of those around him at the AFI event but smiling sometimes, Hitchcock was more than aware of who Bergman was and what she meant to him. At the end of the ceremony, Bergman went to give Hitchcock the all-important wine cellar key that she had kept from *Notorious* (she found out beforehand that it wasn't the actual key but she had to pretend that it was). Hitchcock was seated next to a white-haired and blithely smiling Cary Grant, who actually had been made to toast Hitchcock with the words, "The best is yet to come!" earlier in the evening.

When Bergman came down to him, Hitchcock reached out for her desperately and they embraced desperately and intensely. There was a heart-rending look of worried, dutiful, embarrassed love on Bergman's face as she tried to console Hitchcock while Grant looked on, still smiling. Somehow this series of shots was the real end of Hitchcock's career, the painful reality of what was happening between Bergman and himself offset, splendidly, by Grant's lying camera savoir faire.

There was nothing there now behind Hitchcock's face. He was "doing nothing" for the camera at the AFI event, and this was much like the deadpan look he had offered on his TV show. Behind this "nothing" was the creativity of a man who could be termed a genius, which is not a term that should be used lightly. And not the least part of Hitchcock's genius was his ideas about what acting for the camera could be.

Notes

ix "Actors are like children. They have to be coddled, and sometimes spanked." (*Mr. and Mrs. Smith* DVD featurette)

x "I said I heard worse things when I was in convent school, and he loved that," Kelly said. (*Spellbound by Beauty*, Donald Spoto, Crown Archetype, 2007, pg. 205)

xii "long tracking shots, which cannot be tampered with" (*Alfred Hitchcock: A Life in Darkness and Light*, Patrick McGilligan, Dey Street, 2003, pg. 373)

xiii "Hitch knows more about the mechanics and the physical technique of acting than any man I know," Slezak said. (McGilligan, pg. 343)

xiii "moronic logic." (Mike Scott, TV interview, 1966)

xiii–v "I do not know whether his famous 'Actors are cattle' remark was coined for my benefit, but I well remember his saying it in my presence," Redgrave said. (McGilligan, pg. 210)

xiv "I have a phrase for that," Hitchcock said in 1966. "I call that, 'All the drama on the set and none on the screen.' " (Mike Scott, TV interview, 1966)

xv "It is more true to life and it is more believable," Hitchcock said in the 1930s. (*Hitchcock on Hitchcock*, Faber and Faber, pg. 265)

xv "Because the image is too big" (*Hitchcock on Hitchcock*, pg. 297)

xvii "The poor cabbage had a wonderful soul, I know." (McGilligan, pg. 551)

3 "To tell the truth, she bossed him" (*Spellbound*, pg. 30)

9 "He had a fetish about glasses," Stevens said. (*Hitchcock and Selznick: The Rich and Strange Collaboration of Alfred Hitchcock and David O. Selznick in Hollywood*, Leonard Leff, University of California Press, pg. 267)

14 "Strictly speaking, you shouldn't have a matinee idol in a role of that kind." (Mike Scott, TV interview)

15–6 "He was always at ease with homosexual and bisexual people." (*Spellbound*, pg. 17)

16 Dropped "h's": (*Spellbound*, pg. 19)

20 "Lilian was a good actress" (*Spellbound*, pg. 32–33)

44 "a fairly obvious homosexual" (McGilligan, pg. 145)

44 "The conversation took a very Rabelaisian turn" (*Spellbound*, pg. 40)

54 "He sent me up mercilessly" (*Spellbound*, pg. 41)

55 *Hitchcock's Films Revisited* (Robin Wood, Columbia University Press, 1989, pg. 368)

57 Yarn gag: (*The Man Who Knew Too Much* DVD, Philip Kemp audio commentary, Criterion)

59 Novak, smile on his face (*Washington Post*, Tom Shales, Oct. 14, 1996)

61–2 "queer combination of determination and uncertainty." (McGilligan, pg. 173)
trousers (*Spellbound*, pg. 56)

68 "I only worked for him once" (*Sir John Gielgud: A Life in Letters,* Arcade Publishing, 2012, pg. 482)

69 "Lorre was a great scene-stealer" (*Spellbound*, pg. 58)

71 "When Robert Young came" (*Hitchcock on Hitchcock*, pg. 94)

78 "She could not piece together in her mind what Hitchcock was after" (McGilligan, pg. 188)

79 "In an older style of acting" (*Hitchcock on Hitchcock*, pg. 256)

90 "It isn't possible to direct a Charles Laughton film" (*Charles Laughton: A Difficult Actor*, Simon Callow, Fromm Intl, pg. 130)

77 "What I'd Do To The Stars" (*Hitchcock on Hitchcock*, pg. 92–93)

96–7 "Imagine Margaret Sullavan being pushed around by Mrs. Danvers right up to the point of suicide!" (George E. Turner essay, *Rebecca* Criterion DVD liner notes)

98 "Yiddish art theater rather than British repertory theater." (Leonard Leff commentary, *Rebecca* Criterion DVD)

98 "She was not a good enough actress to play in *Rebecca*—she really was not." (*Spellbound*, pg. 95)

99 "Well, Miss Bates—when did you start playing with yourself?" (*Spellbound*, pg. 97)

120 "comedy face" (*Spellbound*, pg. 116)

121 "The camera lies, you know" (*Shadow of a Doubt* DVD featurette).

123 "I think our secret" (McGilligan, pg. 316)

127 "her eyes were not eyes for movies." (*On Cukor*, Putnam 1972, pg. 38)

129 "My dear, you're sitting on it," Dick Cavett interview

130 "The poor man didn't have an easy trip" (*Tallulah, Darling*, Denis Brian, Macmillan, 1972, pg. 136)

130 "The whole point about Tallulah was that she had no inhibitions" (*Tallulah, Darling*, pg. 138)

134 "He watched what you're doing" (*Spellbound*, pg. 138)

134 "I never got angry when it came back to me" (*Spellbound*, pg. 139)

142 "I almost frightened myself" (*New York Times*, Edmond J. Bartnett, Sept. 1, 1946)

156 "How do I know?" (*Spellbound*, pg. 177)

157 "I must say much better than being cut up and edited" (Ingrid Bergman, *My Story*, Delacorte Press, 1980, pg. 183)

159 "Miss Dietrich is a professional." (*Marlene*, Stephen Bach, William Morrow, 1992, pg. 341)

160 "Ladies must be well fed" (*Marlene*, Marlene Dietrich, Avon Books, 1987, pg. 116)

161 "This is my real first film" (*Strangers on a Train* DVD featurette)

162 "Wouldn't it be interesting if something happened on our film?" (Farley Granger, *Include Me Out*, St. Martin's Press, 2007, pg. 108)

167 "As striking and improbable as Farley's looks were, he seemed unaware of them;" (*Original Story*, Arthur Laurents, Applause, 2001, pg. 100–101)

182 "You know, it's almost like leaving home, leaving this stage." (*Rear Window* DVD featurette)

183 “When I first came to Hollywood five years ago” (*Grace of Monaco: The True Story*, Jeffrey Robinson, Da Capo Press, 2015, pg. 10)

185 “He didn’t direct” (*Doris Day: Her Own Story*, William Morrow, 1975, pg. 189)

186 “Everyone’s frightened” (pg. 192)

186 “What happened to me in that scene seemed very real to me” (*Doris Day: Her Own Story*, pg. 194)

186 “What if it was Terry?” (*Doris Day*, David Kaufman, Virgin Books, 2008, pg. 198)

187 “altogether a lovely man.” (*Doris Day: Her Own Story*, pg. 194)

188–9 “He didn’t believe in rehearsals” (pg. 195)

192 “He was funny all the time” (McGilligan, pg. 537)

194 “Through this camera movement” (*Godard on Godard*, pg. 51)

196 “I tried to please him, but I couldn’t” (*The Making of Psycho*, Rebello, pg. 64)

198 “Let me explain to you” (McGilligan, pg. 555)

206 “All I have to do is disregard everything he says” (McGilligan, pg. 570)

209 “Here was this incredibly beautiful movie he had made that nobody went to see or said nice things about it” (*Alfred Hitchcock and the Making of Psycho*, Stephen Rebello, HarperPerennial, 1990, pg. 50)

214 “It just wouldn’t be very nice” (Rebello, pg. 109–110)

219 “I never show her face” (Hitchcock on Hitchcock, pg. 301)

221 “Hitch, I love you . . . I’ll always love you.” (Spoto, 1983, pg. 472)

226 “That man was physically so unattractive” (*New York Times*, Andrew Goldman, Oct. 5, 2012)

226 “This poor man was desperate for something he never had in his lifetime” (*Spellbound*, pg. 277)

227 “She did what no one is permitted to do” (McGilligan, pg. 646)

234 “Barbara, *I’m* scared” (McGilligan, pg. 726)

234 “Why do they always organize this kind of ceremony when it’s too late?” (*Hitchcock/Truffaut*, pg. 345)

Hitchcock Bibliography

Agee, James. *Agee on Film*. Modern Library, 2000.
Allen, Richard. *Hitchcock's Romantic Irony*. Columbia University Press, 2007.
Bach, Steven. *Marlene Dietrich*. William Morrow, 1992.
Bergman, Ingrid, with Alan Burgess. *Ingrid Bergman: My Story*. Delacorte Press, 1980.
Bosworth, Patricia. *Montgomery Clift*. Harcourt, 1978.
Brian, Denis. *Tallulah, Darling*. Macmillan, 1972.
Callow, Simon. *Charles Laughton: A Difficult Actor*. Methuen, 1987.
Chabrol, Claude and Rohmer, Eric. (Translated by Stanley Hochman.) *Hitchcock, The First Forty-Four Films*. Frederick Ungar Publishing, 1979.
Day, Doris. *Doris Day: Her Own Story*. William Morrow, 1975.
Deschner, Donald. *Complete Films of Cary Grant*. Citadel, 1983.
Dietrich, Marlene. *Marlene*. Avon, 1987.
Dietrich, Marlene. *Marlene Dietrich's ABC*. Ungar, 1961.
Donati, William. *Ida Lupino: A Biography*. University Press of Kentucky, 2000.
Gallagher, Tag. *The Adventures of Roberto Rossellini*. Da Capo Press, 1998.
Gottlieb, Sidney (editor). *Hitchcock on Hitchcock*. Faber and Faber, 1995.
Granger, Farley. *Include Me Out*. St. Martin's Press, 2007.
Greven, David. *Intimate Violence: Hitchcock, Sex, and Queer Theory*. Oxford University Press, 2017.
Harris, Robert A. and Lasky, Michael S. *The Complete Films of Alfred Hitchcock*. Citadel Press, 1976.
Harvey, James. *Movie Love in the Fifties*. Knopf, 2001.
Hedren, Tippi. *Tippi: A Memoir*. William Morrow, 2016.
Humphries, Patrick. *The Films of Alfred Hitchcock*. Bison Books, 1986.
Kobal, John. *People Will Talk*. Knopf, 1985.
Krohn, Bill. *Hitchcock at Work*. Phaidon Press, 2003.
Lambert, Gavin. *On Cukor*. G. P. Putnam's Sons, 1972.
Laurents, Arthur. *Original Story*. Applause, 2001.
Leff, Leonard. *Hitchcock and Selznick: The Rich and Strange Collaboration of Alfred Hitchcock and David O. Selznick in Hollywood*. Grove Press, 1987.
Mangan, Richard (editor). *Sir John Gielgud: A Life in Letters*. Arcade Publishing, 2012
McGilligan, Patrick. *Alfred Hitchcock, a Life in Darkness and Light*. HarperCollins, 2003.
Milne, Tom (editor). *Godard on Godard*. Da Capo, 1986.
Modleski, Tania. *The Women Who Knew Too Much: Hitchcock and Feminist Theory*. Routledge, 2005.
Morley, Sheridan. *James Mason: Odd Man Out*. HarperCollins, 1989.
Ott, Frederick. *The Films of Carole Lombard*. Lyle Stuart, 1984.
Pomerance, Murray. *A Dream of Hitchcock*. SUNY Press, 2019.
Price, Theodore. *Hitchcock and Homosexuality*. Scarecrow Press, 1992.
Rebello, Stephen. *Alfred Hitchcock and the Making of Psycho*. HarperPerennial, 1991.

Riva, Maria. *Marlene Dietrich*. Ballantine Books, 1992.
Robinson, Jeffrey. *Grace of Monaco: The True Story*. Da Capo Press, 2015.
Rusk, Howard. *A World to Care For*. Random House, 1972.
Spoto, Donald. *The Dark Side of Genius: The Life of Alfred Hitchcock*. Little Brown, 1983.
Spoto, Donald. *Spellbound by Beauty: Alfred Hitchcock and his Leading Ladies*. Harmony Books, 2008.
Taylor, John Russell. *Hitch: The Life and Times of Alfred Hitchcock*. Berkley Publishing, 1978.
Truffaut, François. *Hitchcock/Truffaut*. Simon & Schuster, 1966.
Vanderbeets, Richard. *George Sanders: An Exhausted Life*. Madison Books, 1993.
Wood, Robin. *Hitchcock's Film Revisited*. Columbia University Press, 2002.
Youngkin, Stephen, D. *The Lost One: A Life of Peter Lorre*. University Press of Kentucky, 2005.
Ziegler, Philip. *Olivier*. MacLehose Press, 2013.

Index

Abel, Alfred, 41
Ackland, Rodney, 4, 15, 53
Addinsell, Richard, 156
Addison, John, 230
Agate, James, 67
Aherne, Brian, 98
Albertson, Frank, 210
Alfred Hitchcock Presents, 123, 188, 190, 199
Alice Adams (1935), 210
All About Eve (1950), 170
Allardice, James, 188
Allen, Jay Presson, 222
Allgood, Sara, 32, 35
Allyson, June, 158
Altman, Robert, 189
Amann, Betty, 45
An American Tragedy (1931), 78
Anderson, Judith, 58, 100, 101, 102, 104, 105, 106, 169
Anderson, Mary, xiii, 129
Andrews, Julie, 230, 231
Angel, Heather, 117, 129
Anger, Kenneth, 211
Antonioni, Michelangelo, 232
Arendt, Ekkehard, 41
Armstrong, Charlotte, 199
Ashcroft, Peggy, xiv, xvii, 63, 64, 65, 68, 219
Astaire, Fred, 97, 206
Astor, Mary, 189
Auber, Brigitte, xvii, 183
Ault, Marie, 14, 17
Austen, Jane, 50
Autumn Leaves (1956), 190
Aventure Malgache (1944), 130
The Awful Truth (1937), 113

The Bad Seed (1956), 202
Bagdasarian, Ross, 174
Baker, Diane, x, xi, 222, 224, 226
Balestrero, Emmanuel, 190, 191
Balfour, Betty, 24, 25
Balsam, Martin, 215
Bankhead, Tallulah, ix, 28, 127, 128, 129, 130, 135, 136, 158
Banks, Leslie, 55, 56, 60, 61, 82, 90
Barclay, J. Searle, 12
Baring, Norah, 36, 37, 38, 39, 41, 148
Barrie, James M., 230
Barron, Jack, 215
Barry, Joan, xvii, 27, 30, 31, 44, 45, 46, 47, 50, 52, 53, 61
Barrymore, Ethel, 142, 148, 149
Barrymore, John, xi, xii, 12
Bass, Saul, 199, 209
Bassermann, Albert, 107, 133
Bates, Florence, 99
Baxter, Anne, 18, 96, 170, 171
Baxter, Jane, 62
Beck, Kimberly, 223
Bel Geddes, Barbara, 4, 135, 198, 199, 202, 224
Bellamy, Ralph, 111
Belle de Jour (1967), 232
The Bells of St. Mary's (1945), 137
Benchley, Robert, 107
Bendix, William, 129
Benjamin, Arthur, 60
Benson, Sally, 121, 124
Bergman, Ingmar, 232
Bergman, Ingrid, xii, 17, 75, 83, 94, 130, 131, 132, 133, 134, 135, 136, 137, 138, 139, 140, 141, 143, 144, 145, 147, 155, 156, 157, 172, 179, 196, 234, 235
Bernhardt, Sarah, 37
Bertolucci, Bernardo, 147
Best, Edna, 55, 60, 61, 82
Beville, Dickie, 42
A Bill of Divorcement (1932), xii

Billy Liar (1963), 231
The Birds (1963), x, xi, 10, 32, 56, 217, 218, 220, 221, 224, 226
Bjork, Anita, 170
Black, Karen, 233
Blackmail (1929), 19, 27, 28, 30, 33, 34, 35, 44, 62
Bloch, Robert, 209, 212
Blood and Sand (1922), 12
Blow-Up (1966), 232
The Blue Angel (1930), 61
Bogdanovich, Peter, ix, 163, 220
Bon Voyage (1944), 130
Borzage, Frank, 11, 30
Bow, Clara, 46
Brace, Clement, 155
Brando, Marlon, 206
"Breakdown" (1955), 123
Bresson, Robert, xvi
Bridges, Jeff, 196
Bringing Up Baby (1938), 113
Brisson, Carl, 19, 20, 26
Brooks, Louise, xv
Bruce, Nigel, xv
Buchanan, Jack, 51
Bumstead, Henry, 200
Buñuel, Luis, 88, 232
Burks, Robert, 171, 230
Burr, Raymond, 155, 175, 181

The Cabinet of Dr. Caligari (1919), 14
Calhern, Louis, 140
Calthrop, Donald, 29
Capa, Robert, 136, 141
Capra, Frank, 94
Cardiff, Jack, 156
Carey, Macdonald, 122, 126
Carme, Pamela, 82
Carroll, Leo G., 2, 132, 163, 165
Carroll, Madeleine, 62, 63, 64, 66, 67, 68, 69, 70, 71, 86, 87, 93, 96, 99
Cartwright, Veronica, 220
Casablanca (1942), 137, 142, 143
Cassavetes, John, 189
Cavanagh, James, 209
Cavett, Dick, ix, 1
Chabrol, Claude, 26, 81, 155, 184
Champagne (1928), 24, 25
Chandler, Joan, 152, 153
Chandler, Raymond, 161
Chatterton, Ruth, 117
Chekhov, Michael, 133, 134
Christie, Julie, 17, 231
Citizen Kane (1941), 197
Clare, Mary, 83
Clift, Montgomery, xvii, 150, 160, 168, 170, 171
The Clock (1945), 161
Clyde, Vander, 40
Coburn, Charles, 146
Cohn, Harry, 197
Colbert, Claudette, 93
Collier, Constance, 20, 151, 154
Collinge, Patricia, 121, 122, 149
Colman, Ronald, 147
Compson, Betty, 110
Connery, Sean, 222, 223, 224, 225, 226
Conrad, Joseph, 46, 71, 72, 73, 81
Conwell, Carolyn, 230
Cooper, Gary, xvii, 93, 106, 120, 172
Cooper, Gladys, 106
The Corn Is Green (1945), 155
Cotten, Joseph, 9, 121, 123, 125, 126, 156, 157, 181
The Count of Monte Cristo (1934), 66
Coward, Noël, 23, 30, 56, 68, 137
Crawford, Joan, 176, 180, 183, 190, 222
Cronyn, Hume, 121, 150
Cukor, George, xii, 94, 97, 98, 127
Cummings, Robert, xvii, 120, 172
Curzon, George, 82, 84
Cutts, Graham, 2, 13, 110

Dahl, Roald, 198
Dale, Esther, 109
Dalí, Salvador, 131, 133, 201
Dall, John, 18, 150, 151, 153, 155
A Damsel in Distress (1937), 97
Dane, Clemence, 36
Darcy, Georgine, 175, 177
The Dark Side of Genius, 1, 153
Darwell, Jane, 106
Davis, Bette, xvi, 94, 106, 142, 155, 191
Dawson, Anthony, 173
Day, Doris, 55, 60, 184, 185, 186, 187, 188, 217

Day, Laraine, 107
de Banzie, Brenda, 187
de Havilland, Olivia, 123
De Marney, Derrick, 82, 83
Della (1964), 222
Deneuve, Catherine, 232
Dern, Bruce, 228, 233
Destiny (1921), 2
Devane, William, 233, 234
Dial M for Murder (1954), 172, 173
Diary of a Lost Girl (1929), xv
Dick, Douglas, 152
Dietrich, Marlene, 61, 70, 158, 159, 160
Dinner at Eight (1933), xii, 93
Disney, Walt, ix, xii, 75, 86
The Docks of New York (1928), 110
Donat, Robert, 61, 62, 63, 64, 66, 67, 68, 72, 73, 82
Dor, Karin, 231
Dors, Diana, 189
Douglas, Kirk, 157
Downhill (1927), 20, 22, 24
Dr. Jekyll and Mr. Hyde (1920), 12
Dr. Jekyll and Mr. Hyde (1941), 137
du Maurier, Daphne, xv, 96
du Maurier, Gerald, xv
Duel in the Sun (1946), 136

Eagels, Jeanne, 37
Easy Virtue (1928), 22, 23, 24
Elliott, Laura, 163, 164, 165
Elstree Calling (1930), 36
Emery, John, 135
Enter Sir John, 36
Epper, Margo, 215
Esmond, Jill, 42, 43
Evanson, Edith, 153, 224
Evelyn, Judith, 48, 175, 178, 180

Falkenberg, Karl, 9
Family Plot (1976), 233, 234
Farebrother, Violet, 20, 21, 22, 38, 48
The Farmer's Wife (1928), 20, 22, 23
Farrell, Charles, 11, 30
Fassbinder, Rainer Werner, 224
Fast, Howard, 232
Female on the Beach (1955), 180
Ferrer, Jose, 180
Finch, Jon, 232
The First Born (1928), 62
Fitzgerald, Barry, 35
Fleming, Rhonda, 131
Fleming, Victor, 46
Fonda, Henry, 120, 191, 192, 193, 195, 196, 197
Fonda, Jane, 196
Fontaine, Joan, 96, 97, 98, 99, 100, 102, 103, 104, 106, 113, 114, 115, 118, 119, 198, 201
Ford, John, 161, 190
Ford, Wallace, 134
Foreign Correspondent (1940), 106, 107, 121, 133
Forsythe, John, 184
Foster, Barry, 92, 232
Frenzy (1972), 92, 232, 233
Fresnay, Pierre, 55
Fry, Christopher, 41
Fury (1936), 78

Gabel, Martin, 222
Gable, Clark, 66, 172
Galsworthy, John, 41, 42
Garbo, Greta, 93, 94, 147, 155
Garland, Judy, 161
Gaslight (1944), 132
Gavin, John, x, 72, 209, 210
Gaynor, Janet, 11, 30
Gelin, Daniel, 191
Geraghty, Carmelita, 4, 7, 8, 11, 25
Gielgud, John, xiv, xv, xvii, 67, 68, 69, 71, 87, 142
Gigi (1958), 24
Gilda (1946), 223
Gilliat, Sidney, 84, 89
The Girl (2012), 221
Glaser, Vaughan, 120
Godard, Jean-Luc, 194
Granger, Farley, 18, 150, 151, 152, 155, 162, 166, 167
Grant, Cary, xii, 17, 24, 67, 94, 113, 114, 115, 116, 117, 118, 119, 137, 138, 139, 140, 141, 143, 145, 150, 154, 170, 179, 182, 183, 205, 206, 223, 235
The Grapes of Wrath (1940), 106
Greene, Graham, 168

Greenwood, Joan, 183
Greet, Clare, 2, 3, 58
Gregg, Virginia, 215, 216
Grenfell, Joyce, 160
Grey, Anne, 54
Griffies, Ethel, 219
Griffith, D.W., 92
Gun Crazy (1949), 155
Gwenn, Edmund, 42, 183

Haas, Dolly, 171
Hall-Davis, Lilian, 19, 20, 22
Haller, Ernest, xvi
Hamilton, Patrick, 149
Harding, Ann, 189
Hardwicke, Sir Cedric, 115, 154
Harker, Gordon, 20
Harlow, Jean, 93
Harris, Barbara, 233, 234
Harrison, Joan, 89
Harrison, Rex, 173
Harvey, Laurence, 208
Hasse, O.E., 168
A Hatful of Rain (1957), 206
Hawks, Howard, xv, 48
Hayes, John Michael, 173, 174, 176, 184
Hayward, Leland, 177
Hayworth, Rita, 223
Head, Edith, 136, 141, 182, 198, 201, 231
Hecht, Ben, 132, 134, 136, 138, 139, 143, 161
Hedren, Tippi, x, xi, xv, xvii, 12, 48, 196, 217, 219, 220, 221, 222, 223, 224, 225, 226, 227, 229
Helmore, Tom, 199
Henreid, Paul, xvi
Hepburn, Audrey, 182, 208
Hepburn, Katharine, 94, 106, 210
Herrmann, Bernard, 184, 199, 201, 202, 203, 204, 205, 209, 211, 215, 217, 222, 223, 230
High Noon (1952), 172
High Society (1956), 183
Higham, Charles, 147
Highsmith, Patricia, 161
Hitchcock, Alma, x, xiii, 3, 4, 6, 12, 34, 36, 44, 45, 47, 50, 53, 62, 84, 97, 135, 148, 150, 165, 168, 170, 205, 210, 221, 234
Hitchcock, Emma, 1, 18, 122
Hitchcock, Patricia, 3, 6, 150, 158, 199
Hitchcock, William, 1
Hitchcock's Films, 55
Hodiak, John, 129
Hogan, Dick, 151
Holden, William, 162
Holiday (1938), 113
Homolka, Oskar, xvi, 72, 73, 80
Hopper, Edward, 231
Hull, Henry, 128
Hume, Benita, 24
The Hunchback of Notre Dame (1939), 90
Hunter, Evan, 219, 221, 222
Hunter, Ian, 19
Huppert, Isabelle, xi

I, Claudius (1937), 90
I Confess (1953), 18, 168, 169, 170, 171

Jamaica Inn (1939), 2, 89, 90, 91, 92, 95, 146, 159
James, Henry, 151
Jannings, Emil, 61, 93
Jasmin, Paul, 215
Jeans, Isabel, 23, 24
Jewell, Estelle, 124
St. Johns, Adela Rogers, 189
Jones, Henry, 202
Jones, Jennifer, 136, 161, 162
Jourdan, Louis, 99, 146, 148, 149
June, 16, 17
Juno and the Paycock (1930), 35

Kahn, Florence, 69
Kanin, Garson, 113
Karloff, Boris, 25, 142
Kazan, Elia, x, 198
Kedrova, Lila, 231
Keen, Malcolm, 15, 26
Kehr, Dave, 218
Keith, Slim, 48, 177
Kelly, George, 172
Kelly, Grace, x, 17, 69, 172, 173, 174, 175, 176, 177, 182, 183, 196, 201, 221
Kendall, Henry, 44, 45
Kieling, Wolfgang, 230
Kitty Foyle (1940), 106

Knight, Esmond, 54
Knipper, Lev, 41
Knipper, Olga, 41
Knott, Frederick, 173
Konstantin, Leopoldine, 103, 142
Krasna, Norman, 108
Krohn, Bill, 121, 207
Kruger, Otto, 120
Krumschmidt, Eberhard, 143

L'Avventura (1960), 87
L'Herbier, Marcel, 25
The Lady Eve (1941), 191
The Lady Vanishes (1938), xiv, 84, 85, 86, 87, 88, 89, 101, 121, 231
The Lady's Not For Burning, 41
Lamarr, Hedy, 147
"Lamb to the Slaughter" (1958), 198
Lancaster, Burt, 157
Lanchester, Elsa, 91
Landau, Martin, 206, 208
Landis, Jessie Royce, 182, 206
Lane, Priscilla, xvii, 120
Lang, Doreen, 193, 194, 195, 220
Lang, Fritz, 2, 57, 78, 191
The Last Laugh (1924), 2, 93
Latham, Louise, 222, 228, 229
Laughton, Charles, xvi, 89, 90, 91, 92, 93, 142, 148, 159
Launder, Frank, 84
Laura (1944), 149
Laurents, Arthur, 150, 151, 152, 167
Laurie, John, 63
Lawrence, Gertrude, xv
Le Diable au Coeur (1928), 25
Lean, David, 64, 147
Leaver, Philip, 87
Lee, Anna, 62
Lee, Auriol, 117, 118
Leff, Leonard, 105
Lehár, Franz, 121
Lehman, Ernest, 207, 208
Leigh, Janet, xvii, 16, 48, 209, 210, 211, 213, 214
Leigh, Vivien, 42, 87, 96, 97, 103, 177
Leigh-Hunt, Barbara, 232
Leighton, Margaret, 156, 157
Lejeune, C. A., 74
Les Misérables (1935), 91
The Letter (1929), 37
The Letter (1940), 106
Letter from an Unknown Woman (1948), 98
Levy, Louis, 72
Lewis, Joseph H., 155
Lifeboat (1944), ix, xiii, 127, 128, 129, 130
Lindstrom, Pia, 89
Lion, Leon M., 53
The Little Foxes (1941), 122
Lloyd, Norman, 120
Lockwood, Margaret, 84, 86
Loder, John, 72, 73, 75, 80
The Lodger (1926), 13, 14, 15, 16, 18, 20, 62, 146
Lombard, Carole, ix, 108, 109, 111, 112, 113, 158
Longden, John, 29
Lord Camber's Ladies (1932), xv
Lorimer, Louise, 222
Lorne, Marion, 164
Lorre, Peter, 57, 58, 59, 60, 61, 68, 69, 71, 82, 186
The Lost Weekend (1945), 173
Loy, Myrna, 93
Lubitsch, Ernst, 134
Lukas, Paul, 86, 87, 88
Lunt, Alfred, 142
Lupino, Ida, 198

M (1931), 57
MacLaine, Shirley, 183
Mademoiselle Coeur Solitaire (novel), 180
Main, Marjorie, 215
The Man Who Knew Too Much (1934), 44, 55, 56, 57, 61, 62, 69, 71, 83, 90
The Man Who Knew Too Much (1956), 55, 184, 185, 191
The Man with the Golden Arm (1955), 198
Mander, Miles, 9
Manners, Margaret, 199
Mannheim, Lucie, 61, 62
Mansfield, Jayne, 189
Mantrap (1926), 46
The Manxman (1929), 25, 26
Marmont, Percy, 45, 46, 47, 69, 83

Marnie (1964), x, 8, 217, 221, 222, 223, 225, 226, 227, 228, 230
Marshall, Herbert, 37, 38, 39, 56, 107, 148
Marshall, Noel, 226
Martin, Mary, 30
Mary (1931), 41
Mary Poppins (1964), 230
Mary Rose, 230
Mason, James, 37, 150, 154, 206, 207
Massey, Anna, 233
Matthews, Jessie, 54
Maugham, W. Somerset, 67, 93
McCabe & Mrs. Miller (1971), 189
McCowen, Alec, 233
McCrea, Joel, 106, 108
McGilligan, Patrick, 1, 163, 183
Meeker, Ralph, 190
Meet Me in St. Louis (1944), 124
Merchant, Vivien, 233
Metcalf, Nondas, 117, 118
Miles, Vera, 190, 192, 196, 197, 198, 211
Milland, Ray, 172, 173
Minnelli, Vincente, 24, 161
Mogambo (1953), 172
Monkman, Phyllis, 32
Monroe, Marilyn, 28
Montagu, Ivor, 13, 16, 78
Montgomery, Robert, ix, 108, 110, 113
Moran, Joseph, 177
Moranis, Rick, 40
The Morning After (1986), 196
"The Morning of the Bride" (1959), 199
The Most Dangerous Game (1932), 60
The Mountain Eagle (1926), 12, 13
Mr. and Mrs. Smith (1941), ix, 108, 109, 110, 112, 113, 151
Mr. Smith Goes to Washington (1939), 154
Muhly, Nico, 228
Murder! (1930), x, 22, 29, 36, 37, 39, 41, 45, 56, 58, 62, 148
Murnau, F.W., 2, 6, 93, 204
Mutiny on the Bounty (1935), 91
My Best Girl (1927), 11
Mycroft, Walter, 36

Nalder, Reggie, 187
Naldi, Nita, 10, 12, 13
Natwick, Mildred, 183
"Never Again" (1956), 189
Newman, Paul, 230, 231
Newton, Robert, 146
Nicholson, Jack, 233
Night Life in Reno (1931), 11
Night Must Fall (1937), 84
No Bail for the Judge, 208
No Bed of Roses (1978), 98
Noiret, Philippe, 231
Nolan, Jeanette, 215
"None Are So Blind" (1956), xii
North by Northwest (1959), 205, 206, 208
Nosferatu (1922), 6
Notorious (1946), 17, 94, 103, 136, 137, 139, 140, 142, 143, 144, 154, 170, 179, 183, 207, 221, 228, 235
Novak, Kim, 4, 12, 59, 197, 198, 199, 201, 202, 204, 205, 208
Novello, Ivor, 13, 14, 15, 17, 18, 20, 22, 24, 146
Now, Voyager (1942), xvi
Number 13 (1922), 2, 3
Number 17 (1932), 29, 53, 54

O'Brien, Margaret, 124
O'Casey, Seán, 35
O'Connor, Una, 39
O'Hara, Frank, 151
O'Hara, Maureen, 90, 91, 92
O'Neill, Maire, 35
Oakland, Simon, 216
Oates, Cicely, 57, 61
Olivier, Laurence, xvii, 42, 97, 98, 104, 105, 142, 147
Olsen, Christopher, 184
On the Waterfront (1954), 206
Ondra, Anny, 25, 27, 30, 31, 32, 34, 44
Ophuls, Max, 98
Ormonde, Czenzi, 161, 163
Ortiz, Sébastien, 180
Osborne, Robert, 197

Pacino, Al, 233
Pandora's Box (1929), xv
Pappritz, Elizabeth, 10
The Paradine Case (1947), 94, 146, 147, 148, 149
Parker, Cecil, 84

Parker, Dorothy, 120
Parker, Eleanor, 170
A Passage to India (1984), 64
Peck, Gregory, 83, 131, 132, 133, 146, 147, 148, 203
Peeping Tom (1960), 74
Penny Serenade (1941), 118
Percy, Esme, 37, 38, 39, 40, 41
Perkins, Anthony, xiv, 17, 18, 123, 209, 212, 213, 214, 215, 216, 218
The Philadelphia Story (1940), 106
The Piano Teacher (2001), xii
Piccoli, Michel, 231
Pickford, Mary, 3, 11
Pilbeam, Nova, 55, 56, 83
The Pleasure Garden (1925), 4, 5, 7, 8, 9, 10, 11, 13, 25, 54, 219
Pleshette, Suzanne, 218
Poe, Edgar Allan, 2
Porter, Cole, 159
Poulenc, Francis, 151
Powell, Michael, 27, 74
Powell, William, 85, 93, 123, 233
Preminger, Otto, xiv, 149, 198
Priestley, J. B., 89
The Private Life of Henry VIII (1933), 91
Providence (1977), 68
Psycho (1960), xi, xiv, xvii, 6, 16, 18, 22, 31, 33, 47, 48, 72, 74, 77, 196, 209, 211, 214, 215, 216, 217
Pushover (1954), 197

Quine, Richard, 197, 204

Rabwin, Marcella, 98
Radford, Basil, 84, 88
Rains, Claude, 23, 140, 142, 144
Randolph, Elsie, 3, 16, 48, 49, 51, 153, 233, 234
Raymond, Gene, ix, 110, 111
Rear Window (1954), 6, 17, 48, 91, 173, 174, 175, 176, 177, 180, 182
Rebecca (1940), 14, 96, 97, 98, 99, 100, 102, 106, 107, 119, 163, 169
Rebello, Stephen, xvii
Redgrave, Michael, xiv, xvii, 85, 86, 87, 88
Rembrandt (1936), 91
Renoir, Jean, xv
Resnais, Alain, 68
"Revenge" (1955), 190
Rich and Strange (1932), 44, 46, 48, 50, 51, 53, 61, 69, 109, 148, 153, 233
Riggs, Rita, xvii
The Ring (1927), 19, 20
Ritchard, Cyril, 28, 30, 31
Ritter, Thelma, 174, 176, 177, 181
Riva, Maria, 61, 159
The River (1929), 11
Roar (1981), 226
Robbins, Richard, 194
Roberts, Ruth, 156
Robertson, Peggy, 159, 231
Robeson, Paul, 63
Rogers, Ginger, 106
Rohauer, Raymond, 5
Rohmer, Eric, 26, 81, 155, 184
Roman, Ruth, 163, 167, 170
Rope (1948), 18, 149, 150, 152, 153, 155, 215, 224
Rowlands, Gena, 189
A Royal Divorce (1938), 117
Rozsa, Miklos, 131, 132

Sabotage (1936), xii, xvi, 67, 71, 72, 73, 77, 80, 81, 83, 118, 180, 203
Saboteur (1942), xvii, 120, 121, 126
Saint, Eva Marie, 206, 207, 208
Sanders, George, 101, 105, 106, 107, 142, 154
Schmeling, Max, 34
Schnell, Georg H., 6
Scott, Gordon, 190
The Searchers (1956), 190
Secret Agent (1936), xiv, 46, 67, 68, 69, 71, 84
Seiter, William A., 113
Selznick, David O, 94, 96, 97, 98, 100, 104, 123, 131, 136, 142, 146, 148, 149, 161, 162, 205
7th Heaven (1927), 30
Shadow of a Doubt (1943), 9, 121, 122, 123, 126, 127, 149, 165, 166, 168, 182, 225
Shaw, George Bernard, 37
Shaw, Janet, 124, 125, 126
Sheridan, Ann, 163
"Shopping for Death" (1956), 189

The Shrike (play), 180
Sidney, Sylvia, xii, xvi, 71, 72, 73, 75, 76, 77, 78, 79, 80, 82
Sim, Alastair, 160
Simpson, Helen, 36
The Skin Game (1931), 41, 42, 43, 46
Slezak, Walter, xiii, 128, 129, 130
The Sound of Music (1965), 230
Spartacus (1960), 155
Spellbound (1945), 83, 130, 131, 132, 133, 136, 203, 227
Spellbound by Beauty, 42
Spoto, Donald, x, 1, 42, 153, 187
Stage Fright (1950), 18, 158, 160
Stanislavski, Konstantin, 133
Stanwyck, Barbara, xvii, 94, 107, 120, 166, 191
Stefano, Joseph, 209, 214, 215, 221
Sternberg, Josef von, 78, 90, 110, 158
Stevens, Carol, 9
Stewart, James, 6, 55, 150, 153, 154, 174, 175, 177, 178, 184, 186, 187, 188, 191, 198, 199, 200, 204, 205
Still of the Night (1982), xvi
Strait-Jacket (1964), 222
Strangers on a Train (1951), xvii, 161, 162, 167, 208
Strangers When We Meet (1960), 204
Strasberg, Lee, 134
Strauss, Richard, 184
Streep, Meryl, xvi
Street Angel (1928), 11
Stuart, John, 9, 54
Sullavan, Margaret, 96, 97, 120
Sunrise (1927), 204
Sunset Boulevard (1950), 102
Suspicion (1941), 24, 113, 116, 117, 119
Swanson, Gloria, 56, 102
Swerling, Jo, 127
"Sybilla" (1960), 198

Tandy, Jessica, 32, 218, 219
Tanner, Peter, xii
Tarnished Lady (1931), 127
Taylor, John Russell, 4, 227
Taylor, Rod, 218, 225
Taylor, Samuel, 231
Tennyson, Alfred, 83
Tennyson, Penrose, 83
Tester, Desmond, 72, 73, 81, 83
Tetzlaff, Ted, 136
Thaxter, Phyllis, 189
The 39 Steps (1935), xiv, 61, 62, 63, 65, 66, 67, 71, 73, 84, 120, 121, 219
Thesiger, Ernest, 3
This Above All (1942), 98
Thomas, Jameson, 22
Tiomkin, Dimitri, 124
To Catch a Thief (1955), xvii, 182, 183, 184
Todd, Ann, 147, 148
Todd, Richard, 158, 160
"Together" (1958), 226
Tomasini, George, 230
Topaz (1969), 231, 232
Torch Song (1953), 176
Torn Curtain (1966), 230, 231
Torn, Rip, 189
Touch of Evil (1958), 159
Tracy, Spencer, 71
Travers, Henry, 122
Travers, Linden, 84
Trevor, Claire, 189
Tristana (1970), 232
The Trouble with Harry (1955), 183, 184
Truffaut, François, xi, xiii, xvi, 2, 26, 46, 106, 146, 156, 181, 193, 194, 207, 234
Tschechowa, Olga, 41
The Turn of the Screw, 151
Turner, Lana, 209
Twin Peaks, 125
Two-Faced Woman (1941), 94
Tynan, Kenneth, 68

Ullmann, Liv, 230
Under Capricorn (1949), 155, 156, 157
Uris, Leon, 231

Valentino, Rudolph, 12
Valli, Alida, 146, 147, 149
Valli, Virginia, 6, 7, 8, 11
Van Druten, John, 117
Van Fleet, Jo, 189
Varden, Norma, 167
Veidt, Conrad, 14, 41
Vertigo (1958), 4, 10, 59, 104, 135, 196, 197, 198, 199, 202, 205, 208, 209, 224

Vidor, King, 7, 94
Viertel, Peter, 120
The Vortex, 68
Vosper, Frank, 56

Wagner, Richard, 38
Wakefield, Hugh, 58
Walker, Robert, xvii, 17, 123, 161, 162, 164, 166, 167, 168, 169
Waltzes from Vienna (1933), 54, 113
Wanger, Walter, 106
Ward, Edward, 108
Watson, Wylie, 61, 67
Waxman, Franz, 97, 118, 174
Wayne, Naunton, 84
Webb, Clifton, 142
Welles, Orson, 123, 159
The White Shadow (1923), 110
Whitty, Dame May, 84, 85, 115
Wild Oranges (1924), 7
Wilder, Thornton, 121, 126
Wilding, Michael, 155, 156, 159
Williams, Emlyn, 55, 91
Williams, John, 173, 208
Williams, Tennessee, 201
Wilson, Carey, 11
Wilson, Josephine, 86
Winston, Irene, 175
Winters, Shelley, 109
Withers, Googie, 67, 84
Woman to Woman (1923), 110
A Woman Under the Influence (1974), 189
The Women (1939), 97
Wood, Robin, 55, 56, 165, 227
Woolrich, Cornell, 174
Wright, Frank Lloyd, 208
Wright, Teresa, 121, 123, 124, 125, 126, 127
The Wrong Man (1957), 190, 191, 192, 194, 195, 196, 209
Wyman, Jane, 158

You Only Live Once (1937), 78, 191
Young and Innocent (1937), 46, 82, 83, 84
Young, Loretta, 96, 183
Young, Robert, 71
Youngkin, Stephen, 61

Zorba the Greek (1964), 231

1

jump summer into up

one
skipping
rope

one
summer
day

these
feet

these
shoes

this
place

and me
equals

some
thing
        extra
                ordi-
                        nary

fetch
willow
wallow
hollow
sprout

words chime
in my mind
like bells

fetch
willow
wallow

my
feet
my
feet
they
skip

hollow
sprout

this
rope
this
rope
this

fetch
willow
wallow
hollow

rope

I am the
rope-skipping
word queen
of the worl—

HONK
HONK HONK HONK

I miss my skip

HONK
HONK HONK HONK

Mylegsfreeze

BOOGEYMAN BOOGEYMAN
Old Man Whitley

HONK
HONKHONKHONK

BOOGEYMANBOOGEYMAN

inching towards me
in his old man truck
thick glasses glaring
mustache mouth moving

HONK

I
BOOGEYMANBOOGEYMAN
dropmyrope

I back up

the truck

I back up

chugs on

I smack into
JULIA-CICELY-ALIX

Boogeyman Boogeyman Boogeyman
Alix chants

        fetch winter marshmallow
                Cicely sings

They step over my rope
        with their knee high boots
        with their ice white shorts
        with their purses
        slung over their shoulders like
        rock star guitars

        Kids
                says Alix
        Yup
                says Julia

        our
        Julia

and I stand there
        like a

        like a

        like a

WAIT UP! I say

They
        one plus
        one plus
        one
                look at each other
                look back at me

        No
                Cicely says

No

says Alix

Well

says Julia

Come ON, Julia
says Cicely

Yeah

says Alix
Come on
We're going to walk past
Kid's house
See if he sees us

Phoebe
Julia says to me in a hard voice
she didn't used to use

You're
only
ten

BUT

Why don't you find Henny or
play with the other little kids

BUT

Isn't Mercy coming to her dad's this summer?
You could play with Mercy

BUT

BUT BUT BUT Cicely says
Word girl's out of words

They're going to
eat
her
alive
at Southside says Alix

and

one plus
one plus
one minus
me
they
stride off into infinity

But

I

just

turned

ELEVEN!

and
Mercy
doesn't
PLAY
with
any
body
any
way

I grab up that knot of words and dread
Southside Southside
word girl word girl
eat her alive

and I

stand
on the garbage can
step
onto the fence post
lean
into the old rough trunk I

clutch
the limb stump and
shift
pull
climb
to the third branch up on the left where
one long board
a throne
overlooks my kingdom

37th street

47th Avenue

	Houses	
onthecorner	stagger	onthecorner
house	between	house
	two	
empty	streets	manywindows
house	a garage	house
	behind	
my	each one	Lunch Lady
house		house
	an empty lot	
Kid's	like a	empty lot
house	missing	empty lot
	tooth	
blueandwhite	bleeds	Mr Whitley's
house	weeds and	house
	tossed out	
lotsofweeds	junk	rhubarb yard
house		house
	and	
Jennica's	down the	Julia's
house	middle	house
	like a	
?'s	zipper	Hen's
house		house
	a narrow	
onthecorner	road	othercorner
house		house
	our alley	

48th Avenue

38th street

Here is where
I've been every age
up to now

Here is where
I met Henny

Here is where we
run
climb
roller skate

where we
hopscotch
jump rope

Here is where I
make up our rope chants
I am a champion worder

where
Julia
used to jump rope with us

counting our skips
backwards from 100
by threes
or sevens
or eights and a half

Julia was a champion counter

but
not

any
more

Julia
thirteen
the queen
of Southside Middle

Sometimes we spy
through the spaces
in her fence
as she sunbathes
with her new friends
from across 38th Street
who wear lipstick
and carry those beautiful purses

Julia's purse is real cowhide
and in the shape of a saddle
no one has seen inside it

Henny and me
wish we
had one too

We wish Julia would
invite us in
fix our hair
like she used to

let us hold her purse
try on her shoes
show us her closet
ask us

What do you think?

I don't have a purse
but I do have something
all mine
with secrets inside

Standing
tiptoe
on my
board

I can

just

reach

the hole
in the trunk
of the tree

better than a
lock and key

(Hen hasn't had
her growth spurt
yet)

a place for

my notebook
purple with birds
and a silver spiral
just the size of
my hand curved
corners frayed
filled with words
purple with birds
a poemnotebook

a poem is
a fistful of words
wringing my insides out

I tuck my notebook away and lay

back on my board between the branches

legs
dang
ling

hands under my head

looking into the sky and leaves

umbrella of a thousand greens

closing my eyes to see them print on my eyelids

breathing in all that green

breathing in all that green

waiting

listening

waiting

and there
I hear it

slap slap
jump rope

shush shush
sidewalk chalk

whirr whirr
lawn mower

wheeze whap
screen door

bzzzz
bee

izzzzz
mosquito

phee
bee

phee
bee
birds in the tree

It's coming for me
like it does every year

phee
bee
phee
bee
who will
you
be

SUMMER

2

dare don't do dolls do don't dare

Best friend Hen
brings up popsicles
which drip purple
into the empty wren nest
and green
onto my little brothers' heads

Go away! we say to Anton and Cam

I was waiting and waiting and waiting for you Hen says
and you're just up here doing NOTHING

So? I say

It's vacation
We have to DO things

Nothing is something I say
but Hen isn't listening

Remember when we brought Sweet and Heart up here last summer? Hen says

Yup

our dolls went everywhere with us
last summer

Mercy tormented us about our dolls
last summer

Hen I say
needing to tell her about Julia+Cicely+Alix and being eaten alive

We could build them a fort she plows on

Nah
dolls don't look at you
dolls don't answer back
Julia doesn't play with dolls

Hen I say a little louder

We could tie them to a branch and swing them like acrobats
she says

when is she going to realize
dolls aren't real
anymore

Well we could

HENRIETTA!

What? You don't have to use my whole name!

middle
school

SO? At St Mary's I won't have those divisions she says
It's K-8
Sixth grade is just another year

but Alix said

What does Alix know? At St Mary's I'll have lots of teenage friends Hen says
in that tone that is meant to remind me that
Catholic School is so wham bam superior
Well, are you going to tell me or not?
What did Alix say?

But

now I don't want to tell her

Having a best friend means:
no waiting alone
secrets
shield from bullies
story swapping
sharing skates
girls against the world
brushing out snarls
braiding hair
winding string into friendship bracelets
two kitchens
two yards
someone to yell at when you're mad
someone who's not your sister but is almost
double wanting something
double chance of getting it
secret notes
sometimes fights
bottle cap trades when we make up

someone who knows how it is
except when she doesn't

and then
it feels like
the
end
of
everything

but

Hen is the only girl
around here
exactly
my
age
so we're stuck with
each other

Lentil doesn't belong to anyone Hen says
We could put a leash on Lentil

Nah

cats can't be kept

Come ON Hen says

This is what we like *to do*
This is what we always *do*

Well

Come ON Phee
DO something with me
something besides daydreaming in your tree

I can't hold it in any longer

Alix said they're going to
eat
me
alive
at Southside

She could be right says Hen

HEN!

If you want my advice

I don't
but I do

What?

You need to DO *something*

Something extraordinary

What?

There is
Hen says
a dog in the alley

Hen is annoying but she
is the kind of person who sees possibilities

but

a dog in the alley?

not…

BULL?
I am not the kind of person

Mr Whitley's BULL?
who can see
Old Man Whitley's
killer dog BULL
as some kind of creature to play with

Yes, BULL!

But he's a MONSTER!
BULL with those muscly haunches
with those teeth in his wide drooley jaw
BULL's the kind of dog whose fangs show when he barks
the kind of fangs that could rip an arm to slivers
like the time he

I dare you to –

NO!

I hit Hen with my popsicle stick

to—
she hits me with hers

NO!

I can't help myself
I'm laughing

Idareyoutostickyourarmthroughthefenceandcounttoten

NO!

I guarantee you that Alix would never do it

. . .
. . .

but

. . .
. . .

or Cicely

. . .
. . .

but

. . .
. . .

Mercy would do it

but Mercy isn't here
and
if we're lucky
she won't show up at all
this summer

Julia would be impressed she says

and that does it

I'll count to three I say
. . .
. . .
six she says
. . .
. . .

Plus you give me one of your Mr Pibb *bottle caps*
the luckiest kind
. . .
. . .
O
. . .
. . .
kay

We're in the empty lot
by Mudville

Come on, Phee Hen says

it's the thing
my brothers are building
all out of mud
digging
dousing
molding
sticks for trees
small rocks for people

You can't put it off Hen says

it's going to be
a miniature of our
whole block

I dared and you accepted

A dare!
say my brothers at exactly the same time

What are you going to do, Phee?
They say at exactly the same time

Maybe do I say
I said maybe I would

No
No
you did
not
say maybe

says Hen in that teacher voice she gets
looking up at me as if she isn't
six to eight inches shorter than me

You SAID
you'll put your whole arm
up to your shoulder
through
Mr Whitley's
fence

Ooooh Phee
says Anton
leaving his bucket and shovel and standing up

think about Southside
says Hen

What about BULL
says Cam
picking up his raggedy old doll
and grabbing my hand

What about Mr Whitley
says Anton reaching for Hen's hand
Hen swatting him away

You're the bravest of the brave
says Cam

It's no big deal I say
but inside I am a jellyfish

You better have that bottle cap ready, Henrietta

We're statues
by Mr Whitley's fence
listening

shreeeeeech
the 21A bus stopping on 38th Street

boom dalla boom dalla boom boom
Julia and her radio and Alix + Cicely
boom dalla boom dalla boom boom
sitting on Julia's garage roof watching

pap pap pap
Kid and his baseball and his bat

shush shush
little Jennica with her
shush shush
sidewalk chalk

shreeeech boom dalla pap shush shush
but no
RUFF
no BULL
he must be sleeping
dreaming of who he'll eat next

Six Mississippi seconds
Hen shout-whispers
holding up the
bottle caps

I crouch next to the spot in the fence with the loose board

I can feel Julia and them watching
eat her alive

my hand is on the loose board
bravest of the brave

ready to move it aside

I hold my breath

will this be the last time I see these fingers?

All the way to your shoulder! Hen says

and I

Southside Southside

stickmywholehandandmyarmuptomyshoulderIN
oneMississippitwoMississippithreeMissi

RUUUUUUFF

aaaEEEEEEEEE

my brothers scream

fourfivesix I
yank my arm out
just
in
time
and I

cradle my
rescued hand

WHAM SLAM
back door

Mr Whitley
Boogeyman
Boogeyman
Old Man Whitley!

WHO'S THAT?

WHO'S THERE?

YOU BETTER

SCRAM

OR

ELSE

Quick! I hiss

We duck behind the broken down shed
Mr Whitley's voice like the muffler
on his rusty old truck
loud low blasts
threatening to squash us

We

breathe

as

quietly

as

jellyfish

We

breathe

as

quietly

as

jellyfish

We

breathe

as

quietly

as

jellyfish

Was he this mean when Mrs Whitley was alive?
Anton whispers

Who's Mrs Whitley?
Cam says out loud

Shhhh!

His wife
and I don't remember I say

but I do remember

I remember
tumbling rocks avalanche laughs
a wide hat

seeds for Mrs Peg Leg
the one-legged crow

and the way she sang my name

phee
bee
phee
bee
like the bird she'd say
Phoebe like the poem

like the poem she gave me

But I don't remember
Mr Whitley
from when
Mrs Whitley
was around
She was this whole house

He has a gun you know
Hen says in her not-quiet-enough voice

Anton and Cam gasp and huddle closer
a shiver goes all down my spine to my toes

A GUN?

with bullets

lots of bullets

silver bullets

I don't believe you I say
even though I mostly do

It's true she says

I heard my mom on the phone

very recently

He's killed a man

Maybe two

REALLY? I say out loud

Who?

wheeze whap

He's gone back inside

the coast is clear

we all deflate and sprawl on the ground

Who
Hen
Who?

No one we know she says
His name was Buck

My mom says it ought to be illegal

But it is *illegal* I say
Why isn't he in jail?

Beats me Hen says
All I'm saying is that you better watch out

ME?

ME?

You're the one who told me to put my arm
through the fence

AND

I

DID

I DID put my arm through the fence
I felt BULL's breath!

I hold my hand out for Hen's bottle cap

He nearly took my hand off!

You didn't Mississippi on four-five-six
Hen closes her fingers around the cap

Yes I DID!

DIDN'T
say my brothers at the same time

Well it's your fault
That stupid pair

Kids says Hen
She puts her bottle cap back in her pocket

Did he kill Mrs Whitley with that gun Cam says
I want to see the gun Anton says

RUFF!

Words to Say While Running Away

rifle
stifle
or else
or else
or else

From my tree I see
our houses are like
lots of pockets
in the same pants

hiding things inside

sometimes there's a rip
and our secrets fall out

Caw

Caw

Caw

Caw

Ink black
razor beaked
one legged

crow

CAW CAW CAW

Mrs Peg Leg
scolding me out of
my

CAW CAW CAW

own

CAWCAWCAW

tree

shimmy
step
reach
drop

alley

3

crouch crush luck luck babies

Crouching
Hen and me
and her doll Sweet

Don't you want *to come to Southside?*
We've never not been in school together

by a knothole in

My mom says
Mr Whitley's
gate
there's drugs at Southside

but
watching Bull
on his side
in the sun

Southside was supposed to be our school
we were supposed to be together forever

and daring each other to
drop acorns
through the hole

How am I supposed to make new friends all by myself

to see if
he
sees us

HEY!

It's
KID JONES

We stand up fast

fourteen-year-old
next door
KID JONES

going to be in the big leagues someday
KID JONES

KID JONES

talking to

just
us

I wouldn't mind so much
being a sister if
Kid was my brother

It would be like being
Superman's sister

We were just making sure Bull's okay says Hen
tossing her acorns into the alley

Um is all my mouth will say

Um

Um

Um I

and as if this isn't embarrassing enough

there
is
Julia

in sunglasses
holding her turquoise adult size bike

with that white basket in front
full of her saddle purse and her radio

Hi Kid she sings

I stuff the acorns in my pocket

Hi Julia I say
but Kid is already talking

My sister is coming from our mom's for the summer
he says
looking at me
and then at Hen
You guys should try to be nice to her this year

Us? Hen says
but Mercy…

But Mercy what?

Um… I say

Doesn't Kid know what his sister is like?

They'll be nice to Mercy, Kid says Julia
We'll all be nice to Mercy

If she's nice to US Hen says

Kid shakes his head
Just give her a chance he says
and walks away

Okay, Kid! Hen shouts after him
We will!
but she's got her fingers crossed behind her back

HI JULIA I try again

You shouldn't play in the street she says

It's not a

and in one slick motion Julia is
throwing her leg over the bike bar
and gliding away
her hair billowing out behind her
like a movie star

street

* * *

I've got a rope
and Hen's got a rope
and I'm trying out a new
jump rope rhyme
wishing Julia were here
to count for us

Minn
e
sota
North
Dak
o
ta
Penn
sylva
nia
Maine

we
can
jump
all
fif
ty
states

then
jump
them
all
a
gain

Phee Hen Phoebe Henrietta

It's little Jennica
with her bucket of chalk
hanging from her wrist
like a purse

You could forget she's here

flat shadow behind the gate
but nagging

like the memory of something you did wrong
a long time ago

You could forget

except she's got the biggest eyes
behind her glasses so that you think

when you do see her that she
sees right through your skin

and hair and into your head
even though she's only seven

It's like clover which is all over
(so you don't notice)

had a superpower

Jennica hands me a thick chunk of yellow
then
she
lays down flat
smack in the middle of the alley
both arms up in a Y

Trace me
she says in her little mouse voice
Phee Phoebe Phee pleeeeeeeease

You should get up
a car could come

but more than that
Julia could show up again
and witness this

draw me draw me
Phee Phee Phoebe Phee please

Yes! says Hen
We'll do all of us!
and she drops her rope
and flops down
arms and legs bent
like she's running

and if it isn't bad enough
here come Anton and Cam

Draw us too!

everyone posing on the ground
like dead people

and I'm the only one standing

me
Phoebe
Phee
e
lev
en

with a stick of chalk in my hand
like a magic wand
wishing to make them disappear

is this how it's going to be
all
summer
long

just me and these

BABIES

Walking Backwards Away From Them Words

ground play
lace shoe
bow rain
fish gold
fly butter

Blue bag
    hanging
    in my tree

Blue bag
    full of
    ruffle edged
    bottlecaps

clattering like coins when I shake it
clattering like coins when I shake it
clattering like jingling jangling word coins when I shake it

Grape Crush Orange Crush Pepsi Cola Pepsi Cola Hamm's
7UP the Uncola Dad's Root Beer Have a Dad's
CocaCola CocaCola CocaCola Mountain Dew

Make a wish
make a wish
make a wish and
shake it

shake it up
pick three caps

a poem
for my pocket

three!
all the same!

ORANGE
CRUSH
CRUSH
CRUSH

ORANGE
CRUSH
CRUSH
CRUSH

orange crush crush luck

4

erupt disrupt possible what

From up high I spy

Hen Henny Henrietta
jumping rope
tripping once
jumping twice
hair bouncing up, down

Old Man Whitley
behind the tall board fence
trimming his yard like it's his own bald head
    is he scheming
    how he's going to get us

BULL
lunging at the mower
pawing the ground
shaking his boxy head
like he's trying to get rid of bad thoughts
    is he dreaming of
    how he's going to eat us

Anton and Cam
with a bucket of water and two shovels
making another house in Mudville

Jennica
crouched below me
drawing on the asphalt with chalk
symbols only she can read

Julia-Cicely-Alix
leaning against Julia's fence watching

        the screen door slamming at Kid's house
        Kid bouncing out with his
        baseball and his mitt

A not-from-the-alley car
        blue
        with windows rolled down

Oh no is it

driving slowly
        horn tooting

Uh oh yup it is

                scattering Hen and Jennica
                igniting growling Bull
                        the fence shaking
                        where he heaves his body against it
                                Anton and Cam throw down their
                                shovels and run

        and stopping
        stopping!

right
next
door

THINGS I SEE

Kid and Mercy's mom
in a blue track suit

putting a lumpy black duffle
in Kid's driveway

Mercy Jones getting out with
something sleek under her arm
something with wheels

THINGS I HEAR

Kid: *Hey Mom*
Hey Mercy
a skateboard!

Mercy:

Their mom: *mumble mumble*

Kid: *Can you stay for a while, Mom?*

Their mom: *mumble mumble*

Mercy:

Car: *sput sput sput*
right under my feet
toot toot
and away

Kid: *Come on, Mercy*
Let's take your things to your room

Julia-Cicely-Alix:
Hey Kid
Hi Mercy

Mercy:

Julia-Cicely-Alix:

Your skateboard
is really cool, Mercy

Let's see it, Mercy

Let us try it, Mercy

THINGS I THINK

Mercy: Taller than last year
Not a sapling

SKATEBOARD

Mercy: Older than last year
Not a stripling

SKATEBOARD

They wouldn't eat Mercy alive at Southside

SKATEBOARD

MERCY

SKATEBOARD

No one in our alley has ever had a

SKATEBOARD before

luck
lucky
orange crush
lucky
luck

Luck let me ride on that
skate
board
skate
board
skate
board

I'm dragging Hen

Let's get a try on that skateboard

but she's not budging

We don't like Mercy. Remember?

but I'm ready to give her a chance because

I want to get a turn on that skateboard

but Hen's shaking me off

Remember how she grumped everything up last summer?

I'll give you a 7Up cap if you just come with me to the door

Well…

I'm dragging Hen and we're
at Kid and Mercy's door and we're

ready to give Mercy a chance because we're

ready to get a turn
on that skateboard

maybe we'll be three
like Julia + Cicely + Alix

We're

Hi Mercy!

we say at exactly the same time

Look out
she says
and she pushes past us
out the door with her skateboard
and into the alley

Have you turned twelve? I call

YUP
she shouts
as she pushes off and
rides right away
from us

luckier and luckier
Twelve
finally
someone who's not a fledgling

WAIT UP!
Hen and I say
at exactly the same time
as she
glides
all the
way
up the
alley
right
up
to

MERCY!

we holler

LOOK OUT FOR 38th STREET!

we go
along
38th Street
we never go
across
38th Street
but Mercy Jones rides

car car Mercy car

right
across
and
away

Maybe all this time she's just been shy I say

Nope she's just mean says Hen

Maybe I say

but I hope

car car bus motorcycle

it's shy

5

back up back up honeysuckle splat

Henny and me hover over
alley honeysuckle

listening for Bull
You're going to have to try again with Bull
you're going to have to do something
Julia Cicely and Alix will notice

by Old Man Whitley's fence
popping buds between our fingers

listening for Bull

I know
I know
I know

pop pop honeysuckle bud pop

Maybe we could TRY being friends with Mercy this summer I say

No way says Hen

But she's got that skateboard.
That's notable
noticeable

Why aren't we friends with Mercy

We're not friends with Mercy because she's not friends with us

But Julia is being nice to her

Besides, my mother says I'll stay away from Mercy Jones if I know what's good for me

Why?

I'm not supposed to tell

But I'm your best friend

pop pop honeysuckle bud pop

Then why do you care about Mercy

Hen
ri
etta!

All I will say is if we're best friends
we don't need Mercy barging in on our fun

pop pop honeysuckle bud pop

It's you and me and me and you

But

LISTEN she says
trying to distract me

But I'm just saying maybe we should give her and her skateboard a chance like Kid said

Listen

Mr Whitley's window is open
we can hear him playing the piano
how he does
his sad melodies
floating out the window and over the fence
holding the notes like he's tasting misery

Do you think he's sad about who he shot? she says

Hen! What did your mother say about Mercy?

Look she says

and even though I know she's trying to distract me
I look

It's an empty Mr Pibb bottle by Mr Whitley's trash can
which starts a race to find the cap
which makes me bump into the fence
which makes BULL

RUFF

which makes us scream
which makes Mr Whitley stop playing
which gives Hen an idea

Here she says
holding out the bottle

I dare you to throw this
over

Mr
Whitley's
fence

What about Mr Whitley's GUN I hiss
What about Bull?

I'll give you this
Hen's found the cap

I
grab the bottle by the neck bring it over my head and fling it

CHUNK

It hits the fence but doesn't break
which is good luck but now BULL is barking
which is bad luck and I back up

Throw it higher!

I KNOW!

Quick!

I KNOW!

I wipe my sweaty palms on my shorts
back up and
underhand it
up high and

OVER!

Hen hands me the Mr Pibb and I take out my lucky caps and I

SLAM!
Mr Whitley's door

SCRAM!

Henny and me

BOOGEYMANBOOGEYMAN!

smack into

the path of

Mercy and her skateboard

I am so surprised I drop my bottle caps

I'll take that says Mercy
and she flips her skateboard up with one foot
grabs it with her hand
and in the same motion dips down and
snatches my Mr Pibb and
my Orange Crush Crush Crush
then tosses out her board
hops on and
skates away
with all my luck

We run down the alley after her
right up to 38th Street

Julia-Cicely-Alix are waving to Mercy from the
other side

Mercy glides
through the gap
speeding cars
and the 21A
missing her again

but not

splat

my bottle caps

38th Street
river of
cars
buses
motorcycles

the road between
here and where
Mercy goes

between
here and where
people we don't know
like Cicely and Alix
are living
lives we don't see

Come ON says Hen
turning back
Who needs her

I would rather
GO

car car van *get my flat* bike car car

bottle caps

6

impress regress best best nest

Balance
is something you have
or you don't

that's what Mercy says
but she's got it
so she can talk

Mercy's got a skateboard
so she can talk

skateboard skateboard

not from the alley Mercy

twelve year old skateboarding Mercy

sails down the alley on her skateboard
arms wide
neck pulled away from her shoulders like a turtle trying to escape its shell
the wheels *chick chick chick*ing across cracks

chick chick chicka could be should be would be
me Phoebe Phee skateboarding Southsider
skate skateboarding me Phoebe Phee

Henny and me
we plead
Let us try
let us
let us
let us

'til Mercy says
You sound like a couple of rabbits begging for food

Huh? says Hen

Salad I say
Lettuce

And we feel dumber than ever
poking along on eight wheels each
old timey little kid roller skates

let us
let us
lettuce
lettuce
balance
rabbits
balance
beg

I'm done with roller skating I say

Unskated
these feet are
          more than ordinary
the biggest feet of all the alley
          almost
great long boards
          they could skim across water
          they could skip down a hill
          they could stomp out a fire

they could make big prints on the halls of fame
they could stomp through the halls of Southside

these feet
          they can balance
if Mercy
only
gives
them
a
chance

I need Mercy
to give
me
a chance
on that skateboard

MERCY!

My voice is
loud
proud
bold
cold

I stand smack in the middle of the alley
legs apart hands on my hips

she's coming fast
she's coming straight for me
and I

PHEE! Hen grabs me tugs me pulls me to the side

and Mercy

STOPS

Okay
PhoeBE
HenriETTA

What's
my
full
name?

Huh? we say
Um we say

Mercy?

I thought so she says

Mercy flips her skateboard up on
two
wheels
and spins
all the
way
around

You never wanted me before I had a skateboard

But

But

But

But

and chick chick chicka chick
away and back
away and back

chick chick chick away

Without our skates

without Mercy to torment us

the day yawns

sleepy old long old day full of
nothing
notable

until

Hen says
Let's jump the long rope

Hen may be annoying but she is the kind of person
who can always think of something
good to do

One long rope
plus Henny and me

could be
extra
ordinary

One long rope
plus Henny and me
could be but

one long rope
plus Henny and me equals
zero

we need three

Twirl for us, Julia!

she glides past us
glued to Cicely and Alix

Twirl for us, Mercy!

She rides
right through the middle of us
Outtamyway!
right over our rope after Julia-Cicely-Alix

Twirl for us, Jennica!

Jennica takes one end
loops it on the fence
and walks away
that's just like Jennica

One long rope
    plus the fence
    plus Hen and me

equals trouble

How can I twirl
    while she whines

    Slower!
    Faster!

    Slower! Faster!
    You're doing it all wrong!

All I say is

YOU'RE SUCH A BABY

and she stops jumping

    Takes one to know one she says

That's what babies say I say

I start twirling again
but Hen
won't
jump

    You just want to impress Mercy she says

I
I
I
    and you follow Julia around like a little kitten

like a little kitten
does Julia think that too?

I
I

Well that's exactly what Catholic School babies say I say

Hen flinches

Well I'll tell you this
even my mother says

Phoebe will
never
survive
Southside

Well you're
um
um
um

Um
Um
Um she says

and I drop
my end of the rope

we fight but
Hen has never
made fun of me before

Ugly Words to Say While Stomping Away

fungus
sickle
liverwurst
phlegm

I could help Anton and Cam with Mudville
I could spy on Julia-Cicely-Alix

but
sometimes
it feels good
to feel bad

all that mad
expanding inside me
like rocket fuel

filling me with energy
until I
could climb a forest of trees
          if there was a forest of trees to climb

          run
          dash
          zip
          sashay

          I'm fast as a dog
          after a yellow ball

Southside
Southside

          after a yellow ball
          I'm fast as a dog

eat you alive
at Southside

          sashay
          zip
          dash
          run

I climb into my tree
at record speed
and pant like a
worn out dog

ENEMY I shout into the tree
EN
EM
EEEEEE
ENEMY
ENEMY

Enemy is a

satisfying

word to say out loud

WHO ARE YOU TALKING TO?

It's Mercy

Mercy skateboarding
Mercy Jones

standing under my tree
talking up at me

and suddenly
with all this mad stored up

I feel bold
like Mercy

I feel old
like Mercy

Hi Mercy I say
and before I think I say

Do you want to come up

Me
Phoebe Phee
asking
Mercy skateboarding Mercy Jones
to come up into my tree

It all spins out in my mind

Mercy and me: friends
forget Hen

sharing Mercy's skateboard
laughing with Julia

who won't even need Cicely and Alix anymore

like I won't need Hen

the bold feeling builds in me
a Southside feeling

and I scoot over
making room for

Mercy skateboarding
Mercy Jones

will she think this is stupid
just a board in a tree
not a real treehouse
do people in middle school even like treehouses

You don't have to I say but

Mercy tucks her skateboard behind the tree and
stands on the garbage can
steps onto the fence post and
climbs
right
up

she edges in next to me
still
silent
a big bulk of breathing

I am used to sitting close to Hen but
Mercy is different
not from the alley

What's that? she says

I am holding my
very private
purple
with birds
notebook
with poems

which no one has
seen inside
ever

Nothing I say and I tuck it
under me

She shrugs
reaches for my blue bag

What's this?

and suddenly bottle caps
seem like a fledgling thing to collect

but she's got the bag and she's opening it
she's pulling out a handful of bottle caps
dropping them back in

Cool she says closing the bag
shaking it so they jangle
You didn't have these last summer
hanging it back up

Cool I say
liking the sound of it
liking the sound of us
Cool

We neither of us have much to say
but it's okay

Me Phoebe Phee
Southside girl
with

Mercy ...

What is your full name? I say

Why do you care? she says

I
um

Where do you live with your mom?

How come we never wondered this before
we never wondered anything about Mercy before

You wouldn't know it she says
It's a place with lots more people
people who leave you alone

not like here where
everyone's crowded in on
everyone's business

That's more words than I've ever heard Mercy say in a row
I want to hear her say more

I've been in the country I say
to a farm
which is not the same but

Expansive she says

expansive
yes

someone like Mercy
knows expansive things

I don't know how you can stand living here
just LOOK at this dump

I look out on my alley
really look
and all at once my big beautiful alley
looks small
crowded
ordinary

Then why do you come here I say

My dad gets me in the summer

Why doesn't Kid live with your mom, too

Mercy shrugs

I imagine living somewhere
without Anton and Cam
somewhere expansive
it puts a flutter in my stomach

I look up into the leaves

Your best friend is still annoying Mercy says

I look at the shape the sky makes between them

She's not my

best

friend I say softly

but Lentil is meowing howling below us

WHAT?

SHE'S NOT MY BEST FRIEND I say louder

So why are you always together?

and even though Lentil runs off
my voice doesn't notice and I
keep on loud

HEN'S THE ONLY GIRL AROUND HERE
EXACTLY MY AGE
SO WE STUCK WITH EACH OTHER

Not anymore Mercy says

I look where she's looking and

there's Hen

who's heard me

Hen

staring up into the tree
at me

and Mercy

My words hang in the air like darts

not
my
best
friend
stuck
with
each
other

Hen! I say
but she's running away

I want to go after her
I want to tell her I didn't mean it
even though she said things too
I didn't really mean to mean it
but

Mercy's here

and everything is

comp
li
cated

7

rough tough enough enough

Mudville
morning

again again
brothers
lure me in when there's nothing to see from
my tree

I'm Hen-less

cup of water
stir up mud
shape a tiny brick
set it in the sun
do it all
again

they've been working on this
longer than anything

cup of water
stir up mud
shape a tiny brick
set it in the sun
do it all again

        The news cameras will come says Anton

        We'll be famous says Cam

I wish it were still so easy to be happy

Whatever floats your boat I say

They think I am
hi
        lar
                i
                        ous

when really I'm
just passing time in this dump until
Hen comes by
        I miss her

or
Mercy
        I wish for her

or Hen
and Mercy

or
and
Julia
Julia
Julia

        cup of water
        stir up mud
        shape a brick
        set it in the sun
        do it all
        again

If it's Hen
will I be her friend again
will she be my friend again

    cup of water
    stir up mud

if it's Mercy
will we —

    shape a brick
    set it in the

do I have to give up Hen
to be Mercy's friend

    cup of water
    stir up mud

Mercy-skateboard-twelve-expansive

Hen-routine-comfortable-friend

    shape a brick
    set it in the sun

all those mean things I said
she won't want to

    Hi Phee

It's Hen
    she's quieter
    she's wilt-ier
    but she's here
    holding our long jump ropes

like
nothing
was
ever
wrong

that's the notable thing about Hen

a bubble of warm rises up in me
I'm so happy I could nearly play dolls
if she asked me

We don't need three to jump she says
What if we both twirl one string
Hen is the kind of person who calls ropes strings
without a skipper

ONE ROPE!

Pennies
nickels
silver dimes
we can twirl it
ninety-nine times

one
          two
three
          four
...

TWO ROPES!

left rope
right rope

Hen! faster

left rope
right rope

          Phee! slower

left and
right and
over and
under and
left and
right and
Hen and
I can
swing this
string
and

swing this
string
one and
two and

We are the best in the West!

No one twirls like Hen and me
best friend Hen
she's not so annoying

You're too far apart
shouts Mercy as she wheels by
It's got to snap the ground
now that's annoying

WE KNOW, MERCY
we shout
at exactly the same time

how could I have ever thought
I would give up Hen for Mercy?

she wheels by again

JINX
we shout
at exactly the same time

We were all just fine here
before Mercy came back

she stops wheeling

DOUBLE JINX
we're laughing so hard
we can't stand up

why is she just standing there looking at me?

We know how to TWIRL, MERCY
We know how to SKIP, MERCY
We know how to WALK, MERCY

We know

I do want to ride that skateboard but

we KNOW

I'm so relived to be
Hen+Phee

WE KNOW

Phee+Hen
again that I

Who do you think you are? shouts Hen

GOD?

say it
too

Who do you think you are? GOD?

Now it feels like the way things always are

Anton and Cam and Jennica come out
to see what the shouting is about

Who do you think you are?
God?
Who do you think you are?
they chant
laughing

Why doesn't she skate away?
Why does she stay?

BANG!

GUN!
RUN!

I grab Anton and Cam
Hen grabs Jennica's hand

and we run

to the empty lot
with the empty shed

where I fling open
the lopsided door

pull
everyone
in and

pull
the
door

SHUT

everyone

except

Mercy

So dark in here
I can hear
spiders
spinning webs

so dark in here
I can hear

everyone breathing

Here
in the
deep
dank
dark

we listen
for Mr Whitley's gun

What about Mercy whispers Jennica

Things we hear:

laughing
laughing?
yes!

running pounding feet
SHOUTING

and POP POP POP
    BANG

    no Boogeyman voice shouting

    no screaming

    so I

    c
    r
    e
    a
    k

    the door open a

    c
      r
        a
          c
            k

Things We See:

Three teenagers not ours
    crouching in the middle of the alley

Julia+Cicely+Alix
    and Mercy
    standing by Kid's garage

What are they doing? says Henny in her not quiet enough voice

Shhhh! we all say

and everyone crowds around me to see

Should we go out there I whisper
Mercy's out there

Not me says Hen

They look tough says Anton

and *rough* says Cam

rough
tough
gruff
enough to hurt us

rough tough gruff enough Jennica whispers
clutching my shirt

rough tough gruff enough Cam joins in
and lets Jennica hold his doll

rough tough gruff enough they chant

then

CRACK pop pop

BANG

Firecrackers!

Things that happen:

BULL bark bark BARKING
lunging at the fence

Mr Whitley marching into the alley
with his stiff leg walk
waving something in the air
something that looks like a …

and just like that my
legs have an idea and

before my mind can catch up
I am running into the alley shouting

JULIA! LOOK OUT!

HE'S GOT A GUN!

I'm throwing my arms around her

and

everything
everything
everyone
stops

Things I see

Get off!

Julia's unlocking my arms
backing away

GO ON! GET!

Mr Whitley's waving a wrench
turning back into his garage

Cicely and Alix and Julia
and the teenagers
Relax Old Man!
are striding off
down the alley
laughing

at me?

and Mercy
Sheesh Phee
plops down her skateboard
and
Wait for me!
skates after
them

Now I know what
normal is not

I want to be fog
and evaporate

8

eve even evening night

In the after supper hour
when shadows are the longest
we stand in the alley
Henny and me

it's the safest feeling
just familiar Henrietta
and
me

We walk around to make our shadows touch things

I stand way back by Kid's garage
so my shadow enters the empty lot

I step forward
and forward

until my shadow's head covers the old pipe that sticks up out
of the ground

What lives down there? I say
and Hen has to move her shadow over the pipe to tell
that's how it's played

That's where you'll go when you die she says
Down that pipe to a wide tank
floating like a bathtub in an underground sea

There you'll float away to your next destiny
You'll come out of a pipe in someone else's empty lot
Somewhere where you don't know anyone

Somewhere like Southside?

Probably

Hen steps away but I grab her so
her wisp of a shadow covers
the pipe again

Then you'll come too I say

but

RUFF RUFF RUFF

we scream
we take our shadows
and run

and
run
run
just
run

up
the
alley
down
the
alley

shadow pullers
reeling in night

Mercy's brother Kid
hits baseballs
in the alley
in the night
by streetlight

He pitches to himself
one after another
while we catchers hover
with flashlights
at the other end
listening to the

crack
whoosh
crack
whoosh
times three

hoping that Mr Whitley
is asleep

then we race for the balls
and Kid does it again

Kid never misses
never hits a garage
never breaks a window

What are you going to do when you're trying out Mercy calls
When you're supposed to hit left field

we stop
no one talks to Kid while he's batting
even Julia
and he misses

Hit to left field, Kid says Julia who's not a catcher
but a looker on

I can tell because I know Julia
that she tries to say it in a strong voice but it comes out
like a question like everything does since she met Cicely and Alix

Leave him alone Julia he's my brother says Mercy

Hey Kid
You'll only be practiced at center

I could say something
do something too but
I still feel
sheepish
around Julia and

their voices are drifting on the night
floating on the air from all down the alley

all crowded in on each other in each other's business and

I just want to listen

I've got the ball
Anton running

Hit the ball hit the ball
Cam's violin string voice

COMING, MOM!
Hen answering her mother's
bed-time whistle

Hit it to me
Julia jumping off the fence

Hit the ball hit the ball
Mercy joining in

Here comes a homer
Kid

hear
hit
homer
ball
ball
coming
her
hit
homer

CRACK

all of it sounds to me
one voice
like music
two voices
and a poem rises up in me
our voices
and I have to cut away
sounding
and run to my tree

one voice
two voices
our voices
sounding

resounding
pounding
abounding
surrounding

9

drip drop drizzle sop

R
A
I
N
R
A
I
N
R
A
I
N
R
A
I
N
R
A
I
N
R
A
I
N

R   R R   R R R R   R
A   RA A R R A A A A R A
I   AI I A A I I I I A I
N   IN N I I N N N N I N
R   NR R N N R R R R N R
A   RA A R R A A A A R A
I   AI I A A I I I I A I
N   IN N I I N N N N I N
R   NR R N N R R R R N R
A   RA A R R A A A A R A
I   AI I A A I I I I A I
N   IN N I I N N N N I N
R   NR R N N R R R R N R
A   RA A R R A A A A R A
I   AI I A A I I I I A I
N   IN N I I N N N N I N
R   NR R N N R R R R N R
A   RA A R R A A A A R A
I   AI I A A I I I I A I
N   IN N I I N N N N I N
R   NR R N N R R R R N R
A   RA A R R A A A A R A
I   AI I A A I I I I A I
N   IN N I I N N N N I N
R   NR R N N R R R R N R
A   RA A R R A A A A R A
I   AI I A A I I I I A I
N   IN N I I N N N N I N
R   NR R N N R R R R N
A   RA A   R A A A A
I   AI I   A I I I I
N   IN N   I N N N N
    N   R   N R R R R
    R   A   R A A A A
    A   I   A I I I I
    I   N   I N N N N
    N   N

```
R R   R   R   R     R R   R   dr
A A   A R A   A R   A A   A   ip
I I   I A I   I A   I I   I   dr
N N   N I N   N I   N N   N   ip
R R   R N R   R N   R R   R   dr
A A   A R A   A R   A A   A   ip
I I   I A I   I A   I I   I   dr
N N   N I N   N I   N N   N   ip
R R   R N R   R N   R R   R   dr
A A   A R A   A R   A A   A   ip
I I   I A I   I A   I I   I   dr
N N   N I N   N I   N N   N   ip
R R   R N R   R N   R R   R   dr
A A   A R A   A R   A A   A   ip
I I   I A I   I A   I I   I   dr
N N   N I N   N I   N N   N   ip
R R   R N R   R N   R R   R   dr
A A   A R A   A R   A A   A   ip
I I   I A I   I A   I I   I   dr
N N   N I N   N I   N N   N   ip
R R   R N R   R N   R R   R   dr
A A   A R A   A R   A A   A   ip
I I   I A I   I A   I I   I   dr
N N   N I N   N I   N N   N   ip
R R   R N R   R N   R R   R   dr
A A   A R A   A R   A A   A   ip
I I   I A I   I A   I I   I   dr
N N   N I N   N I   N N   N   ip
R R   R N R   R N   R R   R   dr
A A   A R A   A R   A A   A   ip
I I   I A I   I A   I I   I   dr
N N   N I N   N I   N N   N   ip
R R     N     R N     R       dr
A A     R     A       A       ip
I I     A     I       I
N N     I     N       N
        N
```

MUD

Steam's rising from the ground
the world smells like an oven

all over the alley
pink
squishy
slick
wriggling
EARTH WORMS

Hen and I are a two person Worm Rescue Team
one wet slimy squirmer at a time
    pick it up
    drop it by my tree
    a worm colony

NO!
OH NO!
PHEEEEEEEEEEEEEEE!

We drop our worms and run to the empty lot

Anton and Cam have their shirts off
trying to sop up water

Mudville is a
lumpy
bumpy
mud puddle

one lone dandelion still standing beside it

NO NO NO Anton is saying over and over

Cam is crying
    muddy shirt
    muddy face

I hope everyone got out okay Hen says

We can rebuild it I say

NO NO NO

Lentil is lurking

Get away
Get away
Cam cries
shooing her with both his hands

but she's stubborn
nosing the rubble

pressing her paws into the mud

NO LENTIL
we all shout

Leave the cat alone!

It's Mercy
She's swooping in
scooping up Lentil

who YOWLS and
squirms and
scratches

and Mercy yowls
and drops her

And there we all are

all of us and Mercy
with bleeding scratches on her arm

and it is
all of us

and Mercy

and Julia-Cicely-Alix walking by
huddled together

and it's all of them
all of us

and Mercy

even Lentil
has run away from Mercy

in my mind I'm saying
come look Mercy
come help with Mudville

but nothing
comes
out
of
my
mouth

and she takes her bleeding arms
and walks away

We're running up the alley
following Mercy on her skateboard

          Quit following me!

Anton's at 38th Street
with his stopwatch

We want to know
how fast she goes

          Get away from me!

She's passing Hen's house
one more push

          BUS! Anton yells
          but Mercy doesn't slow

                              BUS! We all yell

Mercy screams and
jumps off
just
in
time

but the skateboard keeps going
rightinfrontofthe

THAT COULD HAVE BEEN YOU! Hen shouts

but Mercy ignores her

we all ignore her
as one car
two cars
three cars
crunch and spew wheels and wood
and the shoe that flew off Mercy's foot

When the coast is clear
we run into the street

collecting splintered wood
bent metal four wheels

we carry it all to the curb
lay it out like a dead body

Leave it alone! Mercy hollers

You'd think she'd be grateful

Get out of here!

We retreat
a few feet

My heart's thumping hard
the honking splintering echoing in my head

Mercy stretches her shirt into a sling
puts in all the pieces

walks to Hen's trashcan
lifts the lid

stands on her toes and
drops those skateboard bones

right in

37 seconds Anton says
a world record

Without her skateboard
Mercy is suddenly
an
ordinary
girl
walking on
ordinary
feet
looking for something to do

just like
the rest
of us

so why won't she
play
with the
rest
of
us?

Wondering Words

carburetor
instigator
alligator
thud

10

squeak   retreat   gone   gone   gone

Single
skipping
rope
genius

Mercy
Julia
Hen and
Phee
…
…

how
compli-
cated
can
…
it
…
be

Mercy
Julia
Hen and
Phee

. . .
. . .

how
compli-
cated
can it

PHEE! COME SEE!

Hen comes out from the empty lot where

Anton
Cam and
Jennica are
hunched
and hushed
over in the corner
behind Mudville
by Anton and Cam's shirt heap

What are you looking at?

SHHH!
Look!

A nest of baby mice

nine tiny pink hairless aliens
the cutest things
we've ever seen

and their cloud white mother

right here
in Anton's muddy shirt

we crouch

still as stones
all we can hear is

the trash truck rattling through the next alley
and Anton breathing
his loud mouth-breathing

They're breathing, too
    the mice
we see it
    their little chests going in out in out in out

and I love them already
their tiny bud ears

there is one
bigger than the others
I imagine having her as my very own

    big little mouse
    named Pink

to keep in my pocket
and go everywhere with me
    even Southside

and she will twitch her tiny nose
I will tell her secrets
    and keep her in my tree
I'll make a little nest for her th…

LENTIL!

Quick as a lick
Lentil darts between us
snatches a mouthful of
mama mouse
and runs

Drop it!
Drop it!

We're racing after Lentil
the mama still in his mouth
her skinny tail drooping over his lip
as Lentil darts into the alley
around the trash can
out of sight

We comb all his places
high
low

Here!
Over here!
Cam and Anton are at Mr Whitley's back gate

Lentil has circled back
hopped up top
and we're all moving
slowly
towards
him
arms
outstretched

kitty kitty kitty
here kitty kitty

sweetly as we can
getting so close
that mouse-tail still dangling
then

squeeeeeeak

our mouse

squeeeeeeak

Mr Whitley's screen door

ruff ruff ruffruffRUFF
BULL!

plop
Lentil drops our mama mouse

down
into
Mr Whitley's yard

NOOOOOO!

and strolls along the fence and into a tree

We're all moaning
groaning

I'm hollering

Mr Whitley!
Mr Whitley
please!

and we all holler

MR WHITLEY
PLEASE HELP!

Big square face
over the fence
two brown eyes
and a pinched frown
glowering down
at us

even I
feel small
            as Bull *RUFF*s
            as Mr Whitley glares

                                    WHAT IN TARNATION?

no one says anything so

Please I say
            in a thread thin voice
there's a mama mouse in your yard

                                    THERE'S A WHAT?

                                    WHERE?

Lentil just dropped it
right there
and she has babies
in the empty lot
Can you get her?

Mr Whitley looks down
shakes his head
            back
            forth
                                    YOU'RE TRESSPASSING

                                    ALL OF YOU

HAVE YOU BEEN LOOKING IN MY GARAGE?

We're shaking our heads
shaking our heads
backing up
and I'm thinking
    of the three billy goats gruff
    and the troll and
    Who's that tromping over my bridge

IMPUDENT CHILDREN!
GET!
GET!

and we get
with all we've got
back to the empty lot

where nine motherless mice
lay sleeping

WORDS TO WHISPER
impudent
tromp
impudent
tromp
billy goat billy goat billy goat
gruff

WORDS THEY WHISPER WITH ME
impudent
tromp
impudent
tromp
billy goat billy goat billy goat
gruff

WORDS WE SHOUT-WHISPER
impudent
TROMP
impudent
TROMP
billy goat billy goat billy goat
GRUFF

WORDS THE DOOR SAYS
WHAP
SLAP

We can't leave the babies here Hen says

I could put them in my tree
there's a hole up by my branch

I imagine the little orphans tucked in safe
I'll feed them little sips of water with Cam's old baby spoon

Owls
says Anton

and Lentil
says Cam

I know they're right but that doesn't stop me from
wishing they were mine

While we sit
watching the babies
Jennica dumps out her chalk bucket

She pulls hands full of clover
squats down
slides her slim little hands under the little nest
lifts the whole thing up
sets it in the bucket

and walks away

HEY! we all shout
They aren't yours!
Where are you going?
Wait UP!

We're following Jennica
down the alley

past Mercy
    What are you doing? What's she got?

    None of your beeswax says Hen
    blocking Mercy from seeing the bucket

Baby mice! I say
    elbowing past Hen

    PHOEBEEE!
    Hen elbows past me and past Mercy

Jennica stops at her back gate
bumps it open with her hip and
we all follow her in
even Mercy

There's a small tree
a miniature
in a pot on a rock
    like a regular tree
    only tiny

We've never been inside the fence at Jennica's
    it's a tall fence
    like Mr Whitley's

Jennica's yard is small like all the yards
There's a garden of delicate flowers
    all red
Bricks make a circle path around a small fountain
    burbling water
Green feathered plants grow in clumps
There's a cape of leaves over us

It's cooler here than in the alley
the bricks are swept clear
    no weeds growing between them
a baby swing hangs on its own metal frame
    for Jennica's baby brother Miles
    the loudest crier on the block
There's a small table just Jennica's size

And that tiny tree
    an elf would be too big to climb it
    it is exactly the size for those baby mice

Jennica lifts out the nest and sets it under the tiny tree
    we all huddle around

My eyes are watery and I don't know why
    the perfect smallness of the tree
    the perfect smallness of the mice
    Jennica's perfect smallness
    it's like a poem
I am a giant in a fairy tale

    They aren't going to live says Mercy

    What do you know about it says Hen

They might not live I say
    my heart feels sharp
Mercy's right
without their mother
They might not live!

    You just want to be like Mercy says Hen
    You can't be my friend
    and her friend
    both

Mercy shrugs and
walks
right
out

Maybe I don't want
to
be

ANYONE'S
friend
HEN!

Jennica stands
between
us
and the
mice

Maybe if everyone leaves says Jennica
the mama will come find her babies

simmering

stewing

brooding

in my tree too
long I'm
not the first
one
back
to
Jennica's

Anton is there
crouched by the tiny tree
and Cam
standing by hands-on-her-hips-Hen
and Jennica
holding Miles's hands
as he tries to walk
but no Mercy

THEY'RE GONE Hen says

THEY'RE GONE says Anton

GONE?
They can't just be gone

I push Anton aside and
there is the
empty
nest

Jennica let them get away says Cam

Did not Jennica says

Maybe did says Cam

They've got to be here I say
their bucket is here
their nest is here

I think Mercy took them says Hen

I think Mercy took them, too says Anton
She's not here

And she's mean enough says Cam

I bet the mama mouse took them to her mouse hole says Jennica

Probably that's what happened says Cam

That's what happened I say
I want to believe it

Miles lets go of Jennica's fingers
toddles to the tree
and
before I can stop him he's
knocked that nest
to the ground

Mercy took them says Hen
you'll see

Mercy took them you'll see says Anton

Stop it, Anton says Hen
Anton is in love with Hen

I hope they're wrong
but I think
they might
be right

Hot again late again

lazy feeling sleep feeling watchinglightscomeon feeling

Phee! Phoebe!
PheePhoebePhee!

stringy brother voices
springing from the house
out of tune violins

Com

ing!

If I could sleep here in my tree I would dream
green and green and

STOP!

THINGS I SEE

blue shirt
blue shorts

Mercy

carrying that big black duffle

Mercy

followed by

baseball cap
long legs

Kid

THINGS I HEAR

Kid:

Mercy!

Mercy:

Leave me alone

Kid:

Mercedes! Hold up

Mercy:

Nobody told me I was
STAYING here
PAST summer
Nobody told me
I was STAYING

Kid:

It was just decided
Come back home

Mercy:

You know this
isn't
my
home
Nobody wants me here

Kid:

I want you here Mercy
This is your home now
You are staying
You are going to Southside

Ambulance:

EEEEEooooEEEEooooo
RoooooOORooooOOOOO

BULL howling along

ripples of chills are ruffling me and
I can't hear what they're saying

Kid is taking Mercy's duffle
          Mercy Mercedes
                    Kid is taking Mercy's hand
          Mercy Mercedes
                    Mercy is yanking it away but
Kid and Mercedes are walking back home

PheePhoebePhee!
          PhoebePhee!

Com

          ing!

Words to Whisper

no
body
home
home
body
no
no
body
home
now
now
now

Southside

11

no no no no no

We are looking for Mercy
and for the mice
around every garage
over every fence
I am full to bursting with wanting to
know for sure

is Mercy staying
is Mercy going to Southside

too?

We are knocking on the back door
at Kid's house
at Kid's and Mercy's house
no one is answering

and suddenly
there's a
storm
of feet
and
yelling
and
that pack of teenagers
is back

sauntering
laughing

with Julia+Cicely+Alix

Hey LOOK! shouts one of the
ones we don't know

A treehouse!

I run out to the alley
with Hen+Anton+Cam+Jennica

and one of the teenagers is
jumping up on MY trashcan
climbing into MY TREE

I am KING of the Forest!
he yells

I'm coming up!
shouts another
and she climbs up

Phee! gasps Hen
They can't do that!

But they can

and they are

They're standing on

my
board
in
my
tree

and one of them is snapping
up
my blue bag and
shaking it
and rattling
it
and

what is it
everyone is shouting

and
she opens it up
and dumps it out

and there are bottle caps
scattered

every
where

and while everyone is
scrambling to pick them up

the other one is reaching
reaching
into
reaching into the
hole in the tree

pulling out —

Look at this! the boy shouts
he's waving my notebook
purple with birds
my poem notebook

my chest is cement

my mouth is sand

they are sitting on my board
big feet dangling

they are opening up my notebook
laughing

everyone is gathered under my tree

What does it say? Alix shouts

It looks like a diary the girl says

Read it read it read it! calls Cicely

They're on a stage
and their audience is

rapt
I'm
trapped

My words coming shooting out of their mouths

Julia
used to

everyone laughs
everyone
except Julia

Hen
empty plate

except Hen

brothers
bother

except Anton and Cam

Julia
Julia
Julia

they're reading in funny voices
all of my words
all of my words
all of my words
exposed to the world

one voice
two voices

like a body
without its skin on

my own words

pounding
sounding
resounding

I run

listening for someone to come after me
tell me it will be okay
someone

I run

but no one
comes after me

they all hate me now

I stop

There are chalk marks all down the alley

a cast of people
by Jennica

it's a story of our summer
there's me with a jump rope

there are the mice

Here's Fe B
          me
big as a tree

her face an empty plate

and Fe B
me
with a jump rope

infect us with her rivers of giggles

and with a little girl
JENNICA

holding my hand

Julia Julia

Fe B here and here
and here

my chest is boiling

I feel as mean as Mercy
I feel the power of meanness

before my mind can catch up
my feet are

smudging
smearing
demolishing

PheeBEEEEE

voices are coming
feet are coming

but

I can't stop

PheeBEEEEE

a cacophony of voices

but

I'm in the empty lot

by Mudville

catching my breath

Anton and Cam have been rebuilding since the rains

digging
dousing
molding
sticks for trees
small rocks for people

one voice
two voices

my feet are stomping

no Phoebe no

the buildings
squish
squash
collapsing

my footprint
on the floor of fame

PHEEEEEEEEE
BEEEEEE

PHOEBE

PHOEBE

PHEEEEEE

I turn

I see feet

Hen
Anton
Cam
Jennica

not Julia
not Mercy
not Alix Cicely

not the teenagers
with my notebook

I can't look at them
they all hate me now

my feet
take me
out of the empty lot
back down the alley

I
stand
on the garbage can
step
onto the fence post
lean
into the old rough trunk I

clutch
the limb stump and
shift
pull
climb
to the third branch up on the left where
a hole in the trunk of my tree
is empty

no
clattering bag of bottle caps

no
notebook
purple with birds
poem notebook

where
one long board
just a stupid old board
overlooks my ruin

Cam and Anton in the empty lot
kneeling by Mudville

Julia with the teenagers
at the end of the alley

crossing 38th street

with my notebook?

no Mercy anywhere

and Hen
Henny
Henrietta
standing
right
under
my
tree

How could you
how could you
how could you

say
those things

write
those things

about me

about everyone

her face an empty plate!

I'm an empty plate?

What does that even mean?

Phoebe
how could you

just so you know
I'm not speaking to you

and then you scuffed up Jennica's
art
and you destroyed Mudville

how could you

and just so you know
they have your notebook
they took it with them
they'll take it to Southside
everyone
will know what you wrote

WELL
aren't you going to say something

words stupid words
I'm all done with words

why won't you say something

words stupid words
I'm all done with words

never mind
and anyway
Just so you know
I'm not speaking to you

We're

not

speaking

words stupid words
I'm all done with words

12

morning

afternoon

evening

night

morning

afternoon

evening

night

always it

happens

over

again

morning

afternoon

evening

night

Words the Birds Say

phee
bee
phee
bee

I lay back on my board between the branches

luck *luck* *luck* *luck*

looking into the sky and leaves

umbrella of a thousand greens

we

see

you

we

see

you

closing my eyes to see them print on my eyelids

breathing in all that green

breathing in all that green

cheery
up up up up

up

I
sit
up

I
sit
up
up
up

I
climb
down
down
down

13

again begin us

I'm bouncing
whump
a tennis ball
thwap
against the garage door
whump
thwap
the loneliest hitter
whump
this city's ever
thwap
seen
whump
when
swish
I miss
and
wuff
wuff wuruff wuff
he appears
like a dream
and I'm not waking up
wuff
wuff wuruff wuff

this handsome
long haired
red orange color of fall maples

DOG

sniffing my hand
sniffing my leg and foot
slobbering all over my tennis ball
offering it
slimy gift
tail wagging like a flag in a tornado
a windshield wiper of a tail

I laugh
he opens his mouth to bark some more
and the ball rolls out
all slobbery
I grab it with the edge of my shirt
and he stands with his snout at my belly
right where I'm hunched with the ball
        wuff
        wuff wuruff wuff
in that rhythm I already understand
        wuff
        wuff wuruff wuff
        until Henny comes running to see what's up

        A DOG! Hen yells
        PHEE! PHEE! PHEE!
        YOU GOT A DOG!

Hen

here

talking to
me

and it's true

this dog came right up to me
he must be mine

I have rescued him from an awful fate
like being hit by a car
like being homeless

WHAT'S HER NAME? says Hen

Him I say quietly

Red

Hen
are we
speaking again?

RED! shouts Hen

wuff
wuff wuruff wuff

Hen grabs the ball and throws it

wuff
wuff wuruff wuff

He fetches and brings it
to me
not Hen
to me
and just like that I have a

red
wuffing
running

tennis ball fetching
DOG

and my best friend Hen

> *WHERE DID YOU GET HIM?* Hen shouts
> When Hen is excited she shouts everything

Here I say softly

though I want to shout
I don't ever want to use an inside voice again

a dog a dog a dog
my friend my friend my friend

I have a DOG!
I got him HERE!

When I woke up today
I didn't even think

DOG
except BULL
or Hen
as my friend
or the possibility of

DOG
except BULL
or Hen
as my friend
and now
I have

a real
live
beautiful
slobbering
sweet

extraordinary

DOG
named
RED

He looks at me and I look at him
like we already know each other

Hen crouches next to my dog

What are you going to feed him?
Where are you going to keep him?
Does he have fleas?
Do you have a leash?
Is he hungry?

I pet his velvet ears
and he sniffs me all over

Are you hungry, boy?
Are you hungry?
Are you
are you?

wuff
wuff wuruff wuff

Henny had a dog
so now she is the expert
even though Buster ran away
when we were five
and never came back

Dogs take a lot of responsibility, Phee
she says in that tone
that is meant to remind me
that she is older
even if it is only by eight days

He's not hungry I say
patting Red's belly

It's a well-fed belly
now that we look at it

We look at it some more
pat it
flap flap flap
slap
his tail hits me in the face

You've been missing everything Hen says
I got my school uniform and supplies list
and Melanie who I know from religion class
called me and

No one has seen Mercy
My mother says she's probably grounded

My mother says she's probably done something terrible
and we just don't know what yet

Hen I try to break in
I try to tell her about Mercy and Southside but

My mother says – wait what's this?

Hen is combing Red's neck fur
with her fingers and

uncovers a leather collar
with a silver tag
in the shape of a bone

a leather collar
a silver tag

a collar
a tag

You can't keep him she says
He's not a stray
He belongs to someone
He's not yours

I KNOW HEN
I KNOW
I KNOW
I KNOW

Hen is still Hen
is still Henrietta

I toss the ball and Red runs

Attaboy!

and Red and me
we chase that ball
all the way
to the end of the alley

where I have to grab his neck
to keep him from
running into the street
coax him to the curb
where he puts his head
in my lap

In the world of right now
Red is my dog
Hen is my friend again
and I wish I could write it all down

Maybe says Hen
who catches up and sits on Red's other side
Maybe his other owners got tired of him
maybe they were mean

Maybe I say
but
I know she was right before
he's not mine

I lay my head on Red's silky fur
then my fingers find
that silver tag

Hen gets her head close to mine and we read:

Daisy
729-0442

Daisy?

They didn't deserve him Hen says
Daisy

Daisy's a poodle
Daisy's a shy calico cat
Red is no Daisy

We will call the number
but first we play
What if Red were yours to keep?

I'd take him everywhere I say
He'd wait under my tree for me
we'd play ball
he'd fetch
he'd walk me to Southside

I'd have him pull me on skates Henny says

I wish I'd thought of that

We'll probably call the number
but first

Hen runs home for skates and a jump rope
which we tie to Red's collar
a leash

Hen gets to go first
because it was her idea

She stands but Red doesn't
so we switch

But Red just lies there with his head in his paws
looking at us with his hubcap eyes

Phee says Hen
Shouldn't we

A DOG! A DOG! A DOG!

just in time to stop Hen from saying IT
the little kids have found us
my brothers and Jennica

DID WE GET A DOG?!
DID WE GET A DOG?!
Oh, Phee

and Red's tail wagwagwags
and the kids look up at me
like they used to

and I'm going to explain to them
that he's not for sure ours

but Julia
our Julia

comes out of her yard

I can't bear to look at her but

Phee Phoebe Phee! Julia says
like she used to

she crouches by Red

and suddenly I am me again
we are we again

me
Phoebe
Phee
my friends
and my beautiful dog

His name is Red I say

I feel warm and generous

You can pet him

Julia kisses Red on the snout
her fingers are in his fur
and that tag looms in front of me

what if she sees the tag?
what if she sees the tag?

She's really nice, Phee Julia says
not seeing the tag

He's a he Hen says

Red growls
we look

Alix + Cicely
do they have
my notebook?

It's Poem Girl

Poem Girl

It's Julia Julia Julia I LOVE YOU *girl*

Julia stands up
she looks at the girls
she looks at Red
she doesn't look
at me

Don't she says softly to Alix + Cicely

Kiss your girlfriend goodbye Alix says
and makes kissy noises with her mouth

Don't Julia says again a little louder

Shawn and Rania are waiting for us
says Cicely

Julia puts her head in Red's fur

she gets up
not looking at me

Alix winds one of her arms through Julia's
Cicely takes her other

and

See you, Word Girl

Red is warm

Red is soft

Red is soothing

Red rests
in the middle
of the heap of the
rest of us

Hen reaches in her pocket
and hands me a fist full of
bottlecaps

Anton reaches in his pocket
and hands me some too

and Cam

and Jennica

no

words

needed

Red's ears pop up
　　　　wuff

there's a *rattle*
　　　　clunk
　　　　rattle
　　　　clunkachunka

a slow driving van

Red lifts his head
　　　　wuff

a *honk honk honk*
　　　　wuff
　　　　WUFF WURUFF WUFF

　　　　　　　　　　　　　　DAISY!

the van stops and out jump about a hundred kids
all with red hair

and Red is jumping
and running in circles
pulling that snake of a rope
his tail whirring
a *wuff wuff wuruffing*
as one of them unleashes the snake

Red is jumping into that van
and riding away
like he was
never
even
mine

The rope hangs
limp

in my hand
lighter than a box of spaghetti

when I pull
nothing tugs

It's the bluest feeling
this limp rope

limp
rope
limp
rope

two words that sound so good together
but I won't make them into a poem

Easy come, easy go says Hen

she grabs one end of my rope
and tugs
and ruffs like a puppy

and Anton ruffs
and Cam and Jennica ruff

and we all of us

ruff

and

huff

and

run

14

crumple thump get up get up

They're hopping behind Mrs Peg Leg
the one-legged crow
Anton
Cam
Jennica
and
Hen

Come ON
Come ON
Come ON PHEE

and I remember how it
used to be

before Southside was coming

before I was eleven

and I look around
to see Julia's not watching
and

I'm hopping
on one foot

shouting
        on one foot
hopping
        and shouting
with

Anton
Cam
Jennica
and
Hen

Mrs. Peg Leg flies off
but we keep hopping
we're a storm of up-and-downing
thundering whoops and hollerings
a flock of angry crows

My hop scuffs
more in place than forward and

HONK!
HONK HONK HONK!

TRUCK! Anton yells

HONK!
HONK HONK HONK!

TRUCK!

MR WHITLEY!

HONK

Mr Whitley stops and
erupts from his truck

shaking his fist

GET
OUT
OF
...
THUD
hush

Mr Whitley's hunched against the hood
hand at his heart
eyes open wide
looking at the sky not seeing

his head bobs
down with the rest of his body
down
to the ground
like a jacket
fallen
off
a back hall
hook

Mr Whitley is on the ground

I am first to him
first to
reach out a hand
touch his cheek
pull off his cap
lay my hand on his naked head

HELP! I holler

Henny kneels with me

GET HELP! she yells

Anton and Cam run
as Mr Whitley's truck idles

Mr Whitley's head is bumpy
with one wisp of hair that tickles my palms

My hands are damp
or the head is damp
I worry it will slip
it leans
it's heavy
it's warm

I've never touched a bald head
but I've held an apple when we went to Mr Good's farm
thirteen inches around
Mr Good's grafted-tree state-fair-winning apple
plucked from the sun warm branch
into my hand
big as a head
big as this head
smooth like this head
with bumps
one vein thumps through Mr Whitley's scalp
I lift my hand to look at the thin blue line

IS HE DEAD?

I look up
and there
is skinny
skitterish
run like a fawn
Jennica

Jennica who never says a word above a whisper
and now she shouts again

IS HE DEAD?

There's a vein
I put her hand where my hand is

He could be dead
but I don't say it
dead with the blood still pulsing
like the chicken that ran around the Good's yard
after Mrs Good cut off its head

Jennica stands up
balancing on one foot
arms out
like maybe she'll fly away
like Mrs Peg Leg

Did we kill Mr Whitley
all our
hopping
yelling
unyielding
stirring the earth with our
scuffing feet
Did we do this?

Julia is coming
with Anton and Cam and Kid
but not Mercy

Back up! says Julia
Back up! Make room!
The ambulance will be here soon!

Mr Whitley
mean old man
don't you go dying in our alley
in front of us

Jennica
run home
bring a blanket

Julia sits down on the scruff and cracks of the alley
takes Mr Whitley's head from me

He moans
and all around
everyone shuffles back in one quick step
like Mr Whitley's going to jump up and get us

The weight and warmth of his scalp stays on my hands
I wipe them on my shorts
clamp them at my sides
tuck them up under my arms

We hear a siren far off

Run to the end of the alley Kid says
Flag them down
The alley is not an address

We race to be ready
to wave and holler
and flag that ambulance in case it races by

It's a thin sound
we strain our ears to hear it
we run down 38th towards the growing wail

Lentil got stuck once
Mr Whitley had left out a nailed board by the garbage cans
Lentil had screamed like this
He'd wail high then whimper low
high low high low until we all came

Julia rescued her
She wasn't afraid of the blood
She got the leg out
held Lentil close to her
until the cat scream stopped

The siren is louder
red flashes blink then grow a white box
the ambulance comes up fast
passes us
we spin around
there's Jennica at the alley
a statue, pointing

the siren stops
the ambulance slows
a flashing hum

We pound our feet loud and heavy
careen into the alley

Everyone swarms around that silent red flashing
more people now than there are houses
drawn in by the siren and the light
hushed like Sunday service or the library
or when someone's mother has a headache

all hushed and pushed together
as close as the paramedics let us
as they work on Mr Whitley

who is not dead

he lifts his hand when Jennica touches him
as they strap him
into
onto
a bed on wheels

Mr Whitley moans

doors slamming
lights flashing
siren screaming
thc ambulance speeds down the alley
BULL howling with the siren sound
the crowd drifts away
leaving us
with nothing to see but each other

Kid drives the truck into Mr Whitley's garage
and we follow

LOOK!
Anton shouts

There is a

HEAD

of a deer

up on the

garage wall

a
deer

with

ANTLERS

That's his buck Kid says

WHAT? Hen says

But Kid is striding away and I

Wait Kid I say

and I run right up to

Kid Jones
Fourteen year old
going to be in the big leagues someday
Mercy's brother

Kid Jones

looking at me

Um
I
Um

> *If you're wondering about Mercy* he says
> *She's inside Phoebe*
> *watching tv*
> *because*
> *no*
> *one*
> *here*
> *will play with her*

But she doesn't like us, Kid

> *Because you don't like her*

But

> *Close the door Phoebe* Kid says
> *I've got to go to practice*

Is he right?

I slump back into the garage

We edge all the way around
the still warm truck

it's cool and damp in here
musty tarpaper walls

> *Don't touch anything* Hen says
> *He'll know*

If he lives Cam whispers
and a shiver quivers down my back

that deer staring at us
Buck

rakes
brooms
shovels
a long string of twine on a hook
a family of daddy long legs
push mower
can of oil
silver metal toolbox
rusted up bike leaning against the back wall
dog food

There's scratching in the walls
and we freeze

Mice? whispers Anton

scritcha scritcha scritcha

Could it be?

Mice!
we all shout-whisper

I put my hand on the wall where the sound is
the noise stops
but I know they're in there
Pink
and her mother and brothers and sisters

Mercy I say

She didn't take them

I want to find Mercy
I want to say

sorry

I want to try again

but there's a THUMP at the yard door
and *RUFFRUFFRUFF!*

BULL

we run out

I stretch to close the garage door but can't reach it
I grab a rake
thread the handle through the garage door handle and
pull
and that door creaks down
until we can grab the edge and
pull and
bend my knees and
pull until
the handle is there
I take it and creak Old Man Whitley's
garage door
closed

Henny grabs my hand

Anton and Cam crowd in on us
smelling like peanut butter and dirt

Jennica grabs my other hand
and we all move around
in a big silent clump

My head is a jumble of
sirens and horns
Mr Whitley
Kid and Mercy
and suddenly
I'm running

we're all running

Jennica
Anton
Cam
Henny
and me

feet pounding
lungs stretching
        like birthday balloons

running
past
Julia's
Jennica's
Hen's
        scaring up Lentil
to 38th Street where the ambulance turned in

and back

past Mr Whitley's
the empty lot
Mrs Peg Leg on a post
under my tree
and all the way to the 37th Street where Red
was my dog
until he wasn't

and I stop

BULL! I shout

    BULL! They shout back

        What about Bull?
        We all say at once

    Someone's going to have to feed him Hen says
    and it's not going to be me.

Everyone looks at everyone else

    We're not doing it Anton and Cam say together

Jennica shakes her head

Henny I say
you've got experience.

    No! she says
    Besides I was only five
    And Buster ran away, remember?

Maybe Kid will do it I say
Or Julia

        Julia!
        everyone says

Julia's on the phone
we can see in her kitchen window
we've let ourselves through her gate
and across her back yard
past a stack of buckets
and the ladder leaning up against the garage
we're on the back stoop squashed in close together

she's got her back to us
she's hunched over the counter

Uh-huh she's saying
uh-huh
UH-UH!
yup
uh-huh
Come over!

It must be Cicely or Alix Jennica says
and she opens and closes her fingers and thumb like a talking mouth
Julia babysits Jennica and Miles sometimes
for a second I wish I were small like Jennica
and could get babysat too

I sit on the top step
Hen sits next to me
Anton and Cam sit on the bottom step
Jennica sits on the ground

the birds are still chirping
cars are still passing

How is everything going on like before

Anton looks back at me
Is Mr Whitley going to die
Cam turns around fast

Do you think he's going to die

They all look at me
but Hen stands up

He's not going to DIE
People don't just die
she snaps her fingers
just like that

Yes they do
Jennica says in her tiny voice
my grandma died
right in my house
right after dinner
before Miles was born
he never even met her

Mr Whitley fell
Anton snaps his fingers
just like that

He was yelling then he fell
says Cam

The ambulance came fast
says Hen

we all nod
and remember

It feels good in Julia's yard
safe
with the white fence all around
like a sheep's pen
and we are the little sheep
huddled together

I touched him
I hold out my hands
I held his heavy head

What I don't say is
maybe we did this

We did this
says Hen sitting next to me again
holding my hand

Did what?
It's Julia
she's coming out the screen door
You did what?

Maybe we…
I start
but I can't say it out loud

We killed Mr Whitley
Hen says

Julia takes too long to answer
my stomach tightens into a hard ball

She's supposed to say
no
you did not do this
but what she says is

How?
What did you do to him?

We were hopping I say

We didn't stop says Hen

He was honking says Anton
And yelling says Cam

But he honks and he yells all the time says Julia

and my stomach untightens
He does

He shouted at us
about the mouse

And he didn't die then says Julia

Jennica pushes through us
up the steps
and puts her arms around Julia

It's hot in the sun on Julia's porch
I'm tired
like I've been running and climbing all day

and as if things couldn't get worse
here come Alix and Cicely
on their bikes
leaning against
looking over
the fence

Come on, Julia

Wait says Julia

Wait for what? Alix says

Babysitting again? says Cicely

So many babies coos Alix
and they laugh

Julia come ON Alix says

JUST WAIT says Julia

and we all look up

that was Julia's
old
strong
counting voice

Come here, Phee she says

Julia's unwound herself from Jennica

she's got her saddle purse

it's open

and she's beckoning me

Standing close to Julia
I can feel myself nearly as tall
taller than when she used to jump rope

She smells like strawberry lip gloss
she's got blue eyeshadow on

Here she says

her purse is open
it's full of

her tiny brush
a tiny mirror
lip gloss
a pen
and

my notebook
purple with birds
and a silver spiral
just the size of
my hand curved
corners frayed
filled with words
purple with birds
a poemnotebook

Julia holds my notebook between her two
hands
hands with strawberry nails

She takes out her pen
She opens my notebook
She turns to the next blank page

and she
writes
something
inside

and hands it to me

> *Mr Whitley will probably be all right*
> she says to all of us

We follow her to the garage
watch her wheel her bike out to the alley
plop her purse in the basket
watch her hop on and ride away

What did Julia write?
they all clamor

I clutch my notebook
not ready to look
not ready to look
not ready to look

my notebook my notebook
purple with birds
a place for words
private just for me
words from Julia

No one wants to play kick the can
No one wants to follow Mrs. Peg Leg
Everyone wants to know

Is he alive or is he dead
Mr Whitley
Mr Whitley
Boogeyman
Boogeyman
Old
Man
Whitley

If he died will there be a funeral

If he did not die will he be an invalid

What's an invalid

An invalid is someone who's always sick

How much does an ambulance ride cost

More than a taxi
Remember when the car was broken
and we took a taxi to Red Owl for groceries

What will happen to the food in Mr Whitley's house

Who will move into Mr Whitley's house if he is dead

Maybe people with kids

Why didn't he just wait for us

We're sitting in the empty lot
in the shade of Mr Whitley's tree that hangs over the fence
Hen's got her doll Sweet and is letting Jennica hold her

cloud
I say

cloud *cloudy* *cloud*

cloud
is a nice word
to say out loud

cloud

I say it
soft and slow

cloud *cloudy* *cloud*

and it's happening again

words
I thought they had deserted me

words
rising up in me

cloud
is a nice word to say out loud

cloud

they all say

cloud   *cloudy*   *cloud*

soft and slow

and all together we sound like a
poem
or a song

Let's rebuild Mudville
says Cam
and they go off like it's any old day

cloud
cloud
cloudy cloud
Hen whispers

while we
lay back
and look into the
blue spaces between the
green leaves

almost

forgetting about

RUFF
RUFFRUFFRUFF

BULL

15

urgent urgency once when now

We're going to have to feed him, Hen

I get up but Hen just takes Sweet from Jennica
and keeps on doing nothing

A hungry dog always barks

I KNOW Hen says
I had a dog you know

I did too

Red doesn't count

Does so

You didn't feed him
she says

she's right

So I guess you should feed Bull I say

Maybe Jennica will do it Hen says

But while we were arguing
Jennica has gotten up and gone

RUFF
RUFFRUFFRUFF

I look at that fence
think about Mr Whitley's gate
imagine walking through it
and Bull latching his teeth
onto
into
my leg

It's nearly suppertime I say
He's going to be hungry

Maybe he won't miss just one meal Hen says

Bull?
Bull's the kind of dog who would absolutely mind missing a meal

Mercy would do it
Mercy Jones would just no nonsense do it
if we were friends with Mercy she would do it

I put my hand on the loose board
slowly move it aside
and look in
at the hungry pacing monster

Kibble doesn't have to be in a bowl I say
I bet he will eat off the ground
We can just drop a handful of it through this loose board space

Dogs don't have to eat out of a bowl
Hen says

which is exactly what I just said

It's hard to believe someone holding a doll
could know

EVERYTHING

We stand in front of Mr Whitley's garage door a long time
We look around to make sure no one's watching

It's not against the law
if we're just breaking in to get dog food
to feed his own dog I say

but I still feel jumpy as I
pull
pull
pull on the garage handle
it squeaks and creaks

and Hen just stands there

Can't you put Sweet down and help me?

What's wrong with Sweet?
Hen says but she sets Sweet against the fence

We get the door up as high as Hen's waist
crouch down
and crawl in to the
cool
dark
place
and wait until our eyes can see again

The dog food is all the way in the back
under Buck

We stop where we heard the mice before
there's a little scritch scratching

Pink I say
and we smile at each other
Here it is
I've found the bag

it's big like those gunnysacks when we did races at school

There's a scooper inside
I scoop up the food pebbles
and hand the scooper to Hen

No she says putting her hands behind her back
You do it

We'll both do it I say

Cam and Anton see us standing at the fence and come watch

Bull isn't barking
but we can see through the hole that he's sitting at the back door

He knows it's time I say

We try to hold the scoop and bring it to the hole together
but we can't get both arms in

I peek again at Bull at the back door
he doesn't hear us
yet

I take the scoop from Hen
shove my arm in

tipthecupover
spillfoodontheground
pullmyarmout

and tip the loose board back in place

RUFFRUFFRUFFRUFFRUFF

We back up fast
and look at each other
smiling

Hen holds out

a brand new Mr Pibb bottle cap

For bravery she says

Standing on my tree board
I put my arm around the trunk
I look out between the branches

bravery is
opening up
this
embarrassing
notebook

what
did
Julia
write

2 4 6 8

I think you're
great

♡ Julia

p.s. there is
a poetry club
at Southside.

Lights coming on

kitchen lights

bedroom lights

but one house is dark tonight

one house is empty

one dark empty house

Reaching up
I tuck my notebook in

> *2 4 6 8*
> *you're great*
> *you're great*
>
> Am
> I
> great?

and drop my new Mr Pibb in
my blue bag and
shake it rattle it

a bag full of words

I fed a dog
I fed a dog
I
fed
Bull

It's morning
Mr Whitley's not back
I'm watching through the fence
waiting for Hen
to come along

Bull is white all over
with a brown pirate patch over one eye
brown over his nose
and a big brown spot the shape of Africa
on one wide side

What are we going to do about Bull?

He is pacing the yard
in his slow heavy way

back

and

forth

from the back door
to the gate

back
door
to
gate

he gives a small
uff
uff
uff
like he's trying to clear his throat

Bull yawns
his jaw opens like a car hood
his tongue lolls out
thick slab
I see his big sharp teeth

He's bulky
a potato sack with legs
and four hamburger bun feet

Bull was the first thing I was ever afraid of
We all
have always
been afraid of Bull

Mrs Whitley used to walk him
with a thick leather leash and
we all
always
screamed when we saw him

Once Bull pulled the leash too hard and got away
We watched him catch a squirrel and
shake it
until it was limp
dead

So why am I worried that Bull won't get breakfast?

Lentil just eats from back steps
where people leave him little bowls of this and that
chicken from supper
or tuna from a can

Once I left three little pieces of cheese
in my tree
and the next morning they were gone

Could have been Lentil
could have been raccoons

Bull can't roam around like Lentil or raccoons
he needs us to feed him

Why can't Bull be easy like Lentil
or nice like Red

I got it
Hen's here with the scoop of kibble plus Sweet
so you can drop it in again

I do
do it again
even though I'm thinking about that limp squirrel

I am fast
reachingin
spillingfood
armout
calling *BULL!*
and backing away

RUFFRUFFRUFFRUFFRUFF

We hear him over there
gobbling up the food
sniff sniff sniffing at the place where the loose board hangs

he's whining a little
a pitiful sound
like a monster baby

What if
I say
reaching out
touching the loose board

thinking upside down thoughts

What if
Bull barks because he likes us?

...

...

...

Nah
we say at exactly the same time

Jinx
we say at exactly the same time

DOUBLE JINX

*RUFFRUFF**RUFFRUFFRUFF***
RUFF RUFF RUFF

RUN!

We run we run we
climb we climb we
breathefast
breathefast
until we
can
b r e a t h e
s l o w

w e w a t c h
a l l t h e n o t h i n g
h a p p e n i n g
e v e r y w h e r e

just
Anton Cam Jennica Mudville
tree garage fence garage
caw caw caw

just
summer

What will it be like when we're grown up? I say

We'll just have to wait and see says Hen
She makes Sweet sit between us

But what will be invented?
Will we still be friends?
Where will we live?

We'll just have to wait and see

What's going to happen to Mr Whitley?
What if he dies?
What's going to happen to Bull?
Will Mercy ever come back outside?

We'll just have to wait and see

HEN!
Doesn't Henrietta wonder an
y
thing

What about

But Hen isn't listening
she's pointing

at Mercy

Mercy! She is here
she is here again
outside again

I have another chance
again

hitting a tennis ball
against Kid's garage

Why doesn't SHE
go back
where
she
came
from

Hen says in that voice that isn't a whisper
that voice that anyone can hear
that voice that…

WORDS TO SAY OUT LOUD

HERE is
where
she
comes
from
now
Hen

Mercy
belongs
here
as
much
as
you
or
me

Mercy is dropping her racquet
she is
walkingnowrunning

under this tree and away

But
says Hen
she

I am not waiting to hear more from Hen and Sweet

I
am going
after Mercy

Mercy wait up!

Running down our alley

wondering
is he alive
or is he dead
Mr Whitley
Mr Whitley
Boogeyman
Boogeyman
Old
Man
Whitley

Standing at 38th Street

She's gone

there's nothing to see
except

car   car   bicycle   street sweeper

street sweeper rumbling along
spraying water out the front
brushing up dirt leaving the street clean
spraying out
WATER

WATER!

BULL!

it's hot
he'll be thirsty
a dog cannot live without

WATER

Kneeling by Mr Whitley's fence
I
listen
for
Bull

no barking

I
push the loose board aside

no pacing no scratching

he's sprawled on the grass on his side
his tongue hanging out

IS HE DEAD TOO?
Mr Whitley
Bull

IS EVERYTHING GOING TO DIE THIS SUMMER?

Anton and Cam are in Mudville
with Jennica
there are cups scattered around
and a bucket of water
they fill with the hose from our house

I grab the widest cup
WORLD'S BEST DONUTS
dunk it in the bucket

Hey! they say
You can't just take that cup

SHHHHHHHHH!

and I walkrun back to the fence
movetheboard
reachthecupin
setitontheground
pullmyarmout
call
BULL!
and sit back
and wait

They're behind me now
Anton
Cam
Jennica
and Hen comes too
with Sweet

A dog needs water
I whisper

but there's no RUFFING
there's no sound at all

Maybe you need to put it farther in
Hen says

I putmyarmin
get the cup
putmyarm farther in
so far even my shoulder is in

and the loose board
flops back and the loose nail
catches my shirt
and traps
my arm

INSIDE
THE
FENCE!

HELP!
    RUFFRUFFRUFF
HELP!
    RU
     UU
    schlupschlupschlup
he's drinking
Bull's drinking

His head is so close to my hand
I can feel the heat from it

Hen is pulling my shirt off the nail
something soft is brushing my hand
soft like Red's ear
then
something bristly
and wet
and tickly
not teeth

    IT'S FREE Hen shouts
    YOUR SHIRT IS FREE

but
I
don't
move

it's a tongue

    Bull's tongue

licking my arm

not eating it

my saltyelevenyearoldarm

it's like Julia's hairbrush
is brushing my arm

slowly
slowly
I pull away
take my arm back
hold the loose board
and look
in
right in
to soft brown eyes
and a beautiful brown snout

ruff
Bull says

ruff
I say back

Did he bite you?
Are you bit?
What did he do?
What did it feel like?
Why didn't you pull out your arm?

They are full of questions and
I
am
too

Isn't Bull a monster?
Doesn't he kill squirrels?

Why didn't he bite me?

This feeling I have inside
is like the feeling I had when
I
had
Red

and everyone
and Julia were looking
to me

One cup
cannot be enough
for a dog as big as Bull I say

You can't put your arm in there again! Hen says
You can't put your arm in there again! Anton says

Stop it, Anton! Hen says
Stop it, Anton! Cam says

Anton and Cam are laughing and running and Hen chases after them

Jennica lugs the bucket of water over to me
Do it again she says

I feel like I have a superpower

I reach through
Mr Whitley's
FENCE
and give
Mr Whitley's
DOG BULL
more water

He slurps it up
and *RUFF*s
that *RUFF*
that doesn't sound
so
bad
when I'm
touching his
petting his
short haired side
which is surprisingly soft

I have a dog
I got him here
His name is
BULL

You'd have thought I saved kittens
from a treetop
or babies
from a fire
the way my brothers and Jennica
and Hen and Sweet are
following me around
now that I've fed Bull
given him water
petted him

They're all still scared of Bull
and that's just fine with me

And now that I've done this
I want everyone to know

I want to tell
Julia
Kid
I want to tell Mercy

I want
Alix and Cicely
to see

I want to
climb
jump
leap

I want to
write
a
poem

16

alive across infinite

The morning world
is cool and misty

no one's up
but me

I want to see Bull by myself

I pop a couple of damp honeysuckle buds
by Mr Whitley's fence
watch an ant make its way up a stem

I kneel by the loose board
put my ear up to the rough wood
listen

and see
in the alley

Mercy
kicking a can
kicking a can
kicking a can

I felt so calm
when I had Red
I wonder if Mercy
would like to see a dog too

I run out and grab the can

Mercy I say

I...
I...
I...

Come here I say
Come see

and she comes
Mercy
Mercy
Mercedes Jones
comes with me

I kneel by the loose board
put my ear up to the rough wood
listen

What are we doing? she says

Shhhh I say
feeding Bull

she puts her ear up to the fence too

Mercy
here
next to me

there's a snuffling sound

Bull rooting around for breakfast

I knew you would do it if you were me I whisper
but I am scared
what if he's forgotten me
what if I dreamed it

I hold a flattened bottle cap
then put it back in my pocket
breathe in deep and

Mercy pulls the loose board aside

He's there
Bull's right there
his nose in space in the fence
that beautiful big brown nose
like he wants to come right though

RUFF
he says

and Mercy jumps back

I make myself stay put
and look
into his
eyes his
nose his
floppy
tongue

Bull's so excited he squeezes his square head
into that triangle space in the fence
until

HE'S STUCK!
we say

at exactly the same time

PULL!
we say
at exactly the same time

Mercy and me
we pull at the loose board
pull and pull
until it

SNAPS

Bull pops his head back
and gallops around his yard in a circle

*RUFF RUFF RUFF*ing

his short stubby tail
wag wag wagging

Wheeeeeeeeze whap

Mr
Whitley's
screen door!

Mr
Whitley!

Walking alive Boogeyman Boogeyman Old Man Whitley!

He stands staring
leaning on a cane staring
we stand staring
through the broken fence staring
through the gaping hole
that can't be closed staring

Mr Whitley is alive!
Mr Whitley is home!
We have broken Mr Whitley's fence!

Mr Whitley looks at Bull
He looks at the World's Best Donuts cup
He looks at us
Mr Whitley nods his head quick
turns
and
steps
wheeze whap
back
inside

Words Mercy Says

Words I Say

Words Bull Says
Ruff

RUFF
RUFF
RUFF

I crouch by the new space in the fence
reach through
touch Bull's warmsoft snout

ruff he says
ruffruffruffruff

Mercy kneels next to me
touches him too

I almost had a dog named Red I say
but his real family came and got him

Lucky Red says Mercy

But they took him away from me

But he got to go home

But…

I want to go back home

But...

But…

Mercedes I say
trying out Mercy's full name
liking how it sounds

Mercedes
I heard Kid say…
Is it true that you're staying
that you're going to Southside

Come on Mercy says
she's standing
she's striding up the alley
up to 38th Street

and my feet
they follow
and I'm striding too

We pass Hen's house
Hen's coming out the door
Hey wait up!
in her new plaid school uniform

but I can't wait

I'm keeping up with Mercy

Phee wait up!

we're standing at 38th Street

car bus car car car

Phoebe!
We can't—

I dare you, Hen!

car car

we're walking
now running

Phoebe!
Wait for me!

a c r o s s

38th Street

We're walking
Mercy and me

Wait up!

and Hen

Phee we shouldn't

past

different garages
different houses

Isn't this far enough

neat yards
scruffy yards
garbage cans

What's my mom going to say

a leaning tree
two orange cats on a fence
an old lady sweeping

Cicely being yelled at by someone we can't see

across

car bike car

PheeMercyPheeWhereAreWeGoing

another street

turning left

Oh this is kind of exciting
walking

turning right
following

Mercy where are we going

turning
walking right up to the

Phee look

wide flat hot
tar
tar
tar
parking lot

Mercy brought us to

brick
brick
red
brick
three stories high
windows like winking eyes

red brick

expansive

SOUTHSIDE

There's a low wall
we sit on it

Mercy and me

I can't get my new uniform dirty says Hen

we three
away from our alley

we look just look

So this is it Hen says at last
This is where you're going, Phee

it's just like Hen to explain something to me
that I already know

It's bigger than St Mary's
I don't know how you're going to find your way around
Melanie says it's hard to make friends at Southside
Her sister went to Southside so she should know
she

Hen I interrupt
for once I want to be the one giving the news
You've missed a lot

Mr Whitley is alive
he's home

Oh!

and
Mercy

Mercedes

Mercy is staying and

Oh!

This is where we're going I say

Mercy

Mercedes

Mercy and me

Southside together

Oh!

Mercedes says Hen
she looks at Mercy

Mercy
Mercedes

You're going to…
you and Phee

Not yet says Mercy
and she starts running in big circles
around the empty Southside parking lot
it's still summer

Not yet Hen! I shout
and I start running too
around

across

zig zagging

Not yet!
Hen joins in

NOT YET
NOT YET
NOT YET

17

flutter hover over under

It's a hot hot day
we're huddling around
nothing to do
and a jug of water
cold from Henny's hose

Anton says
swing the string
swing the string
and Cam joins in
swing the string
swing the string

Henny runs for the long jump rope
and we swing that string round and around
over and over
slap slap slap on the alley
slap slap slap
and everyone calls
Jump, Mercy! Jump, Mercy!

and Mercy jumps in
and her feet barely tap the ground
She's light
taking flight

a bird contained in this narrow hoop of rope

Two ropes! Cam shouts and we slow

Mercy steps back
Jennica hands her a swig
she takes a swig
a long drink of
cool
cool
water

We wipe our sweaty hands on our pants
and pick up another rope
and everyone grins all around

even Julia who comes out to watch

We are witnessing something here in our alley
We are witnessing something and making something here

Go go go!

We take a few practice twirls, Henny and me
it takes a bit to get the rhythm just right:
one up one down
one up one down
one slaps while the other
slices the air

an arc

Then we've got it
slice and slap and slice and slap
as Mercy stands staring into that space between
bobbing
forward back
forward back

in rhythm
with
the
ropes

then
with a nimble jig
she slips into the slice
and the slap
and she's jumping our double ropes

someone cheers
we all cheer

faster faster Julia calls

and Mercy whoops
and we flick our wrists and make those ropes
whirr like hummingbird wings

and Mercy tips and taps and dances
her feet are lightning strikes
the alley is scorched ground

and we are witnessing something here
we are witnessing

Surely this is something no one has seen before
the likes of Mercy and her lightning feet
her toes through the holes in her shoes
little flashes of red as she

HONK

honk honk hoooonk

and there is Old Man Whitley
in his old-man pickup with Bull
in the front seat
and Mercy
our Mercy
does not skip one beat
she doesn't miss

and we
Henny and me
we don't either

we keep our ropes twirling
even though our arms are burning
our hands are sweating

and someone
someone starts singing
top of lungs singing

one voice
two voices
our voices
sounding

and they all join in this song my song that becomes just a buzz in my ears

resounding
pounding
abounding
surrounding

as Old Man Whitley toots his horn

and the voices ring

and Mercy's toes tap
and the ropes slap
and slice

then

it's Mr Whitley not honking
our Mr Whitley
and Bull barking along

one voice
two voices
our voices
sounding

his door slamming
Bull jumping out

resounding
pounding
abounding
surrounding

Mr Whitley not yelling
Bull running circles around us

his barks the rumbling bass
anchoring our chorus

All of us
Mr Whitley
and Bull

Will it end

I hope it never ends
I will twirl these ropes until we all are lifted

singing
swinging
tapping
slapping

right up
into the
sky and
clouds

right up
into
SUMMER